OTHER TITLES OF INTEREST FROM ST. LUCIE PRESS

The Healthcare Practitioner's

Handbook of Management

The Healthcare Practitioner's

Handbook of Management

Larry D. Grieshaber, Ph.D.

St. Lucie Press
Boca Raton, Florida

Phone: (561) 994-0555
E-mail: information@slpress.com
Web site: http://www.slpress.com

S^t_L

Published by
St. Lucie Press
2000 Corporate Blvd., N.W.
Boca Raton, FL 33431-9868

Table of Contents

This book is dedicated to Marilyn.
She encouraged its undertaking,
emotionally supported its author, and shared the labor it generated.

Preface

*Mark P. was a twenty-six-year-old senior in a healthcare management pro-
gram. He sat in his academic advisor's office trying to make sense of his final
degree requirements, one of which was a management internship. Although he
had read the course description, he did not understand quite what he was expected
to do.*

Mark: *I have an idea. My daughter was diagnosed with diabetes last year.
I learned how to take care of her from her physician and from
the American Diabetes Association. I learned how to fill out all
kinds of insurance forms. I even worked out something with the
school to take care of sugar monitoring and insulin administration.
What if I write a report summarizing my experience to satisfy this
requirement?*

Advisor: *I'm sorry, but you still haven't understood the point. What you
learned by caring for your daughter is important, but the idea of
the internship is to give you **management** experience.*

Mark: *But I **manage** my daughter's care!*

Because Mark's experience of caring for his daughter was unlike the typical
management internship, his academic advisor failed to recognize it as a valid
management experience. Academic imperatives aside, Mark had successfully
completed a healthcare management experience.

Management is achieving objectives with and through others. Mark was not
providing for his daughter's care alone. He was working with insurers to finance
the care. He worked through her physician, the American Diabetes Association,
and her school to provide treatment. Mark achieved his objective of caring for his
daughter by working with and through others.

In today's healthcare environment, clinical practitioners frequently find themselves in managerial positions—positions for which their formal education may
have failed to prepare them. A few of these practitioners take quite naturally to
managerial roles. These are the practitioners who, like Mark, recognize that there
are fundamental similarities between managing clinical care and managing
organizations.

The purpose of this book is to help practitioners transform clinical skills into managerial skills. Each chapter links a management topic to a clinical analogy with which health practitioners are familiar and presents diagnostic and treatment approaches to the management issue. This book was written with the firm belief that clinicians who have strong assessment and intervention skills can successfully transfer those skills to management.

The book introduces the reader to the vocabulary and theory of management that practitioners need to achieve professional growth as managers. Irrespective of their field of study, licensure, or specialty, clinicians share a common language—medical terminology. Possession of this language is a requisite to professional growth and acquisition of new professional knowledge. Acquiring a clear understanding of management terminology is vital to being able to interact with other managers and to access the management literature. Therefore, management jargon is introduced, highlighted, and defined throughout the book.

Management theory helps managers acquire the conceptual framework that allows them to fully develop their managerial problem-solving skills. It also underpins many applicable management principles and guidelines. This book introduces some of the well-known management theorists and theories frequently encountered in the management literature, along with many practical guidelines.

This book and the advice offered herein are presented with two very strong caveats. The first is a warning about strict application of any management principle or guideline. Clinical practitioners are sensitive to the highly variable nature of medicine. Presenting symptoms vary from one person to the next. Treatments that should work sometimes fail, and sometimes treatments that should not work are successful. That same kind of inexactness characterizes the practice of management. Management research provides insight, but no guarantees. There are undoubtedly readers who, based on personal experience with similar situations, will disagree with my approaches to handling specific cases. This is to be expected. My suggestions are based on management research and on the contemporary wisdom of management experts. However, even a well-documented and researched approach is not always the only appropriate way to deal with a specific management problem.

The second caveat regards the legal environment in which management is practiced. Just as relationships between patients and healthcare providers are defined at least in part by law, so are the relationships among managers, institutions, and employees. Clinicians are often frustrated by the law. Not only is it complex and difficult to interpret, but when they ask for concrete answers about applying the law, they often get responses that begin with, "It all depends on...." There are important legal dimensions to relationships that managers establish with their employees and colleagues. Also, managerial decision making has potentially significant legal consequences. Space limitations prohibit a comprehensive presentation of relevant legal issues. Therefore, nothing presented here should be regarded as legal advice, nor should it be regarded as a substitute for independent advice of counsel. The service of a competent legal professional should be sought when legal advice or expert experience is required.

The cases presented in the book are based on the experiences of many practitioners and managers with whom I have worked over the years. Although the examples are based on actual occurrences, the people and healthcare organizations are composites of those that have been described to me. The names of individuals and organizations associated with the cases were chosen at random.

Because I believe that management is an intensely personal endeavor, I have chosen to use the pronouns he and she rather than the less specific and impersonal them. In a similar vein, I tried to choose fictitious names that reflect the rich cultural diversity of our country. I have tried to use genders and names in a balanced way throughout the book and I apologize in advance for any inadvertent biases that may be perceived.

As clinical practitioners are aware, the American healthcare system is being rapidly restructured. New evolving team-oriented structures present practitioners with opportunities to expand their roles. Practitioners are finding many new and exciting opportunities to combine clinical and managerial roles. Even recent graduates are finding themselves with opportunities to be team leaders. Students nearing the completion of their academic work and new graduates should find that the material presented here will prepare them for the professional challenges that lie ahead. Clinicians have the problem-solving skills that are required to become effective managers. America's healthcare institutions will be much strengthened by having managers who bring both clinical and managerial perspectives to leadership positions.

I would like to express my sincere appreciation to professional colleagues who have reviewed part or all of this book. Marilyn Grieshaber, M.A., Don Kaufmann, M.S., Rebecca Mann, Ph.D., Patricia Parker, Ph.D., Barbara Petzall, Ph.D., and Karen Tabak, CPA, each provided valuable feedback on one or more of the chapters. (I am particularly indebted to Judith Maserang, R.N., Ph.D. and Kenneth Kirk, R.Ph., Ph.D., who took a great deal of time from their overcrowded schedules to review the manuscript. Their careful reading and helpful suggestions resulted in a much stronger book.) The assistance and support of all these reviewers is much appreciated. Any errors in interpretation or reporting, however, are entirely my own.

Larry D. Grieshaber
St. Louis

Introduction

1

Management in the Healthcare Context

In this chapter the reader will learn how:
- ◆ management is commonly defined
- ◆ to identify the functions of managers
- ◆ to identify managerial roles
- ◆ clinical skills compare to managerial skills
- ◆ management in the healthcare environment differs from management in other environments
- ◆ to cope with the transition from clinician to manager.

Kathy B. is the evening charge nurse on a medical-surgical floor of a teaching hospital. This is her first week after her promotion from staff nurse. She was confident she could do the job when she applied for the position, but now she is not so sure of herself.

As she rides the elevator to her floor, Kathy thinks back to one of her favorite patients, Mr. Kilmer. Mr. Kilmer and his family had been one of her biggest challenges. He was a cancer patient with multiple physical problems including incontinence, stomatitis secondary to his chemotherapy drugs, generalized muscular weakness, and depression. His family was also financially distressed. Kathy had been alerted to Mr. Kilmer's impending admission and informed of his condition by his oncologist. Even before Mr. Kilmer arrived, Kathy had ordered appropriate supplies for his incontinence and had sent medication orders to the pharmacy to be processed. She had also scheduled the passive range of motion therapy the oncologist had prescribed. Once Mr. Kilmer was admitted, she rearranged the small items of furniture in his private room to accommodate both his motor deficits and the personal items his family brought with him. Kathy found Mr. Kilmer's family to be very interested in participating in his care, and she helped them learn how to monitor his skin condition and to care for the sores in his mouth. They followed her instructions with accuracy and enthusiasm. Before his discharge, she worked with the home health agency that would provide ongoing care to Mr. Kilmer in his home. By the end of his hospital stay, Mr. Kilmer had regained considerable physical strength and his stomatitis was much improved. He and his family were so pleased with Kathy's personal attention that a week after his discharge, they surprised her by having a dozen red roses delivered to the hospital.

Her first week as a charge nurse has not gone smoothly. She has already received two nasty calls from the patient care scheduling personnel because she did not let them know soon enough about staff shortages on the next shift. One nursing assistant has filed a grievance against her because Kathy reprimanded her about taking too long for her dinner break. Kathy had an argument (complete with shouting and personal insults) with a staff nurse about the appropriate administration of prn pain medications. Kathy was very upset about the argument because she had considered this nurse to be a friend. Not only is she dealing with difficult staff problems, but it is now her responsibility to respond to the constant complaints from physicians about anything from the proper care of a patient to a lack of supplies on the floor to calling in important lab results in a timely manner. Her staff is also referring most of the complaints from patients and their families to her. Every time she starts working on one thing, she is pulled away to resolve another crisis. For the first time in her nursing career, she feels she cannot get all of her work done. She is so overwhelmed that she feels disoriented.

As the elevator comes to a stop on her floor and she takes the first dreaded step off, one thing she knows for sure is that there will be no roses from her head nurse, her staff, the physicians, or the patients.

Kathy's feelings are probably familiar to anyone who has been promoted from a clinical position to a management position. This is not a situation that is unique to nursing. Radiological technicians, medical technologists, pharmacists, respiratory therapists, dieticians, physicians, and other healthcare professionals experience the same feelings of trepidation, and perhaps even inadequacy, that Kathy felt. Unfortunately, it appears that Kathy's hospital did little, if anything, to prepare her for her new role. As health service organizations (HSOs) continue to cut costs, it is not uncommon to find that human resource development funds are minimal. As a result, in-house management development programs frequently are too short and superficial to adequately prepare managerial candidates for their new roles. Kathy is not alone among healthcare managers in being inadequately trained for the job.

In spite of her lack of formal management training, Kathy is not ill-prepared for her new position. She has proven that she is a competent clinician. The same skills that led to her success as a health practitioner will also eventually lead to her success as a healthcare manager. What Kathy has to do is to recognize that she has the right skills to be a good manager and then find ways that she can transfer her skills to her new managerial role. That is what this book is about—helping clinicians to successfully apply their clinical skill set to meeting the demands of managerial roles. The road to achieving that goal begins in this chapter with an exploration of the manager's function.

Management

Kathy seems confused about her new role. Consequently, she appears to be frozen into inaction. She does not know where to begin her job. Instead of getting her work done proactively, she is constantly reacting to the problems of other people. In essence, rather than *managing*, Kathy is *being managed* by everyone else.

Management is the process of accomplishing tasks with and through others. Managers do not work in isolation. Taxi drivers aren't managers because they do all their driving themselves. They are hired by taxi companies to drive, and they are unable to complete their work by having someone else drive for them. The full-time sculptor who works in his studio and sells his pieces on his own is a businessperson, but he is not a manager because he is doing all the work related to the business himself. The essence of management is interacting with people in such a way that they accomplish organizational goals.

One attribute that attaches to all managers, regardless of managerial level in an organization or the type of organization in which they practice, is responsibility for producing results. According to Drucker,

> ...management everywhere faces the same problems. It has to organize work for productivity, it has to lead the worker toward productivity and achievement. It is responsible for the social impact of its enterprise. Above all, it is responsible for producing the re-sults—whether economic performance, student learning, or patient care—for the sake of which each institution exists.[1]

Most healthcare practitioners are managers to a certain extent. In hospital settings, almost all registered nurses direct others (e.g., nursing assistants) in patient care activities. Pharmacists supervise and monitor the work of pharmacy technicians. Medical technologists supervise and monitor the work of laboratory technicians. In these situations, clinicians are responsible for some aspects of the technical worker's performance. When more highly credentialed clinicians supervise and monitor the work of less credentialed personnel, management is taking place. However, it is taking place in a very narrow context. The clinician may in fact have very little control over what the technician actually does. Work content is usually defined by a job description, and clinicians have no authority to change job descriptions and thereby control job content. The role of the clinician in evaluating work is usually limited to the quality of the output as judged by professional criteria. Other work performance attributes (such as attendance) usually are not evaluated by staff clinicians. The relationship between clinicians and technicians is also a relatively fluid one. Different clinicians and technicians may be paired on a daily basis in some HSOs. Management responsibilities pertaining to any one employee may be limited to one shift. Therefore, the managerial role of most clinical practitioners is quite limited.

Management Functions

The work of managers consists of four primary functions: planning, organizing, leading, and controlling. If one were to observe a day in the life of a manager, many other activities could also be observed. For example, going to meetings, counseling employees, writing memos, working on budgets, and responding to complaints are a few of the many tasks managers perform during a typical day. However, each of these activities relates back to one or more of the four basic management functions.

Managerial **planning** includes establishing goals for an organization and developing a strategy for achieving those goals. In an HSO, the goals for the entire organization are established at the highest level of the management hierarchy, typically by the Board of Directors and/or the Chief Executive Officer (CEO). Subsequent to planning at this level, each manager at the next lower level (typically vice presidents) establishes plans for her division that will help the organization to meet its goals. Department heads then formulate goals that support those of the division to which the department belongs. Supervisors establish goals that support departmental goals.

The nature of a manager's planning work changes with the level at which that planning is done. At the top level of the organization, most of the planning activity relates to the development of a **strategic plan**. Strategic plans consist of the organization's overall goals and objectives. These goals and objectives define the organization's ideal position in its environment and describe how the organization is expected to arrive at that position. At the departmental and supervisory levels, planning activities result in **operational plans**. Operational plans are more detailed and specific than strategic plans. Usually they are written for the shorter term. The case of Kortland Hospital demonstrates the different types of planning activities.

The Board of Trustees of Kortland Hospital has just completed its new strategic plan for the next five years. Among the goals enumerated in the plan is the goal of becoming the largest provider of outpatient clinical services in its four-county service area. Subsequent to being presented with the new strategic plan, the Vice President of Professional Services included in her new two-year plan a goal to increase by 50% the number of procedures performed under contract with community providers. After being presented with this goal, the Director of the Laboratory included in his one-year operating budget plan the addition of two full-time medical technologists and three full-time medical technicians to handle the increased workload. After the budget was approved, the evening laboratory supervisor started working on a plan to reassign duties to evening shift technicians and to implement new training programs for them to accommodate the first wave of anticipated increases in workload. The supervisor plans to start the training and reassignment within the next three months. The strategic planning done by the Board of Trustees is outwardly focused (i.e., the competitive position of the hospital in its four-county service area) and long term (five years). The planning of the evening supervisor is inwardly focused (evening shift laboratory technicians) and short term (three months). Managers at other levels develop plans between these extremes.

Of the four management functions, it is appropriate to consider planning first because all other functions follow planning chronologically. Without a plan, engaging in the other functions would be an exercise in futility. Following close on the heels of planning is organizing. **Organizing** is the determination of what work needs to be done, who will do it, and, to some extent, how it will be done. In the Kortland Hospital example, it is clear that the evening supervisor's plan is organizational in nature; that is, it focuses on organizing human resources so that the task of the work unit can be done. Thus, in this case, planning flows seamlessly into organizing.

Leading is the most difficult of the management functions to define. This may be because individuals have different concepts of what constitutes effective leadership. **Leading** may be best defined as the use of noncoercive influence to direct and coordinate the activities of the members of an organized group toward the accomplishment of the group's goals.[2] It is important to note that this definition excludes the use of coercion. Coercion may effectively get a single task accomplished, but it cannot be used as an ongoing management process. Tyrants are not leaders, nor is tyranny management.

Controlling is monitoring activities and evaluating results to assure that planned objectives are met. Because controlling involves monitoring processes set in motion through organizing and leading activities, it is logical that controlling

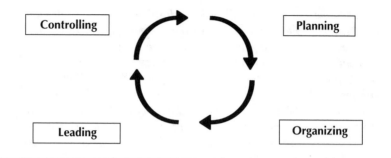

Figure 1.1   The management process.

is usually the last of the management functions discussed. However, controlling is chronologically last only as it pertains to one single organizational plan. In the Kortland example, assume that one of the evening laboratory technicians, whose primary responsibility has previously been inventory maintenance, is retrained and given the additional responsibility of billing physician practices for laboratory work performed. The evening supervisor will obviously evaluate how this change has affected work flow during the evening shift. If the supervisor determines that billing errors have increased by 10% and that the lab has begun to experience out-of-stock situations that did not exist before the change, then a new plan for handling the increased workload may need to be developed. Thus, the controlling function stimulates the planning process. Management is best conceptualized as a continuous process (see Figure 1.1).

Because managers deal with many different issues simultaneously, they typically perform each of the management functions every day. In fact, one of the most common complaints of managers is that their work is so fragmented that they never feel they can devote their undivided attention to any one thing for a significant amount of time. In one often-cited study, it was found that even CEOs have very little continuous time to devote to a single activity. Among the CEOs studied, half of their activities lasted less than nine minutes.[3]

Managing Individuals and Managing Groups

Since the essence of management is working with people, effective managers are expert applied behaviorists. The same can be said for clinical practitioners because the successful accomplishment of healthcare goals depends on the ability of the healthcare provider to work with patients and communities. Clinicians bring to management roles solid experience in dealing with people in a variety of situations. In fact, because clinicians frequently deal with people in stressful and emotion-laden situations, they bring a valuable experiential background to management.

Successful clinicians apply two clinical care axioms in providing patient care. First, each patient is unique and, therefore, requires customized diagnostic and treatment plans. Second, individual patients cannot be treated in isolation from their interpersonal relationships and their environments. The care of a patient with diabetes mellitus is a good example. The clinician has to find the right balance of diet, exercise, and medication to control the disease. The blend that is appropriate varies with the needs of each patient. The clinician may also need to work with the patient's significant others. If the patient is a child, parents will have to be instructed regarding appropriate diet and dealing with potential hypoglycemic and hyperglycemic episodes. If the patient is blind and requires insulin, a caregiver may need to be trained to assist with blood sugar monitoring and/or insulin administration. In these cases, care providers must work with the patient and caregivers as a group so that each person understands the roles and expectations of others. Treating the diabetic patient without the involvement of significant others constitutes inadequate intervention.

Failure to include others in clinical intervention can lead to even more disastrous outcomes in the case of infectious diseases. What would happen if physicians treated individual cases of cholera one at a time without intervening to stop the spread of the disease in the entire community? Obviously the clinician has an obligation to consider the health status of the entire community and to intervene at the community level to stop the spread of the disease.

Management practice is similar to clinical practice in that the primary focus of management activities alternates between the individual employee and the work group. In the role of working one-on-one with an employee, the manager is engaging in **supervisory management**. Supervision includes coaching, counseling, motivating, training, evaluating, and providing feedback. These activities consume so much time and energy that they can easily become overwhelming. However, managers can ill afford to spend all their time in supervising individual employees. Focusing on individual employees to the exclusion of the work group can result in outcomes just as devastating (in managerial terms) as failing to protect a community at risk of an infectious epidemic. No employee functions in isolation from his/her co-workers. The effective practice of management requires that managers not only engage in supervisory activities, but also predict and respond to **organizational behavior**—how humans behave in groups.

The activities of managers with regard to groups also include coaching, motivating, training, evaluating, and providing feedback. However, the group dynamic changes the way managers approach these activities. For example, a very small change in a procedure (such as the completion of a stock order form) may easily be accomplished in some work groups but not so easily in others. If the change is easy to understand and is not burdensome, a simple memo to all department members may work very nicely in one department. However, in another department, employees may resist change of any kind so that department supervisors may have to supplement an introductory memo with one-on-one direction. To ensure successful implementation, one employee may need reassurance, another may have to be convinced of the need for a change, and yet a third may need additional instruction. It is clear that managers have to know their work groups well and to plan their management activities to meet the needs of diverse work groups.

Management is a complex and multilayered process. Years of research have failed to yield simple formulae that guarantee managerial success. However, principles and guidelines have emerged that, when followed consistently, can increase the likelihood of success. Management literature offers managers numerous lists of do's, lists of don'ts, checklists, and lists of suggestions. The multitude of management lists are meant to provide managers with easily remembered guidelines to apply in their daily work. However, day-to-day management is anything but simple. It is far too complex to be distilled into a list of management axioms. If effective management were nothing more than following a checklist, the world would be awash with highly effective managers. Unfortunately, magic bullets are as rare in management as they are in medicine.

The use of management guidelines mirrors the use of treatment protocols. Neither treatment protocols nor management guidelines work equally well in all cases. However, their lack of universal effectiveness does not diminish the usefulness of treatment protocols in providing practitioners with an initial approach to treating patients, even if that approach has to be modified to meet the unique needs of a patient. Even in cases in which following a treatment protocol is appropriate at the beginning of treatment, as the patient progresses, it may become necessary to deviate from the protocol. Likewise, management guidelines provide managers with a framework for developing a plan of action that can be modified to meet the unique needs of different individual employees and work groups. Managers may be required to deviate from management guidelines as the employees and work groups they manage change and evolve.

At this point, it is clear that management is a highly textured process. It consists of four basic functions that occur simultaneously rather than sequentially. It is also a process that is applied in working with individual employees and with groups of employees. It is a process that requires a flexible, rather than a strict, application of guidelines. The conceptualization of this multidimensional process has been clarified by the identification of different roles that managers perform.

Management Roles

Well-known management expert Henry Mintzberg's observation of managers at work led to his identification of ten different management roles.[4] Three of these roles are **interpersonal** roles. As a **figurehead**, a manager performs a ceremonial or symbolic duty. For example, a department head who presents a gift at a retirement party for a long-term employee fulfills the figurehead role. Another interpersonal role is acting as a **liaison**. In this role, the manager maintains contact with persons outside the work group. Those persons may or may not be members of the organization. For example, the administrator of a medical practice may maintain contact with a representative of the local Blue Shield plan. This contact may result in beneficial information being passed along to the administrator and may strengthen the working relationship between the insurer and the group practice. The third interpersonal role is that of **leader**. In the leadership role, the manager directs the efforts of the work group.

Mintzberg identified three **informational** roles. As a **monitor**, the manager searches for and receives information from outside sources. Clinicians are very familiar with this role because they continually monitor what is happening in their fields and in their professions. The information they find helps them to become better practitioners. In the same way, managers monitor the environment for information of significance to their organizations. A manager is also an information **disseminator**. The manager passes along information that is of importance to others in the organization. At times the manager may be a **spokesperson**. In this role, the manager represents the organization to outsiders. A department head who gives a facility tour to a group of students is fulfilling this role.

Mintzberg identified four **decisional** roles. As an **entrepreneur**, the manager searches the organization and its environment for opportunities. Although many people think of entrepreneurs as independent businesspeople, contemporary managers at all levels are expected to assist the organization in entrepreneurial activities. A manager is also a **disturbance handler**. In this role, the manager takes action in response to unanticipated problems. At times, every manager is forced to engage in crisis management. Another decisional role is that of **resource allocator**. The work of allocation includes budgeting, scheduling, and work structuring. Finally, the manager is a **negotiator**. Negotiation occurs with subordinates, peers, superiors, and persons external to the organization.

Special Management Considerations in Healthcare

Is there anything about healthcare that makes the practice of management different in this environment than it is in other industries? The answer is both yes and no. In many ways, providing healthcare services is very similar to providing other kinds of services, and there are valuable lessons to be learned from the experience of managers in other industries. On the other hand, in some ways the nature of healthcare delivery is very different from other kinds of work. Few people see many similarities between running a corner newsstand and a diversified HSO. However, some management principles still apply to both. Perhaps it is the combination of several simultaneous challenges that differentiates the management of HSOs from other types of management. Shortell and Kaluzny have identified several of these challenges:

- The output of healthcare providers is difficult to define and to measure;

- Healthcare delivery is variable, complex, and, frequently, a nondeferrable emergency;

- Healthcare delivery tolerates neither ambiguity nor error;
- Healthcare is delivered by a wide array of highly specialized professionals and necessitates extraordinary coordination;
- Dual lines of authority (managerial and clinical) exist in many HSOs;
- Healthcare providers are professionals with loyalties to both the HSO and to their professions;
- There is little managerial control over the workers (i.e., physicians) with the most responsibility for generating work and expenditures.[5]

In addition, healthcare delivery is a highly regulated process, and it is a service that requires that the client (patient) be highly involved in the delivery of the service. Of course, managers in other industries face very similar challenges. Banking is also heavily regulated; law enforcement has an emergency response component; engineering firms employ highly professional work forces; the practice of law requires a high degree of client involvement in service delivery. There are indeed lessons to be learned from other industries, but it is the convergence of these attributes in one environment that makes healthcare management a challenging undertaking. Providing direct patient care is also difficult and exciting. The clinician who assumes managerial responsibilities exchanges one challenging role for another.

Making the Transition

In the opening case, how can Kathy make a transition from being a competent, effective professional nurse to a competent, effective professional nurse manager? All she has to do is to transfer the very same skills that make her a good nurse to her new managerial role.

First, she needs to apply her considerable patient care planning skills to planning the work of her employees. Note how her planning of Mr. Kilmer's care facilitated both his admission to and discharge from the hospital. Similarly, before each shift, she needs to walk onto her unit armed with as much information as possible. Perhaps her first stop in the hospital each day should be a visit to the staffing office to identify any special staffing problems even before she arrives at the unit. Likewise, she might take a minute to check her unit's current census with the admitting office before she goes to the unit. Until she has the experience to respond decisively and confidently to staffing crises, she can use the few extra minutes in the elevator to plan how she will deal with the very first problem that is going to face her when she gets to the unit. She also needs to spend some time developing plans for dealing with difficult employees and physicians. These people are going to be there each time she reports for duty. She should prepare a plan that will solve ongoing problems so that she will not have to look forward to each shift with dread.

Next, she needs to organize. Her first action on the unit should be to organize the shift's work and assign responsibility and authority to get the work done. Since she is being bombarded with complaints and problems from all sides, she may need to empower her staff to deal with some of these issues so that she can direct her attention and energy only to those problems that really need her degree of expertise.

During the shift, she needs to lead her staff and control the work that is accomplished. This is going to require her presence on the floor and in patient rooms. She will have to find a balance between the extremes of actually doing the work herself and leaving the staff without direction. One of her control activities must be following up to make sure that the unit functions smoothly after she leaves. She also needs to make sure that problems that arose during her shift do not recur. For example, if a nursing assistant's improper transfer technique caused a patient fall, she needs to intervene with the nursing assistant right away so that she does not have to deal with a similar problem caused by this nursing assistant again. She successfully provided this forward-thinking intervention with Mr. Kilmer's family and with his home health providers. She can do the same with her subordinates.

Kathy will be a successful healthcare manager as soon as she finds a way to transfer her clinical skills to the management role. Perhaps if Kathy had had an appropriate management orientation, she could have avoided her feelings of dread and inadequacy. Since her hospital failed to prepare her, Kathy may have to take the orientation initiative. She may have to find a **mentor**, someone higher in the hierarchy who is willing and able to give her support. In choosing a mentor, she should find someone whose management expertise she respects and with whom she has a good relationship.

There is an additional interpersonal challenge that Kathy needs to assess and resolve—her relationship with her co-workers. Kathy was promoted from the ranks, and she is now having some difficulty with a staff nurse that she considered a friend. Is this conflict truly centered on a difference of professional opinion? If so, it cannot be resolved through shouts and insults. Is the conflict a result of Kathy's inappropriate attempt to interfere with professional decision making? Is the staff nurse's response inappropriate to Kathy's legitimate concern for patient care? Is this conflict grounded in jealousy or resentment stemming from Kathy's promotion? Kathy must realize that her authority (exercised or not) over a work group has changed her relationship with the members of the group. Maintaining friendships in the face of this relationship requires extraordinary insight and maturity on the part of both supervisor and subordinate. Disagreements on both the personal and professional levels will arise. Those disagreements must be resolved in their separate spheres for these complex relationships to survive. Most people find this hard to do, and many choose to sever either the professional or personal relationship. Kathy must rationally and objectively analyze this conflict and take the initiative to resolve it. If neither she nor her friend values both their professional and personal relationships enough to put in the extraordinary effort to maintain them, then the relationship will have to be restructured.

The new relationships she must establish contribute to the anxiety Kathy feels about making this career change. In addition, she is going to have to adjust to a new level of ambiguity in her work. Managers are judged by criteria other than the technical quality and quantity of their work. Kathy probably does not yet understand those criteria. Even if she does, she has not had enough time to become comfortable with them. As a supervisor, she probably has more flexibility in structuring her activities than she had as a staff nurse. New managers like Kathy usually require some time to learn how to structure their own work.

She also must deal with the anxiety that comes with making a significant career change. She does not yet know if she likes her new management role and whether she will be successful in it. She does know she was a good staff nurse. There is little she can do to alleviate her anxiety about the nature of managerial work or her choices about career development. With time and success, these concerns will be ameliorated.

The intent of this book is to provide both new and experienced clinicians/managers an overview of management in the healthcare context. Like a classic management text, it is arranged in units that focus on the management functions. Within each of those units, the reader will find chapters that speak directly to the challenges faced by healthcare managers. To help readers see the parallels to clinical practice, analogies to medical science, diagnosis, and treatment are used to illustrate management principles.

Moving from a clinical to a managerial position can be stressful. However, clinicians can be assured that their clinical training and experience have prepared them well for these new responsibilities. Management is not just about problem employees, finance, and handling complaints. It is also about professional growth, fulfillment, and success. Enjoy the journey.

Endnotes

1. Peter Drucker, *Management: Tasks, Responsibilities, Practices* (New York: Harper & Row, 1974), p. 17.
2. A. J. Jago, "Leadership: Perspectives in Theory and Research," *Management Sciences 28* (1982): 315–36.
3. Henry Mintzberg, *The Nature of Managerial Work* (New York: Harper & Row, 1973).
4. Ibid.
5. Stephen M. Shortell and Arnold D. Kaluzny, "Organization Theory and Health Services Management," in Stephen M. Shortell and Arnold D. Kaluzny, eds., *Health Care Management: Organization Design and Behavior*, 3rd ed. (New York: Delmar Publishers, 1994).

Unit I

Planning

2

Goal Setting and Planning: *Disorientation*

In this chapter the reader will learn how:

◆ to diagnose problems related to poor planning

◆ to determine the difference between operational and strategic planning

◆ to develop an operational plan

◆ to develop a strategic plan

◆ organizational planning is similar to managing a disoriented patient

◆ to connect organizational performance to planning.

By 10:40 A.M., 83-year-old Helen Stevens was really nervous. Her new physical therapist was supposed to have been at her house at 10:00 A.M. on the dot. She was not happy about accepting home health services to begin with. She did not like the idea of having strangers in her house. In her frail condition, she was vulnerable to all kinds of abuse by people she did not know. However, Dr. Kern had convinced her that she could not get stronger without the therapy. He had also assured her that the Allmed Agency had guaranteed that she would have the same therapists all the time and that their home health providers were absolutely dependable. This lateness did not equate to dependability as far as Mrs. Stevens was concerned, especially when she had canceled a visit from her church group to keep this appointment. She finally found the phone number for Allmed Home Care and dialed it.

The phone rang eight times before it was answered by Cindy. After Mrs. Stevens explained her problem, Cindy informed her that she was a new employee and that she did not know anything about scheduling therapists. Her job was just to answer the phone. However, if Mrs. Stevens cared to hold, she would transfer her call to someone who could help. Mrs. Stevens did not care to hold, but she had no choice.

After several minutes, Jim came on the line. He identified himself as a nurse. Mrs. Stevens again explained her problem, and Jim said, "I'm sorry. I didn't know this was about a therapy problem, and I'm not your case manager. I don't know who your case manager is or where he or she might be right now. But I can take a message."

"Messages won't do me any good. Let me talk to whoever's in charge down there."

At 11:00, MaryBeth Larson's phone rang.

MaryBeth's day had not gone well. When she went to the closet to pull out her blue skirt for the meeting with Kent Rogers, the skirt was not there. It was several minutes before she remembered that it was at the cleaners. Then she got stuck in traffic and missed the morning briefing. If she had been there, she would have known that the new therapist had torn her right medial meniscus and was going to be unable to work for the next two weeks. At least the traffic jam had given her time to think about her meeting with Kent. Four years ago they had started Allmed. Kent is a businessman and a limited partner in Allmed; MaryBeth is the managing partner. As the only home health provider in the area, Allmed had done very well during its first two years. Now there are three competitors, two of which are branches of national companies. They not only compete for referrals, but also for a short supply of therapists. MaryBeth has found herself working harder and harder, but with the feeling that Allmed is falling behind the competition. Whereas Allmed serves primarily rehabilitation clients, MaryBeth has heard that some of the other firms are also providing high-tech services. She recently heard a rumor that one of the national companies wanted to buy Allmed and maybe that was why Kent wanted to have this business lunch. MaryBeth is not sure she wants to sell because she does not want to work for someone else. However, the pressure is beginning to get to her.

When she got to the office, she had to deal immediately with an equipment supplier who had notified Allmed that it could not process Allmed's latest order for failure to pay an outstanding balance. After an hour-and-a-half of trying to track the missing payment, MaryBeth found that she had failed to sign the check. MaryBeth thought that she had approved payment and signed the check, but it had gotten buried in a stack of paperwork she had never gotten around to, and the bookkeeper had not brought the oversight to her attention.

Then Mrs. Stevens' call came through. MaryBeth had worked hard for months to get a referral from Dr. Kern. Dr. Kern had a large family practice with many older people who were potential home health patients. Mrs. Stevens was extremely upset about the missed appointment. MaryBeth decided that she had to make a personal visit to her to make amends as best she could. As she rushed to the door, she told Cindy to call Kent and tell him she would be half an hour late. Even as she got into the car, she did not know where she was going to be able to get a physical therapist to see Mrs. Stevens today.

Diagnosing Planning Problems

MaryBeth's situation rings all too familiar with owners of small businesses of all kinds. One minute the manager deals with a financial issue, the next minute a professional matter, the next a client complaint, and the next a legal issue. How do managers buffeted by so many stimuli respond? All too often, they respond the way MaryBeth did—by running to put out one fire after another until they burn out, lose their jobs, or lose their businesses.

Although Allmed is a small HSO, managers in large HSOs face the same problems. If MaryBeth headed the home health services division of a healthcare network, she would be in much the same situation. In addition to worrying about personnel, professional, and financial issues, she would have to be concerned about the possibility of the HSO's merging her division with another home health provider, or perhaps the HSO's selling her division.

How do successful managers avoid burnout and find ways to continually renew their interest in their work? How do they minimize the number of crises they have to deal with on a daily basis? How do they steer their firms/work groups around potential pitfalls? Given how many things can go wrong, how do they avoid nervous breakdowns? By planning.

Poor planning and lack of planning manifest themselves in an array of signs and symptoms that may be difficult to recognize as a syndrome. Essentially the signs of poor planning are the same signs that characterize disorientation. The organization is confused about time, place, and person. Notice how many signs of disorientation are present in the Allmed case.

1. No physical therapist appeared to keep an appointment at the correct time or place.

2. No one answered the telephone in a timely manner.

3. Cindy did not recognize the correct person to whom to refer the problem.

4. Jim did not know where the correct person was to deal with the problem. He also did not know the next appropriate place to refer the problem.

5. MaryBeth did not coordinate the time and place of her wardrobe.

6. MaryBeth did not know how her firm ranked competitively in the market.

7. MaryBeth did not know where the check was nor when it was due.

8. MaryBeth did not know which person would provide Mrs. Stevens' therapy, nor the time therapy would take place.

9. MaryBeth did not know where her firm was going, who would take it there, or how long it would take to get there.

Confusion on the part of managers and staff alike is the hallmark of lack of planning.

Treating Planning Problems

Treating organizational disorientation is very similar to the treatment of clinical disorientation. The cornerstone of clinical management of disorientation is identification of an underlying etiology. Common causes of disorientation include trauma, drug toxicity, and neurological disorders. When a definitive etiology is identifiable, the appropriate intervention is treatment of the underlying problem. For example, discontinuing toxic drugs or decreasing dosages will generally result in reversing disorientation. When a manager notices the first signs of organizational disorientation, the first inclination is to search for underlying causes. Among the possible causes of Allmed's problems, the following come immediately to mind:

1. There are not enough staff members to handle the workload.

2. It is almost impossible to hire good help these days.

3. Stiff competition cannot be avoided in today's environment.

4. A competitive environment makes managers nervous, and excess stress leads to oversights and mistakes.

5. The process for handling accounts payable is faulty.

6. Allmed needs a managing partner with vision.

Although these factors frequently contribute to organizational problems, perhaps none of them are operative in the Allmed case. For example, although Allmed's work is not being completed in a timely manner, there may be plenty of staff members. Their failure to produce an acceptable quantity of high quality work may be due to a lack of training, poor communications, lack of supplies, or a multitude of other factors. If this is the case, the reflexive response of hiring more workers will not result in a better outcome. Likewise, the poor performance of Allmed's staff may have nothing to do with a lack of skilled labor in the market.

One possible underlying cause that seems to be irrefutable is that MaryBeth is not a visionary leader. Lack of vision may have contributed to Allmed's weak market position. However, replacing MaryBeth with a visionary will not solve all of Allmed's problems. For example, vision will not get a therapist to Mrs. Stevens' home on time. Responding to organizational disorientation with interventions that address only one aspect of disorientation at a time is symptomatic treatment. The underlying etiology of the many symptoms observed in this case is lack of planning, and the only viable intervention is to introduce and adhere to a structured planning process. Without such a process, MaryBeth will continue the frustration of putting out one fire after another until she and/or Allmed no longer have sufficient resources and reserves to continue.

Planning is very much like providing the organization with reality orientation. In the clinical setting, reality orientation requires two things. First (and so obvious in clinical settings as to be taken for granted), the staff must be oriented to effective procedures. Obviously, the blind cannot lead the blind. Imagine how unproductive it would be for two Alzheimer's patients to provide each other with reality orientation. Second, the staff's knowledge of reality must be communicated to disoriented patients repeatedly and in different ways. For example, in nursing facilities, the day of the week, the date, and the weather may be posted on a bulletin board in each unit and/or in the dining room. Disoriented residents are also reminded verbally of these facts several times through the day.

In the organizational context, the first step in orienting the organization is for managers to be cognizant of the "when, where, and how" of organizational activities. That is, managers must have a plan. Second, that plan must be communicated to staff repeatedly and in several different ways. Providing all members of the staff with a plan helps them to anchor their work activities in a realistic context. It gives them guideposts by which they can determine whether what they are doing and how they are doing it is consistent with the expectations of managers.

Planning is required to keep an organization moving toward its goals, to assure that projects are completed in a timely manner, and to facilitate the accomplishment of daily work. The lack of planning at Allmed left the firm without direction in its market. Allmed started as the only home care provider in its market. Through lack of planning, Allmed had not taken advantage of this competitive position. Effective planning may not have kept competition from entering the market, but it could well have kept Allmed ahead of the Johnny-come-latelys. Instead of enjoying a captive market, Allmed is apparently facing extinction as an independent provider.

Planning is also required to move projects forward. For example, moving from one business location to another is a project that requires careful planning. The new location has to be readied for occupancy, arrangements have to be made for continuing care of patients during the move, physical relocation must be completed, and clients and suppliers must be notified of the change. The importance of planning one-time-only projects is obvious.

Finally, day-to-day activities must be planned. All of the tasks to be accomplished must be identified and a plan of action formulated for successful completion. At Allmed, there is no indication that a well-defined plan to accomplish the work of the agency existed. If there was a plan, it is clear that the staff was unaware of it. It was lack of planning that led to the failure to care for Mrs. Stevens. It was lack of planning that caused an important bill to go unpaid. Had appropriate policies and procedures been written and implemented, these crises could have been avoided.

Planning to get work done on an ongoing basis and planning one-time projects is **operational planning**. Planning for the purpose of providing overall direction to the organization is **strategic planning**. In large organizations, operational planning is usually done at the middle and lower levels of management. Strategic planning is usually done by top level managers and the board of directors or board of trustees. However, in many health systems, lower level managers are expected to participate in strategic planning. For example, if MaryBeth headed a home health department of a large health system, she would probably be called on to do strategic planning for her unit. In small organizations with few levels of management, the same manager(s) may be responsible for both operational and strategic planning. For example, as the managing partner at Allmed, it is primarily MaryBeth's responsibility to formulate a strategic plan as well as to develop policies and procedures for completing the daily tasks of the agency. The same would be true of a medical practice manager.

Operational Planning

In the healthcare service industry, planning takes on special importance. Poor operational planning can put patients at risk. Poor planning of work activities in a hospital, for example, can result in missed or delayed treatments, laboratory tests, and diagnostic procedures. In the Allmed case, poor planning caused Mrs. Stevens to become anxious and reaffirmed her initial distrust of home health providers. The result may well be a compromised clinical outcome.

Operational planning in healthcare must be more flexible than it is in many other industries. For example, in the steel industry the goal of an operations plan is to produce a given number of tons of steel in a given period. The plan describes how that level of production is to be accomplished, how long production will take, and what resources are required for that level of production. The production plan is derived through analysis of current orders and a forecast of future orders. Changes in the production rate are usually small because demand for steel changes slowly. In healthcare, demand may swing rather wildly from one day to the next (or even from one shift to the next). Patient volume in an emergency department may vary by 100% from one day to the next. Some of that change in demand may be foreseeable, but often it is not. Planning under conditions of uncertainty must take into account periods of high demand and periods of low demand. In healthcare, excess production capacity is unavoidable because providers must be capable of handling periods of unexpectedly high demand.

Operational plans that relate to ongoing activities are called **standing plans**. In HSOs standing plans are usually expressed as policies, procedures, rules, and regulations. **Policies** are broad guidelines that establish boundaries for behavior which contribute to advancing the goals of the organization. **Procedures** are more specific in defining actions within the scope of policies. **Rules and regulations** narrowly specify how procedures are to be implemented. A policy of Allmed might be:

Allmed providers are available to patients and physicians by telephone 24 hours a day.

A supporting procedure would be:

Calls will be taken during normal business hours (8:00 A.M–5:00 P.M.) at the Allmed central office (phone number 555-6600). After hours calls will be routed through Midstate Paging Service (phone number 789-3705).

A supporting rule would be:

All incoming calls at the Allmed central office are to be answered by the fourth ring. If the receptionist has not been able to respond by the third ring, it is the responsibility of any other staff member who hears the phone to answer it.

Recall that planning has two important components: formulating the plan and communicating the plan. Writing policies, procedures, and rules is formulating a standing plan. Carefully crafted policies, procedures, and rules are crucial to effective operational planning. After policies, procedures, and rules are written, they must be communicated. Once everyone in the organization understands the operational plan, decision making becomes simplified. Rather than having to solve recurrent problems anew, the staff should be able to solve them routinely by applying policies and procedures. For problems that occur infrequently, employees should be able to consult a policy and procedure manual for guidance. The well-written policy and procedure manual can also be an invaluable training and orientation tool for new employees.

Crafting and implementing policies, procedures and rules is no simple task. The following difficulties are commonly encountered in HSOs.

1. Policy and procedure manuals lack contingency plans. **Contingency plans** are prepared in anticipation of out-of-the-ordinary events. At Allmed, for example, there were probably procedures for establishing a care plan, assigning a case manager, and scheduling therapists. There was apparently no standard procedure to be followed in the event a therapist was unable to keep an appointment.

2. There are too many policies, procedures, and rules. Healthcare delivery is a complex process, and having a large volume of policies, procedures, and rules is not uncommon. However, too many of them can become unduly burdensome. One way to avoid this problem is to require a written justification for each item in the policy and procedure manual. Any manager responsible for authoring policies and procedures should impose this burden on him/herself.

3. Policies, procedures, and rules are misunderstood by the staff. Writing is a very difficult task, especially for managers whose jobs do not normally consist of large amounts of writing. Therefore, all policies, procedures, and rules must be reviewed for clarity. Having several people from outside the work group (and even outside the profession) review them is helpful. If the uninitiated can understand them, the work group should have no difficulties.

4. Policies, procedures, and rules are inappropriate. Times change. Organizations change. Staff changes. Eventually even the best policies, procedures, and rules must change. Policy and procedure manuals should undergo constant review. Having an employee team take on this task not only results in manuals that realistically reflect the work of the group, but also helps disseminate and reinforce the content of the manual.

5. Policies, procedures, and rules are not followed. This situation usually occurs because employees either do not know policies, procedures and rules, or are unmotivated to adhere to them. Lack of employee motivation is easy to understand in those cases in which managers themselves are not fully committed to the operational plan. Unfortunately, this happens too often in healthcare because a policy and procedure manual may be written only to satisfy external accrediting and licensing agencies.

Because the work of managers is less repetitive than the work of staff employees, managers need something in addition to policies, procedures, and rules to assist them in planning their own activities. Some managers seem to be able to do this effortlessly. Others, like MaryBeth, continually seem to be at loose ends. Because their work is somewhat unpredictable and one day seldom duplicates any other, managers need an agenda to keep them on track. The agenda needs to be formalized in writing. It may be as simple as a "To Do" list, or it may be as complex as a computer-generated calendar. Formalization of the agenda in writing is important because it makes the agenda real in substance as well as in concept. In the course of a tumultuous work period, it is easy for managers to lose track of their own work plan as they respond to the needs of others. The written agenda keeps managers moving towards the completion of the work they know needs to be done. This process is particularly important for new managers who can easily be distracted from their plan of action. The written agenda can be considered as a peripheral memory bank. It can be suspended in the presence of more pressing needs, but returning to it once a crisis is resolved brings back into focus the manager's short-term goals.

Project Planning

Not all work of the organization is repetitive. Some actions of a nonrepetitive nature must also be planned. Policies, procedures, and rules are not appropriate planning tools for nonrepetitive activities. However, there are several other tools that can be used by managers to plan projects. The Gantt chart, Program Evaluation Review Technique (PERT), and Critical Path Method (CPM) are commonly used in project planning.

The **Gantt chart** is a diagram of the steps required for the completion of the project. The time to complete each step is included in the chart. Once all the steps to be completed are listed, the result is an outline of the plan for completing the project. The Gantt chart is built from this list. Figure 2.1 is a simple Gantt chart for relocating a group medical practice. The dark lines on the chart represent the amount of time that the manager originally estimated each of the steps of the project will take. Once the chart is prepared, the manager notes the progress of the project on the chart. In Figure 2.1, the actual progress that occurred is indicated by the light lines. This Gantt chart shows that the project was completed in about eleven weeks, about one week longer than the manager anticipated.

Because projects tend to be nonrecurring tasks (How many times in a career does a medical practice manager coordinate a relocation?), identifying the steps

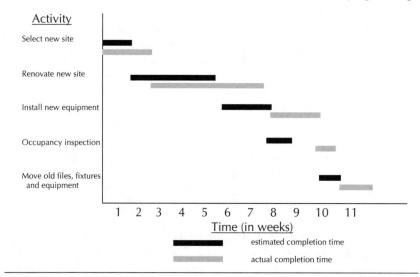

Figure 2.1   Gantt chart for relocating a medical group practice.

of the project and estimating the amount of time required to complete each one are both difficult. One of the most helpful things that managers can do is to talk through the process several times. Talking through the process with staff members can be very helpful. Some staff members may have had experience with similar projects and can offer insight gained as a result of that experience. Also, because staff members are directly responsible for production of services, they will be able to identify steps and/or problems that the manager may overlook.

The manager should also discuss the project with outsiders, as long as those discussions do not disclose information that actual or potential competitors may find useful. Other managers who have been involved with similar projects may be willing to share their expertise. Even friends and family may have had experiences that are relevant to the project. This is a source of advice that managers tend to forget, but it is very important. Seeking the viewpoint of someone outside the business unit and the industry can provide the manager with a fresh way of looking at a project and may lead to a more effective and/or efficient way of approaching it.

Besides talking through the project, managers need to do some research. Today's healthcare environment is information rich. Frequently, when managers do not think there is enough information to plan a project, the problem is not that the information does not exist; rather it is that the manager has not accessed the information that is available. Most healthcare professionals receive more information than they can organize and utilize effectively. The challenge of healthcare managers is to have information available when and where they need it. For example, the medical practice manager who needs to relocate a practice would need information about evaluating practice sites and office design. Short of hiring a consultant to perform these functions, where can the office manager go for the necessary information?

One place is to professional organizations. Many professional organizations publish journals, books, and pamphlets that are specific to the needs of their members. Since office design and location are important issues to medical practice managers, professional associations are likely to have addressed them.

An often underutilized source of information is the library. In fact, reference librarians should be among the healthcare manager's best friends. Managers too often overlook libraries as an inexpensive source of timely information. Healthcare managers can take advantage of libraries that specialize in healthcare. For example, libraries associated with teaching hospitals, medical schools, or schools of allied health would be good places to start finding material about medical practice management issues. Most of these libraries have easily accessible electronic catalogs of their materials. They also allow users to do literature searches through CD-ROM technology. Reference librarians can also assist with searching for material held by other libraries by using the Internet.

Public libraries are also good sources of local information that is important to project planning. These libraries may have local census information, information about local and national businesses (including healthcare firms), and information about pertinent government agencies. This information may be of considerable importance in planning projects and developing realistic Gantt charts.

Program Evaluation Review Technique (PERT) is another useful project planning tool. PERT is a slightly more sophisticated planning tool than the Gantt chart because it includes three different time estimates for completing each step of a project. Note in Figure 2.1 that the process of moving the medical practice was estimated to take ten weeks. Instead, the relocation actually took eleven weeks. If the organization had entered into the project without allowing for a delay in completing the move, the practice could have been in trouble. It might have been without a place to conduct business, much like people who have to move out of one house by a certain date, but who cannot yet occupy their new residence. During that time, makeshift arrangements would have to be made. For an ongoing practice, makeshift arrangements are unacceptable. PERT results in an estimate that takes into account worst case and best case completion scenarios so that trauma due to inaccurate forecasting can be minimized.

Like a Gantt chart, PERT requires that the steps of a project be identified and that they be sequenced. Table 2.1 is a table for the activities required to install a new computer system at an independent home health agency. In this table, the expected time has been calculated using the following formula:

[optimistic time + 4 (most likely time) + pessimistic time]/6[1]

Table 2.1   New Home Health Computer System Project

Activity	Description	Immediate Predecessor	Time (days)
A	Evaluate, choose, and order a new system	—	26
B	Delivery of new system	A	10
C	Rewire facility	A	6
D	Install hardware	B,C	2
E	Install software	D	1
F	Train staff	E	7
G	Transfer records to new system	E	5
H	Notify staff of switch-over date	F,G	1
Finish	Switch to new system	H	1

For example, activity B is an activity in which there is considerable variability. The manager uses the vendor's estimate of delivery time as the most likely time. However, he knows from experience that manufacturers sometimes exceed their expectations and that other times they fall woefully behind. He uses this experience to make the following estimates:

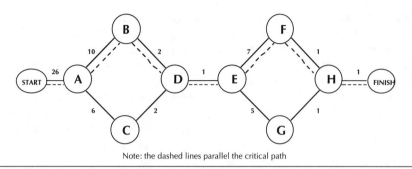

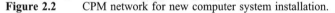

Note: the dashed lines parallel the critical path

Figure 2.2   CPM network for new computer system installation.

optimistic time = 6 days

expected time = 9 days

pessimistic time = 18 days

The manager makes the optimistic estimate based on the knowledge that some hardware and/or software may be ready to ship ahead of the salesperson's expectation. He also allows that transportation of the products may be faster than expected. On the other hand, he knows that if the materials are not ready to be shipped, any number of production problems could result in delays. Given the information he can gather from the salesperson and from his own experience with supplier delays, he estimates that it could take up to twice as long as the salesperson promised (i.e., eighteen days) to get the product. By putting these values into the above formula, he estimates that it will take ten days for delivery. Although there is only a one day difference in the estimate derived by using the formula, it is an estimate that takes into account the possibility of extreme variability in delivery. In terms of operational planning, even one day can be significant. This method of estimating the time to complete each step is not foolproof, but it does force the manager to give considerable thought to what it is reasonable to expect.

The next step in the PERT process is to add the expected values to get the total amount of time that the project will take. In this example, the estimated completion time is 58 days. However, note that not all these steps are exactly sequential. For example, activity C (rewiring the facility) can be started as soon as the system is chosen and ordered. It does not depend on delivery. Likewise, the process of transferring records to the new system can also be started before the entire staff is trained. Because some steps can be completed simultaneously, this project could be completed in less than 58 days. Identifying the sequence of events that requires the longest period of time to complete is the Critical Path Method (CPM).

Figure 2.2 shows the critical path in the new computer system project. (Note: the times shown in this example come from the PERT calculation. The PERT calculation does not need to be included in CPM, but it may improve the project time requirement estimate.) Notice that in this schematic of the project activities, those steps that can be done simultaneously are shown opposite each other. The critical path is the sequence of steps that takes the longest amount of time to complete. Any delay in completing these steps will result in a delay in completing the project. Therefore, it is the progress of these activities that the manager must monitor most closely if the targeted completion date is to be met. Some delay in the other steps can be absorbed without altering the amount of time to complete the project. In this case, the expected completion time is 48 days. In the first set of steps that can be completed simultaneously, there are four days of slack time in the shorter pathway. In the second set of simultaneous steps, there are two days of slack time. On-time completion of these steps is not critical to the completion schedule of the project unless the time required to complete those steps grows beyond the available slack time.

The PERT and CPM methods of project planning are obviously time-consuming. However, they are valuable planning tools that are well worth the time to undertake. They force managers to give serious thought to each step required to complete a project. By completing this planning exercise, managers initiate projects with a clear picture of which steps can be completed simultaneously and which steps require the most attention by virtue of being in the critical path.

Strategic Planning

Strategic planning precedes operational and project planning. A business unit has to have direction before completing projects and carrying out everyday activities have any meaning beyond merely getting through the day. Strategic planning is the lifeblood of organizational survival. Unfortunately, the uncertainty surrounding the formulation of strategy makes this a task with which many managers are uncomfortable.

There is, however, a systematic approach that can help managers deal with the ambiguity of strategic planning. This approach is called **SWOT analysis**. The goal of SWOT analysis is to enable managers to formulate organizational goals and objectives so that they are appropriate to the environment in which the organization exists. SWOT analysis requires that managers identify the **strengths** and **weaknesses** of the business unit, and the **opportunities** for and **threats** to the business unit that exist in its environment. Juxtaposing these factors in tabular form can help managers visualize how they are related. Table 2.2 is an example of how this might be done for a home health agency. (Note: This is a rudimentary example that lists only the most obvious strengths, weaknesses, threats, and opportunities. A thorough SWOT analysis might easily have ten or more entries under each category.)

Most managers know their organizations well and can develop a list of strengths and weaknesses rather quickly. After all, managers deal with these issues daily. However, managers should go through a reality check to validate their assumptions. One way to validate is to have evidence. For example, the manager who prepared the SWOT analysis shown in Table 2.2 should be able to quantify and document an increasing caseload. Providing quantitative evidence may help the manager to put this factor into proper perspective. For example, a 4% annual growth rate in caseload is certainly a sign that the organization is growing. An increase of this magnitude may seem very significant to a manager who is struggling to pull together enough resources to meet the demands of the additional workload. However, if similar home health agencies have an annual growth rate of 10% in the same time period, then the manager has to look for internal weaknesses and external threats that may account for this relatively weak performance. If the agencies experiencing the 10% growth rate are in the same service area, then this home health firm is actually losing ground in terms of its share of the market in spite of its growth. Also, this 4% increase needs to be evaluated qualitatively. Is the increase in high-revenue, low-cost services, or is it coming from low-profit services? By including evidence as part of the SWOT analysis, the manager begins to open the door to generating the kinds of questions and answers that will eventually result in a solid strategic plan.

Another way the manager should validate the internal analysis is by asking staff for feedback. The manager of the home health agency may feel that a high

Table 2.2   SWOT Analysis for a Home Health Agency

STRENGTHS	OPPORTUNITIES
1. Very committed, hard-working management	1. Expansion of geographic service area to surrounding counties
2. Steadily increasing caseload	2. Hospital and rehabilitation average length of stay continuing to decrease in service area
3. Good relationships with referring physicians	3. More public acceptance and demand for home health services
	4. State is considering ways to further decrease Medicaid spending for hospital and nursing home care
	5. Expanding patient population in service area
WEAKNESSES	**THREATS**
1. Too little capital	1. Two national home care providers have entered the market in the past year
2. Hard to recruit new professional employees	2. Third party payers are concerned about rising home health costs
3. High turnover of technical employees	3. Managed care organizations could start their own home care divisions

turnover rate among technical employees is a weakness because hiring and training new employees is expensive, and the consistency of care that is provided to patients is interrupted. However, the remaining staff members may see the turnover as a strength if they feel that their former colleagues were poor workers. In that case, the turnover of employees could be counted as both a weakness and a strength. These two factors do not cancel each other out. They merely indicate that the organization must work at maintaining a more stable work force and, at the same time, continue to weed out employees whose work is unacceptable.

When a manager is formulating a strategic plan for a business unit that is part of a larger organization, seeking the feedback of colleagues can also be a way of validating the SWOT analysis. For example, the head of home health services in a hospital might submit the departmental SWOT analysis to head nurses of units that refer patients to the service. The director of Pharmacy and the director of Central Services might also be able to provide feedback on strengths and weaknesses from their interactions with the home health personnel.

Doing the external analysis is a more difficult task for managers because managers (especially lower level managers) tend to be more focused on their organizations than on the world outside. Uncovering opportunities and threats comes from studying the market, the economy, competitors, politics, and government. All factors that affect healthcare delivery in general, and the service(s) provided by the HSO, in particular, must be observed and evaluated. Managers must tap the same sources of information about the external environment that they use to plan projects (i.e., professional organizations, individuals in other organizations, and libraries).

Strategy Development

Once the SWOT analysis is complete, the manager can choose a strategy that is appropriate for the organization and its environment. The choice of strategy is guided by both the SWOT analysis and the mission and goals of the organization. The chosen strategy must be consistent with the organization's mission. For example, a home healthcare agency's SWOT analysis may show that one of the firm's strengths is the staff's expertise in geriatrics. The environmental analysis may show that an opportunity in the market arises from a lack of adult day care. Putting one and one together would seem to indicate that diversification into adult day care would be appropriate. However, if the mission of the firm is limited to providing care in the home environment, then this diversification strategy should not be pursued. This may seem like an inflexible approach to business development, but, in the long run, it is a wise policy. Many businesses have failed because they strayed from their mission by trying to take advantage of every attractive opportunity that came their way. Deviating from the mission causes firms to spread their financial and human resources so thin that they end up serving their wide range of clients poorly. This is not to say that mission statements are carved in stone. Every organization's mission should be periodically reviewed. However, frequent changes to the mission are ill-advised. Changes that occur at intervals of less than five to ten years result in organizational behavior that zigzags across the highway of business activity and eventually causes the organization to career off the road.

Some strategies (i.e., **corporate strategies**) relate to the nature of the business. Other strategies, **market strategies** or **competitive strategies**, deal with the way that businesses compete in their markets. These strategies are listed in Table 2.3.

Table 2.3   Generic Strategy Options

CORPORATE STRATEGIES	MARKET (COMPETITIVE) STRATEGIES
EXPANSION	COST LEADERSHIP
Horizontal integration	
Vertical integration	DIFFERENTIATION
Diversification	
RETRENCHMENT	FOCUS
Divestiture	
Downsizing	
STABILIZATION	

At the corporate level, there are three basic (sometimes called generic) strategies that a business unit could pursue. The first of these basic strategies is **expansion**. A business that pursues expansion may attempt to achieve an increase in the volume of its current business activities, or it may seek to increase its volume of business through adding new products, services, and/or markets to its current business. There are several actions that businesses can take to achieve expansion.

Horizontal integration is the affiliation of two organizations that perform the same kind of work. In the opening case, MaryBeth was concerned that Allmed would be acquired by another home health agency. An acquisition of this nature would be an example of horizontal integration. A business **acquisition** occurs when one firm purchases another. In the process, the acquired firm loses its separate identity and becomes fully integrated into the acquiring firm. Sometimes two firms decide that a **merger** is an appropriate strategy. Mergers occur when two firms come together to create a new firm. In the process both firms lose their separate identities, and a new business is created. Sometimes similar firms recognize the advantages of working with each other, but prefer an arrangement that preserves the separate identity of each. Such an arrangement is an **alliance**. For example, several home health agencies might come together to form an alliance for the purpose of purchasing supplies. Alliances are not often easy to maintain because of constantly changing personnel and business environmental conditions. There may also be legal obstacles such as antitrust laws. **Joint ventures** are alliances in which each participant contributes resources to begin a new business.

The new business may be jointly managed by alliance members, or it may operate independently. Profits and losses are shared by members of the alliance.

Vertical integration also involves merger, acquisition, and alliance. However, in vertical integration these relationships are entered into with suppliers and/ or customers. This has been a common corporate strategy of HSOs in recent years. Hospitals have integrated with third party payers, nursing facilities, medical equipment suppliers, and physicians. In a vertically integrated health system, patients move from one component of the integrated system to another to receive a wide range of health products and services.

Another way to pursue an expansion strategy is **diversification**. The firm that diversifies adds to the kinds of businesses it operates. These businesses may be related or completely unrelated. A hospital might purchase a food packaging firm or a travel agency as part of a diversification strategy.

Most managers like to think in terms of expansion because it creates new jobs, sources of revenue, and opportunities for personal growth and advancement. However, there are times when it is appropriate to pursue the opposite strategy— **retrenchment**. During retrenchment, the emphasis is on reining in business activity, which may mean a sale of some assets, office and/or site closings, or layoffs (downsizing). When the business is extended beyond the capabilities of its resources, or when the market for its product or service is shrinking, retrenchment may be the best strategy. Retrenchment may involve **divestiture**. Divestiture is the sale of a business unit. For example, an HSO could decide to divest its home health service unit by selling it to another HSO.

A third basic corporate strategy is **stabilization**. A business unit following a stabilization strategy essentially stays its course. Its strategy is to make small improvements in its performance without making major changes in its volume, structure, or market served.

Besides formulating corporate strategies, the firm has to formulate **market strategies** that define how the firm will compete in the market place. One market strategy is **cost leadership** (i.e., competing on the basis of having the lowest price). Of course, this is not the only way that any HSO competes because buyers of health services also expect quality. But setting the lowest price in the market and promoting that fact can effectively position an HSO in its market.

Another market strategy is **differentiation**. This strategy requires making a product/service distinctly better than competing products/services in the eyes of potential buyers. In healthcare, this is not an easy market strategy to pursue because consumers and buyers of health services are inconsistent in their demands regarding what it is they value in healthcare delivery. Also, at the current stage of quality assessment, the quantitative focus is on outcomes, and the criteria for judging outcomes are still evolving. Therefore, differentiating healthcare services is very difficult to achieve.

Another market strategy option is **focus** strategy. This strategy has been effectively employed in healthcare services because it flows directly from medical specialization. A focus strategy requires that a firm focus its efforts on a specific segment of the market. Home health agencies that emphasize respiratory care and hospital-based spinal cord injury services are examples of business units that use focus strategy.

Using SWOT analysis helps business units to identify and choose from among the generic strategies described above. Upon choosing a generic strategy, the unit must customize and apply that strategy to further meet its mission and goals. However, there is one caveat to using the SWOT technique. The SWOT analysis results in strategy selection that matches current organizational strengths and weaknesses with the opportunities and threats that currently exist. The goal of the strategic plan, however, is to carry the organization into the future. If the future is neglected in the formulation of a strategic plan, the organization may find itself beautifully positioned to meet the challenges of a world that no longer exists.

Forecasting

Forecasting is never easy or precise. But it is necessary if the strategic plan is to successfully guide the organization into the future. The place to start forecasting is from knowledge of the past and the present. "The future can be predicted only by extrapolating from the past, yet it is fairly certain the future will be different from the past."[2] The past, and to some extent the present, is comfortable because it is a known quantity. It can be studied and analyzed from an evidentiary base that is not available for the future.

Most managers recognize major changes in their environment. How many HSO managers did not realize by 1994 that the healthcare system was changing to a system dominated by managed care? By 1994 it was too late, however, for many managers to develop a strategic plan that would position their organizations to compete effectively in a managed care environment. How do managers identify changes in the environment early enough to develop strategic plans? Managers need to be constantly on the lookout "for people messing with the rules, because that is the earliest sign of significant change."[3] It is the changing rules of the game, also called a **paradigm shift**, that present managers with the greatest threats and biggest opportunities. In healthcare, there were two trends that signaled a change to managed care: (1) a growing body of literature that extolled the virtues of preventive medicine, and (2) increased monitoring of utilization of health resources by the government and other third-party payers. Managers who extrapolated these trends and foresaw that there would be a change in the rules governing the application of expensive specialized medical interventions were better able to position their organizations in this evolving market.

As today's managers plan for tomorrow, they have to look for similar indications of changing rules of the game. Here is one example. In a 1993 article, Eisenberg et al. reported that 10% of visits to primary care physicians were made to nonconventional practitioners. This is a higher level of utilization of nontraditional therapists than previously thought.[4] To the astute healthcare manager, this is an indication that there may be a shift in the way people choose their care providers. The manager should monitor the literature for additional factual verification of this data, determine if a trend in changing utilization of traditional medicine exists, and determine the importance of that trend as it might affect his business unit. A course of action can then be taken that will allow the business unit to meet the challenges presented by this change.

Other indicators of paradigm shifts can be found in applications of technology. As electronic mail, teleconferencing, long-distance electronic clinical monitoring, and robotics are increasingly used in patient care, the nature of medical work and patient/clinician interaction will change.[5] HSOs will have to reconfigure physical facilities, reorganize their work processes, and reengineer their work force. There is no doubt that technology will change the infrastructure of the entire healthcare system. That new infrastructure is not yet clearly defined. However, it is the job of the manager/planner to look for clues as to which technologies will change his business unit and how they will do so.

Orienting the Organization

There are several techniques that are commonly used to reorient disoriented patients. Some of these are:

1. *Reminding.* Patients may need to be reminded who the people around them are, what the date is, and where they are.

2. *Prompting.* Patients can be assisted in the use of memory aids such as reality bulletin boards and written notes.

3. *Correcting.* Patients need to have their mistaken perceptions of reality corrected.

4. *Instructing.* Simple, step-wise direction of activity is required.

5. *Focusing.* Patients should be given one instruction at a time and asked one question at a time.

6. *Reinforcing.* Oriented responses should be reinforced with praise and repetition. Even the attempt to respond should be reinforced.[6]

These same activities, integrated into a cohesive, systematic managerial process can reorient an organization. **Management by objectives** (MBO) is a process that combines these activities and turns plans into performance.

MBO is a management process that requires setting performance objectives for employees at all organizational levels. The performance of each employee is then evaluated based on the degree to which objectives are met. To effectively tie the strategic plan to organizational performance, all objectives must support the plan. Table 2.4 demonstrates how this can be accomplished in a home health unit. Note how each employee's objectives directly relate to the strategic plan. If J. Walters learns to use the new information processing system and subsequently increases his patient load by one patient, the manager of clinical services will

Table 2.4   Partial List of Employee Objectives for a Home Health Unit

Strategic Plan: To increase market share and profitability in the current geographic market

Employee: B. Gates

Position: General Manager, Home Health Services

Objectives: 1. Increase market share from 23% to 30%

Completion date: October 31, 1997

Measurement: Number of home health visits reported in the December issue of the *Journal of the Mid-South Association of Home Agencies.*

2. To assume the cost leadership position in the service area

Completion date: July 31, 1997

Measurement: Cost data for ten most common services provided by competing home health agencies. Cost survey will be conducted by J&S Marketing Services.

3. To increase operating margin from 8% of sales to 10% of sales.

Completion Date: December 31, 1997

Measurement: Profit and loss statement for the quarter ending December 31, 1997.

Employee: W. Wayne

Position: Marketing Manager, Home Health Services

Objectives: 1. Determine price schedule required to achieve cost leadership role in the market

Completion date: June 1, 1997

Measurement: Completed cost survey conducted by marketing staff.

2. Increase sales calls to physicians by 10%

Completion date: August 15, 1997

Measurement: Internal sales calls records.

3. Recruit and hire new part-time sales representative

Completion date: July 20, 1997

Measurement: New sales representative at work.

4. Design and mail new promotional materials to referral sources

Completion date: August 1, 1997

Measurement: New materials distributed.

Employee: F. Crane

Position: Manager of Clinical Services, Home Health Services

Objectives: 1. Increase nursing and therapist efficiency by 10%

Completion date: October 31, 1997

Measurement: Increase patient-to-care provider ratio by one as reported by operating data for the fourth quarter.

2. Implement new data processing system to improve care planning, charting, and billing efficiency and effectiveness.

Completion date: August 15, 1997

Measurement: All clinical employees trained and using all new information processing capabilities.

3. Decrease active patient attrition from 10% to 7%

Completion date: October 31, 1997

Measurement: Data from audit of patient service records for the third quarter.

Table 2.4 cont. Partial List of Employee Objectives for a Home Health Unit

Strategic Plan: To increase market share and profitability in the current geographic market

4. Decrease patient care supply cost by 2%
   Completion date: October 31, 1997
   Measurement: Expense data for the quarter ending December 31, 1997.

Employee: J. Walters, RN
Position: Staff Nurse, Home Health Services
Objectives: 1. Decrease active patient attrition from 12% to 10%
   Completion date: October 31, 1997
   Measurement: Data from audit of patient service records for the third quarter.

2. Learn and begin using new information processing applications
   Completion date: August 1, 1997
   Measurement: Observation by trainer and field supervisor.

3. Increase average caseload by one patient
   Completion date: October 31, 1997
   Measurement: Operating data for the fourth quarter.

4. Identify five ways to decrease supply costs without jeopardizing quality of care
   Completion date: October 31, 1997
   Measurement: Written report.

come closer to her patient-to-provider objective, which will in turn move the unit manager closer to his goal of decreasing costs. In the end, the business unit's strategic plan will be successfully implemented.

The success of an MBO system rests on several key points. First, the objectives must be achievable. In this example, no one is being asked to double the size of the business or cut costs in half. Both of those goals would probably not be realistic, and holding anyone to them would probably lead to failure. Realistic goals are best established through consensus of individual employees and their managers. If both parties can comfortably live with a goal, then it is probably realistic.

Second, each goal has a completion date. Adhering to timetables keeps the business unit on track. At each of these predetermined dates the employee should be held accountable for completion of the objective.

Third, completion of the objective (and progress toward completion) is measurable. In this example, the objectives have been quantified, and they are specific. The yardstick for measuring achievement has also been identified. When the general manager and his superior(s) evaluate market share gains, they know that market share will be defined by number of visits rather than by revenue. And they also know which data source they will use for retrieving market share figures.

It has been suggested that objectives should clearly identify rewards associated with their achievement.[7] This is the concept behind executive pay-for-performance programs. If the executive meets specific organizational performance objectives (such as earnings per share or return on investment goals), then the executive earns predetermined salary or stock bonuses.

Like most management techniques, MBO has been viewed by management experts alternately as a panacea and as a waste of time. MBO is never likely to be a panacea. Its sole function is to connect planning to performance. Its application cannot and will not do any more than that. Moreover, MBO can become a frustrating exercise when it is inappropriately implemented. For example, frustration results when deadlines and measurement of outcomes are poorly defined, when managers and subordinates fail to reach agreement about what constitutes reasonable objectives, and when objectives are revised before an employee has an opportunity to achieve them. However, when managers use orientation activities with MBO, it works well. In addition to going through the exercise of writing objectives, managers need to:

1. Respectfully and constantly remind employees what their objectives are, where they are in terms of achieving their objectives, and when the objectives must be met;

2. Prompt employees with memos, scoreboards, and reports as appropriate;

3. Correct employees when they stray from their objectives (correction must be ongoing instead of at the completion date when it is too late to salvage performance);

4. Instruct employees on how to achieve objectives (some employees can meet their objectives on their own, but many others will need assistance from managers with more knowledge and/or experience);

5. Focus employees on their objectives by not overloading them and their schedules with too many conflicting demands; and

6. Reinforce achievement of intermediate goals and signs of progress. Immediate feedback is important in letting employees know they are on the right track.

By using the same techniques that are commonly used to orient patients, the manager can successfully orient the organization.

Conclusion

MaryBeth and Allmed Home Care are in trouble. Intervention must be definitive and swift.

First, MaryBeth has to start planning and planning fast. Her planning will start at her luncheon meeting, if it is not too late and her partner is willing to allow her to continue managing Allmed. Her primary planning task will be to formulate a strategic plan by conducting a SWOT analysis. A thorough, carefully researched and written plan is crucial to Allmed's survival. Second, it is clear that MaryBeth cannot handle the operational planning required to get Allmed's work done. Adding the ominous task of strategic planning to her workload makes the situation even worse. She will have to designate an operations manager to be responsible for planning at least part of the operational work. Writing policies, procedures, and rules and communicating them to the employees need to be done expeditiously.

MaryBeth and her new operations manager will have to work together to assure that everything Allmed and its employees do supports the firm's strategic plan. Implementing an MBO system will help both of them to keep the organization focused on its goals. Successful implementation of MBO will require that they remind, prompt, correct, instruct, focus and reinforce employees in their work activities.

Allmed Home Care's prognosis is guarded. Unless MaryBeth acts decisively and treats the organization vigorously, this firm will be beyond resuscitation.

Endnotes

1. Robert Albanese, *Management* (Cincinnati: Southwestern Publishing, 1988).
2. Spyros G. Makridakis, *Forecasting, Planning, and Strategy for the 21st Century* (New York: The Free Press, 1990), p. 66.
3. Joel Arthur Barker, *Future Edge* (New York: William Morrow & Company, 1992), p. 38.
4. David M. Eisenberg, Ronald C. Kessler, Cindy Foster, Frances E. Norlock, David R. Calklins, and Thomas L. Delbanco. "Unconventional Medicine in the United States: Prevalence, Costs, and Patterns of Use," *The New England Journal of Medicine 328*, no. 4 (1993): 246–252.
5. "In 2010—A Survey of the Future of Medicine," *The Economist 330* (1994): 15–17.
6. Adapted from Mark A. Edinberg, *Mental Health Practice with the Elderly* (Englewood Cliffs, NJ: Prentice-Hall, 1985).
7. Karl Albrecht, *Successful Management by Objectives: An Action Manual* (Englewood Cliffs, NJ: Prentice-Hall, 1978).

3

Budgeting:
Malnutrition

In this chapter the reader will learn how:

◆ to diagnose problems that arise from inadequate and/or erroneous budgeting

◆ budgeting is like nutritional planning and support

◆ to develop an expense budget

◆ to strengthen capital budget requests

◆ budgetary performance is monitored.

Steve stared at the large manila envelope on his desk. He knew what was in it. He had been warned that it would be coming. But the warning had not helped him to prepare for the inevitable.

Steve had been Director of Radiology at Kingsford County Hospital for the past three years. For the most part, he enjoyed his work. He got along well with the radiology staff and other department heads in the hospital. He had come to the administration's attention as a potential management candidate when he had successfully organized the radiology department's mobile radiological services several years ago. Under Steve's direction, sales of the mobile services increased rapidly. Purchasers from medical practices, nursing facilities, and home health providers were pleased with the quality of the diagnostic work and the rapid and accurate reporting of results. Steve brought the same commitment to providing high-quality services to his position as director.

But there was the envelope. Steve slowly opened it and found what he expected. Instructions and forms to be used in preparing next

41

year's budget. Everything about this process unnerved him. When the next fiscal year did not start for another six months, how could he even begin to guess what his budgetary needs would be? He did not understand how the controller expected him to predict his exact needs up to eighteen months in advance.

During the first year he was director, he spent much more on labor and supplies than was budgeted, but he was able to keep equipment expenses well below the budgeted level. Although there were large budget variances, his performance appraisal did not suffer because the previous director had prepared the budget, and it had been easy enough to blame the variances on poor budget preparation. But last year, and so far this year, the story had been different. He had prepared the budgets, and he still could not seem to bring expenses into line. Every month he spent at least 5% more for labor than had been budgeted. He tried to control payroll costs, but he just did not see how he could get the work done with any less labor. His equipment requests had been denied by the administration, and he did not know how he could continue to do good work with the current equipment. Besides continual hassles from the controller, he had plenty of trouble with his boss, the Vice President of Professional Services. His failure to bring expenses in line with the budget had been noted in his performance evaluation, and he was even afraid that his job might be in jeopardy.

But he did not know how to do any better. He felt that he was blamed for many expenses that were really caused by other departments. For example, all the film and personnel costs that went into doing the work in the Emergency Room came right out of his budget. Yet the Emergency Room was credited with all the revenue that came from those procedures. The system was not fair, and it had him cornered.

There was nothing left to do but begin making the best guesses he could and keep arguing that if the hospital wanted his department to keep putting out good work, it would have to pay the price.

Steve is one of many HSO managers to whom budgets and the budgeting process are mysterious, frustrating, and even painful. In the well-run HSO, this should not be the case. Because budgeting requires forecasting of future workload and resource requirements, actual performance is never exactly equivalent to budgeted performance. However, by applying some of the basic tools presented in this chapter, the manager can minimize the difference between the two.

Diagnosing Budgeting Problems

Budgeting problems are among the most easily recognized managerial anomalies. The people at the top of the organization establish the criteria for determining financial illness and health. The financial performance of Steve's department is outside the limits that his controller and immediate superior find acceptable. Steve's task is to determine the etiology of the problem and intervene at that level.

The information in this scenario suggests several possibilities.

1. Steve spends more money than he needs to.

2. Steve underestimates the resource requirements of his department.

3. Steve cannot convince financial decision makers of his needs.

4. Steve cannot achieve budget goals because he failed to balance his spending appropriately in the past. If he would have purchased efficiency-improving equipment when he had the chance, his current problems might not exist.

Two less obvious possibilities are that: (1) Steve does not yet understand how to play the budgeting game in his HSO, and (2) there are inherent flaws in budgeting methodology that prevent Steve from preparing accurate budgets. To save his job and continue the good work he is doing at Kingsford, Steve is going to have to take the initiative to discover the problem's etiology and take corrective action.

Purpose of Budgeting

Contrary to what may be a widely held belief, budgeting was not invented as an instrument of torture by a sadistic financial manager (at least as far as we know). Rather than making life miserable for managers, budgets should make the management job easier. Once the purpose and the terminology associated with budgeting are understood, the mystery disappears, and budgets become user-friendly tools.

A **budget** is a financial statement of a business unit's plan. (Thus, it is natural that a chapter about budgeting should directly follow a chapter about planning.) Most budgets are prepared for a fiscal year. A **fiscal year** is a twelve-month period, which may or may not coincide with the calendar year, that is used for financial reporting.

As a written plan, the budget serves as a blueprint for action. It is a device for communicating plans throughout the organization. It also provides a measure of performance. As the fiscal year progresses, financial performance is measured against budget projections, which provides a mechanism for monitoring and controlling costs.

The Budgeting Process

The budgeting process is actually a collection of simultaneous processes that result in separate components of an organization's overall budget. For example, in the case of Kingsford County Hospital, Steve is apparently required to generate an expense budget for the radiology department. Depending on the organization of the hospital, that budget probably will be added to the expense budgets of the dietary, rehabilitation, laboratory, and pharmacy departments to result in a professional services expense budget. The professional services expense budget may be added to the marketing, patient care services, physical plant, administration, and ambulatory care services expense budgets to result in an expense budget for the entire hospital. If this hospital is a unit of an integrated health system, then its expense budget will be added to the expense budgets of other units to result in an expense budget for the entire health system. From this perspective, the budgeting process looks like a bottom-up process.

While the accumulation of expense budgets occurs, revenues are also being budgeted throughout the organization. Revenue projections are based on forecasts of business volume that are derived from operating experience and from the organization's strategic plan. Revenue projections are frequently made by financial managers because department managers seldom have much control over the volume and pricing of the output of their operating units. Because revenues must exceed expenses, some negotiation and revision will occur as these simultaneous processes progress.

Making sure that the budget reflects and supports the organization's plans requires that the budgeting process be well-planned and executed. This is usually the job of the **controller**. The controller (also called the **comptroller** in some organizations) is the chief accountant. In some organizations budgeting responsibilities are delegated by the controller to a budget director. It is important to realize that the controller does not make the final decisions about how much money to budget for specific purposes or how much money goes to different business units. It is the controller's job to oversee the budgeting process, provide supporting information that will result in accurate forecasting, monitor financial performance, and report financial performance to decision makers. To report performance, the controller makes comparisons to budgeted performance and reports discrepancies in the form of **variances**. Because controllers take the lead role in the budgeting process and because they monitor expenses on an ongoing basis, most managers believe that they have more decision-making authority than they actually do.

There is no generally accepted sequence of steps in budgeting. The specifics vary from one HSO to another. The one constant is that the process always begins well in advance of the start of the period being budgeted. In some large HSOs, the process is so complex that as soon as one budget is completed, work begins on the next one.[1] The envelope that Steve received in the opening case contained the documents that initiate the process among operations managers. The initial package usually contains a calendar of deadlines by which various steps of the budgeting process must be completed. Included in the package are two sets of support documents that assist the manager with budget preparation. The first is a **projection package**. The projection package is a forecast of estimated workloads for the institution for the upcoming budget period. Not only does the projection package contain overall workload data, such as the anticipated number of patient days, but it may also provide workload forecasts for departments whose costs vary greatly with changes in volume. For example, the in-patient radiological examination volume varies with patient days. Therefore, Steve may receive a workload projection for his department. The second set of documents, the **administrative package**, provides other helpful information such as new program plans, forms to be completed in support of budget requests, and instructions for completing the forms.[2]

The first deadline in the budget calendar usually requires managers to submit a preliminary budget to their superiors. After review and revision, the proposed budgets are sent to financial decision makers. In many large HSOs, this means that proposed budgets go to a broadly representative budgeting committee. In smaller HSOs, there may be only one financial decision maker, the chief financial officer (CFO). At this step, budgetary requirements and resource availability are reconciled through a process of review and negotiation. The final proposed budget is presented to and approved by the CEO and the board of directors before it goes into effect.

During the budgeting process, resource availability and requirements are translated into financial terms. This process is very similar to nutritional assessment and prescription. Nutritional assessment requires that nutritional needs be determined and stated in common units (calories). Each individual's caloric needs are determined from an assessment of activity levels, size, age, and nutritional status. The nutritional status assessment yields data that dieticians use to determine appropriate forms of caloric intake. The prescribed diet identifies the relative amounts of protein, fat, carbohydrates, and other nutrients that must be taken in to meet nutritional needs.

Whereas the quantity of nutrition required to maintain normal physiologic function is expressed in calories, the quantity of resources required to maintain a business unit is expressed in dollars. When caloric needs are not met, the patient is unable to function optimally. When a business unit does not have enough resources, it also fails to perform optimally. Caloric intake must consist of the appropriate balance of protein, fat, and carbohydrates, and mineral, electrolyte, and vitamin content must be balanced. The resources taken in by a business unit must be made up of the proper balance of labor, equipment, supplies, and overhead.

Because an HSO's budget is a multifaceted statement of resource availability and utilization, it is usually broken down into parts. The **statistics budget** provides estimates of activity in each business unit. This part of the budget identifies the workload that each business unit should anticipate. Most managers have little input into the development of the statistics budget. However, when they detect what they think are errors in workload estimation, they need to point these out because the statistics budget becomes the basis on which other budgets are developed. The **operating budget** is that portion of the budget that describes financial resource availability and needs that are directly related to doing the work of the HSO. Within the operating budget, the **revenue budget** is a statement of anticipated receipts from the sale of services. In large HSOs, many department and supervisory managers do not have to be concerned with the preparation of a revenue budget. For example, a hospital's security service generates no revenue so the chief of security does not have to be concerned about budgeting revenue. The other component of the operating budget, the expense budget, is a concern of all managers because each business unit incurs expenses. The expense budget is a statement of the resources that will be required to continue operating the business unit for the next fiscal year.

The **capital budget** is a statement of the financial resources needed to purchase items like large pieces of equipment or buildings during the upcoming fiscal year. Because of special concerns about spending large sums of money for items that will be used for a long time, capital expenses are budgeted separately from ordinary operating expenses.

The **cash budget** is the portion of the budget that describes inflows and outflows of cash. Knowing when cash is going to be available to cover expected expenses is obviously important to the people responsible for paying the bills. For a general manager who is responsible for cash disbursements, like a physician practice manager or a manager of an independent home health agency, it is crucial to make these projections. For department level managers in large HSOs, paying bills is not a direct responsibility. Because not all healthcare managers prepare revenue and cash budgets, the remainder of this chapter will focus on the two kinds of budgets that are of universal interest: expense budgets and capital budgets. The guidelines and suggestions for preparing these budgets are also applicable to revenue and cash budgeting.

Perhaps the best way to understand how budgets are generated is to work through a simple budgeting process. Some managers react to the budgeting process much like Steve did in the Kingsford County Hospital case. They experience severe anxiety. They are often overwhelmed by the volume of information provided, and they have difficulty knowing how to sort it out and how to use it effectively. In their effort to be supportive and comprehensive, financial managers and controllers may overload managers with data. The data presented here are kept to the minimum needed to illustrate the budgeting process. Two important assumptions are also made here. First, it is assumed that this is a **fixed budget** (i.e., that it is fixed for the upcoming fiscal year). Some facilities use an ongoing budgeting process (that results in a **rolling budget**), in which the budget is continually extended while it is in progress. As soon as one month in the budget passes, another month is estimated and added to the end. Second, it is assumed that the budget is a **forecast budget**. Forecast budgets remain in effect irrespective of changes in volume. This a common way of budgeting in HSOs. The alternative, the **flexible budget**, moves budgeted figures in a predetermined way to reflect changes in activity level. The budgeting process will be illustrated by developing expense and capital budgets for the laundry department of Modrian Hospital.

Budgeting for Expenses

Protein is a key component of most anatomical structures. Among its many locations are hair, blood cells, internal organs, and skin. In all these structures, it has different functions and is composed of different lengths and sequences of amino acids. The expense budget is similar to protein in that it is made up of component parts (expense categories) that are distinct entities. They must be present in correct proportions for the expense budget to meet the organization's needs. Because no two HSOs or parts thereof perform exactly the same function, no two expense budgets will be the same. Common expense categories are listed in Table 3.1. In the administrative package, Mr. Morgan, Director of Laundry and Linen Services, is instructed to put estimated expenses in the right-hand column.

Because the laundry department is a **labor intensive** department (i.e., a department in which the ratio of labor expense to other expenses is high), accurately forecasting labor expense is perhaps Mr. Morgan's most important budgeting task. In the projection package, Mr. Morgan finds information about the history of his department's labor costs (Table 3.2). One thing that strikes Mr. Morgan immediately about this information is that labor expense has increased constantly over the past five years. (It might also strike the reader that all labor expenses are evenly divisible by 5,000. This is a simplification created for purposes of illustration.) His first inclination is to make his labor cost estimate by simply extrapolating this trend out to 1999. He sees that this is easy to do by

Table 3.1   List of Expenses, Laundry Department, Modrian Hospital

Expense	**Budgeted Amount (1999)**
Labor	
Supplies	
Administrative and General	
Interest	
Depreciation	
Utilities	
Travel	
Equipment Maintenance	
Insurance	

Table 3.2   History of Labor Expenses, Laundry Department, Modrian Hospital

Year	Labor Expense
1993	$100,000
1994	110,000
1995	115,000
1996	125,000
1997	140,000
1998	75,000 (1st 6 months)
1999	to be budgeted

plotting the data on a graph (Figure 3.1). By drawing a line through the points and then noting the point at which the line intersects the 1999 line, he can estimate the labor cost. A line drawn parallel to the horizontal axis from the intersection to the vertical axis yields an estimate of the 1999 labor cost (Figure 3.2). Labor cost estimated in this way is about $158,000. This type of forecasting is **time-trend analysis**. Under certain circumstances, it can yield acceptable cost estimates. These circumstances include:

1. when the environment and the business unit have a stable history free of significant fluctuation; and

2. when the next fiscal year is expected to continue the historically stable pattern; and

3. when a quick, imprecise estimate of expenses is sufficient for decision-making purposes.

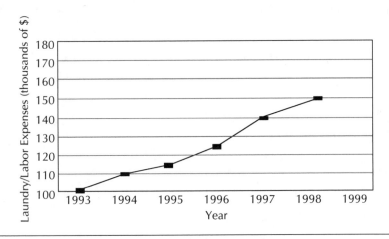

Figure 3.1   Historical data, laundry/labor expense.

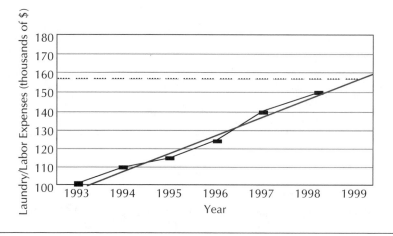

Figure 3.2   Time-trend extension, visual method.

The inherent risk of using this method is that Mr. Morgan does not have complete knowledge of the causative factors that contributed to labor cost increases. He may have no idea what factors contributed to the trend of cost increases. Not knowing this, he does not know if, or how, these same factors may contribute to future costs. For example, has turnover influenced labor costs? Have overtime hours and pay policies fluctuated? Additionally, this prediction technique fails to consider future factors that may help determine labor costs. These factors may not have influenced labor costs before, but may do so in the future. For example, a recent union certification may change labor costs. A final knowledge deficit results from the fact that 1998 data is incomplete. If 1998 is ignored, then the most recent data (and possibly the most relevant) may be left out of the calculation. If 1998 data are included under the assumption that the second half of 1998 will duplicate the first half, the trend line is contaminated by the inclusion of estimated data. In other words, an estimate is being based on an estimate.

There are mathematical techniques that could replace the ruler method of extending the line. One way of finding a line that best represents the data points on the graph is the **least squares** method. The least squares method incorporates the historical data into a formula (the calculation of which is beyond the scope of this text) for a straight line. Alternatively, some calculators and computers are capable of calculating a regression analysis which yields the same results. In this case, the application of the formulas results in anticipated labor cost expenses of $158,413. Although this method is more accurate than using a ruler to draw a line through the points, it still uses historical data out of context and does not take into account any foreseeable operational changes.

Another mathematical technique that could be used to extend the line is to apply an average annual increase percent to estimated 1998 data. The first step in

Table 3.3   Average Annual Percentage Increase in Labor Expense

Year	Labor Expense	% Increase
1993	$100,000	—
1994	110,000	10.0
1995	115,000	4.5
1996	125,000	8.7
1997	140,000	12.0
1998	150,000 (est.)	7.1
Five-year average		**8.5**

this calculation requires that a percentage increase be calculated for each year. To do this, the increase between year one (the base year) and year two is divided by the base year's expense. For example, to calculate the percentage increase between 1993 and 1994 labor costs, the following calculation is made:

$$\frac{(\$110,000 - 100,000)}{\$100,000} = .1 = 10\%$$

In other words, the 1994 labor expense was 10% higher than the 1993 labor expense. The same calculations are made for all the reported data (Table 3.3). As the table indicates, the average annual increase in labor expense over the five years of reported data is 8.5%. Applying this average increase to the estimated data from 1998 yields an estimated labor expense for 1999 of $162,750. This calculation illustrates more clearly than either the least squares calculation or using graphic estimation, a weakness of using time-trend analysis to project expenses. The annual average percent increases vary in this example from 4.5% to 12.0%. If the

Table 3.4   Laundry Workload and Labor History

Year	Laundry Production (thousands of pounds)	Laundry Labor (hours)
1993	1,200	17,170
1994	1,202	17,183
1995	1,218	17,310
1996	1,227	17,529
1997	1,239	17,914
1998	1,241 (est.)	17,775 (est.)
1999	1,250 (projected)	(projected)

Table 3.5   Laundry Output per Labor Hour

Year	Laundry Production (thousands of pounds)	Laundry Labor (hours)	Pounds of Laundry (per labor hour)
1993	1,200	17,170	69.9
1994	1,202	17,183	70.0
1995	1,218	17,310	70.4
1996	1,227	17,529	70.0
1997	1,239	17,914	69.2
1998	1,241 (est.)	17,775 (est.)	69.8
1999	1,250 (projected)		

low and high percentage increases are reproducible, then the 1999 labor expense could range from $156,750 to $168,000. There is too much variability in these data to lead to a satisfactory estimate of labor expense.

Better labor expense estimates can be derived by working from predicted workload levels. The manager's budgeting job is easier when he is given a workload estimate in the statistics package. In this example, a report of historical and projected workload is included (Table 3.4). To get from workload data to labor expense, Mr. Morgan must first determine how many hours of labor will be required to produce 1,250,000 pounds of laundry. If he is confident that the additional 9,000 pounds projected for 1999 can be produced by the same staff working the same number of hours as in 1998, and if he is confident that 1998's first-six-months' data indicate that 17,775 hours is a valid estimate for the entire year, then he could budget for 17,775 hours of labor. However, the department's history indicates that since 1993, every increase in laundry output corresponded to an increase in labor time. By dividing the number of pounds of laundry produced by the number of hours worked, Mr. Morgan can calculate how much laundry is produced by each hour of labor. The results of this calculation are reported in Table 3.5. Including the 1998 data in the calculation yields an average output of 69.9 pounds of laundry per one hour of labor. Dividing the estimated output of 1,250,000 pounds by 69.9 pounds per hour yields an estimated labor requirement of 17,883 hours. The final dollar amount budgeted for labor expense will be determined by each individual staff member's wage or salary, and by the amount of time he is expected to be at work (Table 3.6). In this case Mr. Morgan has predicted that the increased workload will be absorbed by the existing staff. If a workload of 17,883 hours would have necessitated hiring another person, then Mr. Morgan would have to budget for that position. Note how going through this process of projecting from workload data may have saved Mr. Morgan from a significant labor budget shortfall during 1999.

Table 3.6   Schedule of Labor Expenses by Employee, Projected for 1999

Employee	Position	Salary/Wage ($)	Projected Number of Hours	Labor Expense
M. Morgan	Department Head	$41,000	2,080	$41,000
C. Drums	Supervisor	$12.25/hr.	2,080	25,480
B. GoricSupervisor	11.75/hr.	2,080	24,440	
P. Brown	Clerk	6.00/hr.	2,080	12,480
S. ClarkStaff	8.45/hr.	2,080	17,576	
B. Gordon	Staff	7.80/hr.	2,080	16,224
L. ReyesStaff	7.25/hr.	2,080	15,080	
L. TrangStaff	7.10/hr.	2,080	14,768	
G. BlackStaff	6.00/hr.	1,243	7,458	
TOTALS			17,883	$174,506

Expense Budgeting Pitfalls

Unfortunately, many managers learn how to do budgeting well by attending the infamous "School of Hard Knocks." The following items are some of the lessons that are often taught there:

1. *Working from inappropriate or incomplete data.* Given historical labor expenses, why could Mr. Morgan not have simplified the projection by calculating an average labor cost per pound of laundry? He could have correlated labor expense with output quite easily. By dividing the historical workload by labor cost, he could have calculated the average cost to produce one pound of laundry (Table 3.7). Averaging the cost over six years results in an average

Table 3.7   Average Labor Expense to Produce a Pound of Laundry

Year	Laundry Production (thousands of pounds)	Labor Expense ($)	Labor Expense (per pound of laundry)
1993	1,200	100,000	$0.0833
1994	1,202	110,000	0.0915
1995	1,218	115,000	0.0944
1996	1,227	125,000	0.1019
1997	1,239	140,000	0.1130
1998	1,241 (est.)	150,000 (est.)	0.1209
1999	1,250 (projected)		

cost of $.1008 per pound of laundry. Given the history of increasing labor expense per pound, a sharp decrease to $.1008 seems unlikely to occur in 1999. Obviously, something is happening to the labor cost in this department that makes using an average figure inappropriate. Perhaps there has been little turnover so that the department is staffed by senior employees who earn more. Perhaps there has been a change in the local labor market that has resulted in inflated wages. Perhaps new overtime and/or shift differential policies have raised average wages.

2. *Using the wrong historical data.* Why did Mr. Morgan use data from 1993–1998? Should he have ignored the incomplete data from 1998 or should he have done the opposite and based workload projections only on the latest output data (i.e., the first six months of 1998)? Or was he correct in using all the data available? There is no definitive answer to this question. Given the very stable productivity of the department since 1993, it seems to make sense to strengthen the projection by using as much historical data as possible. However, if something had happened to significantly change the output per hour, then only the data after the change should be used. For example, if more efficient equipment had been installed on January 1, 1998, then using only the output data for the first six months of 1998 would be appropriate.

3. *Using erroneous statistical data.* In some institutions, managers have to estimate their own anticipated workload based on projected data such as patient days, outpatient clinic visits, or surgical procedures. In other cases, the projected workload is provided. In the latter case, the manager must learn how the projection was made because it is possible that the managerial accountant who calculated the figure may have made an error. For example, an increase in the laundry workload may have been forecasted on the basis of a projected increase in in-patient days. The projected increase is due to an increase in the anticipated number of OB cases to be handled under a new managed care contract. Mr. Morgan knows that each OB-GYN case uses more laundry per day than the average in-patient. If the accountant failed to take this fact into consideration, the increased workload for laundry is underestimated. Mr. Morgan has to work from the best possible workload estimate if his expense budget is going to be accurate. An inaccurate workload forecast will result in poor budget performance throughout the year.

4. *Insufficiently differentiated workload analysis.* The laundry example was chosen for illustrative purposes because it is easy to

imagine a laundry that has only one kind of output—clean linens. This is not true of most HSO units. The laboratory performs many different tests. Physicians see different kinds of patients and provide both consultative and procedural services. Pharmacists process different types of medication orders as well as consult with patients and other health providers. Different kinds and amounts of resources go into these outputs. If expense estimates are to be made on the basis of output, then the estimate of output must include all the entire array of outputs a unit produces. For ease of projection and calculation, this is done by converting all outputs to a common unit of production. These standardized units of production are called **relative value units** (RVUs).

Because providing clinical care is a labor intensive process, different kinds of outputs in most clinical departments are converted to RVUs on the basis of how much time is required to produce them. In the pharmacy, for example, processing and filling a new order for an oral dosage form may take 10 minutes. If this function is equated to one RVU, then all other outputs can be numerically related to it. For example, if processing and filling a new order for an intravenous fluid requires 15 minutes, then this output is equivalent to 1.5 RVUs. A chemotherapy order may require 25 minutes (2.5 RVUs) and a total parenteral nutrition order 30 minutes (3.0 RVUs). Converting different kinds of output to RVUs forces managers to do a complete analysis of workload that results in more accurate labor expense forecasting.

Fixed and Variable Expenses

Some expense items are more sensitive than others to changes in workload. In the laundry example, the assumption was made that there was a clear correlation between the amount of the laundry produced and the labor that went into that production. Would the same correlation hold up for insurance expense? No. Insurance costs are more highly correlated with the type of activity than they are with the amount of activity. Those expenses that change directly with workload (like most labor costs) are called **variable expenses**; those that are consistent irrespective of workload (like insurance) are **fixed expenses**.

Not all expenses fit neatly into one of these categories. A good example of a difficult expense to classify would be the laundry's utility expense. A laundry must have access to electricity, and there is a basic charge for electric service. This would lead one to classify electricity as a fixed expense. On the other hand, the more laundry equipment is used, the more electricity is consumed. Thus, one would conclude that electricity is a variable expense. Neither conclusion is entirely correct or incorrect. Expenses with such clearly distinct components may be called **semivariable** or **semifixed**. This distinction is important because knowing how an expense behaves regarding workload determines the best way to budget the expense.

Variable expenses should be estimated from the anticipated workload just as the laundry labor expense was estimated above. This is not the case with fixed expenses. Since fixed expenses do not vary with volume, it is usually best to start estimating by extending historical data forward. However, any other changes that could affect this extension must be considered. For example, if the insurance expense allocated to the laundry has increased on the average of 2% per year over the past five years and that increase has been fairly constant, then a 2% increase is a reasonable preliminary estimate. But that estimate must be modified to take into account any factors that could make the upcoming budgeting period different from the preceding years. For example, the manager may have read a report by an insurance industry trade association that indicates that because of a spate of high damages awards for personal injuries, it is anticipated that businesses can expect to see an increase of 10% in their insurance rates over the next two years. The preliminary 2% increase is inappropriate in light of this report.

Even if there are no detectable external changes, there may be internal changes that could influence the expense. The hospital may allocate property insurance costs to departments based on the physical size of the department (i.e., on its square footage as a percentage of the entire facility). If the hospital has increased its total square footage by 8% over the past year while the size of the laundry remained constant, then less insurance expense will be allocated to the laundry, and a 2% increase may be unrealistically high.

Segregating fixed and variable portions of semifixed/semivariable expenses, will increase the accuracy of budgeting. But it is not always possible. How will the fixed and variable portions of the laundry's electricity usage be determined? If there is only one electric monitoring device for the whole facility, it may not be practical to trace the use of electricity to specific functions. Therefore, it makes sense to treat electricity as a fixed expense, even though it has a variable component. The estimate would then be made based on past expenses with some adjustments made for anticipated rate changes and internal expense allocation changes.

Whenever it is possible and practical to do so, breaking labor expenses into fixed and variable components increases budgeting accuracy. This is particularly true in cases where workload forecasts are difficult to make. Budgets for labor expenses in nursing units are sometimes made this way. Consider the following example.

The core personnel to keep a unit open consists of a head nurse, an assistant head nurse, 5 staff nurses, 10 nursing assistants, and a ward secretary. Below this level of staffing, the floor could not function because there would not be enough staff on any one shift to handle the work. The wages and salaries of these people are considered fixed expenses. Assume further that this core group can care for a census up to and including 12 patients. If the census reaches 13 or more, then additional staff is needed (Table 3.8). The additional staff requirements represent the variable portion of labor expense. Obviously, different patient levels above 12 will call for different levels of staff. By separating out the fixed expense, the budget estimate has been improved in two ways. First, a minimum level of expense has been identified that will be constant irrespective of patient volume.

Table 3.8   A Flexible Budget for Labor Expense of a Hospital Nursing Unit

Patient Load	Staff	Labor Expense (annual)	Labor Expense (daily)
0–12 patients	Core Staff	$398,360	$1,091
13–15 patients	Core Staff + 1 RN + 1 Nursing Assistant	$445,840	$1,221
16–20 patients	Core Staff + 2 RNs + 3 Nursing Assistants + 1 Ward Secretary	$520,360	$1,426
21–24 patients	Core Staff + 3 RNs + 5 Nursing Assistants + 1 Ward Secretary	$580,320	$1,590

Core Staff = head nurse, assistant head nurse, 5 staff nurses, 10 nursing assistants, and ward secretary

The wages and salaries of the core personnel are relatively easily estimated. Second, the kinds (and, therefore, wages) of personnel associated with increased volume have been identified. There will not be another head nurse with increased volume in the unit. Therefore, any estimate of labor expense above the fixed expense will not be based on historical data that includes this salary. Instead, the estimate clearly reflects the actual staffing expenses associated with specific workload levels. Notice that in this example, it does not cost twice as much to take care of 24 patients as it costs to care for 12.

The ability to categorize expenses as fixed, variable, and semifixed/semivariable gives rise to the possibility of developing flexible budgets. Remember, flexible budgets project expenses on the basis of volume. In the nursing unit example, a flexible budget would predict labor expenses over a range of volumes. Throughout the fiscal year, if the unit's workload exceeds 12 patients for any reporting period, then the labor expense budget is automatically increased to the new budget targets. Under conditions of changing workloads, flexible budgeting results in better estimates of expenses than fixed budgeting. It also eliminates some unnecessary reporting and investigation of budget variances.

The Capital Budget

The capital budget is less complex to forecast than the expense budget. However, it is more difficult to get approved. Financial managers expect that all business units require a certain number of resources to maintain operations. Salaries, utilities, and maintenance are universally recognized as essential expenses. New facilities and equipment are also recognized as being necessary resources. However, because they are of a nonrecurring nature, the necessity of each individual purchase is not evident. For example, it is obvious that a computerized billing system requires printers. However, when the billing supervisor asks for six new state-of-the-art color printers, it is not immediately obvious that six is the appropriate number of printers, that state-of-the-art equipment is required to do the job, or that the expenditure cannot be delayed to a later fiscal year. Therefore, capital budget requests require justification.

There is no definitive rule for determining which expenses are operating expenses and which are capital expenses. All capital expenses involve plant (i.e., buildings and building modifications) and equipment. But not all equipment expenses are treated as capital expenses. A magnifying glass is a piece of equipment but is not treated as a capital expense. In general, expensive items with long useful lives are treated as capital expenses. This kind of expense does not recur annually. New washers and dryers, laminar flow hoods, and imaging equipment are usually capital expense items.

The criteria for determining if something is a capital expense item are usually found in the administrative package along with capital budget request forms. Because the money spent for new equipment may represent only a portion of the total cost of a project, the manager will also have to estimate related expenses such as installation, training costs, and downtime. Furthermore, limiting the capital budget request process only to investment in tangible assets may lead an HSO to underestimate its true budget needs. Therefore, some organizations require that all new programs or projects be budgeted through the capital expense request process. This assures that all relevant costs of any new program are considered.[3]

Each HSO also has its own procedure for submitting, processing, and evaluating capital requests. Therefore, capital request forms vary considerably. Whatever their format, they all attempt to elicit the same kind of information:

1. how the capital expense will help the HSO to meet its objectives;

2. why the proposed expense is the most appropriate solution to a problem;

3. evidence that the proposed expense is the most cost-effective way to achieve an objective; and

4. evidence that the proposed expense request has been completely researched and represents a realistic estimate of the total cost.

The fourth point is particularly important. For example, if new imaging equipment requires new wiring, the cost of that wiring must be anticipated and added to the projected price of the equipment to prevent budget shortfalls.

Budget Variances

If the budget is to be an effective planning tool, actual financial performance must meet the goals established by the budget. The controller periodically provides managers with reports that compare actual financial performance with budget estimates. To allow managers to intervene quickly when actual performance deviates substantially from budgeted performance, budget reports are usually issued on a monthly basis. Because so many factors influence expenses, even the best budget estimates seldom exactly match actual expenses.

Among the controller's functions is to assure that actual expenses are in line with budgeted expenses. However, because actual expenses for any one month rarely match budgeted expenses, the controller must decide when to intervene and what kind of intervention is required to correct variances. Controllers establish guidelines for actual performance within which it is usually not cost effective to investigate variances. For example, if a department's supply expense was budgeted at $153 for January and the actual expense was $154, it is not worth anyone's time to explore the reason for the variance. If the actual expense was $2,980, then obviously there is some cause for concern. There may be a perfectly legitimate reason for such a large expense. However, without investigating, the controller would not know the reason. If the controller allowed such variances to occur without intervention, the organization would soon be far away from its targeted budget. If the expense is justifiable, then investigation may indicate that changing the budgeting process is required so that similar expenses can be anticipated and budgeted. To separate the expenses that require investigation from those that do not, the controller may establish a dollar limit beyond which an investigation would occur.

Another guideline that could be applied would be to establish a percentage variance that would trigger an investigation. In the above example, $2,827 is 1,847% over budget. However, assume that a $2,827 variance occurred in a $3,000,000 budgeted payroll. The variance would then be only 0.094% of the budgeted amount. This difference would probably not be worth investigating. A 1% variance guideline may be appropriate for an expense of this magnitude. However, if the $2,827 difference were to continue for many months, it may represent an ongoing budgeting problem or a problem with overspending. That is why some organizations include guidelines based on the consistency with which budget projections are unmet. For example, overspending of any magnitude for three consecutive months might prompt an investigation.

If the controller investigates a budget variance, the manager responsible for the budgeted expense will be called on to justify the variance. This requires that the manager review the budget derivation and the expenses for the month in question. The manager needs to be able to explain why the expense was unavoidable and why the budget did not anticipate the expense. Some of the common reasons for budget variances include unanticipated increases in the cost of supplies and raw materials, changes in wages/salaries, and changes in workload. Even after the most meticulous forecasting, some unanticipated and unavoidable changes will occur. In addition, the manager needs to search for timing as a reason for variances. For example, due to heavy volume in the July, the laundry may have had to place two orders for a special linen softener. However, lower volume during the Christmas holidays may result in no purchases of the softener during that month. Seldom do expenses in all categories even themselves out into 12 equal parts. Yet budget reports seldom take cyclical changes in volume into account.

Sending less than budgeted amounts should also trigger investigation by the controller. By investigating positive variances, the controller may uncover money-saving practices that can be utilized throughout the organization. For example, an investigation of a positive variance in the pharmacy supply budget may reveal that the pharmacy found a less expensive supplier of custom-designed pressure sensitive labels. If similar labels are used by patient accounts, the controller can let the business office manager know about the new vendor so that similar savings may be realized by that department as well.

Improving Budgeting

Much like dietary planning, budgeting is an inexact science. Just as each individual's nutritional requirements vary, so do the financial requirements of HSOs. In spite of the fact that there are no definitive rules to follow, managers can develop better budgeting skills. The following suggestions should help most managers.

1. *Talk. Talk. Talk.* Managers cannot discuss budgets too much with their superiors, financial managers, and colleagues. The more managers know about the organization and about the budgeting process, the better they will be able to formulate budgets. It is vitally important to understand every item in the statistical package. If the manager bases the budget on erroneous assumptions about workload or about the relationship between workload and expenses, then there is no hope of developing a meaningful budget. Managers must also reach consensus with their immediate supervisors and with financial managers about budget estimates. If everyone is in agreement about departmental objectives and about the resources required to meet those objectives, then there will be far fewer disagreements about expenses during the budgeted period. Reaching a clear understanding of and agreement on goals and expenses requires copious communication.

2. *Start early.* Budgeting should be an ongoing process. Managers should not start thinking about budgeting only when the budgeting forms and a budget calendar arrive on their desks. The manager who has the best chance of getting the minimum daily requirement of financial resources is the manager who best anticipates and justifies needs.

3. *Learn from mistakes.* Some managers think that they are superheroes when it comes to controlling costs. Unfortunately, they have

a tendency to overestimate their ability to save money and end up underbudgeting for their needs. In the face of consistent over-spending variances, they continue to underbudget while they promise themselves that they can do better next time. Other managers seem to have a constant fear of starvation and consistently overbudget. Each individual seems to have a psychological comfort zone in which he places his budget estimates. When that zone is consistent with actual expenses, the manager's financial performance is appreciated. However, when actual expenses consistently deviate from the comfort zone, financial managers and superiors become frustrated. In the face of consistent budgeting inaccuracies, managers must leave their psychological comfort zones and budget objectively based on the facts.

4. *Learn and play the budgeting game.* Budgeting is an organizational process. There are certain rules that the organization imposes on this process. The formal rules come in the budget packet. The more important rules, however, are frequently the informal rules. The informal rules are, at worst, unspoken, and, at best, are whispered over a table for two in the back corner of the employee dining room. The informal rules frequently include such important information as:

    •   who to see in the accounting department for fast and accurate information;

    •   what financial managers really want to see in a budget before they will approve it;

    •   which managers always seem to get what they request in a budget and why;

    •   whether it is necessary to spend overbudgeted amounts in the current budget to avoid having them pared from the next budget; and

    •   whether (and how much) to overbudget in the first draft of the budget to get what is really needed after the obligatory cutting of the proposed budget.

These last two rules are crucial. It is unfortunate that some financial decision makers feel that if an expense was overbudgeted one year, then the business unit does not need as much the next year. This is like telling an athlete who suffered a sprained ankle and missed a month of training one year that her total caloric intake would be decreased by 6% next year because she had used only 94% of her budgeted calories in the current year. This is obviously nonsense. However, it is done in organizations every day. To avoid financial malnutrition in the future, managers tend to spend down to the last budgeted penny. While some of this spending undoubtedly contributes to the organization's well-being, it is certainly not an optimal way to use the organization's resources. Too much inadequate and overpriced equipment has been purchased in the race to spend down capital allotments. Too many underemployed personnel have punched in and out for the sake of consuming the last morsels on the staff budget plate.

It is also unfortunate that the budgeting process in many organizations involves deliberate deception. Budgeting is a process of dividing up an organization's financial resources among its constituent units. Managers find themselves in competition with each other for those resources. As soon as one manager employs deception to get a bigger piece of the resource pie, other managers feel pressured to use the same tactic defensively. Not only are managers pitted against each other, but they are frequently in conflict with their superiors and with financial managers. This is due to the ill-conceived notion of many higher level decision makers that anything lower level managers request in the budget is inflated and must be cut to a realistic level. Managers also work from the equally ill-conceived notion that anything they ask for will be cut, so they overstate their needs. Mutual distrust quickly becomes a self-fulfilling prophecy. The practice of mutual deception has become ingrained in most organizations so that these ill-conceived perceptions have, in fact, become a fact of life. Until strong-willed CEOs formally state that honesty is one of the budgeting ground rules and act vigorously to enforce the ground rules, managers need to find out who is deceiving whom and by how much if they are going to be successful at playing the budget game.

This is a more important issue than most HSO CEOs realize. Once deception is accepted in the budgeting process, it becomes a value that permeates the entire organization. An HSO that incorporates deception into its corporate culture is well on the way to becoming an organization where trust, loyalty, and respect have no meaning. What a high price to pay for saving a few dollars.

Conclusion

For many managers, budgeting never feels comfortable. Preparing a budget always involves the imprecise task of forecasting. The inherent uncertainty that goes along with forecasting does not allow many managers to reach a level of comfort with the process. Add to that discomfort the fact that in many organizations, the budgeting process is characterized by adversarial negotiations and deception, and there is small wonder that budgeting generates negative emotions.

Yet the budget should not cast a pall over everything that the manager does. It is nothing more than the financial statement of plans and goals. As with any plan that is handed him, the manager should make a good faith effort to carry out the plan and adhere to the agenda that the plan establishes. But if the manager allows a short-term plan to be his overriding concern, then he may well end up subordinating efficiency and efficacy to the fiscal plan. That sacrifice may not even be fiscally responsible. If, for example, a new kind of light bulb was developed that would cut electric consumption by 32%, but the price of the bulb was 20% higher than the old type of bulbs, it would make fiscal sense for a physical plant manager to exceed the supply budget to purchase the new bulbs. His priority is to work with his superior and the controller to do the most efficient thing, rather than to adhere to an inefficient budget just because it is there.

Clinicians are trained to place quality of patient care at the top of their professional agendas. When they move into management positions, higher level managers give them additional performance objectives. Because their superiors and colleagues spend so much time focusing on objectives other than high quality care (many of which are related to resource utilization), they begin to sense that there is a conflict between quality-of-care objectives and financial objectives. Sometimes this conflict is openly stated. "No margin, no mission" is a frequently repeated axiom that, roughly translated, means, "If we don't make a profit, there won't be anybody here to provide quality care." The obvious counterpoint is, "No mission, no margin," which can be restated as: "If we provide poor quality care, then no one will come here, and there won't be any profit." This is the dilemma faced by Steve in the opening case. He opted to overspend his labor budget to achieve high quality care. But what would happen if every manager did the same thing? Would the hospital be able to pay at least 5% more in labor expense and remain in business?

Managers are in the difficult position of having to make these seemingly contradictory objectives compatible. That is, they have to find ways to provide high quality care while using no more resources than necessary so that organizational viability is assured. Steve may have been able to do this by more efficiently using the budgeted staff or by selling the administration on his capital requests, which may have cut labor expense. Meeting both quality and financial goals is one of the healthcare manager's greatest challenges, and it is what makes budgeting so difficult. But, at the same time, by meeting both goals, the manager does his organization and the people it serves the greatest possible service.

Endnotes

1.   Bruce R. Neumann, James D. Suver, and William N. Zelman. *Financial Management: Concepts and Applications for Healthcare Providers*, 2nd ed. (Dubuque, IA: Kendall/Hunt Publishing Co., 1993).

2.   Howard J. Berman, Lewis E. Weeks, and Steven F. Kukla. *The Financial Management of Hospitals*, 7th ed. (Ann Arbor, MI: Health Administration Press, 1990).

3.   William O. Cleverley. *Essentials of Healthcare Finance*, 3rd ed. (Gaithersburg, MD: Aspen Publishers, 1992).

Unit II

Organizing

4

Organization of Work and Jobs:
Anatomy and Physiology

In this chapter the reader will learn how:
- ◆ signs of dysfunctional organizational structures appear
- ◆ formal organizational structures and functions are related
- ◆ healthcare services are organized as integrated systems
- ◆ healthcare institutions are organized
- ◆ alternatives to departmentalization are used
- ◆ different approaches to job design are employed
- ◆ authority is effectively delegated.

It was a day for reflection. One year ago today was Kevin's first day on the job. It had been a year of accomplishment. He had strengthened his staff through selective termination and sound hiring. He had done a financial analysis that resulted in shedding unprofitable accounts. He had cut inventory by 35%, although sales volume had remained constant. He had instituted quality control procedures that minimized dispensing errors and had made on-time delivery the rule rather than the exception.

When Kevin came to NH Pharmacy, Inc. (NHP) as general manager, the company was in trouble. NHP had been founded by Dalton Mack, a pharmacist who had a successful career in wholesale pharmaceuticals. Through his involvement in the community, Mr. Mack recognized the need for a pharmacy that specialized in providing pharmaceutical products and related services to long-term care facilities. A combination of strong sales ability, good service, and lack of competition converged to make NHP a success. Then Mr. Mack died.

Following Mr. Mack's death, NHP was managed poorly by Mr. Mack's heirs for two years. Clients fell away and competition became intense. Eventually NHP was sold to Brighton Medical, Inc., a diversified health system that included three hospitals, two nursing facilities, a managed care product, a physician practice group, mobile diagnostic services, and an ambulance service. However, NHP suffered a year of corporate neglect under the absentee management of Brighton's Chief Operating Officer (COO).

Kevin was hired to turn around the unprofitable, noncompetitive business. In spite of his successes, Kevin was not happy with NHP's progress. Neither was Brighton's COO, to whom Kevin reported. Kevin had spent a considerable amount of time working with his 15 employees to define and simplify their jobs. As a result, productivity increased, which freed employees to complete quality control procedures that Kevin developed. Yet they seemed less satisfied with their jobs than when they were performing less effectively. Kevin was really concerned to hear a rumor that the data entry clerk was thinking of leaving. She was one of NHP's best employees.

He was also concerned about the number of internal communication problems at NHP. The need for special-order items wasn't always communicated to Kevin. He also was not made aware of client complaints or about special service requests. Policy and procedure information communicated to clients by the staff nurse consultant was frequently at odds with that communicated by pharmacists. Among the pharmacists, there was little consistency of communication.

Communication between NHP and corporate headquarters was not much better. Corporate headquarters handled NHP's marketing and sales. Two sales contracts had been negotiated and signed without Kevin's input. In both cases, Kevin was given so little time to prepare for servicing the new accounts that the start-ups did not go smoothly, and both new clients voiced several complaints. Through his own field work and personal contacts, Kevin had two strong leads on new clients. However, he was unable to close either deal because Brighton's Chief Financial Officer (CFO) insisted on approving all new contracts. NHP's competitors were sole proprietorships that were able to respond to buyers' demands quickly and efficiently without waiting for any outside approval.

Kevin also knew that NHP's largest competitor was upgrading its data processing system. However, when he mentioned this to the

CFO, the CFO told him that NHP would not be getting any more infusions of capital until it began to show a profit.

Kevin had the feeling that in his first year he had emptied his bag of tricks for dealing with NHP's problems. He had used up his ideas for ways of making operations more efficient and effective. The work he had done was enough to stop NHP's backsliding. No more good accounts had been lost, but he had the feeling that he was trying to win the game by playing defense. NHP was no longer providing worse service than its competitors. Nor was it any better. The only way NHP would have a chance to grow to a profitable size would be for a competitor to make a mistake. As he turned out the lights to go home, he wondered what he could do to get the business moving forward.

The human body is an amazing assembly of parts and processes. From the biochemical metabolic processes catalyzed by enzymes, to the electrochemical transmission of nerve impulses, to the musculoskeletal production of movement, the body is a complex and elegant model of the integration of structure and function. The integration of electrical, chemical, and mechanical activity that results in cardiac function is one of the most intriguing phenomena in anatomy and physiology. A malfunction of any one of the components or processes involved may result in severe disease or death. The importance of structure and function in normal cardiac activity is such a powerful construct for clinicians that it will be used as a medical analogy for this and the next two chapters.

The anatomy of the heart includes coronary vasculature, valves, myocardium, membranous linings, and nerve tissue. When impulses originating in the sino-atrial (SA) node are transmitted through the network of cardiac nerves, the myocardium is stimulated to contract in a sequential pattern that moves blood through the body's vasculature. Nerve impulses and contractile activity are mediated by biochemical processes that involve the passage of ions through membranes.

The most immediately fatal of all cardiac pathologies is the total failure of a component of the cardiac structure. For example, if a weak ventricular wall ruptures, the result is electromechanical disassociation (EMD). No matter how much harder the other chambers contract or how many more impulses the SA node initiates, no compensation is possible. Theoretically, the only possibility of saving the patient would be immediate surgical repair. However, given the current state of diagnostic and surgical technology, it is impossible to intervene quickly enough.

Human organizations may also suffer structural defects that inhibit their proper function. Fortunately, these structural defects may be detected and corrected soon enough to avoid the demise of the organization. These defects are also usually easier to repair than a ventricular rupture. Unlike the static anatomy of the heart, human organizational structure is dynamic. Because human organizations are constantly evolving, some structural problems may be corrected merely by directing the natural evolution of the organization in the right direction.

Organizational structure is comprised of the working relationships that exist among individual members of an organization. The relationships that are established and defined by top management constitute the **formal organization**. Relationships that arise from the members themselves as they work together are the **informal organization**. The formal organization is legitimized through its recognition and sanction by managers. It is the anatomy of the organization. The informal organization is no less important than the formal organization, but it is a more amorphous and fluid set of relationships that are not as amenable to managerial control. The informal organization is the subject of subsequent chapters. The focus of this chapter is formal organization.

Anatomy and physiology are usually studied together because it is difficult to separate the structure of a biological entity from its function. The link between structure and function is observable in all levels of physiological organization, from the subcellular level up to the integration of organ systems. Likewise, the formal organization of healthcare delivery exists at different levels (Figure 4.1). The terms *microstructure*, *metastructure*, and *macrostructure* are used here to refer to the three different levels of organization for healthcare delivery.

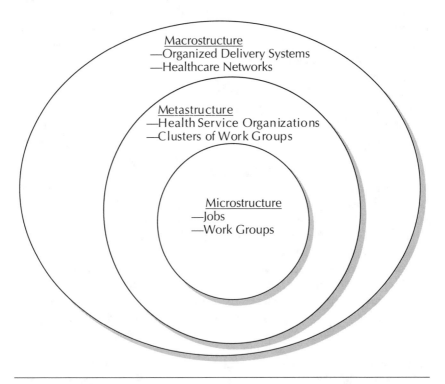

Figure 4.1   Layers of organization.

At the core of the formal organization is the individual job. The range of structure and function of individual jobs is as diverse as that of individual cells. Jobs are grouped together into units on the basis of something they have in common. For example, the cells of the cardiac anatomy are juxtaposed so that they can achieve the objective that they have in common (i.e., cardiac output). The individual cells of the myocardium, the lining membranes, and the nerves are linked together in such a way that they collectively do what no individual cell could do alone. In healthcare, analogous groupings might consist of nurses, laboratory technologists and technicians, or interdisciplinary clinical rehabilitation teams.

In the heart, the myocardium, nerves, linings, and valves work together to produce cardiac activity. In an HSO, work groups interact to achieve a common purpose. For example, in a nursing facility, the dietary department, nursing personnel, maintenance workers, and administrators work together to care for residents. At this organizational level, integrating the work of diverse work groups requires extensive coordination. In the heart, coordination of cardiac activity is primarily the responsibility of the nerve impulse initiation and conduction cells. In organizations, coordination is primarily the responsibility of managers.

At the highest anatomical level, the various organ systems (integumentary, cardiovascular, nervous, etc.) come together to allow an individual to pursue his personal objectives. At the highest organizational level in today's healthcare environment, healthcare institutions are becoming integrated into healthcare systems whose function it is to provide for the healthcare needs of their communities.

The process of establishing an organizational structure at any level is **organization design**. This process includes aligning the goals of an organizational unit with its workers, coordinating the work of groups of workers, and defining patterns of division of labor.[1] The formal organizational structure that results from organization design is represented by an **organizational chart,** which graphically indicates the authority and responsibility relationships that exist among the components of the organization.

Diagnosis of Dysfunctional Formal Organizations

Some of the signs of dysfunctional organizational structures are:

- delayed and/or poor decision making;
- lack of communication (especially, the "left hand doesn't know what the right hand is doing" syndrome);
- moribund organizational growth and development;
- lack of motivation and job satisfaction; and
- inability to adapt to changes in the competitive environment.

In the NHP case, all of these signs were present. However, any one or all of them may be signs of other problems that have nothing to do with the formal organization. Therefore, the final diagnosis of dysfunctional organizational structure would have to be made by ruling out other working diagnoses such as poor decision-making skills, poor communication skills, lack of planning, and poor human relations.

Macroorganization

There are two schools of management thought regarding the right way to structure an organization. One school of thought (the classical school of management) holds that there is one best way of designing organizations.[2] Management theorists who adhere to this view believe that the one best way of organizing can be discovered by observing effective organizations and determining the organizational structures they have in common. Their successful structural elements can then be copied and assimilated into all organizations. However, research has indicated that there does not seem to be one best way to design an organization. Rather, the appropriate design may depend on a unique set of constituencies served by each organization and a set of variables (contingencies) that characterize each organization and the environment in which it operates. Among the contingencies that may affect organization design are the organization's size, age, strategy, and use of technology. In addition, environmental stability, complexity, diversity, hostility, and the power relationships among internal and external constituencies help shape the organization.[3,4] The contingency view makes intuitive sense, especially to healthcare practitioners who, in recent years, have witnessed a macrostructural revolution in their industry.

Prior to the 1980s, healthcare was delivered by a set of relatively independent institutions (Figure 4.2). The only thread that held these units together was the patient. In fact, it could be argued that there was no formal macrostructure because

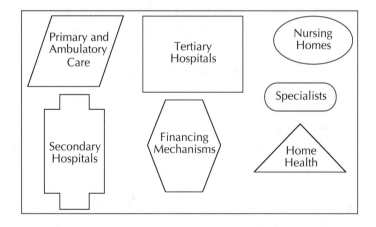

Figure 4.2   Traditional healthcare delivery.

most of the responsibility and authority relationships which existed among providers were established by law, not by the providers themselves. Moreover, the law only addresses these relationships on a piecemeal basis. The intent of the law has never been to create a comprehensive organizational structure. Also, patients were largely free to determine for themselves the point at which they would enter and exit the healthcare milieu.

The contingency factors that have led to the development of formalized macrostructures in healthcare are widely recognized. They include extraordinary growth in the cost of healthcare (from 9.3% of the gross domestic product in 1980 to 14.2% in 1995),[5] new technologies that shorten hospital stays by making treatment in ambulatory settings and at home possible, and a turbulent economic, political, and regulatory environment. The pressure on hospitals to lower costs in the face of decreasing occupancy caused many of them to integrate horizontally (i.e., to merge or form alliances that would allow them to take advantage of economies of scale).

Economies of scale occur when businesses lower operating costs by combining their resources. Economies of scale are achieved in the hospital industry when hospitals combine their purchasing power to negotiate for lower prices from suppliers. Economies of scale also accrue through sharing equipment and/or facilities. Combining jobs in such a way that labor costs are reduced may further contribute to economies of scale. For example, if hospital A has an underemployed risk manager and hospital B has an underemployed risk manager, the two positions might be combined to save one salary. As boards of trustees, who are responsible for institutional survival, see smaller profit margins, they become more amenable to trading institutional independence for financial security. In healthcare, financial pressure has fostered pursuit of linking strategies that bring institutions together for mutual benefit.

Even more traumatic for individual institutions and managers has been the vertical integration of healthcare providers. Recall from Chapter 2 that vertical integration occurs when institutions form alliances, acquire, or merge with their suppliers or customers. In other words, firms at different levels in a chain of suppliers of goods and services come together. In healthcare, vertical integration results in a macrostructure called an **organized delivery system (ODS)**.

An ODS is "a network of organizations that provides or arranges to provide a coordinated continuum of services to a defined population and is willing to be held clinically and fiscally accountable for the outcomes and the health status of the population served."[6] These systems have resulted from two of the contingencies noted above (i.e., shorter hospital stays and increasing application of technology in ambulatory settings). Through vertical integration, ODSs are formed in which patients never leave the system to receive their care. They merely move from one component of the system to the other. In theory, the ODS results in an orderly process of care that meets the changing health status and needs of individuals. The orderly flow of patients from one component of an ODS to another is a **continuum of care**.

A hypothetical ODS is represented in Figure 4.3. This is not a traditional organizational chart in that the lines do not represent responsibility and authority. Rather, they represent the flow of patients through the system. The lines are doubled to represent the back and forth flow of patients. The financing mechanisms are encapsulated in the center of the system. Payers (be they patients, private insurers, public programs, or managed care providers) interact with every component of the ODS. Many ODSs have a financing component, usually a managed care product. In those ODSs, the managed care product may be the most powerful component of the system in that it regulates the flow of patients and determines care pathways. Marketers would call the managed care product the **channel captain** because it is has more control than any of the other entities in the ODS.

Because the environment of healthcare delivery is unstable, the macrostructure needs to be very adaptable. Because they contain diverse components, ODSs have the potential to respond rapidly and vigorously to changes in the environment. However, there is one organizational issue that must be resolved if their full potential is to be realized—that is the question of where to place decision making in the system. In **centralized organizations**, decisions tend to be made by top managers and handed down (or out) to constituent groups. In **decentralized organizations**, decision-making authority is pushed to lower levels. Centralized organizations may achieve consistency in decision making by concentrating the process. They also tend to focus on the goals of the system rather than the goals of individual operating units. On the other hand, in centralized organizations, decisions pass through more layers of management, which slows down the process and, thereby, compromises the organization's ability to respond to environmental changes in a timely manner. This is what happened in the opening case. NHP missed out on getting new accounts due to the slow, centralized decision-making process. Also, centralizing removes decision making from the point of service delivery. When that happens, cost concerns may become more important in decision making than responding to market demands because centralized managers deal more with financial pressures, whereas decentralized managers deal more with consumers. Shortell et al. note that overemphasizing financial considerations at the expense of consumer satisfaction, marketing research, and assessment of community health needs hinders the ODS's ability to align its strategy and achieve full integration.[7]

Macrostructures in healthcare will continue to evolve in response to the rapidly changing environment. Not only are the economic, political, and regulatory dimensions of the environment unpredictable, but new (and highly unlikely) competitors are springing up. Now large employers like John Deere & Co., Delta Airlines, Bethlehem Steel, R.J. Reynolds, and Goodyear Tire & Rubber Co. have formed their own healthcare units that perform some of the functions currently

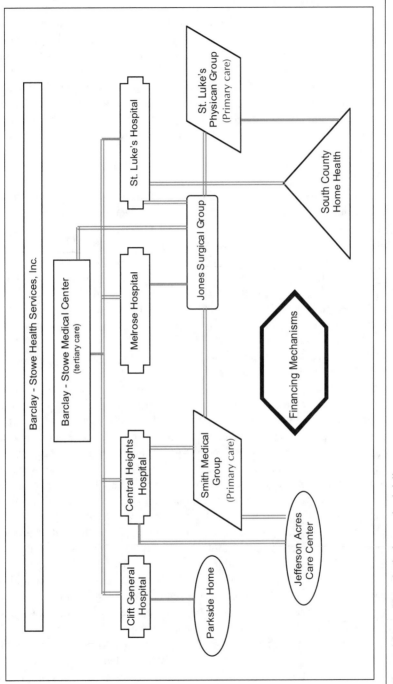

Figure 4.3   Hypothetical organized delivery system.

done by ODSs.[8] As ODSs respond to intense external pressures, a high human toll will be paid. Each structural change sends stress waves throughout the system. At the metastructure level, managers will have to deal with stress and concerns of employees. They will have to devote considerable energy to making sure that the linkages among their institutions are intact and functioning optimally. They will have to continually modify the structures of their organizations to meet external demands. Managing structural change is difficult and causes stress and burnout. However, there are some managers who thrive on being engaged in creatively reconceptualizing the delivery of healthcare and who are energized by restructuring their organizations.[9]

Metastructure

When most healthcare providers think of organizational structure, they think of the structure of an institution. Anyone who has worked for more than one employer probably knows that there is more than one way to structure an organization. Size is an important contingency factor at this level. Small firms of 12–15 employees seldom have more than one layer of management. The NHP case provides a good example. At NHP, there were different kinds of employees (bookkeeping, pharmacy, nursing, and maintenance), but Kevin was the only manager. Organizations that have few levels of management are called **flat organizations**. Many larger organizations tend to have several layers of managers and are therefore **tall organizations** (Figure 4.4). There are both flat and tall organizational structures in healthcare. The flatter an organization, the more subordinates report to each manager.

The number of employees that one manager supervises is the manager's **span of control**. There is no magic number that defines the ideal span of control. Managers who supervise employees whose work is well-defined and who can complete their work in relative isolation can usually supervise several employees. However, there are some employees who require more supervisory attention. For example, physician relations coordinators have jobs that require diverse activities and that require them to work with many other members of the organization. Supervising their work requires considerable time. Therefore, the manager of these employees usually has a relatively small span of control.

One of this decade's organizational structure trends has been **downsizing**. This is the process of reducing the number of employees of an organization. Much of the cutting has been done in middle management under the twin assumptions that much of the work of middle managers was unnecessary and that middle managers were capable of handling a larger span of control. It is now evident that many firms cut too deeply and have lost their competitive edge. Neither have these organizations realized the cost savings they had anticipated. Shrinking the size of the organization is not the path to overall growth.[10] Some firms are learning the hard way that any structural change should only be implemented pursuant to an objective assessment of the organization and its specific needs. Many traditional

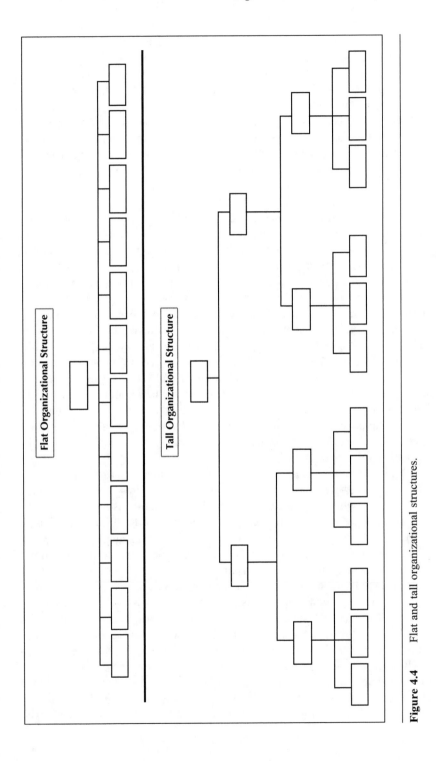

Figure 4.4   Flat and tall organizational structures.

structures meet the needs of their constituencies quite well. Follow-the-leader organizing can lead to very poor outcomes.

Figure 4.5 is a typical organizational chart of a hypothetical health maintenance organization (HMO). At the top is a Board of Directors. In nonprofit organizations, this body is frequently called the Board of Trustees. By law, the ultimate legal responsibility for the operation of a business lies with the **Board of Directors**. The board also is a vital link between an organization and its community. With the emergence of ODSs, the roles of boards are changing. There are several options for organizing the governance of ODSs. At one extreme, all boards could be dissolved except for a single board at the top of the organization. This option makes absolutely clear in whom the responsibility for governing the organization is vested. It also negates the possibility of conflicts among different governing groups. However, a single board structure minimizes the role of the board as a link to the community. At the other extreme, each entity could retain its board. This maximizes each entity's linkage to the community, but sets up the possibility of internecine battles for control. A middle-of-the-road option is to retain separate boards, but to limit their roles to advising an umbrella board and to handling routine governance issues like the granting of medical staff privileges.[11]

Because it is impossible for the board to be in continual session for decision-making purposes, it delegates ordinary decision-making authority to a **Chief Executive Officer (CEO)**, who acts on the board's behalf within limits established by the board. In many organizations, the board also delegates to the CEO the responsibility of representing the organization in the community. Because the CEO has external responsibilities and is frequently the person who is responsible for planning how the organization will meet new challenges posed by the firm's environment, he delegates most day-to-day internal decision making to a **Chief Operating Officer (COO)**.

When the number of employees exceeds the number that one manager can effectively supervise, the employees must be grouped into smaller units. The process of grouping employees is **departmentalization**. Like most aspects of organizing, there is no one best way of doing this. In healthcare, it has been customary to use the employees' functions as a basis for grouping them, which results in **functional structures**. In the HMO example, there are clear functional areas in medicine, nursing, and marketing.

Functional structures have dominated in healthcare because of the high degree of specialization of clinicians. By training and by law, nurses cannot be physicians, who cannot be pharmacists, who cannot be respiratory therapists, who cannot be speech pathologists, and so on. Functional departmentalization, which is used to organize clinical care, is applied in administrative areas where marketing, billing, and human resource departments (among others) are common. There are several advantages of organizing along functional lines. The full benefits of specialization can be realized by having people with similar skills working together. The members of the group can help each other to develop and apply their

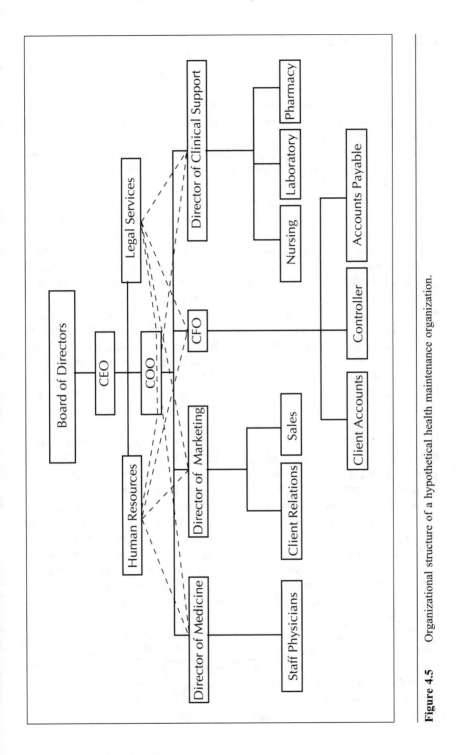

Figure 4.5   Organizational structure of a hypothetical health maintenance organization.

skills, and the manager can focus his energy on supervising the performance of a narrow range of activities. Also, managers of functional groups are frequently specialists in the function themselves, which helps them to mentor and support their subordinates. From the employees' point of view, working with people with similar interests may be attractive. Career paths in functionally departmentalized organizations are also easily identified. The development of clinical career ladders capitalizes on this advantage.

The alternative to functional structure is **market structure** or **divisional structure**. The departmentalization of a market structure reflects a characteristic of the market for the organization's goods or services. Organizational divisions may be formed around the various products/services the firm produces, the kinds of clients served, or the geographic location of clients. This kind of structure is common among firms that sell a variety of products nationally. A diversified media company might be structured by type of product. Many media firms produce a wide array of products (magazines, newspapers, television and radio programming, motion pictures), all of which require different production capabilities and are sold to different audiences. Geographic organization may work well for firms like insurance companies whose primary objective is to sell a limited number of relatively similar products. Geographic organization facilitates the management of the sales force by dividing it into units of manageable size. Using geographic departmentalization allows sales managers to supervise groups without having to crisscross the entire country. The advantages of a market structure include the ability of managers to coordinate all the activities related to a single product/service and the ability to identify the cost and contribution of each product/service to the entire organization.

Some health institutions have adopted market structures based on the concept that not all products/services supplied by the healthcare institution are the same. Johns Hopkins Hospital is a notable example. In 1973, the hospital restructured by organizing around medical specialties. Each department was headed by a physician chief who was assisted by a nursing director and an administrator. Each department then became responsible for its own decision making within a broad set of institutional guidelines.[12] Under the banner of **disease management**, other HSOs are developing processes and structures centered around specific diseases. These organizations are developing guidelines information and delivery mechanisms that focus on the treatment of different diseases.[13,14] In these HSOs, teams of professionals focus on providing services to patients who suffer from the same condition.

There is an inherent trade-off between functional and market structures. Functional structure makes the integration of specialized work groups difficult. Market structure inhibits the collaboration of specialists.[15] In an attempt to achieve the best of both worlds, some organizations choose a **matrix structure** (Figure 4.6). In a matrix structure, employees are assigned both to a functional group and to a project or product group. Hospitals have always had some characteristics of

Clinic Director	*Medicine*	*Nursing*	*Marketing*	*Psychology*	*Client Relations*
Well-child Care	Miller, M.D.	Blanton, R.N.	Sommers	Hilton, Ph.D.	Marler
OB/GYN	Rios, D.O.	Candici, R.N.	Dart, M.B.A.	Parker, M.S.W.	Chen
Occupational Health	Walters, M.D.	Conners, R.N.	Jones	Rivera, Ph.D.	Steuben
Internal Medicine	Song, M.D.	Kwan, R.N.	Lee, M.B.A.	Simons, M.S.W.	Kramer
Mental Health	Yu, M.D.	Black, R.N.	Sontag	James, Ph.D.	Clagget

Columns represent functional departments; Rows represent clinical teams.

Figure 4.6   Matrix organization of hypothetical health maintenance clinic.

matrix organizations. For example, staff nurses report to nursing managers. However, in clinical treatment matters, staff nurses follow orders issued by physicians. Thus, their responsibility and authority to take specific action regarding patients comes, in large measure, from the medical staff.

It is reasonable to expect that more healthcare institutions will adopt matrix structures as they become more responsive to environmental forces. In an increasingly competitive environment, HSOs are required to prove that they offer high quality services at reasonable prices. Purchasers are going to become comparison shoppers. To assess the relative value of healthcare products, buyers will compare certain key services like well-child care, substance abuse programs, and cardiovascular services. As HSOs and ODSs more clearly define specific products for the market, organizational structure will begin to reflect these products. For example, a nurse might be hired by a large managed care organization to be part of a team that manages diabetic patients. However, she would also be appointed to the nursing staff and would be responsible not only to a Clinical Coordinator of Diabetic Services, but also to the Director of Nursing Services. A word of caution about matrix structures is in order. Matrix structure violates one of the tenets of traditional management theory—the principle of **unity of command**. According to this principle, each employee should report to only one supervisor. Violating unity of command puts the employee in the position of serving two masters. For the matrix organization to be viable, the two masters must share common values and priorities and be able to cooperate in the utilization of resources.

Regardless of the basis for departmentalization, it is evident that the key to effective function is *coordination*, which requires that the interdependencies of work units be understood and communicated. Once the nature of the interdependencies is known, appropriate linkages can be established. In healthcare organizations, the flow of information forms the linkages that allow for the efficient and effective provision of services. Clinicians recognize interdependency and linkage concepts in cardiac function. The ventricles depend on the atria for their supply of blood to put into circulation. The cardiac nerves provide the linkage that maintains the sequence of atrial contraction followed by ventricular contraction.

One last crucial element of organizational structure appears in the organization chart depicted in Figure 4.5. This is the differentiation of staff and line positions. **Line positions** are jobs that are directly related to the production of goods and services. In a nursing hierarchy, line positions include nursing assistants, staff nurses, head nurses, and nursing service supervisors. Although some of the people in the hierarchy hold strictly managerial positions, they are still responsible for the patient care that is delivered. **Staff positions** are functional jobs that do not relate directly to production. In organization charts, the lines from staff positions to other positions are usually broken to show that staff personnel have no direct authority over line personnel. Persons in staff positions function in an advisory capacity. They provide guidance and advice based on their functional expertise. However, they do not make final decisions that relate to line positions. For example, the human resources staff places advertisements for line positions, usually screens applications, conducts initial interviews, and checks references. However, human relations personnel do not make final hiring decisions. Even in matrix organizational structures, there are employees in staff positions to provide support and advice to employees in functional positions.

Responsibility and Authority

Responsibility and authority are terms with which everyone is familiar. In ordinary usage, they have rather value-laden meanings. However, in management, these terms have very specific meanings. **Responsibility** is an obligation on the part of the employee to perform in a prescribed manner and/or to achieve established performance objectives. When an employee accepts responsibility, she also accepts concomitant **accountability**. Accountability arises from the necessity of answering to someone for performance (or lack thereof). **Authority** is the employee's right to make decisions relevant to completing his work.

As soon as a task becomes larger than the ability of one person to complete it, the process of assigning responsibility and authority for completing specific parts of the task begins. Take the case of a consultant whose business grows too large for him to handle. There are two ways for him to bring someone into his business. He could find an associate consultant (partner), or he could hire an assistant.

If he takes on an associate, in all likelihood an intricate dance begins in which each of the partners tries to accept the share of responsibility and authority with which he is comfortable. Perhaps the consultant brings in a partner with whom he can agree that the best way to divide the work is by account (i.e., each partner will be responsible for servicing certain accounts). If that is agreeable, then the partners have to determine who gets which accounts and how that decision should be made on an ongoing basis. As the partnership matures, each partner's desires and motives change, with the result that the division of work, responsibility, and authority becomes a dynamic process. After a time, for instance, the partners may decide that a better way to divide the work is on a functional basis (i.e., both partners will work on each account but be responsible for different aspects of the work). One might be responsible for field work and the other for writing reports. The negotiation of responsibility and authority between and among peers is a **horizontal coordination** process. Because there is no one higher in the chain of command, the partners are accountable only to each other for performance.

If the consultant hires an assistant, he would do an inventory of his work activities. Those that could be done by the assistant would be assigned to the assistant. He would retain the responsibility for the other activities himself. Although there probably would be some negotiation between the two parties, there would be a hierarchy, and responsibility and authority would be delegated downward. This arrangement would be accomplished through a **vertical coordination** process.

One advantage of the second alternative is immediately obvious. If the consultant and his assistant cannot agree on the delegation of responsibility and authority, the consultant is in a position to terminate the assistant and replace him with someone who is more in agreement with the consultant's view of the job. However, partners (even junior partners) are usually not so easily cast off. Even if the financial ties in a partnership are not strong, there may be professional repercussions in the future.

As the number of people in an organization increases, the nature of delegation stays the same but grows somewhat more standardized. People move into and out of organizations rather frequently, and they also change their areas of responsibility by changing positions. The effects of this are that (1) there is less negotiation of responsibility and authority, and (2) responsibility and authority attach to positions rather than to people. That is why lines of responsibility and authority can be shown on an organizational chart. Regardless of who fills the positions, the lines of responsibility and authority remain the same.

Although it is required for effective and efficient operations, delegation of responsibility and authority is not easily accomplished in most organizations. One of the biggest problems at all levels of the organization is delegating responsibility without the appropriate authority to achieve the work for which the employee is held accountable. This was part of Kevin's problem in the opening case. He had been hired specifically to turn NHP around, and he was being held accountable by the COO to do that. However, he had not been given all the tools he needed to be successful. He had no authority to sign contracts, someone else controlled marketing, and he could not get the capital he needed to be competitive. Controlling day-to-day operations is only one of the keys to success. Kevin did not have the others.

There are several reasons for the failure of managers to delegate sufficient authority to subordinates. Most managers have achieved their positions as a result of developing skills and knowledge which exceed that of others in similar positions. Managers tend to supervise people who tend to have fewer skills and less knowledge than they do. Under these conditions, it is not surprising that managers are reluctant to delegate authority and responsibility to someone less capable. Many managers tend not to trust in the ability of lower level employees to make good decisions.

Lower level employees undoubtedly make mistakes, and those mistakes are often ones that higher level managers would not have made. When some managers experience subordinate failure, they adopt the philosophy, "If you want a job done right, you have to do it yourself." Unfortunately, it is easy for the considerable amount of good decision making of employees to be overshadowed by a few errors. The manager who adopts the do-it-yourself philosophy is headed for burnout because he tries to do the work of subordinates as well as his own.

Some managers also have a need to be involved in all the details of the unit that they manage. Excessive managerial oversight and decision making is **micromanagement**. There is no definitive indication that Kevin was doing this at NHP, but there are signs of it. He had reshaped and simplified all the jobs. He was concerned about not being told about special order items and service requests. These seem to be the kinds of things that conscientious pharmacists handle on a routine basis in most pharmacies. Perhaps Kevin's efforts would have been better spent working with employees to design a system and then delegating its operation to them. That way he would have had more time to communicate with his superiors and with clients.

Other managers fail to delegate because they have certain activities that they like to do. If Kevin came to NHP from a pharmacy position in which he was responsible for handling special order items, he may be both familiar and comfortable with this activity. He might prefer handling special orders to treading the uncertain and murky waters of corporate politics. Managers need to be aware that their emotional responses to work may color their delegation decisions.

Although the delegation of responsibility and authority flows downward through the organization, managers do not have the luxury of delegating their own responsibility away. A CEO will be held responsible by the board of directors for the performance of the organization. He cannot escape his accountability for performance by claiming that he delegated this responsibility to other employees. If the CEO is neither responsible nor accountable, what is his raison d'être?

In mature, stable organizations, the delegation of responsibility and authority is relatively clear and is usually codified in job descriptions and policy and procedure manuals. Changes occur slowly and incrementally. However, in rapidly changing organizations, delegation is not as clear because new positions and work groups come and go, and the relationships among positions change to meet the needs of the moment. In today's rapidly changing healthcare environment, managers need to be cognizant of the fact that they, their colleagues, their superiors, and their subordinates are going to be less clear about their responsibility and authority. To clarify responsibility and authority, it is necessary to increase communication with everyone in the organization regarding changes. Changes in job descriptions and policies and procedures must be documented, and documentation needs to be disseminated as quickly as possible to avoid confusion. (Waiting until the day before accreditation or licensing visits to update documents will not sustain organizations undergoing change.) In dynamic organizations, managers also have to spend more time strengthening the organization's microstructure.

Microstructure

Forming work groups and designing jobs should be done at every organizational level. That is why Figure 4.1 is presented as layers of organization structure rather than a hierarchy. However, because most of the jobs in an organization are at the lower levels, dealing with microstructure issues seems to consume a disproportionate amount of time and energy. Forming effective work groups is important to the overall success of any organization. In healthcare, it has become critical to organizational survival. Because this is perhaps the most important function of most clinicians who become managers, both Chapters 5 and 6 are devoted to this topic. Some basic concepts and concerns regarding job design are presented here.

Job design is the process of deciding which tasks are associated with a job. The objective of job design is to assign tasks in such a way that the amount of human effort that goes into a job results in the maximum amount of output. In other words, the goal is to maximize productivity. One of the most important factors that influences job design is the context in which a job is performed. For example, because the equipment, resources, and environments of nursing facilities are never identical, the job of an activities director in one nursing facility may never be exactly the same as that in another facility.

Contemporary job design had its birth in the efforts to increase the productivity of industrial workers around the turn of the century. Researchers used techniques like time and motion studies to find ways to decrease the amount of time required to do certain jobs. Efficiency maximization efforts frequently resulted in decreasing the number of tasks associated with each job (**job simplification**) so that employees spent less time moving from one task to another. Work spaces were also redesigned to minimize the number of steps and physical movements employees had to make to accomplish their jobs. Contemporary HSOs use the same or similar techniques to redesign jobs and work environments.

Although efficiency can be improved through job simplification, other problems may be created because this engineering-oriented approach to job design virtually ignores the most important component of the production process—people. Taken to the extreme, job simplification results in the kind of monotonous, mind-numbing work commonly associated with assembly lines. Taking away an individual's ability to do a variety of tasks and to make decisions about how to accomplish work robs employees of their ability to use skills that are inherently part of being human. Not unexpectedly, the result is lack of job satisfaction and low motivation. This may have been one of the problems at NHP. Kevin simplified jobs, and employees became less satisfied. Several techniques can be used to retain the efficiency gains of job simplification, yet make jobs more interesting and satisfying.

Job enlargement is increasing the number of tasks associated with a job. It allows employees to experience some variety in their work. To retain efficiency, tasks have to be chosen that allow employees to move among them easily. This is not an easy task in itself. Some organizations use **job rotation** to give employees some variety. However, because humans are adaptable and capable of learning, they may soon become so accustomed to the simplified jobs added to the rotation that they again become bored. Unfortunately, job rotation does not guarantee that employees will have any control over their work.

Employees do not always view job enlargement in a positive light. A minority will always find comfort in the predictability and lack of challenge of simplified jobs. Others may perceive job enlargement as a way for managers to add to employee workload without increasing compensation. As with all change, job enlargement must be introduced in a nonthreatening and positive way. Because job enlargement is intended to increase job satisfaction and motivation, employees should play a major role in determining how jobs are enlarged.

Job enrichment is a job design technique that does more than merely add tasks to a job. It also loads jobs with factors that employees find psychologically appealing. Hackman and Oldham identified five core job characteristics that contribute to job satisfaction and motivation.

1. *Skill variety*—the array of skills and activities required to do a job.

2. *Task identity*—doing a whole job from beginning to end with a clearly recognizable outcome of job completion.

3. *Task significance*—the degree to which the job affects others, be they clients or colleagues.

4. *Autonomy*—the freedom of the employee to schedule work and decide how it is to be done.

5. *Feedback*—the degree to which job outcomes provide employees with information about the effectiveness of their performance.[16]

The more jobs can be infused with these characteristics, the more appealing they will be to employees. Making sure that jobs have these core characteristics requires significant delegation of responsibility and authority.

Job enrichment is difficult to achieve. It requires intimate knowledge of tasks, work processing, and employees. Implementing job enrichment is similar to playing three-dimensional chess. Employees, tasks, and processes have to be aligned in such a way that organizational goals are efficiently achieved. Like job enlargement, job enrichment does not guarantee that employees will be satisfied or motivated. Several other factors including scheduling, compensation packages, and working conditions also play a role. However, job enrichment is an important tool to be used in improving efficiency and effectiveness.

Conclusion

Organizing work is one of the most challenging aspects of management. Several of the potential problems that result from poor organization have been explored in this chapter. Managers can avoid some of these pitfalls by following some basic guidelines.

1. Delegate responsibility and authority. Employees must be given enough authority to do the job that is expected of them. In growing ODSs, authority and responsibility must be decentralized. The organization of each unit in the ODS must be customized to meet the demands of the various constituencies.

2. Design jobs with both efficiency and human factors in mind. Jobs and the people who do them are inseparable. This is also important advice for supervisors who are responsible for assigning daily operational tasks.

3. Communicate, communicate, and communicate some more. Each employee must be clear about his responsibility and authority. These issues are too important to be left open to interpretation and debate. An employee should never be confronted with, "You should have known it was your responsibility." If the employee should have known, the superior should have told him. Because HSOs are changing rapidly, there is no such thing as too much communication.

4. Minimize the trauma of change. As a result of organizational change, employees live with stress induced by uncertainty about the future. Managers must be cognizant of employee concerns about job security and about the ability to plan their personal lives in relationship to their jobs. Managers need to have a strategy for dealing with stress among their employees and within themselves.

In their book, *American Business: A Two-Minute Warning*, Grayson and O'Dell argued that if American firms did not restructure so that they were more responsive to the pressures and challenges of a global marketplace, they would find that they would have no role in that marketplace. Grayson and O'Dell found that operating units which efficiently produced high quality goods shared several characteristics:

1. Units were structured on the basis of a product, market, or customer rather than a function;

2. The basic work groups were small teams rather than large departments;

3. There were few layers of management; and

4. Each employee had significant responsibility and freedom to take the initiative regarding his job.[17]

The authors also noted that the most innovative firms use teams that cut across functional areas. Their team members have good people skills and activities are coordinated and integrated within the teams. Healthcare managers can learn much about effective organizational structures from successful organizations in other industries.

What can Kevin do to improve the situation at NHP? First, he needs to vigorously argue his case for more authority with the COO and/or CEO. Second, he needs to stop micromanaging and begin directing his attention to those problems that only he is in a position to solve. Third, he must pursue a team-oriented approach to accomplishing NHP's day-to-day work, as well as to achieving its long-term goals. He must delegate responsibility and authority for routine decision making to teams of employees. He should also advocate the formation of a higher level multidisciplinary team that would focus on strategies which would allow NHP to achieve its goals. Kevin is in a position to be the pacemaker who stimulates a sequence of events that will lead to NHP's success.

Endnotes

1. Jay R. Galbraith, *Organization Design* (Reading, MA: Addison-Wesley, 1977).
2. Jay M. Shafritz and J. Steven Ott, *Classics of Organization Theory* (Pacific Grove, CA: Brooks/Cole Publishing Co., 1992).
3. Galbraith, op. cit.
4. Henry Mintzberg, *The Structuring of Organizations* (Englewood Cliffs, NJ: Prentice-Hall, 1979).
5. Sally T. Burne and Daniel R. Waldo, "National Health Expenditure Projections, 1994–2005," *Healthcare Financing Review 16* (Summer 1995): 221–242.
6. Stephen M. Shortell, Robin R. Gillies, David A. Anderson, John B. Mitchell, and Karen L. Morgan, "Creating Organized Delivery Systems: The Barriers and Facilitators," *Hospitals & Health Services Administration 38* (Winter 1993): 447–466.
7. Ibid.
8. Alden Solovy, "New Power Strategies: The Battle for Control," *Hospitals & Health Networks 68* (December 20, 1994): 24, 26, 28, 30, 32, 34.

9. Jill L. Sherer, "Managing Chaos," *Hospitals & Health Networks 69* (February 20, 1995): 22–27.

10. Bernard Wysocki Jr., "Some Companies Cut Costs Too Far, Suffer 'Corporate Anorexia'," *The Wall Street Journal LXXVI* (1995): A1, A5.

11. Jeffrey A. Alexander, Howard S. Zuckerman, and Dennis D. Pointer, "The Challenge of Governing Integrated Healthcare Systems," *Healthcare Management Review 20* (Fall 1995): 69–81.

12. Robert M. Heyssel, J. Richard Gainter, Irvin W. Kues, Ann A. Jones, and Steven H. Lipstein, "Decentralized Management in a Teaching Hospital," *New England Journal of Medicine 310* (May 31, 1984): 1477–80.

13. "Disease Management," *Modern Healthcare 25* (June 12, 1995): 30–33.

14. Kevin Lumsdon, "The Heat and Headaches Over Retooling Patient Care Create Hard Labor," *Hospitals & Health Networks 69* (April 5, 1995): 34–36, 38, 42.

15. Arthur H. Walker and Jay W. Lorsch, "Organizational Choice: Product Versus Function," *Harvard Business Review 46* (Nov/Dec 1968): 129–138.

16. J. Richard Hackman and Greg R. Oldham, *Work Redesign* (Reading, MA: Addison-Wesley, 1980).

17. C. Jackson Grayson Jr. and Carla O'Dell, *American Business: A Two-Minute Warning* (New York: The Free Press, 1988).

Selecting Team Members:
Mitral Valve Defects

In this chapter the reader will learn how to:

◆ diagnose functional problems that stem from poor team composition

◆ avoid common errors in choosing team members

◆ identify attributes that team members should have

◆ detect potential problems through pre-employment screening and interviewing

◆ use group decision making in selecting team members

◆ consider important legal issues in hiring decisions.

A Tale of Two Therapists

Physical therapists are hard to find. Susan Heller knows. As the head of Rehabilitative Services at Parkmoor General Hospital, she is in constant competition with private rehabilitation companies for therapists. In spite of the competition, she has been able to hire and retain good people. But nobody bats a thousand, and Susan feels as if she has just hit a slump.

Carl and Chris were both hired about six months ago. It is near the end of their probationary employment period, and Susan has been reviewing their work records in preparation for the mandatory end-of-probation performance appraisal. She recalls that the pre-employment interview with Carl had gone pretty well, although he was definitely not like Parkmoor's other therapists. He was in his early thirties and had been working in a sports medicine practice for six years. He was looking for a change. The standard reference check by the human resources department had not revealed any areas of concern.

About three months into his employment, it became obvious that Carl was experiencing major mood swings. He alternately treated staff members with contempt and effusive friendliness. Sometimes he was distracted to the point that it was difficult to get his attention. After getting off to a good start in his first few weeks, he began clocking in late and calling in sick. He also asked other therapists to change shifts with him, usually on short notice. Susan had engaged him in casual conversation in an attempt to discover if he was having personal problems. Carl denied that anything was bothering him. Susan let him know that, just in case something should come up, Parkmoor had an employee assistance program (EAP) that he could take advantage of. She suspected that Carl either had emotional problems or was abusing drugs.

Susan consulted with the human resources department and was given the standard advice to investigate and document each instance of disruptive behavior. Susan had done that. She was very uncomfortable with Carl's continued employment. His unpredictable moods and attendance were detrimental to staff morale. But she wasn't sure that she had sufficient documentation to terminate his employment.

Then there was Chris, the almost perfect employee. He was good-looking, had a beautiful voice, and an absolutely charming personality. He had brought a professional portfolio to the pre-employment interview with him, something no other therapist had done. In it he had documentation of continuing education (including graduate courses), pictures of himself and some of his obviously happy patients, pictures of some of the social activities he had organized for his former co-workers, and several letters of support from co-workers and former patients. In almost every way his work performance lived up to the picture he painted. He was pleasant to work with, competent, and liked by all. It was just that he couldn't get to work on time.

Susan counseled him from the start about the necessity of being on time. Chris never offered an excuse, so Susan could not advise him on how to improve. She did offer to do anything she could to help. She tried shift rotation. That didn't work. She even tried creating a late day shift. That didn't work. The other employees liked Chris, but they complained bitterly about working harder because of his tardiness and about the favorable treatment he seemed to be receiving.

If she kept either Carl or Chris, she knew she was in for months, if not years, of problems. If she let them go, she might have open positions for months, and there might be legal complications. She wondered how it was that she had so misjudged these two as employment candidates.

Diagnosis of Team Member Selection Disorders

Susan has made an erroneous assumption in her analysis of her dilemma. She has assumed that she made two hiring errors. This may not be the case. The unacceptable behavior of both Carl and Chris may be new behavior. She is ignorant of the causes of these behavioral patterns, so without any evidence to the contrary, she cannot assume that there is something fundamentally wrong with the selection process. In fact, given her successful track record she should have considerable confidence in the process. Managers should suspect that there is a problem with the selection process when they see a pattern of behavioral problems among new employees, not when there are isolated, dissimilar cases.

Even when the selection process is sound, mistakes do happen. Therefore, to guard against recurrences, Susan should review the hiring decisions made in these two cases to discover if she overlooked any clues that would have indicated potential problems and to determine if any of the steps in the selection process were completed in a slipshod way.

With the wisdom of hindsight, she should review all application materials (including interview notes) to determine:

1. that all of Parkmoor's policies and procedures for recruitment and selection were followed;
2. that applications were complete in every material detail;
3. that references had been checked and verified;
4. if references had provided useful information about job performance and work-related behavior;
5. that interviews had been conducted in such a way that these potential problems could have been discovered; and
6. if indications of potential problems had been overlooked or ignored.

She should also review the circumstances surrounding the selection. Was she, for instance, under extraordinary pressure to fill these positions? If so, she may have been predisposed to overlook some indicators of performance problems or to have failed to probe for them.

Employee selection errors are costly. Not only do they drain the energy of the manager, but they potentially affect the entire organization. Having an employee whose performance is substandard is like having a defective mitral valve. A mitral valve defect sets off a cascade of events that results in the signs and symptoms of heart failure. Some of these include weakness, confusion, dyspnea on exertion, peripheral edema, abdominal discomfort and distention, nocturia, and pulmonary congestion. Because of anatomical and physiological interdependencies, this one structural defect can affect almost every other system.

Carl's and Chris' malfunctioning may affect almost every other work group at Parkmoor. Co-workers are already compensating by carrying larger workloads. If their ability to function deteriorates significantly, additional staff might have to be hired. (This is similar to the myocardial hypertrophy associated with heart failure.) In addition, anyone outside the rehabilitation department with whom Carl interacts may have negative responses to his erratic behavior that could result in strained interdepartmental relationships. Uncomfortable staff relationships detract from efficient and effective patient care. In fact, patients themselves may suffer from being exposed to Carl's exaggerated moods or from being denied services due to Chris' absence. Parkmoor is also at financial risk. If either employee's behavior results in a liability action, a loss of patients, or a lawsuit related to his employment or termination, Parkmoor could incur significant losses.

The New Healthcare Team

Team building in healthcare is changing. Susan is dealing with a traditional team-building problem. She is trying to build and maintain a staff of competent, effective physical therapists. Because she heads a rehabilitation services department, she probably has another team of occupational therapists, and another of speech therapists. In other words, she is building teams of functional specialists. Some team members may come together intermittently when they are providing services to the same patient (e.g., patients in a skilled nursing unit), but otherwise, the teams are independent. In the evolving healthcare delivery system, this kind of functional team will be increasingly displaced by multidisciplinary teams.[1]

Where the specialist team predominates, filling vacancies is usually done by searching outside the organization. In the Parkmoor case, when Susan needed a physical therapist, she conducted a search outside the hospital. As multidisciplinary teams become more prevalent, team leaders may conduct internal searches before turning to outside sources. For example, if a physical therapy vacancy occurs on a geriatric rehabilitation team, the team leader may search among other teams in the institution before undertaking an external search. The internal search is already frequently used by nursing service departments in hospitals. It is through this mechanism that nurses transfer from one department to another.

Internal searches (also called **job posting** programs) have the advantage of allowing managers to select from among candidates with a verifiable work history within the organization. But there is a downside to job posting. The objective of any search should be to find the best candidate for the job. Unfortunately, internal searches are even more prone to political contamination than external searches. In the name of fair play, some employees exert pressures on managers to always choose internal applicants with the most seniority. That way, everybody gets a chance at the best positions if they stay around long enough. Some employees play the games of office politics well and end up scoring enough points with certain managers so that they are favored for internal openings irrespective of merit. Managers may also use internal searches to even out the distribution of "good" and "bad" employees among departments. At its worst, in organizations characterized by managerial adversity, internal selection may become another weapon in organizational internecine warfare.

Building strong teams begins with selecting the right team members. As with so much of the work of managers, there is no one formula or set of procedures that will guarantee success. However, there is a common set of steps that most organizations follow. These steps do not ensure that all hiring decisions are wise ones, but they do encourage managers to do an in-depth evaluation of candidates, and they help organizations to avoid the wide range of legal consequences that can result from the hiring process. Anyone who has held a job recognizes these steps. They include recruiting, accepting and screening applications, checking references, interviewing, evaluating candidates, and selecting. Whether the search is internal or external, the steps in the process are the same.

One additional step needs to be added to this list. It is one in which candidates do not participate but which is absolutely vital and must be done before recruiting is initiated. The characteristics of the ideal candidate must be determined.

Characteristics of Ideal Team Members

It is impossible to determine what attributes to look for in potential team members without having a clear understanding of the jobs that team members do. This understanding is attained through performing job analysis. As its name implies, **job analysis** is a process of defining jobs by breaking them down into their component parts. In large HSOs, job analysis is a standard operating procedure that is done for each position in the organization. Job analysis yields information that is used by human resources specialists to plan for future human resource requirements, to develop pay scales, and to establish recruitment parameters.

Information derived by job analysis includes information about a position's tasks and responsibilities. A statement of these tasks and responsibilities is a **job description**. The items that are listed in a job description are observable in the activity of employees. In fact, one of the techniques used in performing job analysis is observation.

It is only after tasks and responsibilities are identified that a determination of the skills and knowledge which are required for successful job performance can be determined. A statement of these skills and knowledge is a **job specification**. The difference between a job description and a job specification is that the focus of a job description is the job itself, while the focus of a job specification is the employee. Therefore, the job specification is the document that forms the basis of recruitment efforts. Job postings and employment ads are written directly from job specifications so that candidates can determine whether they have the requisite skills and knowledge. Because the knowledge base required for many positions is extensive, it is common to use a knowledge-base indicator such as a degree or professional licensure as a surrogate measure of knowledge. If specialized knowledge beyond the basic credential is required, that is also listed. For example, an employment ad for a physical therapist might read:

WANTED

Physical therapist for private rehabilitation company. Must be registered in Missouri or registration-eligible. Graduate education and/or experience in working with children with developmental disabilities required.

This ad clearly indicates that skills and/or knowledge above and beyond the basic certification are required. Unfortunately, the ad does not reflect the specific advanced requirements. How many graduate hours would qualify a candidate? How many weeks, months, or years of experience? Because ads are usually developed to fit small spaces and limited recruiting budgets, they usually highlight only the key points contained in a job specification. For example, the job specification for this position would probably contain specific information about educational and experiential requirements. It would also probably contain a statement about the physical capability required to perform the job. For example, the job might require that the employee be able to lift 50 pounds. If minimum skill or knowledge levels are required, stating them helps some potential candidates self-select out of candidacy. Spending a little more money on advertising might save human resources personnel and managers a considerable amount of time in screening and interviewing potential candidates. It is more efficient to have potential candidates disqualify themselves.

Job specifications are extremely helpful to managers who are responsible for choosing new team members. However, they cannot be relied on exclusively to identify the attributes of ideal employees. For example, there was no indication in the Parkmoor case that either Carl or Chris was technically incompetent. However, their on-the-job behavior prevented them from effectively applying their technical skills because they were incapable of working effectively as part of a team. To increase the likelihood that they will choose employees who can function as team members, managers need to look beyond the attributes derived from the job specification.

Several personality traits have been studied as possible predictors of job performance. The traits that have generated the most interest among researchers are extraversion, agreeableness, conscientiousness, emotional stability, and intelligence or openness to experience.[2] Although the empirical evidence that links these traits to job performance is meager, there is certainly face validity to using them to evaluate candidates. People who do not function well in teams frequently prefer to do all their problem solving internally rather than sharing the process and their thoughts with others (introversion). People who are disagreeable and/or emotionally unstable have difficulty maintaining smooth working relationships with their colleagues, like Carl in the Parkmoor case. People who fail to perform in a conscientious manner also have difficulty working in teams. The other team members frequently have to pick up the slack and sooner or later, they end up doing so with resentment. This was the case with Chris' colleagues. People who are not open to new experiences are not good candidates for most healthcare teams. Change, whether technological or organizational, is a constant and often dramatic feature of healthcare delivery. Change is also evident in the healthcare work force. Team members come and go often. Healthcare teams are also growing in diversity. People who see change as a negative, rather than as an exciting and stimulating learning experience, are likely to have trouble functioning in a group.

In addition to job specification requirements and personality characteristics, another factor the manager should evaluate is the fit between a candidate's value system and the organization's corporate culture. Before managers can begin to make that determination, they must be able to describe the corporate culture. **Corporate culture** includes the values and philosophy of organizational members that ultimately lead to the informal rules that define how individual members of the organization are expected to behave.[3] Finding a fit between corporate culture and candidates is fundamental to the selection process.

If a selection error is made and a candidate is hired who does not have the skills or knowledge to do a job, some interventions may correct the mismatch. For example, the employee can pursue additional training or skills development programs, or perhaps the job can be redesigned so that the employee could function at an acceptable level. However, there is virtually no way to change an individual's values. Take, for example, a candidate in rehabilitative services who believes that the best way to treat stroke patients is to custom design a therapeutic program for them and then to push them to their maximum capability to comply with that program. This approach, which places a high value on professional autonomy, might well be in direct opposition to an approach that would involve the patient both in planning a therapeutic program and in determining how quickly to move through that program. The latter approach places a high value on patient autonomy. What might happen if the clinician were hired as a team member on a rehabilitation team that values patient autonomy more than it values professional autonomy? There would be immediate conflict about care planning and progress. Every treatment failure (and in rehabilitation there are bound to be a few, regardless of the competency of caregivers) will reinforce the clinician's feeling that he is right and the rest of the team is wrong.

Some HSOs have begun to realize that screening candidates for personality traits and values is an important part of the selection process.[4] Unfortunately, none of the screening tools (reference checks, interviewing, testing) are so reliable that hiring mistakes will not occur. However, using them can help to minimize the errors. In the Parkmoor case, if Susan were to discover that Chris' tardiness was due to a day-care problem or due to unreliable transportation, she could work with him to find ways of dealing with these issues. However, if punctuality is something that Chris doesn't value, then there is little or nothing that Susan can do to change his behavior. The only way to avoid this kind of hiring error is to be sensitive to indicators of individuals' values in the selection process.

Recruiting

Effective team building begins with recruiting. Anyone who has read a sports page is aware of that. In fact, reading sports media could lead one to believe that at the collegiate and professional levels, recruiting is by far the most important aspect of team building.

Internal recruiting is more easily done than external recruiting. Internally, recruiting is frequently done through job posting. This is a formal procedure that is usually coordinated through a human resources department if the HSO is large enough to have one. Internal recruiting should be done on a formal basis so that all qualified employees have an equal opportunity to be considered for internal openings. Employers have an ethical obligation to treat each and every employee in an evenhanded and fair manner. Opening up the process to all qualified candidates does that. Following a formal process can also provide employers with evidence that they have not filled internal vacancies in a discriminatory way which would violate any of the employment laws discussed below.

HSOs tap into a number of sources when it is necessary to recruit externally. Sometimes internal job postings will generate external applications. Some people in the job market visit potential employers with the idea of finding out if there are any internal postings. At the same time, they may leave an application on file even if there is no opening currently available. Therefore, the HSO may have to go no further than the current file of applications to find the right candidate for a position.

Recruiting on college campuses may be appropriate for some positions. Campuses can be good places to find part-time employees. As the cost of higher education continues to escalate, there will be more students who need to finance their educational expenses through part-time employment. The campus is also a good place to look for candidates who can fill positions that require relatively little experience. Many students and prospective employers use internship (or equivalent) experiences as a way of getting to know each other for possible employment purposes. As colleges and universities continue to strengthen their ties with alumni, regular recruiting through alumni associations may become feasible.

One of the most popular and successful techniques for finding jobs and employees is networking. **Networking** is the process of meeting and interacting with professional colleagues from a variety of organizations. Networking may be done to discuss mutual problems and concerns or to discover opportunities. From a recruiting perspective, networking can be thought of as professional scouting. It can lead to the discovery of professionals with exceptional qualities that managers would like to have playing on their teams. Professional associations provide important networking opportunities. Potential employees found through this network usually evidence significant interest in their field.

One of the most useful sources of informal information among HSOs is the salespeople who call on different HSOs in a geographic area. As part of their jobs, salespeople are expected to get to know the people with whom they conduct business. This includes not only purchasing agents, but whoever might play some part in purchasing decisions. Pharmaceutical sales representatives not only spend time with physicians, but also with pharmacy buyers, pharmacy managers, and staff pharmacists. Medical equipment sales representatives spend time with purchasing agents, nurses, therapists, dietitians, and others. Through extensive interaction, they learn who needs what kinds of personnel and which individuals might be thinking about making a job change.

HSOs also advertise job openings in the newspaper. This may be done even though there are active applications already on file and managers may know of potential applicants through other sources. Advertising broadens the pool of applicants. Newspaper advertising is very important in recruiting the kinds of employees who may not have access to networks, professional organizations, and salespeople. These kinds of employees would include clerical employees, maintenance staff, and lower level caregivers such as nursing assistants. Although the applicant pool generated by advertising may contain the one best applicant, it usually includes many applicants who must be screened out.

Screening Applications

Screening applications can be an arduous process. In healthcare, it is common to use both standard employment applications and resumes. Having candidates complete standard applications is useful as an information gathering tool. Most of the data on applications relates to job specifications. This data forms the basis for the initial screen. If the applicant's qualifications do not fit the job specification, the applicant can be eliminated from candidacy. Also, the data should be verified before investing additional time in screening and selection. Applicants for virtually any position can present falsified credentials. Because the information requested on application forms is relatively simplistic and relates to technical skills, it is not very predictive of what kind of team member the applicant would be.

Resumes present another set of opportunities and problems. Opportunities come from the fact that applicants have the freedom to develop their own presentations of qualifications. They can inject elements of their values and personality into the resume. Unfortunately, one can never be sure how much a resume reflects the candidate and how much it reflects good writing skill (or that of the person hired to write the resume).

A manager faced with a stack of applications and resumes to go through sometimes loses sight of his mission. The manager may find himself looking exclusively for ways to screen people out rather than for reasons to screen people in.[5] The manager has to remember that the real job is not to whittle the stack of resumes down to one. It is to eventually select the one best person for the job. That person may not even be among the applicants or that person may not have submitted the best application and/or resume. Manor Healthcare Corp. has added a videotaped scenario assessment to its application process for nursing and administrative personnel. By evaluating how candidates would respond to the videotaped events, candidates "who have a strong sense of pride, are team players and independent problem solvers, and can provide optimum customer service" are screened in rather than out.[6] These are traits that candidates may have some difficulty communicating on a resume.

Reviewers typically look for **red flags** in the resume. These are factors that the interviewer intuitively feels would make a candidate a poor choice. Table 5.1 summarizes some of the characteristics of applicants that reviewers commonly see as red flags, along with an explanation of what potential problems they could signify. The important point to remember about these red flags is that they vary greatly from one reviewer to another because each reviewer comes to the selection process with a different set of experiences and biases. The empirical data that would relate any of these red flags to job performance is virtually nonexistent. Because the ultimate goal is to find the best candidate for the position, the manager should spend more time focusing on reasons to keep candidates in contention for the position rather than looking for red flags to screen them out.

Checking references can be done either before or after interviewing. If reference checks are done before interviewing, they can uncover information that would eliminate some candidates. They may also prompt the manager to focus on some specific aspects of work history during the interview. This would obviously save the manager some time. However, if references are checked after the interview, they can be used to confirm or clarify information that was elicited during the interview.

In addition to helping managers to identify ideal job candidates, checking references must be done to help employers avoid liability exposure that could arise from having hired unfit employees. Litigation involving employers has arisen as a result of physical injuries sustained by co-workers or others because of actions taken by unfit employees. Employers may be held responsible for these injuries if they knew or should have known that an employee was unfit and the employee was subsequently hired or retained[7] (see Chapter 13). It has been suggested that one way employers can protect themselves from being held responsible for what they should have known is to check at least three references.[8] That way the employer is relying on more than one outside opinion. While a candidate might find one reference that would provide false information, it is unlikely that he would be able to find three who would collude in providing a misleading picture.

Reference checking is far from a routine matter. In recent years, there has been some fear among employers that sharing negative information about former employees could result in their being sued for defamation. Therefore, soliciting

Table 5.1   Resume Red Flags and Potential Interpretations

Red Flag	Typical Reviewer Assumptions	Valid Explanations
Frequent employment changes	Emotional instability? Lack of loyalty? Inability to work well in an organization? Chronic malcontent?	Each new position added to professional development. Some moves necessitated by family obligations. Lack of employer commitment to the employee. Downsizing. Employer(s) engaged in illegal activities.
Gaps in employment history	Not committed to a career?	Illness of the employee. Pursued education/training during unemployment.
More education or experience than the job requires	Unable to get a better position? Overqualified and would be bored?	Pursued education/experience out of curiosity rather than to move up. More comfortable with lower level employment.
Resume is wrinkled and smudged	Nonchalant about the job?	Resume was damaged by the postal service or by in-house handling.
Resume is long	Doesn't know how to be brief? Long-winded? Full of him/herself?	All information is pertinent. Unusual and exceptional credentials/experience. Leaving anything out would create red-flag gaps.
Resume is short	Inexperienced? Nothing to say?	Trying to follow conventional wisdom of submitting short resumes.

information about anything other than confirmation of employment can be difficult. Fortunately, the courts have held that communication about an individual's job performance between former and prospective employers constitutes a qualified privilege, which means that a former employer cannot be held liable for defamation unless the employer intentionally lied about the employee.[9,10] As long as the information given relates to job performance and the former employer has documentation that clearly verifies that the information is true, there is little risk of liability exposure. All employers, however, should know what information is protected from disclosure under state statutes. In some cases, information about disciplinary reports or actions may not be released without written notification to the employee. However, if the employee has waived this statutory right of privacy in an application to another employer, if a court requires disclosure, or if a government agency requests the information in response to an employee's complaint or as a result of a criminal investigation, then the information can be released.[11]

It is small wonder that most former employers feel it is still better to play it safe and share as little information as possible. However, there are two things that prospective employers can do to get more cooperation from references. First, the applicant should be asked to sign a waiver releasing from liability any former employers who provide a reference. The waiver may also allow the prospective employer to check any of the other credentials (education, court records) that may be relevant to employment.[12] Second, the interviewer needs to frame questions very carefully. Only questions that are clearly relevant to past job performance should be asked. If questions stray into areas about the applicant's opinions or life outside the employment context, reference sources may becomes suspicious of the motives behind the questions and be less responsive. Questions that would lead the source to suspect that the prospective employer might be in violation of the Americans with Disabilities Act (ADA) or the Civil Rights Act of 1964 might also persuade a reference that silence is the best policy. After all, few people want to participate in a discriminatory process, and probably even fewer want to be a party to any legal action that arises from these practices. The kinds of questions that should be avoided are the same kinds of questions that should not be asked directly of applicants.

In spite of the hesitancy of some former employers to provide information, there are some things that interviewers can do to break down the barriers.

1. Ask about skills. Skills are positive attributes that many former employers do not mind talking about. However, in the course of talking about skills, the interviewer can learn several things. Once the source begins talking, not only the positive things about skills come out, but areas in which the candidate is weak or could improve also may be revealed. Also, if the interviewer asks about skills without prompting the reference about which skills she is interested in, the source may shed (through omission) some light on areas in which the applicant is devoid of skills. For example, if the interviewer asks for a list of all the candidate's competencies, and no interpersonal skills are listed, then the candidate's interpersonal skills may be weak. This area may be probed with this source, other sources, or with the candidate during the pre-employment interview.

2. Be persistent. Let sources know that if they refuse to give more than a verification of employment dates, it will be assumed that there is some kind of problem. Because that is not the intent of

most sources and they do not want the interviewer to make such an assumption, they may become more willing to provide information, especially if they feel that they have positive information to share.

3.   Refer to information that the applicant has already made known. If the applicant has already listed certain skills, such as communication skills, as a strength, let the source know that. Frame the questions related to communication skills as questions that are simply meant to verify the accuracy of what the candidate has already divulged. That way the source may feel that the candidate has already opened the door to the questions by supplying information that another employer can only be expected to verify.[13]

Skilled and persistent interviewers can obtain considerable information about candidates from reference sources. However, even sources who know candidates and their work well cannot provide the same degree of insight as candidates themselves.

Interviewing

The pre-employment interview provides candidates and prospective employers an opportunity to exchange information about each other. The employer's objective should be to identify the candidate who best fits the position that is available. The candidate's objective should be to identify a position and organization that best meet his career objectives. If either the prospective employer or the candidate has other objectives, then the integrity of the interview is compromised. For example, an employer who is under pressure to fill a position as soon as possible may have a tendency to oversell a position to a candidate. To the candidate who is trying to find the best possible fit between her professional objectives and a position, this oversell could lead her to believe that the position is more suitable than it really is. Conversely, a candidate who is under pressure to find employment may have a tendency to overstate his capabilities or to lead the prospective employer to believe that he is a better candidate for the job than he really is. The result of anything other than candid exchange of information on the part of the employer or candidate may result in an employment mismatch that harms either one or both parties. However, both candidates and employers need to keep in mind that there may be hidden agendas at work during the interview. Therefore, although the pre-employment interview can be a powerful tool for eliciting information, the results must be interpreted as part of a comprehensive evaluation program.

Even interviewers who have good intuitive interviewing skills should always prepare for pre-employment interviews. No two interviews are identical. Through their conversation, their responses to questions, and the questions they pose themselves, candidates help to shape their own interviews. For interviewers to effectively use interviews to distinguish among candidates, there must be some questions that are asked of all candidates. Otherwise, interviewers will find themselves comparing the proverbial apples and oranges (and plums, bananas, and papayas) if they interview enough candidates.

Planning the interview should begin with preparing a list of objectives for the interview. Assuming that the employer's purpose is to find the best person for the job, the objectives will include eliciting information about the candidate's competency as well as the candidate's compatibility with the organization. In other words, planning the interview begins with a review of the job specification, the corporate culture, and the personality traits that would make for a good fit. A list of possible interview objectives for an interview with physical therapy candidates is listed in Table 5.2.

The first set of objectives may be the easiest to formulate because they come directly from the job specification. Any patient care position requires strong verbal skills. In fact, this is such an important skill that many managers may be tempted to not even list it as an interview objective under the assumption that it is so obvious as to be redundant. However, listing verbal skills assessment as a separate interview objective serves as a strong reminder to interviewers that they need to be mindful that, in many cases, how a candidate says something is every bit as important as what he actually says. Objectives related to the ability to work in a team are also fairly easy to formulate. These objectives are derived from the ideal team member traits mentioned above.

Table 5.2   Some Possible Interview Objectives for a Staff Physical Therapy Position with a Home Health Agency

Job Specification:

Reiterate and determine that the applicant can lift at least 50 pounds without assistance.

Determine how much and what kind of experience the candidate has with pediatric patients.

Determine how much and what kind of continuing education the candidate has pursued in the past year.

Assess the candidate's verbal communication skills.

Determine the candidate's ability to adjust to working in diverse conditions found in home environments.

Corporate Culture:

Determine to what extent the candidate is willing to "go the extra mile" to serve a client.

Determine how receptive the candidate is to change.

Team Skills:

Determine how the candidate works with professional colleagues and subordinates in providing clinical care.

Assess the candidate's intellectual curiosity.

Determine how open the candidate is to new experiences.

Determine how the candidate deals with conflict in the workplace.

Writing objectives relevant to assessing the candidate's fit with the corporate culture is more difficult. To write these objectives, the interviewer has to be able to describe the organization's corporate culture. The interviewer should be able to answer the following questions about the corporate culture:

- What does this organization stand for?
- What kind of behavior is rewarded in this organization? What kind of behavior is punished or discouraged?
- Who are the most admired people in the organization? Why?
- What words best describe the people who seem to fit in here?
- What words best describe people who have not fit in? What words best describe people who have left the organization after a short period of employment?
- What things are important to the people at the top of the organization?[14]

The first objective in Table 5.2 under the corporate culture heading came from the assumption that one of the organization's values is making an extra effort to meet client needs. This kind of behavior is rewarded in the organization. Therefore, the interviewer will try during the interview to determine how far a candidate will be willing to go to meet the needs of the client. In a different organization, just the opposite may be true. The organization may value providing less service to each patient so that caregivers can care for more patients (i.e., quantity may be valued above quality). Therefore, employees who are willing to minimize the amount of time they spend with patients so that they can increase their patient loads are more valued employees. (Note that this is not necessarily an undesirable corporate value. When there is insufficient health manpower to fully meet the needs of a community, it may be to the community's overall benefit to make that manpower available to as many patients as possible, even if it is in small doses.) Managers need to make an unbiased assessment of the corporate culture to determine the best fit between employment candidates and the organization.

In very rare circumstances, it will be the interviewer's objective to screen for employees who do not fit with the existing corporate culture. This is usually the case when it has been determined by top management that a major change in strategy is required. Take, for example, the hospital where providing highly specialized, cutting-edge tertiary care has been the major objective. At that hospital, the reward system has favored clinicians who maintain the highest level of technical proficiency and continually push the boundaries of technical capability. Now what happens if that hospital joins a network and it is determined that the hospital should be a secondary care provider and transfer complex cases to another network member better equipped to handle them? Obviously, the top management of the hospital will have to change the corporate culture and reward job performance that supports the new objectives. However, the people who remain will, by and large, continue to value tertiary care because that was their interest and the key to the fit between them and the organization. For the corporate culture (which includes informal rules of behavior as well as formal rules) to change, a conscious effort will have to be made to hire employees who share the new values of the organization, even if those values are at odds with the values of the majority of current employees.

Formulating Interview Questions

Although interviewers should come to interviews with a list of prepared questions, they should keep in mind that the purpose of an interview is to exchange information. Because the interviewee (particularly the well-prepared interviewee) comes with a different script than the interviewer, there will be some variation in the flow of interviews from one candidate to the next. The interviewer's objective is to get responses to all of his questions, not necessarily to ask all of them. Some interviewees provide the information the interviewer is looking for with very little prompting by questions. Others wait for the interviewer to provide the lead. Interviewers may do well not to read too much into this variability because it may reflect more what candidates have read or been told about job interviewing than anything else.

A well-prepared list of interview questions includes closed, open, and follow-up questions.[15] **Closed questions** result in responses of very few words, usually a "yes" or "no."

Interviewer: Have you ever worked with pediatric patients?

Interviewee: Yes.

The closed question is used effectively to elicit very specific information quickly. In the above example, if the candidate had answered "no," then the interviewer could move very quickly to another part of the interview. The "yes" response would probably prompt the interviewer to clarify the experience of the candidate with pediatric patients.

Open questions require interviewees to provide longer responses.

Interviewer: What do you find attractive about working in home healthcare rather than in an institutional environment?

Interviewee: I really like the idea of getting outside and having a change of scenery.

This response is appropriate, but provides very little insight into the candidate's needs or values. The interviewer can get more valuable insight by using **follow-up** questions. There are two types of follow-up questions: the **mirror question** and the **probe question**. Mirror questions are used to get the candidate to continue talking without directing the candidate to elaborate on any specific point.

Interviewer: You like to work in different locations?

Interviewee: Yes. When I worked in the nursing home, I was pretty much stuck in the therapy room all day because the residents were almost always brought down by the aides. After a couple of months, I felt like I was getting claustrophobic.

Interviewer: Uh-huh.

Interviewee: And it's not just the four walls. But I like working with different people all the time too.

Notice how the lead question is merely a paraphrase of what the candidate has already said. It is a cue to elaborate. Now the interviewer has a much better idea of the candidate's needs. She also has found out that the candidate is open to working with new people. But does his last statement imply that he may have problems maintaining relationships with his co-workers? This is where a probe question may be helpful. **Probe questions** are used to elicit additional information and/or to clarify what has been said.

Interviewer: By different people, do you mean that you got tired of working with the residents or with the other rehabilitation staff?

Interviewee: Not the residents because most of them weren't there more than a month or so. It's just that there were only five of us in the rehab department and after a few months in close quarters like that, you get awfully tired of seeing each other.

Interviewer: I see.

Interviewee: Actually, even though it has been several months since I left the nursing home, I still get together with Joe, the other physical therapist there, every couple of weeks or so to play a round of golf. He's not much of a golfer, but he's a great guy.

Now the interviewer has a clearer picture of what the candidate is looking for in a job. Notice how effectively "uh-huh" and "I see" were used in the dialog. Both of these nondirective interjections cued the interviewee that the interviewer was interested in hearing more about this subject. The interviewer can also use silence as a cue to continue. In fact, interviewers should keep in mind that because only the questions are scripted in an interview, silence will naturally occur as the interviewer and the interviewee consider their responses. The interview will not have the same pace and flow of rehearsed television and movie dialogues.

Conducting the Interview

Because the primary purpose of the interview is to exchange information, the interview should be conducted in an atmosphere that promotes and facilitates such exchange. Therefore, the environment should be comfortable. The more relaxed people feel, the more they tend to talk. And the more they talk, the more they reveal about themselves. The manager also has to set aside an interruption-free time and place. Some healthcare managers have difficulty doing this because there always seems to be some kind of crisis to deal with or other demands on their time. Some of them rationalize the interruptions as just a way of letting the candidate know what working in that organization is really like. However, interruptions break the flow of the interview and divide both the interviewer's and the interviewee's attention. Unless both parties are willing and able to focus their attention on the interview, much of its effectiveness as a selection tool will be lost.

Interviews are structured much like reports, speeches, and letters. They include an introduction, a body, and a conclusion. During the introduction, every effort should be made to put the interviewee at ease. Smiles, handshakes, and small talk all help create a relaxed atmosphere. If the interviewer has any ground rules for conducting the interview, such as a time limit or taking notes, these should be stated during the introduction. That will let the interviewee know that the interviewer has taken time to prepare for the interview and that the interviewee can relax because there will not be any surprises.

The body of the interview consists of the information-gathering and sharing portion. If the interviewer would prefer to get through the information-gathering agenda before opening the discussion to questions by the interviewee, he should state that as a ground rule. If he prefers that the interviewee raise questions as they come to mind, that should also be mentioned as a ground rule. It is recommended that interviewers take notes during the body of the interview. Most managers juggle a variety of tasks at any one time. Even though a specific time for an interview may be set aside, the manager may not return to the evaluation or comparison of candidates until some time later. Having notes to refresh the memory may bring some salient characteristics or responses back to mind.

The conclusion of an interview is very important. Unless the interviewee said something that definitively eliminated him from consideration, each candidate may be the next new employee. Because this may be the first encounter of a long professional relationship, every effort should be made to get the relationship started on solid ground. Even if the candidate is not chosen for the position, the candidate deserves to be treated respectfully. Each candidate should be thanked for the time and effort required to interview. In addition, the manager should let the candidate know what the next step is in the selection process. He should also indicate when the candidate can expect to be notified of a final hiring decision. Following up with candidates is especially important in today's healthcare environment. The interviewer never knows when a candidate that is not right for a position today may be the perfect candidate for a position that may be available in the future. The fluidity of positions and personnel in healthcare makes it imperative that every opportunity to establish goodwill in the community be maximized. Not only is it discourteous not to inform candidates of hiring decisions, it is just plain bad business.

When it comes time to compare candidates, interviewers need to beware of a tendency to overemphasize one positive or negative attribute. For example, if a physical therapist responding to the hypothetical newspaper ad presented earlier were to state during the interview that she had completed a minor in child psychology, that one positive fact might cause the interviewer to come away with a favorable impression of the candidate even though she may have a history of poor relationships with co-workers or a work history which indicates she may not be a dependable employee. Giving a candidate a favorable review on the basis of one positive attribute is the **halo effect**. Likewise, giving a candidate an unfavorable review on the basis of one negative attribute is the **horn effect**. Interviewers should also be sensitive to the power of the first impression. The interviewer's first impression can become the one attribute that colors the overall evaluation of a candidate. It has even been demonstrated that first impressions can influence the way interviewers conduct the remainder of an interview, which, in turn, causes the overall evaluation to be biased.[16]

Hiring Teams

One way to improve selection processes in organizations is to form hiring teams. This is commonly done in higher education where hiring teams are called search committees. One of the values of search committees is that groups of employees bring to the table a broader perception of an organization's corporate culture than any one individual can do. A hiring team composed of prospective peers may also put forth considerable effort to clearly identify the characteristics they would like to see in a peer. Managers should feel confident in empowering groups of employees to make hiring decisions. Nobody has more to lose from a poor hiring decision than co-workers. Prospective peers are motivated to find people who are conscientious and will make their work flow smoothly.

The hiring team concept has been used in several industries, including healthcare.[17] Hiring teams may include employees from several different levels in the organization and from different departments. The latter is especially important if the position requires that the new employee be a member of multidisciplinary teams or be part of a matrix organization. By working as part of a team that chooses employees, individuals can also learn important interviewing and evaluation skills from their colleagues who may come to the task with different levels of experience and different perspectives.

Legal Considerations

As this discussion of selecting team members indicates, the process can be both interesting and creative. However, there are a number of ways in which the selection process can lead employers into a legal quagmire. It goes without saying that the best way to deal with quagmires is to avoid them.

Laws related to hiring employees are extremely complex. Before managers even begin the selection process they need to be well-grounded in this field. Managers need to formulate their search strategies, application and resume review procedures, and interviews with the expert guidance of legal specialists in employment law and/or human resources professionals. The review presented here is meant to be introductory, not comprehensive. It is meant to provide managers with a brief overview of the field of the law that deals with employee selection. Before managers embark on the actual experience, they are advised to seek appropriate assistance. Even managers with years of experience are well-advised to review employment laws. New statutes, regulations, and judicial interpretations create a constantly changing employment environment.

This review is also limited to federal law. Many states have laws that are more restrictive than federal laws. When there is an apparent conflict between the two levels of law, the more restrictive law is the law that should be followed. Table 5.3 presents an overview of the provisions of the major federal laws that influence the selection process.

The **Civil Rights Act of 1964** (also commonly referred to as **Title VII**) is the cornerstone of federal legislation that deals with employment discrimination. The Act prohibits employers from treating individuals or groups of individuals differently on the basis of race, creed, color, gender, religion, or national origin. It created the **Equal Employment Opportunity Commission (EEOC)** to enforce its provisions.

Persons who believe that they have been victims of discriminatory practices covered by the Act first seek relief under a state law if there is one. If not, they may file a complaint with the EEOC. Proving that discrimination existed is difficult in that employers who intentionally discriminate are seldom foolhardy enough to document the discrimination. However, complainants may prove their case by showing that the practices of the employer resulted in discrimination. For example, if 90% of a healthcare firm's entry-level employees are women, but only 20% of supervisors are women, then there may be sufficient evidence of discrimination to win a suit. In order to prove cases, some plaintiffs have resorted to using testers.[18] Testers are impostors who interview for positions. By showing that testers who are members of protected groups receive less favorable treatment than equally qualified testers of nonprotected groups, some plaintiffs have won settlements from employers.

Even employers who never intend to discriminate can find themselves inadvertently doing so by the kinds of questions asked on applications and in interviews. In general, the courts have held that any question that does not directly relate to the job may indicate that there is a pattern of discrimination. Some of the common application items that can lead to problems include:

1. Asking for photographs (obviously alerts prospective employers to race, gender, and possibly age).

Table 5.3   Summary of Federal Statutory Laws that Affect the Selection of New Employees

Law	Employers Covered	Major Provisions
Civil Rights Act of 1964 (Title VII)	Employers with 15 or more employees; unions and employment agencies	Requires employers to hire, retain, and promote personnel without regard to race, color, national origin, gender, creed.
Pregnancy Discrimination Act of 1978	as above	Prohibits employment discrimination based on pregnancy or on having given birth.
Civil Rights Act of 1991	as above	Places burden of proof in discrimination cases on employers; makes victims of intentional discrimination on the basis of race, ethnicity, gender, religion, or disability eligible for compensatory and punitive damages.
Equal Pay Act of 1963	Employers with 2 or more employees, involved in interstate commerce, and with gross sales of at least $500,000	Prohibits gender bias in compensation for the same amount of substantially equal work under similar conditions.
Age Discrimination in Employment Act of 1967	Employers with 20 or more employees	Prohibits discrimination against employees over 40 years of age.
Rehabilitation Act of 1973	Employers doing $2,500 or more in business with the federal government annually	Requires employers to take affirmative action to hire disabled workers; requires primary government contractors to impose the same requirements on subcontractors.
Americans with Disabilities Act of 1990	Employers with 15 or more employees	Prohibits discrimination in hiring against disabled persons; requires employers to make reasonable accommodations for qualified individuals with disabilities.

References:

Clark, Lawrence S., Alberts, Robert J., and Kinder, Peter D. 1994. *Law and Business: The Regulatory Environment*, 4th ed. New York: McGraw-Hill.

Harrison, Bruce S. et al. 1994. *Employment Law Deskbook.*. New York: Matthew Bender & Co., Inc.

Rothstein, Mark A. and Liebman, Lance. 1994. *Employment Law: Cases and Materials*, 3rd ed. Westbury, NY: The Foundation Press, Inc.

2. Marital status and dependents (may indicate that the employer is trying to find out if a woman would have any family obligations that would conflict with performing a job).

3. Arrest record rather than conviction record (African-Americans are more often arrested on charges that lack merit than whites).

4. Maiden name (identifies gender and marital status).

5. Education (Hispanics and Afro-Americans have lower high school graduation rates than whites, which also influences education at higher levels. Only if a diploma or degree is directly related to a job [e.g., a degree in physical therapy for physical therapists] is it appropriate for an educational history to be required upon application).

6. Height and weight (average height and weight of women and some ethnic minorities are less than the average of white men).

The only time that an employer may discriminate in hiring on the basis of race, creed, color, gender, religion, or national origin is when one of these characteristics is a bona fide occupational qualification. For example, women may be given preference in the hiring of employees to model women's clothing. In healthcare, the number of cases in which one of these characteristics is requisite to performing a job is extremely rare.

It is permissible under the Civil Rights Act to administer tests to determine an applicant's ability to do a job. However, these tests must be applied equally to all applicants, and the tests must relate specifically to the ability to perform the job. For example, a hospital might require that all maintenance workers be able to lift 50 pounds without assistance. This test may favor male applicants over female applicants. If a female applicant who failed the test were to file a discrimination complaint, the hospital would probably have to prove that lifting 50 pounds without assistance is really necessary to performing a maintenance job in that hospital. If lifting that amount of weight unassisted is an extraordinary event that few maintenance workers seldom have to do, the hospital would have a difficult time defending this selection requirement.

The Civil Rights Act has long been associated with **affirmative action**. Affirmative action programs are employer plans for ending discriminatory practices and erasing the effects of those practices. Some affirmative action programs are involuntary (i.e., court ordered), and others are voluntary (i.e., as prophylactic measures to avoid charges of discriminatory practices). Although some affirmative action programs establish hiring targets for protected groups (also known as hiring **quotas**), that is not a universal objective. Many affirmative action programs are designed to assure that the pool of applicants for available positions reflects the racial, ethnic, and gender composition of the general population from which the firm recruits its employees. For example, a healthcare firm that recruits locally would strive to have a pool of applicants whose composition in terms of women, races, and religions is essentially the same as the composition of the locality in which it exists. A firm that recruits nationally would use national population percentages as affirmative action goals.

In recent years, there has been considerable debate about **reverse discrimination** (i.e., discrimination against white males). Discrimination against white males is generally prohibited unless it occurs as part of a valid affirmative action program.[19] One practice that has led to reverse discrimination is race-norming, which was the practice of adjusting test scores upwards for certain minority applicants so that they would have an advantage in the selection process. As a result of the Civil Rights Act of 1991, race-norming of test results is illegal.

Because there is no sure way to avoid charges of discrimination under the Civil Rights Act, the best employers can do is to purge the selection process of any discriminatory elements that they can find and, at the same time, make every effort to assure that the pool of applicants reflects as closely as possible the community served.

The **Age Discrimination in Employment Act of 1967** prohibits discrimination against employees over 40 years of age. Obviously age is an issue that should not be addressed in employment applications or interviews unless it is relevant to the job. Applicants should be made aware of any minimum age requirements that apply because of child labor laws. The employer should also avoid asking for information that could indicate an applicant's age. For example, dates of graduation or dates of military service might be indicative of age. So might dates of employment. If these are required for reference checking, they can be obtained after an offer of employment is made, contingent upon verification of application information. Age information and verification can be completed after a hiring decision is made.

The **Rehabilitation Act of 1973** applies to many healthcare firms because it requires employers doing $2,500 or more of business annually with the federal government to take affirmative action steps to hire disabled workers. Under the Act, employers must take certain measures ("reasonable accommodations") to assure that the disabled are given the opportunity to be successful in their employment. Appropriate parking facilities, rest room facilities, and wheelchair ramps are considered among the reasonable accommodations that employers are expected to make.

The **Americans with Disabilities Act of 1990 (ADA)** is an extension of the Rehabilitation Act. This is a comprehensive piece of legislation that deals with many aspects of dealing with disabled persons. The ADA generally prohibits discriminatory hiring, promotion, and termination practices against qualified individuals with a disability who can perform the essential functions of the position. One of the most important components of this legislation is its definition of disability.

"The term 'disability' means, with respect to an individual: a physical or mental impairment that substantially limits one or more of the major life activities of such individual; a record of such an impairment; or being regarded as having such an impairment."[20]

These broadly drawn descriptions reflect the inclusive nature of the Act. However, specific disabilities mentioned by the Act include HIV/AIDS, cancer, heart disease, and cerebral palsy. Persons with certain sexual conditions (exhibitionism, transsexualism, pedophilia) are not considered disabled under the ADA. Homosexuality is also excluded. Compulsive gambling, kleptomania, and pyromania are excluded, as are psychoactive substance use disorders that result from the current use of illegal drugs. However, recovering alcoholics and persons who have been rehabilitated or are currently in rehabilitation programs as a result of illegal substance abuse are covered by the Act. Employers are permitted to verify abstinence from illegal drugs through drug testing.

There are still several aspects of this legislation that will become more clear as individual cases are litigated under the ADA. First, what constitutes the essential functions of a job may be open to interpretation. The ADA states that

> *consideration shall be given to the employer's judgment as to what functions of a job are essential, and if an employer has prepared a written description before advertising or interviewing applicants for the job, this description shall be considered evidence of the essential functions of the job.*[21]

Managers can expect that at some time they will be interviewing candidates who are considered disabled under the ADA. Therefore, before they advertise, accept applications, and interview, they should have a clear understanding in their own minds of what the essential functions of a job are so that they can communicate these to candidates.

The second area which is subject to interpretation is the ADA's requirement that employers make reasonable accommodations for otherwise qualified candidates or employees with a disability. According to the ADA, reasonable accommodations may include

> *(A) making existing facilities used by employees readily accessible to and usable by individuals with disabilities; and*

> *(B) job restructuring, part-time or modified work schedules, reassignment to a vacant position, acquisition or modification of equipment or devices, appropriate adjustment or modifications of examinations, training materials or policies, the provision of qualified readers or interpreters, and other similar accommodations for individuals with disabilities.*[22]

Obviously, requiring employers to meet these conditions imposes a substantial burden on them. In recognition that making these accommodations could threaten the survival of some businesses, the ADA exempts businesses from making them if doing so would impose an undue hardship.

Determining what constitutes an undue hardship is the third component of the ADA that is open to interpretation. The ADA states that the factors to be considered in determining whether making accommodations constitutes an undue hardship are:

(i)   the nature and cost of the accommodation;

(ii)   the overall financial resources of the facility or facilities involved in the provision of the reasonable accommodation; the number of persons employed at such facility; the effect on expenses and resources, or the impact otherwise of such accommodation upon the operation of the facility;

(iii) the overall financial resources of the covered entity;

(iv) the type of operation or operations of the covered entity, including the composition, structure, and functions of the work force of such entity; the geographic separateness, administrative, or fiscal relationship of the facility or facilities in question to the covered entity.[23]

The ADA is enforced by the EEOC. However, complainants may also take their cases to court.

The **Pregnancy Discrimination Act of 1979** prohibits employment discrimination on the basis of pregnancy or on having given birth. Both married and unmarried women are covered by this law. During the selection process, employers should refrain from ascertaining any information about pregnancy (past, current, or planned).

The **Equal Pay Act of 1963** requires that employees receive the same amount of compensation for performing substantially equal work under similar working conditions, regardless of gender. This law pertains only to gender discrimination. The Act does not eliminate, however, the use of seniority, merit, or quantitative measures (i.e., piece rates) as factors in establishing compensation rates. Unfortunately, in spite of the fact that federal legislation prohibiting gender discrimination in pay has existed for more than 30 years, several recent studies have indicated that the compensation of women continues to lag considerably behind that of men.

At best, this discussion of the laws that help shape the hiring process is cursory. It is far from comprehensive and should not be relied on as the final word in avoiding potential legal problems that could arise from the hiring process. It does, however, provide the manager with a framework for planning selection procedures and for refining them in consultation with human resource and/or employment law experts.

Conclusion

Would a better selection process have helped Susan avoid the personnel problems she faces now? Perhaps she will never know. Certainly it is worth reviewing how these employees were hired to help her avoid similar mistakes in the future. In the meantime, she has to deal with the problems at hand. Because she has already given Chris every opportunity to improve his performance and he has failed to do so, the only remedy left to her may be to terminate him and fill his position with someone who is capable of fulfilling the responsibilities (including punctuality) that attach to the position. Chris is analogous to a defective mitral valve. Therapeutic options are limited. Given the severity of the defect, there may be no therapy other than excising the defective structure (Chris) and replacing it with something (i.e., another therapist) that functions properly.

Carl's case is slightly different. Many of the laws that govern hiring also govern how managers may deal with employees who are already in place. Is Carl's behavior a result of drug abuse, or is the etiology of his behavior entirely unrelated to substance abuse? Susan needs the input of professionals in this case. Susan should consult with her human resources department and perhaps even with hospital attorneys. It is unknown whether Carl has taken advantage of Parkmoor's EAP. His doing so would be a positive indication of his willingness to deal with his emotional problem(s). This is a potentially serious case, and the EAP staff may be able to help Susan intervene appropriately even if Carl has ignored her advice. Susan should not ignore her intuition, but acting on intuition is risky. Carl's performance appraisal and Susan's intervention should be based on fact.

One thing is certain. In both of these cases, Susan needs to intervene immediately rather than wait for a probationary review deadline to force her into action. She should probably cut her losses on Chris and plan for his replacement as soon as possible. She should also stop wondering what she did wrong in hiring Carl and head immediately to human resources to get the help she needs to develop a sound plan of action.

Endnotes

1. Larry D. Grieshaber, "Managing the Emerging Organization," *Health Management Quarterly 15* (4th Quarter 1993): 25–28.
2. Mark J. Schmit and Ann Marie Ryan, "The Big Five in Personnel Selection: Factor Structure in Applicant and Nonapplicant Populations," *Journal of Applied Psychology 78* (1993): 966–974.
3. Terrence E. Deal and Allan A. Kennedy, *Corporate Culture: The Rites and Rituals of Corporate Life* (New York: Addison-Wesley Publishing Company, 1982).
4. Paula Eubanks, "Hospitals Probe Job Candidates' Values for Organizational 'Fit'," *Hospitals 65* (October 20, 1991): 36, 38.
5. Bob Smith, "How to Screen Resumes," *HR Focus 72* (January 1995): 24.
6. "New Variations on Recruitment Prescreening," *HR Focus 71* (October 1994): 1, 3, 4.
7. Burr E. Anderson, "Background Checks: Legality Versus Liability," *HR Focus 70* (March 1993): 4–5.
8. Paul W. Barada, "Check References With Care," *Nation's Business 81* (May 1993): 54, 56.
9. Ibid.

10. Chambers v. American Trans Air, Inc. 577 N.E.2d 612 (Ind.App.1991).
11. Lawrence S. Clark, Robert J. Alberts, and Peter D. Kinder, *Law and Business: The Regulatory Environment,* 4th ed. (New York: McGraw-Hill, 1991).
12. Barada, op. cit.
13. Adapted in part from "Reference Checking Gets Creative," *Personnel Journal 73* (August 1994): S22, S24.
14. Deal and Kennedy, op.cit.
15. Marilyn Grieshaber and Larry D. Grieshaber, "The Pre-employment Interview in the Hospital Pharmacy," *Lippincott's Hospital Pharmacy 18* (June 1983): 288–292.
16. Thomas W. Dougherty, Daniel B. Turban, and John C. Callender, "Confirming First Impressions in the Employment Interview: A Field Study of Interviewer Behavior," *Journal of Applied Psychology 79* (1994): 659–665.
17. "How to Form Hiring Teams," *Personnel Journal 73* (August 1994): S14, S16–17.
18. Clark, et al., op. cit.
19. Clark, et al., op. cit.
20. The Americans with Disabilities Act. 42 U.S.C. Section 3. (2).
21. Ibid. Section 101. (8).
22. Ibid. Section 101. (9).
23. Ibid. Section 101. (10).

6 Promoting Teamwork: *Cardiac Dysrhythmias*

In this chapter the reader will learn how:
◆ different kinds of teams function in healthcare
◆ to diagnose teamwork deficiencies
◆ team inefficiency and ineffectiveness are like cardiac dysrhythmias
◆ to diagnose group productivity problems
◆ to recognize effective teams
◆ the evolution of teams occurred
◆ to recognize common roles of individuals in teams
◆ to improve team efficiency and effectiveness.

The Committeeman Blues

Jay Sommers arrived in the conference room at 12:55 for the 1:00 meeting of the Communications Committee (CC). Jay, Vice President of Professional Services of the Sandler Healthcare System (SHCS), has chaired the CC for the past eight months. Chairing the committee was not unpleasant, but Jay wondered if there were not much better things he could be doing.

The committee was formed 14 months after SHCS was created by the merger of three metropolitan hospitals. The idea for the CC came out of a meeting of top SHCS managers during which the CEO had expressed her disappointment that the cost savings envisioned by the formation of the system had not materialized. She said that she thought that if communication among SHCS hospitals and other business units was better, operations would be more efficient. The COO formed the CC to solve this problem.

So far, the only concrete action the CC had taken was to establish a monthly newsletter. However, not one of the first three issues had been published on time. Jay noticed that most of the copies of the last issue remained untouched in the employee hospital cafeterias where they were made available. He inadvertently overheard a couple of nursing supervisors say that the newsletter was a big waste of trees.

Jay had not known any of the committee members when they were appointed. They had been appointed at the suggestion of department heads at SHCS' three hospitals. While he waited for them to show up, he reviewed the list of members and the personal notes he had made about each of them.

Member	Position	Hospital on CC	Time on CC	Personal notes
Craig Morris	Security Officer	St. Mary's	8 months	lots of ideas (usually bad ones)
Beth Weisman	Dietitian	St. Mary's	4 months	pleasant, agrees with everything
Bart Sands	Physical Therapist	St. Mary's	6 months	undependable, doesn't come half the time
Mollie Moelner	Patient Accounts	Barstock	2 months	pleasant enough but doesn't show much interest
Bill Kwok	Ass't. Director of Maintenance	Barstock	8 months	attended only 3 meetings; unprepared; doesn't see communication problems
Pat Watkins	Staff Nurse	Barstock	5 months	attends infrequently but sends other people to replace her when she can find someone
Sandor Kalesh	Respiratory Therapist	Barstock	3 months	has high opinion of himself; loudmouth
Milton Marks	Director of Human Resources	Barstock	3 months	nice to have around; quick to diffuse any disagreement
Sam Henderson	Housekeeping	Barstock	2 months	negative; whines/complains about everything, finds fault with all suggestions
Mitch Morrison	Parking Attendant	Hillside	2 months	nice guy, no input
Sue Morales	Lab Technician	Hillside	0	new member, replaces pharmacist who resigned from CC
Blanton Forsythe, MD	Chief of Staff	Hillside	3 months	has attended no meetings

Jay knew that SHCS was still struggling with communication problems. From billing to patient care to referrals to contract purchasing, it was evident that SCHS' proverbial right hand did not know what the left hand was doing. He also knew that his committee had done little to tackle these problems. In spite of his efforts to hold the group to a communications agenda, CC spent most of its time discussing peripheral issues. For example, the bulk of the last meeting was spent discussing parking problems employees had when they worked shifts in different system hospitals.

At 1:05 Bill Kwok was the first member to arrive. As Jay handed him the meeting agenda, he wondered what the actual topic would end up being. He also wondered if he could get the meeting started by 1:20. In the back of his mind, the thought occurred that CC should just go away.

Teams in Healthcare

Management is inherently complex and challenging because the individuals who are managed are complex. Each individual is made of a different recipe of emotions, values, motives, and physical and mental abilities. Effective managers are attuned to the different needs, strengths, and weaknesses of individual employees and adopt management strategies to accommodate individual differences. Now, multiply the complexity of working with an individual by the number of members in a team, and multiply that result by the number of interactions which must take place among team members to accomplish a task, and the enormity of managing teams becomes obvious.

The SHCS Communications Committee is typical of the dysfunctional teams that can be found in many American businesses. In complex organizations like healthcare systems, managing teams presents several management challenges. These include:

1. determining the correct team size and choosing the right team members;

2. bringing the team members together for meetings;

3. coordinating the work of individual team members;

4. facilitating intragroup interaction and communication;

5. directing team activities toward the achievement of appropriate objectives;

6. maintaining team stability and continuity; and

7. fostering team flexibility and adaptability to changing organizational needs.

Given the difficulty of getting work done through teams, why use them in healthcare? Griffith sees the need to increase productivity as one of the driving forces behind the need to use teams. By his estimate, healthcare institutions must increase productivity by 3% per year for survival.[1] He notes that clinical teams now influence clinical processes that traditionally have been controlled by individual practitioners, that teams work across traditional lines of accountability, and that teams function with less supervision. Not only do teams exist to increase productivity, but also to improve the quality of services provided. He also foresees that "authority to set major operating parameters will pass from technical experts in clinical support services to permanent task forces oriented to specific clinical conditions, led by the specialists most familiar with the clinical activity."[2] Because no one individual can master the range of knowledge and skills that is required to deliver comprehensive clinical care, clinicians must work in teams to provide care.[3] By virtue of their responsibility for setting and achieving objectives, managers also have a role to play in teams.[4] Irrespective of the terminology du jour (team leader, facilitator, resource coordinator), managers assure that teams stay focused on appropriate objectives, facilitate team member interactions, supply information required for team decision making, and coordinate communication among teams.

It is safe to say that virtually no one works in isolation. Even independent businesspeople (writers, house painters, entertainers, etc.) have working relationships with others (agents, suppliers, lawyers, accountants) who help them to accomplish their goals. Because teamwork is a universal characteristic of the workplace, an enormous amount of research has gone into developing an understanding of how individuals behave in teams, how groups accomplish their objectives, what factors are barriers to group performance, and what conditions foster maximal group performance. The research of the past 70 years has produced many insights into group behavior that are useful in the management context. However, the field is so complex that a rich research agenda continues to be pursued and continues to produce important new findings.

Different types of teams are assembled for different purposes.[5] The everyday work of the organization is performed by **work groups**. A rehabilitation care team composed of clinicians from different professions (dietary, medicine, nursing, pharmacy, physical therapy, occupational therapy, speech therapy) is an example. Completion of the routine administrative and coordination work that is required to maintain an organization is accomplished by **management teams**. For example, department directors in hospitals usually meet on a regular basis to review progress toward organizational objectives, to explore and discuss mutual problems, and to improve routine interdepartmental communication and cooperation. **Intermittent groups** also meet periodically but are composed of people who do not normally work together. The purpose of intermittent groups is usually to coordinate work among different groups. A hospital safety committee, for example, is comprised of representatives of different departments. Its purpose is to disseminate safety information, to devise and revise safety policies and procedures, and to assure organization-wide compliance with safety policies and procedures.

Temporary groups are formed to address issues, solve problems, and achieve objectives that are not expected to recur. Temporary teams are frequently called **task forces** to differentiate them from more permanent groups, which are usually referred to as "teams" or "committees." For instance, a large healthcare system might form a task force to recommend ways that the organization can more effectively deal with work force diversity. Once that task is completed, the task force would be dissolved, and its recommendations passed along to a management team or an intermittent group (a standing committee) for implementation.

The nature of the work of large healthcare organizations like ODSs and hospitals usually requires that all these kinds of teams exist. The degree to which management involvement is required in the team's work varies with the type of team. For example, many work groups require minimal ongoing management supervision once they are established. This kind of group is referred to as a **self-managed team**. However, because managers cannot delegate their responsibility to a lower level, the work of self-managed groups must be monitored to make sure that work group performance is acceptable. Also, self-managed teams cannot always manage the interpersonal conflicts that are a part of everyday work life. Therefore, management intervention may be required from time to time. Self-managed teams may also need managerial stimulation to continually improve performance. Like individuals, teams may settle into a comfortable mode of operation that leads to complacency. Managers may have to take the initiative to get these teams to search for better ways of doing things.

Diagnosing Teamwork Problems

The signs and symptoms of dysfunctional teams are similar to the signs and symptoms of cardiac dysrhythmias. Dysrhythmias result in poor vascular perfusion throughout the body (i.e., the cardiovascular system fails to meet its objective of delivering an adequate blood supply). The extremities may become cold and cyanotic. The patient may complain of weakness and lack of energy. Vital organs such as the kidneys and liver may enter pre-failure function patterns, which result in the slow accumulation of toxins in the blood.

In the SHCS case, the CC failed to meet its objective. Its single product, the newsletter, was not only ineffectual, but also the object of ridicule. Parts of the system that needed information still were not getting it and were suffering from impaired information circulation. CC members exhibited no enthusiasm for their work and failed to infuse their efforts with energy. The ongoing lack of communication was continuing to sap SHCS of its energy. Even the chairperson seemed to lack the energy that is required to move a group toward its goal.

The pathological functioning of an ineffective committee clearly mirrors the function of a dysrhythmic heart. Dysrhythmias are caused by inappropriate initiation of impulses or abnormal conduction of impulses. The result is a heartbeat that is too fast, too slow, and/or irregular. Impulses may be initiated irregularly by the SA node, or they may abnormally arise in other areas of the heart (ectopic foci).

Once impulses are initiated, they may be blocked at the AV node or in the conduction fibers. They may also reenter the conduction system inappropriately.

In ineffective teams, the team leader may fail to initiate the team's work effectively. He may not move the team quickly enough toward its goal (resulting in a bradydysrhythmia), or he may push a team too quickly (resulting in a tachydysrhythmia). The team leader may find himself in competition with another team member for control of the team's agenda. In that case, the team member acts as an ectopic focus which initiates action in opposition to or out of synch with the team leader's direction. Some ineffective teams reiterate the same agenda without making progress toward its completion (reentrant dysrhythmia).

The remainder of this chapter will guide the reader through team development, team anatomy and physiology, and team pathology, to prescriptive recommendations for building effective teams. The labyrinthine journey begins with an overview of effective teams and team evolution. It then proceeds to a tour of group processes (role assumption, cohesion, and conflict). The last port of call is a list of practical recommendations for maximizing team effectiveness.

Effective Teams

Several characteristics of effective groups have been identified.[6] Comparing the performance of the CC in the opening case with these characteristics demonstrates how dysfunctional groups can be identified.

1. *Goals are clear, cooperatively formulated, and inspire commitment to achievement among team members.* The goal of the CC was vague. Jay was aware of some specific communication problems. However, there is no indication that he actually brought those issues to the CC. There is also no indication that any of the team members had a stake in better communication or were seriously concerned with the issue.

2. *Group members clearly communicate their ideas.* Most of the CC members seemed to avoid participation either through lack of attendance or failure to contribute in a meaningful, constructive way.

3. *All members share in participation and leadership.* Jay seemed to be the glue that held the team together. Team member participation was erratic and/or destructive.

4. *Decision-making procedures change to accommodate the situation.* CC's decision making was static even in the face of obvious failure.

5. *Constructive conflict is encouraged.* Unanimity is rare. Complete agreement on the nature of organizational problems and their solutions is unnatural. Conflict engages team members in a search for acceptable courses of action. Jay appears to be conflict-averse. Either Milton Marks shares this aversion, or he is acting as a peacemaker to please the ranking committee member.

6. *Power and influence are distributed throughout the team.* By virtue of his position, Jay has formal power in the group. The only power of committee members is the power to obstruct and delay meaningful progress.

7. *Group cohesion is high.* There is no evidence of cohesion in this team. In fact, the high turnover of members and failure to attend meetings may indicate an aversion to working together.

8. *Problems are solved efficiently.* The CC has demonstrated no problem-solving capability, efficient or otherwise.

9. *The personal goals of members are met through participation.* There is no way of knowing how well the CC members' goals are met. However, lack of attendance, turnover, and scant participation may reflect poor personal goal attainment.

Evaluating the CC along these dimensions demonstrates how a dysfunctional group remarkably resembles a cardiac dysrhythmia. The communication (impulse) emanating from the chairperson (SA node) is too weak to cause the group to accomplish its work (contract). The communication that is initiated and expressed through the agenda (AV node) does not get to members either because they do not attend meetings or because the message is inadequately communicated through the meeting process (conduction fibers).

Team Evolution

Understanding the natural history of a disease is a prerequisite to identifying the most appropriate interventions in the disease process. Likewise, understanding the natural history of a team is a prerequisite to appropriate managerial intervention. Just as treating cardiac dysrhythmias differs among pediatric, adult, and geriatric patients, team interventions must be appropriate to the stage of a team's life cycle. The stages of team evolution have been labeled differently by different authors. In one scheme the stages are forming, storming, norming, performing, and adjourning.[7, 8] Other authors use the terms formation, differentiation, integration, and maturity.[9] During the **formation** stage, disorganization and lack of focus are to be expected and require no intervention. In this stage, team members get to know each other. They gather and assimilate the information they need to establish working relationships. This includes finding out about each others' needs, skills, and objectives. Managers and team leaders who value progress toward the completion of objectives may become frustrated with groups that seem to linger very long in this stage. However, going through this process is crucial to the development of effective relationships and should be allowed to play itself out.

During **differentiation**, group members continue to gather information about each other and use this information to establish their roles in the team. During this stage, members also begin to explore the rules of behavior (norms) that will govern how the team conducts its business and makes decisions. The focus of their interactions is on finding how they differ from each other and whether each member can find a role in the group with which he is comfortable. If the members cannot agree on rules and norms (i.e., they get stuck in the differentiation stage), then the team cannot move forward to do its work. This may have been one of the problems with the SHCS task force. The members may have been unable to reach consensus about their roles and how the work of the committee would proceed. Therefore, the individual members of the team never became seriously engaged in their work.

Members who do not accept the norms of the group have two ways of avoiding participation. First, they can leave the group. This is likely when the norms require behaviors about which the members feel strongly. For example, healthcare practitioners who feel strongly that abortion is wrong are likely to avoid being part of a clinical team that performs abortions. Similarly, employee team members who feel that the decision-making process of a task force is dictated by administrators may leave the task force rather than be part of a rubber stamp process. Second, team members may remain part of the team but withhold any constructive contributions. The high turnover among CC members and lack of participation of ongoing members may indicate that several members may not have accepted key group norms.

Like the formation phase, differentiation is a member-driven process. Impatient managers may be tempted to intervene before this process has run its course. As long as group members make progress toward defining roles and operating procedures, intervention is probably inappropriate. As Senge notes, "The team that became great didn't start off great—it learned how to produce extraordinary results."[10] Learning is a time-consuming process. Managers who cannot provide teams with enough time to allow this learning to occur should seriously reconsider the teamwork approach to production.

Integration occurs when the group turns its focus to the group's objectives. Because the nature of a task and the appropriate way to accomplish it are inseparable, agreeing on the team's purpose and norming are integrated processes. This can be a difficult stage of team development. Many managers naively assume that teams accept and affirm the objectives given to them as their charge. However, there are times when teams disagree with charges or reject them as impossible to complete. For example, assume that a task force was formed to recommend ways to deal more effectively with diversity in the work force. The final recommendation of the task force was to establish ethnic hiring targets. The manager who received the recommendation may feel that the team should have dealt only with management issues relevant to the current work force. He may be taken aback that the team exceeded its bounds. However, the team may feel that the only way to deal with diversity issues is to attack them at their source, which is the hiring process.

Discrepancies about perceived objectives and work boundaries are more likely to occur with temporary and intermittent teams because they deal with less routine problems. If the manager feels that there is a discrepancy between the charge to a team and the team's interpretation of the charge, he can resolve the discrepancy in two different ways. First, he can accept the team's assessment and allow the team to continue its work without intervention. The manager must be prepared to accept the fact that the team may have more insight into the problem than he does. After all, the sum of the team's expertise and experience with the issue may well be greater than any one individual's expertise. Second, he can reject the team's direction as inappropriate. The team may have misunderstood its charge or may lack the contextual framework to define the problem appropriately. If intervention is required, the manager must meet with the team to explain how the team's objectives differ from his objectives. This will cause the team to regress in its development and delay its work. It may also make it impossible for the team to function if too many team members are unwilling to adopt the manager's objectives.

The integration step is critical to the team's ultimate success. It is obvious that the manager needs to stay in touch with the team to monitor its progress so that if the work being pursued by the team is inconsistent with its intended purpose, the manager can intervene appropriately.

In the **maturity** stage, progress toward achievement of objectives is made. Unfortunately, progress may not be steady. For example, unavoidable absence, employee turnover, the changing nature of the problem, and environmental changes are likely to disrupt the flow of work. Once the team begins to make progress, managers have generally lost the opportunity to intervene. If they try to realign the team's objectives during the maturity stage, the intervention will likely cause resentment. Team members went through a difficult process of give and take to reach consensus about objectives. They will not appreciate having their hard work undone. The same is true of intervention in the actual work of the team. After the members have gone through the uncomfortable process of role definition and norming, they may feel that they have earned the right to complete the task without interference.

Managers need to continually evaluate the performance of teams regarding objectives. Many teams (task forces and intermittent groups, in particular) outlive their original objectives. When the team's mission evaporates, usually the team should be disbanded (adjourning). However, there may be related work that can and should be transferred to an effective team. For example, a safety committee might be formed to recommend policies and procedures that would reduce the number of back injuries in a nursing facility. If this team performed effectively, the nursing facility administrator might do well to assign the same group a related task, such as developing and/or monitoring a comprehensive risk management program for the facility.

Managers should disband hopelessly ineffective teams. Sometimes it is better to swallow one's managerial pride and admit failure than to continue wasting resources on ineffective teams. However, in the process of adjourning ineffective teams, managers should avoid blaming team members for failure. Managers may have presented the team with an impossible task, or chosen team members inappropriately, or failed to provide the team with sufficient time and resources. In the long term, there is little to be gained by highlighting failure and laying blame.

Roles in Groups

Individuals working in groups assume different roles. A **role** is a set of behaviors that are associated with a position within a group. Some of those behaviors are expected of the occupant of the position by others in the group. For example, the chairperson of a committee is expected to call committee meetings and to run meetings in an orderly manner. These duties are part of the **expected role**. However, a chairperson may perceive that it is her responsibility only to call meetings, set an agenda, and then to step aside and let the members run the meetings as they see fit. In this situation, there may be a difference between the expected role and the **perceived role** (i.e., how the position holder thinks she should behave). Sometimes, due to lack of time or some other obstacle, the chairperson only schedules meetings and neither prepares an agenda nor formally conducts meetings. Thus the **enacted role** (i.e., what the holder of a position actually does) is considerably different from either the expected or perceived roles. The failure of these roles to be in alignment increases the likelihood of dysfunctional performance and conflict among team members.[11] Therefore, it is critical during the differentiation and integration stages that roles and expectations be clarified. When managers sense that role ambiguity is a problem, they may have to intervene by facilitating the role definition process. The more roles "are understood, integrated, and synergized, the better the performance of the group."[12]

Roles in groups can be generally understood by the focus of the activities of the people who are in the roles. Team members focus on either the objectives of the team (**task-oriented roles**), interpersonal relationships among team members (**maintenance roles**), or the needs of the members themselves (**individual roles**).[13] Within each of these categories are a number of more specifically focused roles (see Table 6.1). Task-oriented and maintenance members are constructive, contributory team members. Members that play individual roles are not. Members with individual roles have self-serving agendas that may conflict with the goals of the team and management. In an effort to be inclusive and/or bring perceived troublemakers or dissidents into the fold, some managers intentionally assign people who tend to play individual roles to teams that have controversial objectives. (An employee benefits review team, for example, would undoubtedly deal with controversial issues.) These managers believe that they can make people part of the solution rather than part of the problem. This is an admirable goal. However, when dissident individuals are brought into a team, there is no guarantee that their colleagues will be able to exert enough pressure to cause them to subordinate their personal goals to the goals of the team. The effort to be inclusive and to use colleagues to change behavior may stymie task-oriented and maintenance members by forcing them to deal with members who assume individual roles.

Analysis of the CC in terms of the roles assumed by team members helps explain why the team is dysfunctional. Several members appear to play individual roles. S. Kalesh seems to be a recognition seeker. He will probably slow down the work of the team by diverting attention to himself whenever possible. B. Sands, M. Moelner, B. Kwok, M. Morrison, and B. Forsythe may be avoiders. Their lack

Table 6.1   Common Roles and Role Occupant Activities in Groups

Role	Characteristic Activities
Task-oriented roles	
initiators	Offer new ideas and suggestions about how to do the group's work
information seekers	Attempt to clarify ideas and alternative courses of action by securing information and data
information givers	Provide information that can be used to assess and improve the work of the group
coordinators	Try to effectively link the work of individual team members
evaluators	Monitor the group's productivity and processing quality
Maintenance roles	
encouragers	Provide emotional support and positive feedback to members
harmonizers	Resolve interpersonal disagreements and relieve tension
standard setters	Question group goals and set performance standards
followers	Passively agree in the capacity of friends and colleagues
group observers	Monitor performance without participation unless asked for feedback
Individual roles	
blockers	Resist group progress through negativism and irrational stubbornness
recognition seekers	Place themselves at the center of attention through personal aggrandizement (bragging, boasting, acting superior)
dominators	Attempt to gain control of the group through authority or flattery
avoiders	Resist group progress passively

Adapted from John A. Wagner II and John R. Hollenbeck, *Management of Organizational Behavior* (Englewood Cliffs, NJ: Prentice-Hall, 1992).

of attendance and/or participation may be their way of resisting the work of the team. However, there may also be other explanations for their behavior. They may have been unable to arrange their schedules to attend, or they may be supportive of the team but simply have no ideas to put forth about how to achieve the team's objectives. From J. Sommers' sketchy notes, it is hard to determine whether these people are really avoiders or followers. P. Watkins' efforts to send replacements indicate that she is probably not an avoider. S. Henderson is a blocker. The consequences of his behavior are obvious.

Only a couple of members clearly fulfill maintenance roles. B. Weisman is a follower. Note, however, that her aversion to conflict may indicate that she is not engaged in the work and is, therefore, also an avoider. Because there is little leadership in the group, her influence is minimal. M. Marks is a harmonizer. Given the lack of initiative on the team, it would probably be more beneficial for him to assume the encourager role.

C. Morris is an initiator. It is unfortunate that his ideas are not appreciated by the chairperson because Morris is the only member of the team who is explicitly task-oriented. By implication, J. Sommers is playing the role of evaluator. By scheduling and chairing meetings, he is also playing the role of coordinator. However, his performance in that role is apparently weak.

This team is remarkable for the number of roles that are not being played. No one seems to seek or supply the information that is necessary for this team to solve communication problems. So little actual work is being done that the coordination role has been minimal. No one provides encouragement or positive reinforcement. No one is focused enough on the goal to set a standard of performance. No one who is not actively participating is offering the group any feedback on its performance. The most prominent roles are the individual roles.

It has been suggested that effective teams have a balance of people who perform task-oriented and maintenance roles.[14] Without a change in the willingness of current members to assume important roles, the team membership would have to be altered so that an appropriate blend of members and roles could be achieved. As it is currently constituted, this team is out of alignment. Members are working at cross purposes, which causes the little energy that is going into this team to be wasted. The team needs to be aligned so that the members work with a sense of commonality and harmony.[15]

Cohesion

In a physical sense, cohesion is the tendency of objects to stick together. Similarly, within groups, cohesion is also a tendency to stick together. However, rather than being mediated by physical properties, **cohesion** among members of a group is mediated by the attraction members feel toward each other, their tendency to remain in the group, and the degree to which they influence each other.[16] It is well-documented that cohesion occurs to different degrees in different groups.

What is less obvious and less well-defined is the importance of cohesion to team effectiveness.

There are a number of research studies that have linked cohesion to changes in group performance, increased satisfaction of team members, and lower turnover among team members.[17] It is important to note that not all changes in group performance have been positively related to cohesion. For cohesion to increase group performance, group members must value group performance. If a highly cohesive group values low performance and/or productivity, then the group will act quite cohesively toward ineffective performance.

Conflict

As interpersonal processes go, conflict has a rating in the junk bond zone. For most people, conflict is an uncomfortable process. Defending one's position and negotiating with other team members depletes one's energy. In addition, many people are emotionally uncomfortable with conflict. If conflict is not properly focused, it can damage interpersonal relationships and weaken group cohesion. Conflict is also inconsistent with the managerial goal of smooth, efficient operations.

However, conflict is an unavoidable group process and is, in fact, what most managers unconsciously depend on to produce high quality decision making. Individuals bring different perspectives on problems and issues to the table. It is the engagement in a discussion of different perspectives and perceptions that leads a group closer to an accurate assessment. When differences are aired in a spirit of cooperation, **constructive conflict** occurs. Conversely, **destructive conflict** occurs when disagreement is pursued in a competitive manner. When conflict is constructive, win/win resolutions are possible (i.e., all parties can come away from the conflict satisfied that they have gained something from the process).[18] An example would be a disagreement between a registered dietitian and a purchasing manager over the enteral nutrition system to be adopted by a hospital. Through disagreement and argument about the choice, they may acquire greater knowledge and understanding of the equipment and its suitability for that particular hospital. Irrespective of the ultimate decision, they can both win if they can come to agreement about which system is better for this particular hospital. However, if the real objective of the dietitian and the purchasing manager is to win the argument, then only one party can be satisfied with the ultimate decision, and the other party will be dissatisfied. Even if the final choice is identical to the choice that would have resulted from a cooperative effort, one person loses psychologically because his determination to win kept him from accepting the final choice as the best choice. A recent review of the research on conflict suggests that rather than being avoided, conflict should be managed so that it contributes to team progress.[19] The manager's objective regarding conflict is clear—minimize destructive conflict while encouraging constructive conflict.

Maximizing Team Effectiveness and Productivity

Teams should come carefully packaged and clearly labeled, "Caution: Fragile...Handle with Care." There are so many ways in which teams can malfunction that managers must diligently establish a supportive environment and intervene in team functions with finesse. The following issues should be given careful consideration by team managers.

Team membership. Managers can avoid many problems by choosing team members judiciously. This process requires an extraordinary amount of attention and should never be done haphazardly (see Chapter 5). In addition, managers need to make sure that the team has the knowledge, technical skills, and teamwork skills to accomplish the team's objectives. In the SHCS case, the CC did not have the appropriate knowledge base to deal with the communications issues that it was formed to resolve. It is unlikely that a security officer, a parking attendant, a housekeeper, and a laboratory technician would know enough about billing, patient care, referral procedures, and purchasing to make meaningful contributions. Other members of this team may be similarly ignorant of one or more of the problem areas. A prohibitively long education process would be required to give these team members the requisite knowledge to begin their work.

There is also no indication that most of these team members bring the appropriate technical skills to the team. The problem that this team is trying to solve is a lack of communication among business units that are physically separate. Developing communication links would probably require some combination of reorganization, new policies and procedures, new applications of communication technologies, and development of new interpersonal relationships among employees of various SHCS business units. If the career paths of these team members are typical, most members will have had little, if any, experience in these areas. Thus there is a mismatch between technical skills and the goals of the team.

When a team is used for problem-solving purposes (which is frequently the case with intermittent and temporary teams), the membership should be drawn so that an appropriate variety of viewpoints is represented in a balanced way. In the SHCS example, one wonders why there are six team members from Barstock Hospital, but only three each from St. Mary's and Hillside. Even if Barstock is twice as large as the other two, communication is a proverbial two-way street that requires equal commitment and participation from each party. There is no readily apparent rationale for this imbalance. Team members and outsiders may perceive that Barstock's disproportionately large representation is the result of favoritism.

Many managers use teams as vehicles for providing employees a role in decision making. When using teams for this purpose, managers must resist the urge to appoint team members who share their own beliefs and would likely make the same decision they would. For example, a nursing director may form a team of nurses to develop a shift rotation policy. If the nursing director prefers a policy of regularly rotating shifts as opposed to straight day, evening, and night shifts, she could vicariously implement the policy of her choice by appointing team members she knows support rotating shifts. However, a word of warning is in order about this action. Employees can see through this thinly veiled attempt to make them feel that they have a legitimate voice in decision making when, in fact, the manager is still making the decision, albeit through others. What might have been merely an unpopular decision could become an unpopular decision served on a platter of resentment with a generous helping of distrust on the side. If the nursing director feels strongly enough about a rotating shift policy that she would stack a team with sympathetic employees to get the policy, she would probably be better off to impose her will straightforwardly and honestly, rather than to try to pass the decision off as employee instigated.

Team members also need to be chosen for the roles they are likely to play on the team. Because individual roles are defined only after the team is formed, choosing team members on the basis of their roles appears to be chronologically contradictory. However, this is not completely so. In the absence of an unmistakable metamorphosis, people who have subordinated the organization's and team's goals to individual goals in the past can be expected to continue this behavior. Because individual role players disrupt team performance, they should not be included in teams without compelling reasons. The team should be composed of an array of people who have a history of playing task-oriented and maintenance roles. Individuals choose either maintenance or task-oriented roles because they find comfort in them. ("I'm a people person" describes someone who is likely to play a maintenance role in any team.) The specific maintenance or task-oriented role an individual plays may change from group to group. For example, if Joan H. is usually an encourager but joins a team in which a strong encourager is already in place, she may assume a vacant maintenance role such as harmonizer. Moving from a task-oriented role to a maintenance role (or vice versa) is more unlikely, but not impossible. Assume that Joan H. is assigned to a team in which the only vacant role is initiator. She may assume the role of initiator if it is too uncomfortable for her to share a role that has already been taken. She also may assume the initiator role if she is too uncomfortable being in a team that lacks an initiator. By carefully observing behavior in teams, managers can make informed choices regarding the roles individuals are likely to occupy. This knowledge should then be used to select a team in which key task-oriented and maintenance roles will be occupied.

Group size. Because communication, coordination of activity, and interpersonal relationships become increasingly complex as groups get larger, the intuitive conclusion of most managers is that the smaller the team, the better. There is research evidence that tends to support this conclusion. Smaller groups are more productive, and members of smaller groups are more satisfied.[20,21] Larger groups require larger spaces in which to work, generate more distractions that can divert members from their tasks, and require more coordination to link people and tasks.[22] Managers should strive to form the smallest teams that include all the skills, knowledge, and role diversity required to accomplish objectives.

It has been suggested that as the size of a group increases arithmetically, the number of potential interrelationships increases geometrically. The following formula relates group size to the number of possible interrelationships.

$$C = N[(2^n/2 + (N - 1)]$$

where C = total number of possible
interrelationships, and

N = the number of group members[23]

Once the size of a group reaches six or seven members, each individual appears to find it difficult to relate to other members as individuals. The result is that subgroups and factions begin to form.[24] The formation of subgroups with autonomous agendas weakens group cohesiveness.

Cohesiveness. Teams which lack cohesion cannot accomplish their objectives. The factors that encourage group cohesiveness[25] offer clues as to how managers can foster cohesiveness.

1. Use the smallest possible groups so that physical proximity can be maximized.

2. Facilitate and make possible frequent interaction. If objectives are important enough to merit a teamwork approach, the team members must be allowed to prioritize their work so that they can interact frequently and consistently with their colleagues. In addition, "the physical environment and social climate of the group should be designed to facilitate interaction. For example, meeting rooms should be provided, ambient noise should be reduced, electronic communication systems that facilitate communication might be installed, and communication skills training might be provided."[26]

3. Recognize effective group performance to reinforce productive work. Positive feedback confirms to team members that they are doing the right things and doing them well.

4. Establish and apply a reward system that encourages team interaction and cooperation.

5. Select team members who share similar interests and values (but not the same perceptions of problems and/or solutions).

6. Secure agreement on group goals.

The cohesive team has a good chance of becoming an effective team as long as its goals are consistent with the organization's goals.

Goal alignment. A number of studies have shown that clearly defined goals are crucial to effective team performance.[27] Managers need to monitor teams to make sure that team members agree with team goals and that those goals are aligned with the goals the manager had in mind in forming the team.

Managers can promote team commitment to group goals by allowing team members to participate in goal setting. Team members are likely to vigorously pursue goals in which they hold an ownership stake. Among the skills and abilities required for effective teamwork is the ability to "help establish specific, challenging and accepted team goals."[28]

When group goals are consistent with individual goals, teamwork is more likely to be successful. This alignment represents another win-win situation. The organization wins when its goals are achieved. Individual team members win when their individual goals are achieved. When both goals are one and the same, there is mutual interest in goal achievement. Sometimes a manager can achieve this alignment by choosing team members because their individual goals are consistent with the goals he has in mind for the team. At other times, managers intervene in the goal-setting process to assure that the goals adopted by the team are important to the organization as well as individual team members. Sometimes managers can align organizational, team, and individual goals through an educational process. For example, in the SHCS case, the organizational goal is improved communication. As it stands, the committee members do not seem to perceive that effective, efficient communication has any benefits for them as individuals. However, if Jay can show how the work life of each committee member would be better as a result of better communications, then each member may adopt more effective, efficient communication as an individual goal. Therefore, the goals of all parties are aligned.

Rewards. Managers have at their disposal a variety of tools to motivate employees (see Chapter 8). Some managers attempt to stimulate performance by threatening employees with punishment. More commonly, managers hold out the promise of rewards for satisfactory performance. When faced with the challenge of motivating a team, the manager who uses the "carrot and stick approach" has to decide whether to dangle the carrot in front of individual team members or whether to dangle a whole bunch of carrots in front of the team and make receiving the bunch of carrots contingent on team performance. In other words, should the manager reward individuals for individual performance, or reward teams for team performance?

This is rarely an either/or choice. In most healthcare settings, employees may be members of several different teams. For example, a hospital pharmacist may be part of a critical care team, the Pharmacy and Therapeutics Committee, and an employee benefits task force. In addition, he may be responsible for independently performing utilization reviews of selected cardiovascular drugs throughout the hospital. Rewarding this person solely on the basis of team outcomes does not account for the totality of his performance. Also, any (or all) of his teams may be ineffective irrespective of his performance as a team member. What if they are all constituted poorly (like the CC)? Or what if the goals they were given are unrealistic or inappropriate for the teams? Would the pharmacist feel a reward system based only on team performance to be fair under these conditions? Would he be motivated by such a system? Probably not. Likewise, a system based solely on individual performance is incomplete in that it does not reward team performance and provides no incentive to a team.

Designing an appropriate reward system is not simple. It requires a performance appraisal process that recognizes both individual efforts and teamwork skills and contributions. As teams become more prevalent, the prominence of teamwork in performance appraisal should increase. For reward systems to be effective, they must be strongly linked to the performance appraisal process. In turn, the performance appraisal process must recognize both individual and team performance. It has even been suggested that new performance appraisal systems might punish poor team players whose poor team performance has not heretofore been recognized by traditional performance appraisal systems.[29]

Conclusion

Historically, a number of factors have worked against the use of teams in the provision of healthcare. Not the least of these factors has been the traditional tripod organization of hospitals. The organizational tripod consists of administration, the governing board, and the medical staff. The divisions at the top of the institution that has been the 20th century centerpiece of American healthcare delivery have carried through to the lower ranks of the hospital and have been copied by other healthcare delivery institutions. As the 21st century dawns, new team-oriented organizational structures are evolving. The easy part of this evolution has been changing organizational charts and operating procedures on paper. The real management challenge lies in modifying interpersonal relationships and work patterns.

For teams to be effective, the teamwork concept must be embraced by all components of the organization. Clinicians are slow to adapt to multidisciplinary teamwork because the educational process defines and reinforces professional practice boundaries. Some of these boundaries are of a hierarchical nature in relation to other clinical professions. Medicine is at the top of the clinical hierarchy, and physicians are unprepared for team roles.[30] One factor that may contribute to lack of preparedness to work within teams is the medical education process. "Within clinical medical education, there exists a distinctive authority structure that nurtures competition and collaboration among learners."[31] The educational process also fosters the development of independence and responsibility for individual decision making. This professionalization process works against the development of effective multidisciplinary teams in the clinical setting. Other clinical professions share some of these isolationist characteristics. Distinct and diverse accreditation and licensure requirements provide no incentives for interdisciplinary education and training among the clinical professions. Adding the perceptions, skills, and knowledge of nonclinicians into the team member mix further complicates the teamwork effort.

To overcome the many obstacles to effective teamwork in healthcare institutions, all managers must promote teamwork by pursuing the following strategies:

1. openly dealing with organizational changes, personal values, and beliefs;

2. incorporating evaluation and rewards of team efforts into the performance appraisal system;

3. identifying and eliminating processes that promote competition rather than collaboration;

4. identifying essential team roles and encouraging individuals to assume those roles;

5. encouraging teams to develop and monitor productivity and quality goals;

6. assigning sufficient resources to teams and allowing teams to control those resources; and

7. instituting ongoing programs that encourage team development and improvement.[32]

Over time, these strategies and the success they generate will infuse the organization with a commitment to teamwork.

Reaping the dividends of teamwork requires a considerable investment of time, effort, and thought. SHCS failed to make that commitment. Any one intervention at this point will not guarantee success. Just as many cardiac dysrhythmias require multi-drug regimens to control, this team will probably require several interventions. At best, the prognosis of this ill-conceived, poorly managed team is guarded.

Endnotes

1. John R. Griffith, "Reengineering Healthcare: Management Systems for Survivors," *Health & Health Services Administration 39* (Winter 1994): 451–470.

2. Ibid., p. 482.

3. Daniel A. Shugars, Edward H. O'Neil, and James D. Bader, eds., *Healthy America, Practitioners for 2005: An Agenda for U.S. Health Professional Schools* (Durham, NC: The Pew Health Professions Commission, 1991).

4. Larry D. Grieshaber, "Managing the Emerging Organization," *Health Management Quarterly 15* (1993): 25–28.

5. John A. Wagner II and John R. Hollenbeck, *Management of Organizational Behavior* (Englewood Cliffs, NJ: Prentice-Hall, 1992).

6. David W. Johnson and Frank P. Johnson, *Joining Together: Group Theory and Group Skills*, 4th ed. (Englewood Cliffs, NJ: Prentice-Hall, 1991).

7. Bruce W. Tuckman, "Developmental Sequences in Small Groups," *Psychology Bulletin 63* (1965): 384–399.

8. Bruce J. Fried and Thomas G. Rundall, "Managing Groups and Teams" in Stephen M. Shortell and Arnold D. Kaluzny, *Healthcare Management: Organization Design and Behavior*, 3rd ed. (Albany, NY: Delmar Publishers, Inc., 1994).

9. Wagner and Hollenbeck, op. cit.

10. Peter M. Senge, *The Fifth Discipline: The Art and Practice of the Learning Organization* (New York: Doubleday, 1990), p. 7.

11. Marvin E. Shaw, *Group Dynamics: The Psychology of Small Group Behavior,* 2nd ed. (New York: McGraw-Hill, 1976).

12. Philip A. Harris and Dorothy L. Harris, "High Performance Team Management," *Leadership and Organization Development Journal 10* (1989): 28–32, 30.

13. Kenneth D. Benne and Paul Sheats, "Functional Roles of Group Members," *Journal of Social Issues 12* (1948): 42–47.

14. Harris and Harris, op. cit.

15. Senge, op. cit.

16. Dennis Organ and W. Clay Hammer, *Organizational Behavior: An Applied Psychological Approach* (Dallas: Business Publications, 1978).

17. Kenneth L. Bettenhausen, "Five Years of Groups Research: What We Have Learned and What Needs to Be Addressed," *Journal of Management 17* (1991): 345–381.

18. Morton Deutsch, *The Resolution of Conflict: Constructive and Destructive Processes* (New Haven, CT: Yale University Press, 1973).

19. Michael J. Stevens and Michael A. Campion, "The Knowledge, Skill, and Ability Requirements for Teamwork: Implications for Human Resource Management," *Journal of Management 20* (1994): 503–530.

20. Richard Z. Gooding and John A. Wagner III, "A Meta-Analytic Review of the Relationship between Size and Performance: The Productivity and Efficiency of Organizations and Their Subunits," *Administrative Science Quarterly 20* (1985): 462–481.

21. B. Mullen, C. Symons, L. Hu and E. Salas, "Group Size, Leadership Behavior, and Subordinate Satisfaction," *Journal of General Psychology 116* (1989): 155–170.

22. Wagner and Hollenbeck, op. cit.

23. V. A. Graicunas, "Relationship in Organization," in Luther Gulick and L. Urwick, *Papers on the Science of Administration* (New York: Institute of Public Administration, 1937), 181–188.

24. A. Paul Hare, *Handbook of Small Group Research* (New York: The Free Press of Glencoe, 1962), 330

25. Wagner and Holenbeck, op. cit.

26. Elizabeth Weldon and Laurie R. Weingart, "Group Goals and Group Performance," *British Journal of Social Psychology 32* (1993): 307–334.

27. Bettenhausen, op. cit.

28. Stevens and Campion, op. cit., 515.

29. Ibid.

30. Julie S. Abramson, "Making Teams Work," *Social Work with Groups 12* (1990): 45–63.

31. Donn Weinholtz, "The Socialization of Physicians During Attending Rounds: A Study of Team Learning among Medical Students," *Qualitative Health Research 1* (May 1991): 152–177, 152.

32. Suzanne Smith Blancett, "Self-managed Teams: The Reality and the Promise," *The Healthcare Supervisor 12* (1994): 48–55.

7 Decision Making and Problem Solving: *Cognitive/Affective Disorders*

In this chapter the reader will learn how to:
- distinguish between decision making and problem solving
- describe the problem-solving process
- differentiate underlying problems from their symptoms
- generate alternatives
- evaluate alternatives
- choose an alternative
- make group decisions
- recognize and deal with group decision-making errors.

Paying the Piper

Jim Ferris' new business philosophy: "Hindsight is 20/20 vision."

Two-and-a-half years ago, Jim was promoted by Rehabaserve, Inc. to general manager of a major metropolitan branch office. Rehabaserve is a contract rehabilitation care provider to long-term care facilities. Jim was new to the area, and Rehabaserve's central office gave him a few months to learn the operating details of the branch office and to familiarize himself with the market. However, as the first year of Jim's tenure wore on, it became obvious that his branch was going to fall short of profit projections. Corporate executives began to pressure Jim to generate more business.

Jim had worked with his staff to identify the most lucrative prospective clients in his new hometown. One name that came to the fore was PierPointe Care Facilities, Inc. PierPointe was a local chain of eight nursing facilities with over 1,400 beds. The PierPointe facilities were very attractive and located in high income areas. The monthly charges were the highest in the region. The PierPointe facilities seemed to set the performance standard in the local long-term care industry. Jim quickly realized that service vendors who had contracts with PierPointe had a "seal of approval" in the eyes of other nursing facilities. Jim decided to vigorously pursue PierPointe's business.

As the first anniversary of his promotion dawned, he got a call from Bert Conrad, PierPointe's CEO. Mr. Conrad said that he was fed up with the service he was getting from his current provider and that he wanted to talk business with Jim. This was music to Jim's ears since PierPointe's current provider was the leading rehabilitation firm in the market.

Jim was ecstatic to have a contract with PierPointe in hand at his one-year review. Mr. Conrad was a hard bargainer, so the contract fell short of Rehabaserve's standard fee schedule. But Jim felt sure that he could justify the price discount because the PierPointe account would put Rehabaserve in an enviable market position.

The honeymoon was quickly over with PierPointe. No matter how hard he tried, Jim could not keep Mr. Conrad satisfied. Mr. Conrad demanded to have Rehabaserve's staff available at any time of the day or night. His administrators and directors of nursing (DONs) made it impossible to adhere to treatment schedules. They were also slow to share resident information that was important for treatment and billing. Jim and his staff worked diligently to meet as many of Conrad's demands as possible. Jim spent several hours a week in PierPointe facilities working with PierPointe personnel to resolve scheduling and record-keeping issues. But, in the end, there seemed to be nothing he could do to satisfy the PierPointe staff.

Instead of getting better with age, the relationship between PierPointe and Rehabaserve deteriorated. Mr. Conrad got to the point of cursing Jim over the phone about seemingly trivial issues. He also delayed paying fees so that the Jim's branch office was having cash flow problems. Jim had trouble explaining these problems to corporate financial officers.

Jim knew that he could not afford to renew the contract with PierPointe, but he also knew that there would be repercussions. He would have to explain the loss of volume to his superiors. He would have to lay off some employees. He also knew that Conrad was not above doing whatever he could to discredit Rehabaserve in the market.

Signing that original contract with PierPointe had been a cause for celebration. But now Jim knew that he should never have gotten involved with PierPointe. He just hoped that this one mistake did not jeopardize his career at Rehabaserve.

The Problem-Solving Process

One of the roles that managers assume is the role of decision maker. In the Rehabaserve case, Jim was fulfilling this role in deciding to enter into a contractual relationship with PierPointe. Unfortunately, all decisions (even routine decisions) carry the risk of poor outcomes. Even deciding to tie one's shoes in the morning could lead to a bad outcome. A shoelace could break, and there might not be a replacement in the house, which could result in an unscheduled stop at a convenience store that could result in getting stuck in traffic and arriving at work 45 minutes late. However, deciding to tie one's shoes is not a bad decision because, more often than not, the risks associated with untied shoelaces far outweigh the risks associated with attempting to tie one's shoelaces. Before Jim berates himself for making a bad decision, he needs to review his actions to make sure that he did not make a good decision that unfortunately resulted in undesirable consequences.

If Jim hopes to avoid similar negative outcomes in the future, he needs to evaluate this experience in terms of problem solving, not just **decision making**. Decision making is making a commitment to a specific course of action. That is what Jim did in signing a contract with PierPointe. However, making this commitment is just one step of the problem-solving process. Jim's decision making may have been sound, but based on erroneous assumptions, misconceptions, and limited information generated at other stages of the problem-solving process.

Many managerial decisions are made outside the problem-solving context. Sometimes, managers must decide whether to take advantage of an unexpected opportunity. Although opportunities are not problems, managers must decide what to do about them when they occur. The same is true for planning function decisions. The future is not yet a problem that cries for a solution. However, managers must make planning decisions in anticipation of the future's arrival. All decision making is significant. It is a crucial step in problem solving.

Jim's actions in the Rehabaserve case illustrate how cognitive deficits and affective responses can result in poor solutions. Problem solving occurs as a sequential process (Figure 7.1). Jim first became aware of a problem when he was made aware of a mismatch between current revenue and projected profit. His superior(s) saw this as a problem. There is nothing to indicate that Jim made an attempt to identify the cause of the problem. Jim seems to have assumed that the difference between current and projected profit was the result of insufficient

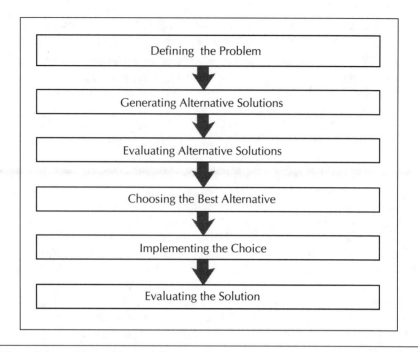

Figure 7.1   The problem-solving process.

business volume. This may have been true, but other possibilities beg for consideration. First, profit projections may have been overly optimistic. All forecasts are subject to error and should be reviewed as intensely as performance when they are not achieved. Second, the market conditions on which the forecasts were based may have changed. Therefore, adjusted forecasts that take market changes into consideration may be the solution to the profit problem. Third, profit may not be perfectly correlated with volume. Adding long-term care residents that require few services but generate large costs will not improve the branch's profit picture. Due to inaccurate assumptions and inadequate analysis, Jim's cognitive perception of the problem and its cause may have been faulty.

The problem-solving process only moves forward from the problem definition stage if the manager is concerned enough to want to solve the problem. In this case, Jim was very concerned with solving the problem and moved forward in the process to generating alternative solutions.

For a firm of Rehabaserve's limited product line, there are few alternative sources of revenue. However, besides contracting with nursing facilities, Rehabaserve's service delivery mechanisms could have been expanded to providing industrial injury rehabilitation services, home health services (independently or under contract), and services to other health institutions. There is no indication that Jim generated any alternative solutions. Perhaps he was too ignorant of the industry and the market to do so. Perhaps Rehabaserve had never provided services to a broad market, so Jim was not sure that any attempt to do so would be well received by his superiors. Perhaps Jim felt so much pressure to increase profits quickly that he did not take the time to generate alternatives.

Although he had only one alternative to consider, Jim did not evaluate that alternative carefully enough to identify potential problems. His staff provided part of the information he needed, but not all of it. They could legitimately speak only to the market reputation of PierPointe. It was from other vendors that Jim could have learned about what it was like to work with Conrad and the rest of the PierPointe staff. Jim should have picked up on the clue that this was a difficult account when the leading firm in the market could not satisfy Conrad's demands. It appears that an account-hungry Jim heard what he wanted to hear.

Making the choice was easy for Jim. He had a potential client that would bring revenue and prestige to his firm. Given the paucity of information and the limited options available, it would be difficult to say that he made a bad decision. However, it is obvious that he made several problem-solving errors on the way to his decision.

It is impossible to tell from the case if the solution was poorly implemented. Certainly Jim and his staff worked hard to make the relationship work. However, effort does not always result in achievement. In his zeal to get the contract, Jim may have oversold the quality of Rehabaserve's service and ability to handle the workload. If so, it is no surprise that Conrad and his staff were unhappy that their expectations had not been met. It is also possible that Jim and his staff were not up to doing even a reasonable job. Therefore, Jim's perception that Conrad cannot be satisfied may be erroneous.

Jim has evaluated the decision and concluded that it was a mistake. However, it is now obvious that his evaluation is flawed. The decision to sign a contract with PierPointe was not bad, rather it was based on an inadequate and possibly inaccurate assessment of the underlying problem, alternative solutions, and implementation. At each of the suspect steps of Jim's problem-solving process, cognitive and/or affective factors negatively affected his actions. Jim's anxiety about his performance and joy over finding a job-preserving client colored his perceptions of the opportunity. His lack of information about alternatives (including the one he chose) was a cognitive deficit that distorted his perception of reality. In addition, he had no data that demonstrated whether Rehabaserve was providing reasonable service to PierPointe. Therefore, he did not know if Conrad's complaints were valid. This cognitive deficit caused him to question the wisdom of entering into the PierPointe contract, rather than whether the contractual problems were really due to Rehabaserve's poor quality of service.

There is a tendency to treat problem solving and decision making as rational, fact-based processes. If the world consisted only of machines working with perfect information, they would be. But in the real world, people make decisions with imperfect, incomplete information. Most problem-solving errors are like Jim's. They involve some degree of affective and/or cognitive dysfunctions. Minimizing mistakes requires recognizing the most common deficits and compensating for them.

Identifying the Problem

This is the diagnostic stage of problem solving. The analytical process that managers engage in should be analogous to medical diagnosis. During the influenza season, physicians should never assume that every patient that presents with a fever, headache, and nausea has the flu. A well-considered diagnosis is only arrived at after the physician has obtained a history of the episode of illness and has performed a physical examination to rule out other underlying causes of the symptoms. Effective problem solvers resist the temptation to rush to diagnostic conclusions. They investigate situations thoroughly before labeling them as problems and classifying them as specific kinds of problems.

Another diagnostic challenge faced by managers is differentiating between symptoms and underlying pathologies. Treating symptoms in management is as effective as it is in medicine. Pain and discomfort may be relieved, but the disease is not cured. Treating a fever secondary to pneumonia may make the patient more comfortable, but it will not cure her. Similarly, consider the executive who is faced with an avalanche of employee complaints about parking spaces. The employees complain that there are not enough spaces because administrators have reserved parking places. The manager solves the problem by slightly staggering shifts, which frees up some parking places. However, a number of employees eventually quit and cite the parking problem as the reason. This executive solved the wrong problem. The complaints about parking were a symptom of employees' underlying dissatisfaction with administrators' prerogatives. The executive could only have arrived at the real problem by probing for other signs and symptoms much like a physician does by palpating an abdomen.

The correct identification and definition of a problem begins with the recognition that something is wrong. Recognition could be precipitated by a simple unmistakable event such as a fire, the unexpected death of a patient, or an employee's stabbing of a supervisor. However, management problems seldom manifest themselves in such dramatic and easily recognizable events. Instead, it is more common that evidence of problems is originally perceived as isolated, unimportant events. For example, on Friday, MaryEllen K., RN, is fifteen minutes late for work. On the following Tuesday, one Tylenol #3 tablet is missing. On Thursday, a nursing assistant comments that MaryEllen "must be going through the change of life" because she has been so grouchy lately. Many people reading those three facts together would perceive that it is possible that MaryEllen has a chemical dependency problem. But how would those same facts be perceived by a head nurse on a medical-surgical unit? Over the course of seven days crammed full of late arrivals, absences, missing supplies and drugs, complaints from employees and patients, and employee squabbles, it would not be at all surprising if these events remained unrelated (and perhaps forgotten) minor incidents in the mind of the head nurse. According to Cowan,

> *Problem recognition rarely occurs as a discrete event. In practice, the process occurs through various time intervals (from seconds to years), amidst a variety of ongoing activities and in different ways depending on both situational and individual factors.*[1]

Being able to recognize a problem over a period of time punctuated by many unrelated events requires strong conceptual skills.

Managers perceive problems when they become aware of dissonance between current and expected events. "Problems are, in effect, created by erecting goals and then detecting differences between the present situation and the goal."[2] In the Rehabaserve case, the profit goal was explicit and quantitatively measurable. Not all goals are so clear or explicitly stated. For example, the manager of an outpatient clinic notices that the carpeting has become unsightly as a result of usual and customary use. She decides to order new carpeting. Replacing worn carpeting in the clinic had probably not been explicitly stated as a goal. However, this manager perceived a discrepancy between the current appearance of the clinic and the general goal of maintaining an attractive clinic.

Once problems are recognized, an attempt is made to categorize and gather information in order to clearly define them.[3] It is in the attempt to define problems that managers seek to get beyond the symptoms of problems to their causes. Although the only way to cure a problem is to treat it at its source, there are times when the cause cannot be found. In the absence of an identifiable cause, the manager has three options. First, he can do nothing and hope that the cause and symptoms resolve themselves. Second, he can try to offset the untoward effects of the symptoms.[4] For example, a manager may notice an unusually high number of absences over a two-month period. After she investigates and fails to find a cause, she decides to use her discretionary budget funds to pay for a few extra hours to be worked by part-time employees. That does not treat the underlying problem, but it offsets the symptoms. Third, the manager can choose to treat the symptoms. A physician who sees a case of contact dermatitis is not always able to determine what caused it. Nonetheless, she usually treats the condition with topical steroids that speed the healing process. When the patient again comes into contact with the antigen, the symptoms will reappear. Likewise, managers sometimes have to settle for the less-than-satisfying option of dealing with problem symptoms when the true cause cannot be found. They are likely, however, to see the symptoms reappear.

Generating Alternatives

The objective of the problem solver is to choose the one best solution to a problem. In order to choose the best solution, that solution must be among the alternatives considered. If the manager terminates the search for alternatives prematurely, the best choice cannot be made. In the Rehabaserve case, for example, Jim did not consider any way to improve profitability other than to increase the volume of services provided to nursing facilities. When managers feel pressure to make decisions quickly, they are more likely to end the search for alternatives too soon. Also, once they identify a solution that they think will solve the problem, they terminate the search. This implies, of course, that managers evaluate alternatives as they arise. While generating and evaluating alternatives are discreet activities, managers do tend to generate and evaluate alternatives concurrently. Discreet activities need not be sequential.

At the other extreme, the best solution may be generated early in the search process, but the manager may continue to expend time and resources until the search is exhausted. The manager's dilemma is that the search for alternatives could theoretically go on forever. The last viable alternative does not come with a label that reads "LAST VIABLE ALTERNATIVE." The decision to quit searching is frequently triggered by the need to curtail expenditures of time and resources rather than by the certainty that there are no other alternatives worth finding. In the Rehabaserve case, Jim's search for alternatives may have been halted by cost considerations. He did not spend much money specifically searching for alternatives, but he and his superiors perceived that doing nothing to increase revenue would result in undesirable financial outcomes.

The degree to which managers search for alternatives may vary according to their experience with the problem. The search will be relatively short when they identify **ready-made solutions**. These are solutions that they have seen or tried before, or that they follow on the advice of others.[5] In other words, the search is short when the manager can find a tried and true solution. This is a likely scenario when the problem is routine and is characterized by common features. However, when problems are not routine, they require **custom-made solutions** that are designed for specific problems. It is generating custom-made alternatives that requires creativity.

Creativity is another of those difficult-to-define concepts that are encountered so frequently in management. It is one of those things that people recognize when they see it, but which they have some difficulty describing. A simple working definition of **creativity** is "the production of ideas that are both new and useful."[6] While it is doubtful whether this definition would hold up under close metaphysical scrutiny, it does have value for managers. Any number of new, unique ideas may be generated in the organizational context. However, creativity "must not be in disagreement with ordinary thinking."[7] In the business sense, for new ideas to be anything other than original thoughts, they must be applicable. In organizations, creativity is bounded by lines of practicality. For example, in the opening case, Jim might have been able to improve profitability by enlarging his bookkeeper's job to include becoming a bookie for Rehabaserve's employees with a percentage of all bets accruing to Rehabaserve. Original? Yes. Creative? Not in the business sense.

Although creativity has been recognized since antiquity as a desirable attribute, how it occurs is still somewhat of a mystery. Anyone who has had a creative idea knows that describing the process of how that idea occurred is difficult. Although people consciously experience thoughts, they do not consciously experience their genesis.

One aspect of the creative process which is generally accepted is that creative ideas rarely occur when individuals first encounter a situation requiring creativity. Writers do not sit down at a keyboard and emerge an hour later with a creative essay. Presented with a unique switch design problem, an electrical engineer does not generate a creative design for a new kind of switch on the spot. When managers are presented with problems that call for custom-made solutions, they do not come up with the solution off the top of their heads. The delay between situation exposure and idea generation suggests that creativity occurs in stages. Wallas proposed that the creative process occurs in four stages: preparation, incubation, illumination, and verification.[8] During the preparation stage, information about the task or problem is collected. In other words, the individual prepares to get down to the business of thinking by learning all she can about what it is she has to think about. During the incubation stage, the task/problem is set aside and the individual goes about other activities. It is during this time that the subconscious mind works on the task/problem. What exactly it is that the subconscious does in this phase is not clear.[9] However, it has been hypothesized that it works to make connections where none have existed before (i.e., what had been viewed as unrelated concepts are brought together into new ideas).[10] At the illumination stage (also frequently referred to as the insight stage), the creative idea comes to the conscious mind. It is the insight stage that cartoonists depict with an electric light bulb and that the word "Eureka" describes. During the verification phase, the idea is tested in ways that confirm its fit with reality. Verification can be achieved through experimentation and by others' review.

Because creativity is not fully understood, there are no guaranteed things that managers can do to make themselves creative problem solvers. However, the creative process itself suggests some ways that managers can foster creativity. First, because the creative idea arises from connections made between and among concepts stored in memory, the more information in memory, the more likely that creative ideas can be generated. A general education and accumulating large amounts of general knowledge set the stage for generating creative ideas.[11] Likewise, regular participation in a wide range of staff development activities may stimulate creativity. Second, since the search for creative ideas is a process of making new connections, flexibility in thinking is required. All activity can grow stale with repetition. Creativity requires breaking out of the confines of routine thinking. Exposing oneself to a constantly changing variety of environmental stimuli may help promote flexibility. Activities that result in mental exercise have been suggested as ways of stimulating the imagination. Among these activities are pursuing diverse, thought-provoking pursuits such as traveling, puzzle solving, game playing, and producing crafts and fine arts. Reading is also important because, "It supplies bread for imagination to feed on, and bones for it to chew on."[12] (Of course, the reading material must be thought-provoking rather than merely entertaining.) These activities may seem remotely relevant to healthcare and to management. However, engaging in mental activity outside the confines of the familiar work environment helps managers view their situations from a fresh perspective. Third, creativity requires time and thinking. Managers have too little of the former to do much of the latter. Creative solutions will not materialize without a commitment of time and effort. Thinking time is difficult to account for in productivity statistics. However, without it, neither managers nor employees are likely to come up with creative ideas.

Finally, managers must learn how to eliminate boundaries to creative thinking. When managers think they know the best way to do something, they tend to write a procedure that tells employees exactly how to do a task. This, in effect, establishes a boundary that employees cannot cross without taking a risk. If they never take that risk, they never find creative and better ways of doing things. By reducing every activity to strictly defined procedures, managers sacrifice creativity on the alter of control. When managers want employees to be creative, they are better off not telling them what to do and how to do it.[13] Very narrowly defined job descriptions also establish boundaries to creative thinking. They tend to lead individuals to think of themselves and their responsibilities in limited ways.[14] For example, if a respiratory therapist has a job description that speaks only to the duties of a respiratory therapist in relationship to the respiratory therapy department, then the therapist is likely to limit the definition of her role to those terms. She will be unlikely to risk stepping out of those boundaries by thinking creatively about how clinical processes in general can be improved or how the organization can better achieve its objectives. As a result, her organization loses an important potential source of new ideas.

This discussion has dealt with creativity as if it is always desirable. This is not true in practice. First, there must be a match between creativity and problems that require custom-made solutions. Creativity is not desirable when ready-made solutions suffice. For example, a department manager who has to deal with morale problems would be ill-advised to offer employees who perform well the chance to leave early. This may be an effective and creative solution, but it could inadvertently create interdepartmental jealousy. Less creative solutions would probably be more appropriate. Second, not every organization encourages or values creativity. In these organizations, creative managers may be so out-of-step with prevailing organizational values that they may become dysfunctional. Finally, not all creative alternatives are good alternatives. The lone creative alternative in a group of tried-and-true alternatives is not necessarily the best alternative. Determining which alternative is best requires evaluation.

Evaluating Alternatives

Evaluating alternatives is a complex process that varies widely from one situation to another. Alternatives are evaluated along several different dimensions including the:

1. probability of successful outcomes;
2. degree to which they are likely to effectively address the situation;
3. time required for results to be achieved;
4. cost; and
5. number of times the alternative would have to be implemented for effectiveness.[15]

It is immediately evident that all these criteria require prediction and estimation. Thus the ability to make the best choices depends, to a great extent, on the ability to accurately forecast outcomes. A short problem-solving scenario shows how alternatives are evaluated along these criteria.

> *Jeanette Sanfilippo, DDS, faces an enviable dilemma. Her practice has grown to the point that several of her patients have complained about the inability to get appointments in a timely manner. A few patients have threatened to find another dentist if the situation does not improve. Dr. Sanfilippo suspects that some patients have already gone to other dentists or are delaying prophylaxis or treatment due to the long appointment lead times. Dr. Sanfilippo has come up with only two alternative solutions. She can either (1) extend office hours for routine prophylaxis by one hour per day, or (2) add and equip an additional examination room. She currently has four examination rooms.*

Dr. Sanfilippo's evaluation of these two alternatives can be classified under the five dimensions identified above. Her evaluation is summarized in Table 7.1.

Because choices are made on the basis of value (i.e., the perceived benefit received in exchange for an expenditure), Dr. Sanfilippo must also determine what outcomes might accrue as a result of her decision. It is sometimes helpful to compare outcomes by constructing a decision tree. A **decision tree** is a graphic representation of possible outcomes of alternative courses of action and the probability that corresponding outcomes will occur. When Dr. Sanfilippo sets pen to paper to do this, she should remember that she actually has three alternatives to evaluate, because doing nothing is an alternative.

In Dr. Sanfilippo's decision tree (Figure 7.2) the outcomes of her alternatives are expressed as changes in revenue per day. She has determined that in the worst case scenario, she stands to lose $100 of revenue per day if patients leave due to long lead times for appointments. In the best case, she stands to gain $600 in revenue per day if she satisfies all the demand she feels exists. The range of possible outcomes lies between these two extremes. Dr. Sanfilippo simplifies the

Table 7.1   Dr. Sanfilippo's Evaluation of Alternative Solutions to the Schedule Overload Problem

Dimension of Evaluation	Alternative 1— Extending Hours	Alternative 2— Add Examination Room
Probability of success	*Probable* enough patient demand that they would probably come earlier or later some staff would have trouble working longer or different hours	*Highly probable* Dr. Sanfilippo has enough time to work with another hygienist patients seem to like current hours
Degree to which situation is addressed	*Mostly*—adds 20 hours/week patient care time (will shorten appointment lead times but not eliminate them)	*Addresses problem fully*—adds 40 hours/week patient care time, which should take care of the whole problem
Time for results	*Short*—could start within 2 weeks of notifying employees	*Long*—construction and equipment installation will require 6 months
Cost	4 more hours of hygienist time/day (about 20% may be at overtime rates) 1 additional hour of Dr. Sanfilippo's time per day about 5% increase in utilities increase wear and tear on equipment	$80,000 one time capital expense 20% increase in depreciation expense ongoing thereafter
Number of times	*ongoing* implementation	*one time only* implementation

evaluation by assuming that the intermediate outcomes will be at two discreet points: no change ($0 revenue change) and halfway between no change and the maximum increase ($300 revenue increase). There is a different probability of occurrence associated with each possible outcome. For example, if she does nothing, Dr. Sanfilippo estimates that there is a 50% chance there will be no change in revenue because she may lose some patients, but their places will be taken by new patients. However, she believes that there is a 40% chance she will lose enough patients that revenue will decrease by $100 per day. She also feels that if she does nothing, the continuing high demand may stimulate the staff to find ways to fit in more patients so that there is a 10% chance that revenue will actually increase by $300 per day. She does not see any possibility that under the current circumstances, revenue could increase by $600 per day. Notice that in the decision tree, these probabilities are expressed as decimals (i.e., a 50% chance of occurrence is expressed as 0.5). She makes similar estimates of the probabilities of possible outcomes for the other alternatives. The **expected value** of each

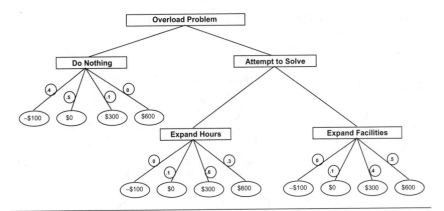

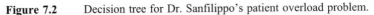

Figure 7.2   Decision tree for Dr. Sanfilippo's patient overload problem.

alternative is calculated by summing the products of the probability of the occurrence of the outcome times the value of the outcome:

$$EV = \Sigma(P_n)\,(O_n)$$

where EV = expected value

P = probability of outcome

O = value of outcome

A **payoff table** is the depiction of this calculation in tabular form (Table 7.2). At the intersection of the rows (alternatives) and the columns (value of the outcome times the probability of outcome) is the expected payoff. By adding the payoffs associated with each alternative, the expected value is determined. As the table indicates, the highest expected value is associated with the facility expansion alternative.

Dr. Sanfilippo's decision can only be as good as the data upon which she bases it. At this point, her probability estimates are based on her intuitive assessment of her patients' behavior and the practice environment. She could strengthen her data by conducting market research that would more systematically and quantitatively describe how her patients would be likely to react in the face of each alternative. The more factually based Dr. Sanfilippo's estimates are, the more likely that her actual outcomes will match projected outcomes.

Choosing

There are two approaches to choosing an alternative. The first is **screening,** which requires that each alternative is determined to be either a satisfactory or unsatisfactory alternative.[16] Dr. Sanfilippo may determine that doing nothing may be an unsatisfactory alternative because it does not meet her minimum criterion

Table 7.2   Payoff Table for Dr. Sanfilippo's Patient Overload Problem

Alternative	Expected Payoff ($100 outcome)[a]	Expected Payoff ($0 outcome)	Expected Payoff ($300 outcome)	Expected Payoff ($600 outcome)	Expected Values[b]
Do Nothing	−$40	$0	$30	$0	−$10
Expand Hours	$0	$0	$180	$180	$360
Expand Facility	$0	$0	$120	$300	$420

[a]expected payoffs = (probability of outcome) (value of outcome)
[b]expected values = sum of expected payoffs in each row

of no likely loss of revenue. Because both expanding hours and expanding facilities result in a likely increase in revenue, Dr. Sanfilippo may find them both satisfactory. However, she still has to choose between them. In order to choose between these two, she could establish another screening criterion. For example, her second criterion may be that she must solve the problem in the next month. In that case, she would decide that expanding the facility is not satisfactory because it requires too much time to implement.

An alternative to screening is scoring. **Scoring** requires that scores be attached to each alternative and the alternative with the highest score is chosen. Dr. Sanfilippo could score each of her alternatives in terms of contribution to net profit within a given time frame. To do so, she would calculate the expected cost of each alternative and subtract that from expected revenue at some future time. The alternative that results in the greatest net profit would be her choice.

Screening and scoring are not mutually exclusive. Dr. Sanfilippo may use screening to eliminate doing nothing from consideration. Then she could use scoring to choose between the expansion alternatives.

Implementation

Problem solving does not end with choosing an alternative. For example, once a cardiologist determines that the best approach to treating a patient with coronary artery disease is to perform a coronary artery bypass graft, the patient is still compromised until the procedure is completed. Once Dr. Sanfilippo makes a decision, she still has to implement it to solve her problem. All kinds of things could happen during implementation that would derail Dr. Sanfilippo's intent. Personnel could quit, dental coverage plans could be cut back, natural disasters could strike, and loan rates could go up. Similarly, Dr. Sanfilippo could benefit from unexpected windfalls. New applicants could appear, dental coverage could expand, the weather could be better than normal, and loan rates could go down. All implementation variables can be neither foreseen nor controlled. However, the better the evaluation of alternatives, the better contingency planning can be done.

Much of the success of implementation will depend on the manager's ability to work with people who are responsible for completing specific implementation tasks.

Evaluation

Evaluation is an almost inescapable consequence of decision making. After having chosen a day-care provider and having sent his child to the provider, a parent will evaluate the care actually provided to make sure that it meets his expectations. In the Rehabaserve case, Jim evaluated his decision to sign a contract with PierPointe and found considerable fault with it. Irrespective of the alternative Dr. Sanfilippo chooses, she will certainly compare the actual outcomes to what she expected to happen. Because her decision is made under conditions of uncertainty, she may always wonder if the choice she made was the best choice. Never knowing for sure how the other alternatives would have worked out is one of the ambiguities with which managers have to live.

Barriers to Effective Problem Solving

In a perfect world, decision makers would be presented with clearly defined problems. They would have all the information they need in readily accessible forms. They would have all the time they need to make and implement decisions, and they would also have all the resources they need to implement them. In the real world, problems are solved under imperfect conditions.

- **Information deficits.** The available information may be insufficient either to define the problem or to evaluate alternatives. Even complete information may be in a form that is not easily accessible. Consider how Dr. Sanfilippo would react if she commissioned a marketing study and was handed 200 pages of phone and interview survey data without any interpretation. These 200 pages of responses would have to be tabulated and analyzed before Dr. Sanfilippo could have the information she needed for problem solving.

- **Perceptual deficits.** *Perception* is the way people see the world. Each individual processes sensory stimuli so as to generate a view of the world that is meaningful and coherent.[17] Perception includes reacting to stimuli, becoming conscious of them, placing them into a conceptual framework, and interpreting them.[18] Because each individual develops different perceptual processing patterns and comes to each situation with a unique set of experiences that influences how stimuli are processed and interpreted, perceptions of reality vary. When actual and perceived reality converge, accuracy in problem identification and solution evaluation is enhanced.

- **Cost and time limitations.** Time and financial resources available to managers are limited. Every decision-making situation is approached by managers within the context of limited resources. The natural reaction is to screen out all alternatives that initially seem to fall outside cost and time boundaries without looking for value (i.e., fully assessing the benefits gained in relationship to their costs).

- **Stress.** Stress compromises the decision-making process.[19] Some extraordinarily stressful situations arise from severe time constraints, which compress generation and evaluation of alternatives. Stress may also arise from the conflict a decision maker feels as a result of having to choose between or among alternatives that have quite unpredictable outcomes. Stress can be intense when choosing the wrong alternative may result in losses for the decision maker.

  Stress may distract the decision maker so that inadequate attention is paid to decision making. It may also distort the perception of problems or situations that require decision making. Stress may heighten an individual's natural tendency toward risk aversion.

  Clinicians deal with a similar phenomenon as part of their professional practice. They help patients work through illness-induced stress so that they can make rational treatment choices. The challenge for managers is to recognize when stress compromises their own managerial decision making.

  Under stressful conditions, a magnified fear of failure may lead to incremental decision making. Decisions that result in small changes and small improvements are favored irrespective of whether they are the best decisions. Decisions that result in significant change are avoided because they are disruptive and, therefore, intensify already stressful situations. As a result, stress causes decision makers to tend to **satisfice** (i.e., choose alternatives that are adequate) rather than to optimize (i.e., make the best possible decisions).

Two additional causative factors that lead to satisficing have been suggested.[20] First, decision makers are incapable of organizing, analyzing, and interpreting all the information pertinent to a single decision. Indeed, information overload may be as much of a barrier to decision making as information deficiency. Second, time and cost constraints limit the extent to which any decision maker can collect and apply information. The decision maker who adopts a satisficing approach to decision making will approach the process by evaluating alternatives in succession rather than by comparing them all at one time. If Dr. Sanfilippo had pursued a satisficing strategy, she would have discarded the do-nothing alternative as not being adequate. However, she would have probably accepted the hour-expansion alternative because it met her objective of increasing revenue. She would not have even considered the facilities expansion alternative, although it had the potential to generate the most revenue. In the end, satisficing may be sufficient for an organization to muddle through. However, it does not yield the best results. One way to increase the capability to collect and process more information is to engage in group decision making. Teams are capable of bringing information processing power and a range of perspectives to bear on problem solving so that less satisficing and more maximizing can occur.

Group Decision Making

There are several potential advantages of using groups to make decisions.[21] First, as noted above, more information and perspectives may be brought into the process than an individual could apply. Second, individuals working in groups may be intellectually stimulated to consider the problem and alternatives differently than they would working in isolation. Third, engaging people in decision making and problem solving increases their understanding of the problem, possible solutions, and rationale for the chosen solution. Understanding leads to a greater likelihood of acceptance, which, in turn, paves the way for a smooth implementation. Consider, for example, how a nurse feels when she learns that her patient care choices are criticized by a nurse who takes over for her at shift change. The second shift nurse may have valid negative criticisms to make. However, the first shift nurse will likely feel defensive because the criticisms are made without full knowledge of the stress, resource, and time limitations that resulted in imperfect choices. Employees are equally likely to criticize and resist imperfect management decisions. However, when they experience the limitations of decision making by being engaged in the process, they are more likely to embrace the imperfect decisions that they themselves help to craft.

Deciding when to engage others in the decision-making process is not easy. In spite of the potential advantages of group decision making, groups require a major commitment of the manager's time and energy. They are also expensive in that several wage earners are required to make a decision. Several guidelines based on research results suggest when it is appropriate to employ group decision making. Groups should be favored when

1. the quality of the decision is important, and the manager lacks the information or expertise required to solve the problem;

2. the quality of the decision is important, the problem is ill-defined, and the information needed to solve the problem is unknown; and/ or

3. the acceptance of the decision by subordinates is required for effective implementation, and it is doubtful whether an autocratic decision will be accepted.

Groups should not be favored when the quality of the decision is important, but the group does not value or share the organizational goals that are furthered by the decision.[22] When the balance between quality of the decision and acceptance is nearly equal and/or the group appears to be in conflict about goals, the manager has to make a situational assessment to determine which decision-making style is more appropriate.

The manager's role in group decision making is twofold. First, the manager needs to facilitate the group's decision-making activity. Second, the manager needs to help the group sidestep common group decision-making pitfalls. Following the suggestions for building strong teams presented in Chapter 6 will contribute to successful group decision making. There are a few techniques that are specific to strengthening the group decision-making process.

Group Decision-Making Techniques

Brainstorming. The purpose of **brainstorming** is to generate ideas. Brainstorming occurs in a meeting format (usually referred to as a brainstorming session) during which the group leader explains the decision to be made and asks for ideas. For this technique to be effective, the rules of brainstorming[23] must be followed.

1. Criticism (positive or negative) is not allowed.

2. Free-wheeling (i.e., unrestrained) ideas are encouraged.

3. Quantity is encouraged.

4. Combination and improvement of the ideas of others is encouraged.

In the hands of an inexperienced or ineffective group leader, brainstorming may fall short of expectations. The leader must communicate and enforce brainstorming rules, especially rule number one. Nothing kills the idea generation process as quickly as criticism. Negative criticism makes participants hesitate to share ideas (especially unusual ones) for fear of being publicly ridiculed. Positive criticism makes people hesitate to put forth new ideas out of fear that they will pale by comparison. For brainstorming to work, the leader must create an atmosphere in which participants feel safe in offering their ideas. Because people are innately judgmental, the leader's role in suppressing criticism is not an easy one.

Because of the incubation period required for creativity, a single brainstorming session may yield few if any creative ideas. Therefore, follow-up sessions are common. At follow-up meetings, the leader must maintain the atmosphere of support for new ideas so that anyone who has had creative ideas in the interim will place them before the group. Only when new ideas have been exhausted can the leader unleash the group's critical tendencies.

The **Delphi Technique** is a procedure for soliciting different perspectives and ideas from several individuals without actually bringing them together for a meeting. This process is named for ancient Greece's famous oracle of Apollo at Delphi. The oracle was a place where people went to solicit prophecies of their future. The oracle's namesake process acquired its name because it was first used as a forecasting technique.

To initiate the Delphi Technique, the decision leader needs to determine what kind of expertise has a bearing on the problem. He then must choose an expert panel composed of people with the appropriate range of expertise. The experts may be internal or external, and they may be geographically dispersed. They remain unknown to each other throughout the process. A questionnaire describing the problem and requesting ideas is sent to the experts, who complete and return it to the decision leader. If the experts concur, the process ends. If not (as is usually the case), the leader prepares another questionnaire based on the original results and repeats the process. The cycle continues until the experts reach consensus.

The anonymity of the Delphi Technique addresses the problem of reluctance to share ideas in front of others. Delphi also has the advantage of using written responses provided in a lengthened time frame. This allows for a more accurate and complete evaluation of ideas put forth, as well as providing incubation time to foster creativity. These attributes suggest two offsetting disadvantages. The Delphi technique is time-consuming. Also, participants who work in isolation are not exposed to the ideas of others that might trigger additional new ideas.

The **Nominal Group Technique (NGT)** is a hybrid process that combines the advantages of brainstorming and the Delphi Technique. Like brainstorming, NGT begins with the assembly of a group and the presentation of a question or decision scenario to the group. Unlike brainstorming and like the Delphi Technique, group members write down their responses. Then the ideas are presented aloud without discussion. After the ideas are presented, they are discussed. After discussion, each member silently ranks or rates each idea and the aggregate rating becomes the group decision.[24,25]

NGT preserves the advantage of brainstorming in that it brings different skills, knowledge, and perspectives of diverse individuals into the decision-making process. However, because some of the idea generation and evaluation is done independently, social conformity pressures are minimized. Although NGT captures the advantage of independent work that is characteristic of the Delphi Technique, the entire process is shortened by having a single meeting. In NGT, the need for creativity is counterbalanced by the need for expediency.

Group Decision-Making Errors

Compliance occurs when individuals in groups behave in ways they think other group members expect them to behave.[26] Compliance was confirmed in one well-known experiment in which individuals knowingly stated that the length of a line was something other than what they knew it to be just to agree with the opinion of a small group of people they had never met before.[27] Imagine how much more compliance there must be in a work group in which individuals perceive that compliance could lead to increased popularity, better working conditions, and maybe even a raise. Individuals may also perceive that there are significant punishments (lack of group acceptance and administrative disfavor) for failure to comply.

Health practitioners are familiar with the relationships between rewards, punishment, and compliance because they constantly use rewards and punishments to manipulate patients into compliance with prescribed treatments. Some of the following admonitions may sound familiar.

"If you don't quit smoking for yourself, do it for your children."

"I can't tell you what to do, but I know if it were my mother, I wouldn't put her through it."

"Most of the moms in the neighborhood have brought their children down for their shots. What about bringing in your son this afternoon?"

These are clearly attempts to make patients perceive that someone else has expectations of them, and if they comply with that behavior, they will be approved and accepted.

The **Abilene Paradox** occurs as an extension of compliance when a group of individuals behaves in the way they believe the group leader expects them to behave. Imagine that on a particularly busy Friday afternoon of a particularly stressful week, the head nurse says, "Wouldn't a big piece of sinfully rich chocolate cake hit the spot right now?" Everyone nods, and, behold, at noon the next Friday, the unit secretary presents a sinfully rich chocolate cake to be shared by the staff. The secretary secretly resents the time and money the cake cost her. The cake creates a mess that no one wants to clean up. It takes up space in the conference room. Most of the staff members are watching their weight so they do not really want the cake but eat some anyway because everybody else does. Why do they all do something they really do not want to do? Because they think the group leader wants to. In reality, however, the head nurse does not even like chocolate cake and was just using it as a metaphor for indulging in something sybaritic. Chocolate cake popped into her head because she assumed that most people liked it. Nonetheless, like everyone on the unit, she digs into the cake. The irony of the Abilene Paradox is that everyone ends up doing something they do not want to do without any real coercion to do it.

The Abilene Paradox is not limited to social interactions. It occurs in operational and planning decisions made by groups. Individuals working in groups try to find the common ground that puts them in sync with other members of the group. It is the group leader who frequently gives (either deliberately or inadvertently) group members a standard to rally around. It has been hypothesized that it is a fear of separation, alienation and loneliness that drives group members to conformity.[28] The operationalizing of this fear can be so strong that, "Organizations frequently take actions in contradiction to data they have for dealing with problems, and as a result, compound their problems rather than solving them."[29] Through speculation about what leaders want, the group ends up at a place no one (not even the group leader) would have gone individually.

Groupthink occurs anytime rational evaluation of problems and alternatives is superseded by the desire for harmony and unanimity.[30] It is obvious that the proximal cause of the Abilene Paradox is groupthink. The symptoms of groupthink include:

1. A sense of *invulnerability* that comes from believing that the collective wisdom of a group precludes decision-making errors.

2. A belief that a group decision *cannot be morally wrong.*

3. A tendency to *rationalize* decisions in the face of data that indicate that they may be wrong.

4. A tendency to *dismiss the opinions of persons outside the group.*

5. Hesitancy of individual members to express *dissenting points of view.*

6. Belief in *unanimity* without submitting the belief to a test such as anonymous voting or polling.

7. *Pressure* on individual members not to disagree.

8. *Selective limitation of information flow* so that all team members do not get information that might disrupt the unanimity of the group.[31]

The result of groupthink is truncated decision making with skewed choices and choice evaluation. Excessive confidence in the group's skills causes it to shorten its search for information and alternatives. The group may gloss over the risks and disadvantages of the favored alternative and fail to reconsider alternatives that were screened out early, even if new information is brought to the table.[32]

Choice shift is the tendency of groups to make more extreme choices than individuals acting independently would make.[33] When the group members see potential gains, they tend to accept more risk than individuals would to receive those gains. When they perceive potential losses, they tend to make more cautious decisions to avoid losses than individuals would make.

It is unclear why choice shift occurs. One explanation suggests that individuals in groups feel more secure in supporting extreme positions. Many people are hesitant to state positions that they believe would be perceived by others as being extreme. Therefore, to avoid alienating people they tend to state more moderate opinions. However, when they are engaged in a group discussion and they hear more extreme opinions that are close to their true position, they may support them publicly.[34] It would require only a small leap of faith to assume that as a group explores more extreme positions, group members become more comfortable with them.

Avoiding Group Decision-Making Errors

No managerial interventions can consistently prevent compliance, the Abilene Paradox, or groupthink. These are errors rooted in emotions. In the usual work environment, the ability of managers to change emotional responses is limited. The following guidelines are not quick fixes and will be met with different degrees of success with different groups.

1. *Severely restrict thinking aloud.* Managers who want to engage subordinates in decision making have a tendency to share their thoughts on problems and alternative solutions with them. Managers

do this to indicate openness and to stimulate employee thinking. However, the manager has to be careful because she may find that her thoughts take on a life of their own. Many managers have tossed out ideas in meetings only to have them show up as full-blown, budgeted projects months later after the manager had long since discarded and/or forgotten them. This is the Abilene Paradox in operation.

2. *Welcome dissent.* Minority opinions need to be encouraged. In meetings managers should positively reinforce novel ideas, even impractical ones. Dissenting opinions should be considered seriously. (Employees recognize when their ideas are being written off without serious consideration, even under the guise of polite rejection.)

It almost goes without saying that performance appraisal should recognize rational decision-making participation rather than compliance. Working effectively with others specifically excludes unthinking compliance with group leadership. Constructive disagreement should be encouraged and rewarded.

Managers may formally institutionalize dissent by assigning individuals the responsibility of playing devil's advocate in groups and requiring written reports of that individual. Similarly, managers can require written evaluations of all alternatives and justification of choices and rejections. The manager should critically review and question all such group reports.

3. *Encourage personal responsibility.* Although individuals should be expected to cooperate when they work in groups, they should also be encouraged to take personal responsibility. Group members should not be allowed to hide behind a veil of group responsibility. When a group fails to make good decisions, the group as a whole and individual members should be held accountable.

Conclusion

Throughout this chapter, it has become clear that decision making and problem solving have both cognitive and emotional components. The rational element has to do with information collection, analysis, and application to the issue at hand. Anything that interferes with information handling has the same effect as a cognitive disorder in an individual. Performance is substandard because it is based on inadequate and/or inaccurate information.

The emotional element has to do with the decision maker's response to the situation. Typical emotions include fear of failure and joy at the prospect of success. Responding only to the dominant emotion at any given moment has the same result as an affective disorder in that strong emotions may cause inappropriate, ineffective behavior. This was Jim's problem in the Rehabaserve case. His joy and relief at the prospect of a big contract caused him to make an irrational, poorly informed decision.

Maximizing decision making requires the same kinds of approaches that are generally used in dealing with people with cognitive and/or affective disorders.

1. *Recognize and validate emotional responses.* People engaged in work will have emotional responses to opportunities and threats. These responses need to be recognized and worked through so that they can be rationally taken into account during the decision-making process. However, decision making (especially in healthcare) should not be approached in an emotionally detached way. To do so might result in institutions "devoid of acts of affection, conscience, and humanity, as well as passion."[35]

2. *Focus on facts.* Constantly ask what additional information is needed to make a decision and make every effort to get it. Once the emotional responses to situations and alternatives are considered, it is time to make rational decisions.

3. *Minimize stress.* The best thing to do to decrease decision-making stress is to allow decision makers time to think. Reasonable deadlines and timetables should be established. When time dictates quick decisions, then decision makers should be relieved of other duties so that they can concentrate more fully on the decision.

4. *Reward creativity and dissent.* Run-of-the-mill organizations reward run-of-the-mill performance. Compliant performance is run-of-the-mill performance. Cutting edge organizations reward employees who dare to offer fresh ideas and alternative perspectives.

Had the top managers of Rehabaserve observed these guidelines, Jim probably would not have entered into a contract with PierPointe. He would have been attuned to his emotional response and would have dealt with it. He would have searched for and paid attention to important facts, and he might have thought of creative and profitable ways to build Rehabaserve's business in his market.

Endnotes

1. David A. Cowan, "Developing a Process Model of Problem Recognition," *Academy of Management Review 11* (Spring 1986): 763–764.
2. Andrew Leigh, *Decisions, Decision!* (Aldershot, England: Gower Publishing Co. Ltd., 1983), p. 12.
3. Cowan, op. cit.
4. Alfred R. Oxenfeldt, David W. Miller, and Roger A. Dickinson, *A Basic Approach to Executive Decision Making* (New York: Amacom, 1978).
5. Thomas S. Bateman and Carl P. Zeithaml, *Management: Function and Strategy*, 2nd ed. (Homewood, IL: Richard D. Irwin, Inc., 1993).
6. Ramon J. Aldag and Timothy M. Stearns, *Management*, 2nd ed. (Cincinnati: Southwestern Publishing Co., 1991), 693.

7. Silvano Arieti, *Creativity: The Magic Synthesis* (New York: Basic Books, 1976), p. 4.
8. Graham Wallas, *The Art of Thought* (New York: Harcourt, Brace, & World, 1926).
9. Alex F. Osborn, *Applied Imagination*, 3rd ed. (New York: Scribner's, 1963).
10. Arthur Koestler, *The Act of Creation* (New York: MacMillan, 1964).
11. J. W. Young, *A Technique for Producing Ideas* (Chicago: Crain Communications, 1940).
12. Osborn, op. cit., 77–8.
13. Robert Simons, "Control in an Age of Empowerment," *Harvard Business Review 73* (March-April 1995): 80–88.
14. Peter M. Senge, *The Fifth Discipline* (New York: Doubleday, 1990).
15. Oxenfeldt et al., op. cit.
16. Aldag and Stearns, op. cit.
17. Bernard Berelson and Gary A. Steiner, *Human Behavior: An Inventory of Scientific Findings* (New York: Harcourt, Brace, & World, 1964).
18. Aldag and Stearns, op. cit.
19. Irving L. Janis and Leon Mann, *Decision Making: A Psychological Analysis of Conflict, Choice and Commitment* (New York: The Free Press, 1977).
20. Hubert A. Simon, *New Science of Decision Making* (New York, 1960).
21. Norman R. F. Maier, "Assets and Liabilities in Group Problem Solving: The Need for an Integrative Function," *Psychological Review 74* (1967): 239–249.
22. Victor H. Vroom, "Decision-making and the Leadership Process," *Journal of Contemporary Business* (Autumn 1974).
21. John A. Wagner III and John R. Hollenbeck, *Organizational Behavior* (Englewood Cliffs, NJ: Prentice Hall, 1992).
24. A. L. Delbecq, A. H. Van de Hen, and D. H. Gustafson, *Group Techniques for Program Planning* (Glenview, IL: Scott, Foresman & Company, 1975).
25. Henry L. Tosi, John R. Rizzo, and Stephen J. Carroll, *Managing Organizational Behavior* (Marshfield, MA: Pitman, 1986).
26. Wagner and Hollenbeck, op. cit.
25. Solomon Asch, "Studies of Independence and Conformity I: A Minority of One Against a Unanimous Majority," *Psychological Monographs 70* (1956): 416–22.
28. Jerry B. Harvey, *The Abilene Paradox and Other Meditations on Management* (Lexington, MA: Lexington Books, 1988).
29. Ibid., 20.
30. Irving L. Janis, *Groupthink* (Boston: Houghton Mifflin, 1982).
31. Ibid.
32. Janis and Mann, op. cit.
33. C. Fraser, C. Gouge, and M. Billig, "Risky Shifts, Cautious Shifts, and Group Polarization," *European Journal of Social Psychology 1* (1971): 7–30.
34. G. S. Sanders and R. S. Baron, "Is Social Comparison Irrelevant for Producing Choice Shifts?" *Journal of Experimental Social Psychology 13* (1977): 303–314.
35. Janis and Mann, op. cit., 45.

Unit III

Leading

**8**

Motivation:
General Malaise

In this chapter the reader will learn how to:

◆ define motivation
◆ diagnose motivational problems
◆ recognize similarities between low levels of motivation and a general malaise
◆ differentiate between motivation and satisfaction
◆ recognize factors that influence motivation
◆ distinguish between job content and job context motivators
◆ distinguish between motivation and behavior modification
◆ establish linkages between reward systems and behavior that make it possible to motivate employees
◆ apply motivational techniques in healthcare.

The Ides of March

March 15. A beautiful day. The first real spring day after a long, almost brutal winter. Anita had never felt so much like playing hooky.

As she carefully maneuvered her car through the morning rush hour traffic on the way to the SouthSide Neighborhood Health Center, Anita mentally reviewed the "to do" list that she had written before she left the office last Friday afternoon. Three major items came immediately to mind.

1. *Management meeting. The main topic of discussion was the budget. She had already found out through the grapevine that SouthSide would not get the amount of federal funding that had been expected next year. The only question was how deep the cut would be. The hard part would be in a few weeks when she would have to tell employees that their already well-below-average wages would be frozen for the foreseeable future.*

2. *Meeting with SouthSide's lawyers about the Allen incident. Louise Allen was a nurse who had been attacked in SouthSide's parking lot. It was the third act of violence involving employees this year. Mrs. Allen had been raped and beaten. Not only was she left with emotional scars, but she was also going to have a long-term disability. In the weeks following the attack, several employees quit SouthSide, and absenteeism was very high. Although the shock of the incident had worn off, employees were still concerned and frightened.*

3. *Place ads for an advanced practice nurse (APN). Joe Kline, a pediatric APN, had given his two-week notice Friday. He told her that when he had taken the job, he thought he could make a difference in the lives of the children of the neighborhood. Instead, he was spending most of his time doing paperwork and the kind of nursing functions that most office nurses do. He said that Dr. Sheets refused to allow him to assess and treat any child with a medical problem and that under these conditions, he felt underutilized. Anita accepted his explanation, but deep down she suspected that he was leaving for the considerably higher salary she was sure he would be making in his new job at a managed care company.*

    As she got closer to the clinic, the more she realized that she did not really want to go there today. In the 19 months since she had been promoted to Director of Therapeutic Services, she had not missed a day of work. Most days she came in early and stayed late. She knew that her work was important. She knew she was good at it. But the job had turned out to be far more difficult and draining than she had ever imagined it could be. It seemed that day after day, all she dealt with were the sad and tragic consequences of living and working in poor urban America. Progress was slow and painful when it was made at all. Moments of joy and laughter were rare.

    By the time she was eight blocks away from the clinic, her eyes began to fill with tears. She drove halfway around the block and started home. For one fine spring day, the clients and employees of SouthSide would have to muddle through without her.

General malaise is a frustrating condition. It is a feeling of not being physically well that can interfere with normal activities. Therefore, sufferers frequently seek treatment. However, medical management is not always effective, nor indicated. In the absence of specific symptoms, discovering underlying causes is difficult. Lack of findings upon routine physical examination can escalate into a wild goose chase of diagnostic procedures. Palliative treatment is unsatisfactory. Treatment aimed at nonspecific targets rarely hits the mark. Even if some benefit is realized, it may be short-lived. Moreover, attempts to treat nonspecific symptoms may mask specific symptoms that might occur if an underlying disease worsened.

In the organizational context, **motivation** is the desire to perform a task well. Note that motivation is future oriented. Therefore, current motivation cannot be discerned by evaluating how well tasks have been done in the past. Managers sometimes mistakenly assume that low productivity and poor quality work are the direct result of lack of motivation. However, many variables contribute to productivity and quality problems. Before a diagnosis of low motivation is made, the manager must have additional evidence that employees lack the desire to perform well. Motivation is very similar to general malaise in that it has an affective component. "I just don't feel very energetic" and "I've really been down in the dumps lately" are expressions of emotional responses that frequently accompany general malaise. An individual's environment and state of physical and/or psychological well-being contribute to these responses. Similarly, "I really want to get this supply room organized today" and "I just don't feel like doing anything today" are expressions of emotional responses that are related to motivation. The person who has these feelings cannot always articulate what gives rise to the them, but that does not mean that they do not exist nor that they are not salient factors in job performance.

Because motivation is an emotional response, it is not always perceived through rational eyes, nor responsive to rational interventions. Some people can mask their emotions so that others cannot determine what they are feeling. They can also usually control behavior that tends to arise from their emotional responses. But they cannot control their emotions, even when they are uncomfortable with them. These sentiments may sound familiar.

"I don't know why I got so mad about the schedule. It's not all that important."

"I know that this picnic is important to the residents, and it's not that much work. But I'm not in the mood, and I don't want to go."

These are feelings that individuals obviously regret and that they believe to be irrational, but that they are, nonetheless, powerless to change. Because employees cannot control their emotions at will, motivating them is never a simple matter of explaining to them why they should feel motivated.

Diagnosing Motivational Problems

Contrary to what many managers believe, motivational problems are difficult to diagnose. The first assumption which can lead to diagnostic errors is that all motivational problems result from lack of motivation. Paradoxically, lack of motivation is only one type of motivational problem. Motivation is dynamic. Therefore, at times, employees may feel highly motivated, and, at other times, they may feel little, if any, motivation. Therefore, what appears to be lack of motivation may actually be *inconsistent* motivation. Like any medical problem that is intermittent, this type of motivational problem is difficult to diagnose and treat. Another type of motivational problem occurs when an employee is highly motivated but what the employee is motivated to do is incongruent with the organization's and the manager's goals. For example, a staff pharmacist may be highly motivated to do patient education, but the organization's primary goal may be for the pharmacist to dispense, an activity in which the pharmacist may have only a secondary interest. This is motivational incongruity, not lack of motivation.

Because motivation is a feeling, it cannot be directly sensed through observation. Many diagnostic errors occur through assuming that actions directly result from specific underlying emotions or motives. For example, what is the motive behind a secretary's giving her boss a bottle of cologne as a holiday gift? Undoubtedly, some people would immediately assume that her motive is to ingratiate herself with the boss (i.e., the gift is given as a way of kissing up to him). Others would assume that the motive is to simply be nice at the holidays. But imagine the other possibilities. She may have a personal interest in the boss. She may feel socially obligated to get him something because he got her something for Secretary's Day. She may have an aversion to his current cologne and is using this opportunity to get him to change to something that she can tolerate. It is obvious that any number of motives may underlie the action.

One of the best ways to determine how someone feels is to ask him. However, even between individuals whose relationship is built on trust, respect, and even love, there is the possibility that incomplete and/or false disclosure could occur in response to the question. (The hackneyed cartoon/sitcom dilemma in which a husband is asked for his opinion about his wife's outrageous new hairstyle or outfit is a good example. He either lies or pays the consequences.) Manager-subordinate relationships are seldom characterized by the same high levels of mutual trust and respect as our personal relationships. How many employees would admit that they are not motivated to do the work the manager wants them to do? Since unmotivated employees are undesirable employees, they would justifiably lie about their lack of motivation for fear of losing their jobs. Therefore, asking directly about motivation is usually not a reliable way of assessing motivational levels.

If observation and questioning are out, then what diagnostic techniques can be used? In an admittedly colossal example of doublespeak, the answer is *observation* and *communication*. The two activities that separately are inadequate must be melded into a diagnostic evaluation process.

Although motivation cannot be observed, behavior can be. However, at best, behavior is a surrogate measure of motivation. The behavior of poorly motivated employees includes the following:

1. *Avoidance behavior.* Employees who are absent or late avoid performing tasks they do not want to do. Loafing while on duty is another form of task avoidance. Quitting is the most extreme form of avoidance behavior.

2. *Substitution behavior.* Employees keep busy with activities that they prefer to do. This kind of behavior is common when there is a mismatch between organizational goals and personal goals. Much of the substitute behavior may result from an employee's prolonging the performance of work that he likes to do.

3. *Affective response.* Motivated employees tend to greet tasks with enthusiasm. Conversely, it may be expected that lack of enthusiasm could be an indication of lack of motivation.

Managers must be careful when interpreting (un)enthusiastic responses. Verbal expressions of enthusiasm cannot always be trusted. There is always the possibility that employees will attempt to ingratiate themselves with managers by feigning enthusiasm and, thereby, creating the illusion of motivation. Managers are vulnerable to being duped by this kind of behavior because they are gratified by warm, receptive responses to their ideas.

What managers perceive as a lack of enthusiasm may not actually be lack of enthusiasm. Some people do not overtly express their feelings and emotional responses. Managers may also have a tendency to evaluate responses according to the way they themselves would react. For example, managers are sometimes disappointed in employees' responses to pay raises. A manager may think, "Gee, if I had gotten a raise like that, I would have been jumping for joy. She couldn't even come up with a 'Thank you'." The employee may be just as happy as the manager would have been but is more reserved in expressing her emotions.

Observation of these behaviors alone is insufficient to diagnose a motivational problem. The diagnosis can be narrowed only through communication. Avoidance behaviors may have many causes other than a lack of motivation. Employees who frequently are late or absent may have transportation difficulties. They may have child care arrangements that frequently fail them. They may suffer from chronic physical problems like migraine headaches or recurrent urinary tract infections. Highly motivated employees may work harder than other employees to overcome these problems, but that does not mean they always succeed. Before managers conclude that avoidance behavior is the result of low motivation, they must know employees well enough to rule out other causes.

What the manager perceives as substitution behavior may be perceived by the employee as a legitimate use of time. For example, consider a head nurse who has nagged a unit secretary for two weeks to obtain a rack for the record-keeping forms used on the unit and to arrange the forms in it. The head nurse observes that the secretary takes significantly longer to process physicians' orders than other secretaries. She suspects that the secretary is drawing out her other responsibilities so that she will not have to organize all the forms. Before she diagnoses this as a motivational problem, she needs to determine why the secretary spends so much time with order processing and why she has not yet organized the forms. The secretary may spend more time with order processing because she is unsure of herself or because she does all of her work more slowly than her colleagues. Or maybe she pays more attention to detail than the other secretaries. She may actually think that organizing the forms is just as important as the head nurse does and may be motivated to get the job done. However, she perceives that she has too little time to get the job done in light of her other responsibilities. The only way for the head nurse to determine if there is a mismatch between her goals and the secretary's goals is to spend time getting to know the secretary and how the secretary feels about her work.

Motivation and Job Satisfaction

Because it is a feeling about work, motivation is often treated as synonymous with job satisfaction. **Job satisfaction** is the degree to which people have positive feelings about their work. Note that there is nothing in this definition that indicates a desire to do work and to do it well. Imagine the rather unlikely case of a physical therapy assistant working in a nursing facility at a salary of $60,000 per year. This salary is guaranteed irrespective of how many residents actually receive therapy. The employee has flexible hours and works with minimal supervision. She may leave anytime there are no residents waiting for therapy. If asked whether she likes her job, it would not be surprising to hear a resounding "yes!" from this employee. However, is she motivated? Some individuals undoubtedly would be. However, others might be motivated to take the money with as little work as possible. For example, they may only show up on Sunday afternoons (during heavy visiting hours) or during dinner periods when no residents are available for therapy. The assistants could then leave without doing anything. Each individual placed in this situation might experience a different level of motivation, but reported job satisfaction might be uniformly high.

While it may be intuitively comforting to believe that there is a causal relationship between job satisfaction and motivation (i.e., happy employees work hard, and unhappy employees loaf), there is little support for this conclusion. In the SouthSide Health Center case, it is evident that Anita is dissatisfied with her job, and on March 15 she was not motivated enough to do it. However, for months before that, she had been motivated enough to go in every day and to try to do a good job. What she will do on March 16, and thereafter, is unknown. Because she knows that her job is important, like many healthcare workers her sense of obligation may overcome her job dissatisfaction, and she will return to work. However, since each individual has a unique psychological composition, no one could predict her behavior with certainty.

Managers frequently ask themselves, "How can I motivate my employees?" A much more appropriate question to ask is, "How can I motivate each employee?" Each employee is an individual with a unique set of reasons for wanting to do something. Therefore, managers who try a one-size-fits-all motivational strategy will almost certainly fail to reach all employees in the group.

In fact, motivating employees may not even be an appropriate way of conceptualizing the manager's role in motivation. Individuals come to the workplace with an internalized set of motives. That is, they already come with a set of reasons for wanting to do a job. It is unrealistic to think that a manager who has little emotional involvement with employees can replace those pre-existing motives. Managers cannot change employees' desires; therefore, managers must choose employees whose motives are consistent with the goals of the organization. They must then establish a work environment in which employees can achieve their goals and the goals of the organization.

Motivational Factors

If managers are to be successful at developing strategies that appeal to employees' motives, it is important to first understand what those motives are. Because each individual operates from a different set of motives, it is inappropriate for managers to assume that their motives are the same as the motives of their employees. While there is no substitute for directly identifying the motives of each individual employee through observation and discussion, managers can learn much from what researchers have discovered about what motives commonly give rise to workplace behavior. Although no single definitive and all-inclusive explanation has come out of the more than 50 years of research into employee motivation, much has been learned about what kinds of things influence motivation. Several theories of motivation and theorists are frequently cited in the management literature. The most widely known and applied of these are reviewed below.

One of the most influential of the motivational theories was proposed by Abraham Maslow. He stated that five different needs stimulate human behavior.[1] These needs are:

1. *Physiological needs* (need for water, food, shelter);
2. *Safety needs* (need to assure that physiological needs will be fulfilled in the future);
3. *Social needs* (need for affection, social interaction, belonging, acceptance);

4. *Esteem needs* (need for self-respect and need to be respected by others); and

5. *Self-actualization needs* (need to reach one's full potential).

These needs are usually shown arranged in the order Maslow hypothesized that people seek to fulfill them (Figure 8.1). Thus, **Maslow's Hierarchy of Needs** is a taxonomy for classifying and organizing motives based on a sequence of need satisfaction. Maslow felt that as long as an individual believed that his existence was threatened, he would be motivated by factors that would meet his physiological needs. For example, he would be motivated to work for money to buy food. However, once physiological needs were satisfied, then sustenance factors such as food, water, clothing and shelter would no longer serve as motivators, and the unmet needs for safety and security would become motivators. After safety needs are satisfied, individuals attempt to satisfy love needs, and so on up the hierarchy.

As an introduction to motivation, Maslow's hierarchy of needs is extremely valuable. It reinforces the notion that each individual's behavior arises from

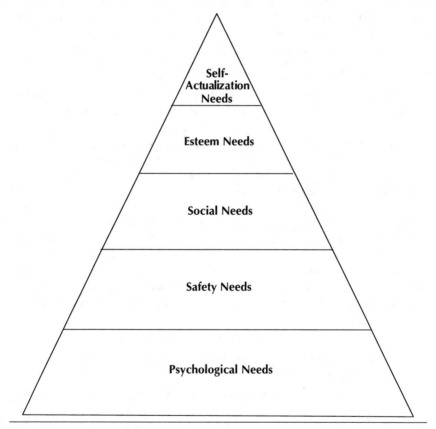

Figure 8.1   Maslow's hierarchy of needs.

different motives. It also suggests that an individual's motives may vary over time. However, the practical application of this theory is limited. Research has not consistently supported the order of the needs in the hierarchy, nor an individual's progression through the needs levels.[2] Most clinicians can relate to the fluidity of motives, even in the course of a single day. When the alarm goes off in the morning, the primary motives to get up and go to work may be remuneration and keeping a job. In the mid-morning, the primary motives may be esteem needs that arise from knowing that one is performing an important service for others. In the mid-afternoon, the primary motive may be acceptance by a group of colleagues working as part of a clinical team.

Since Maslow's theory was published, many researchers have tried to clarify and describe common work-related motives. McClelland found that three motives appear to be particularly important in the work environment: need for affiliation (n-Aff), need for achievement (n-Ach), and need for power (n-Pow).[3]

N-Aff is an individual's need to form positive relationships in the workplace. To people with a high n-Aff, acceptance and belonging are very important. These people may have a tendency to focus their efforts more on establishing and maintaining interpersonal relationships than on accomplishing tasks.

N-Ach is an individual's need to perform efficiently and/or effectively. Unlike people with high n-Aff, high n-Ach individuals tend to focus more on tasks than on relationships. High n-Ach individuals prefer tasks that are neither too easy, nor too difficult. They also like to receive timely, specific feedback about their performance. Feedback helps them to measure their performance. Because performance is important to them, they may prefer to work alone so that they have more direct control over performance.

N-Pow is the desire to control others. High n-Pow individuals focus on the resources (human, financial, and informational) that are required to accomplish a goal. They are more interested in the process of goal achievement than in achievement itself. Although managers must maintain strong relationships with others and must be goal oriented, it is n-Pow that motivates successful managers.[4]

McClelland's Theory of Achievement Motivation is similar to Maslow's hierarchy of needs in that it reaffirms that different individuals have different needs. However, in McClelland's model, these needs are not mutually exclusive. Most individuals probably have at least some of all three. The importance of McClelland's theory is that it is predictive. If individuals can be classified as having a high n-Aff, then situations that offer significant opportunity for interpersonal interactions would probably appeal to them. These individuals would probably do particularly well in situations in which their job performance is based on their ability to interact with others. Interaction-rich situations would probably meet their n-Aff. Client relations associates and ombudsmen positions might appeal to high n-Aff persons. High n-Ach people would tend to do well in project work where they tend to work independently. Some laboratory positions might appeal to these individuals. Home health work may offer a degree of independence and feedback that would appeal to the motives of high n-Ach individuals. As mentioned above, high n-Pow individuals may be motivated by opportunities in management. However, team leaders whose primary responsibility is facilitation may be more successful and motivated if they have a high n-Aff rather than a high n-Pow. Thus, McClelland's theory has practical applications in matching individuals with positions that appeal to their motives.

Herzberg's Dual Factor Theory of Motivation[5] offers yet another way of classifying motivational factors. Herzberg's work led him to the conclusion that there are two distinct kinds of motivational factors—those that cause workers to be satisfied with their jobs and those that cause workers to be dissatisfied. (Notice that in Herzberg's early work, he made the assumption that job satisfaction and motivation were virtually synonymous.) The source of one set of factors is the environment in which the job is performed. These factors include compensation, working conditions, relationships with co-workers, security, status, and policies and their implementation. These factors have subsequently been called **hygiene factors** and **context factors**. The source of the other group of factors is the work itself, and these are inseparable from the job irrespective of where it is performed. These factors include achievement, responsibility, growth, and advancement. These factors are known as **motivators** or **content factors**. Herzberg posited that the demarcation between these two sets of factors was clear. If hygiene factors are absent, employees are dissatisfied. However, increasing these factors *ad infinitum* does not motivate employees. The motivators, however, stimulate people to perform.

Since Herzberg's original work was published, subsequent research has failed to consistently confirm his hypotheses.[6–8] It is possible that the lack of confirmation is as much due to differences in research methodology as to deficiencies in his model. Any emotional response is influenced by so many internal factors that research results which focus only on external factors may not be reproducible in different groups. Even transitory changes in mood influence the level of reported job satisfaction.[9] Nevertheless, Herzberg's contribution to understanding motivation is twofold. First, it helped to distinguish job satisfaction from motivation. Second, it has caused managers to reconsider the potential of specific work environments and job design modifications to bring about a change in employee motivation.

Motivation and Behavior Modification

The surest way to get employees to do what managers want them to do is to administer a good swift kick in the pants (KITA). The KITA may result in the behavior the manager wants, but it does not motivate the employee. In this dyad, the person who is motivated by the task at hand is the manager. The employee is only motivated to escape the KITA and to avoid it in the future.[10] While there is no doubt that the KITA is effective at modifying behavior, it does not motivate.

As such, it has to be reapplied each time the manager wants something done because the employee has no innate desire to do the work.

The elaborate system of punishment and rewards established by some employers in the name of motivation fails to change the level of employee motivation for this same reason. Imagine that Tom K. drives to work every morning on Highway N where the speed limit is 45 mph. One morning, he gets a traffic ticket when a patrolman lying in wait at the side of the road clocks his speed at 53 mph. Is Tom likely to be motivated as a result of the ticket? Perhaps. But if he is like most people, he will not be motivated to drive more slowly. He will be motivated not to get caught again. He may be motivated to look more carefully for predatory patrolmen hiding at the side of the road, or he may be motivated to find a less controlled route. He may even drive more slowly when he believes he is in danger of getting another ticket. However, he has no desire to drive more slowly (i.e., he is not *motivated* to drive more slowly). Control systems that punish employees for poor performance may have the same result. Rather than motivating employees to improve performance, they may motivate employees to find ways to beat the control system.

The same kind of relationship exists between rewards and motivation. Performance bonuses are a good example of a commonly used motivational tool. Employees who reach certain performance standards receive an award such as an additional cash payment or paid time off. These awards can be quite effective at modifying behavior when the awards are attractive and employees believe that they are achievable. However, the motivation that is generated with such a reward program is motivation to get the award, not motivation to do a job. Once again, it is the manager who wants to get the job done, not the employee. As long as the award program is in place and the awards continue to be attractive, the desired behavior may be sustained. However, as soon as the awards are removed, performance returns to pre-award program levels. Rewards and punishments do not change the way people feel about their work. They may change the way employees behave, but they do not change what employees desire to accomplish.

If the manager cannot motivate employees with rewards and punishments, what tools are left? Herzberg suggests that the only way to motivate is to manipulate the motivators (content factors) so that jobs take on characteristics which employees find appealing. This may require that jobs be restructured. Restructuring a job so that it provides opportunity for an employee's psychological growth is job enrichment. In practice, jobs are sometimes restructured so that each employee does more tasks. If the additional tasks do not provide for growth or do not meet other psychological needs, then job enlargement rather than job enrichment has been accomplished (see Chapter 4).[11]

The kinds of job-specific changes that result in motivation include removing controls while retaining accountability for task accomplishment; making individuals responsible for entire units of work rather than oversimplified, disconnected pieces of a process; giving additional decision-making authority; and adding new and challenging tasks that require new skill mastery. These job modifications appeal to motives of responsibility, personal achievement, growth, and learning.[12] Among the current management fads is **employee empowerment** (i.e., giving all employees more decision-making power). (Hopefully, this trend is a result of the recognition that employees are more motivated when they have more responsibility for their own work as opposed to being the consequence of downsizing to the point where there are too few middle managers to make the necessary decisions.) One of the difficulties of empowering employees has been that some managers are reluctant to trust significant decisions to front-line employees. For example, a cashier might be empowered to make a decision about when to empty the office trash but may not be empowered to adjust a patient's bill. Empowered employees have important decision-making authority and responsibility. As long as employees share the same basic values as managers and have appropriate training, there is no reason for their decision making to be significantly different from that of their managers. This phenomenon has been demonstrated in practice.[13]

It is important to remember that the most carefully planned and brilliantly conceived job enrichment program can be an abysmal failure. Neither the program itself nor the managers who implement it may be at fault. Intrinsically rewarding work cannot be created and handed out to employees. For employees to find any job intrinsically satisfying, they must find their own challenges, seek their own accomplishment, and sense their own achievement.[14] The objective of the manager is to create the job and environment that make it possible for the employee to do those things.

The Role of Employee Expectations

One of the difficulties of converting the theories of Maslow, McClelland, and Herzberg to a simple list of things that managers can do to appeal to the inherent motives of employees is that, in practice, it is not only employee motives that give rise to motivation. **Vroom's Expectancy Theory** describes how factors other than a match between motives and job characteristics can influence an employee's decision to put forth a given level of effort toward the completion of work.[15]

Expectancy theory is built on the assumption that people make an effort at work in order to receive some kind of reward or goal (outcome). In the workplace, effort and outcome are linked through performance (Figure 8.2). According to Vroom, the amount of effort that an individual decides to expend depends on the value (**valence**) of the desired outcome and the perceived likelihood that effort will result in the outcome. In other words, the individual determines whether the outcome is worth achieving and whether he is likely to achieve the outcome. It is

Figure 8.2   Key elements of expectancy theory.

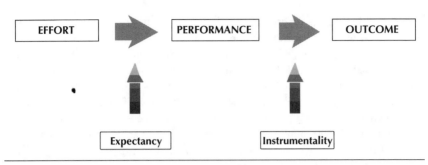

Figure 8.3   Key elements of expectancy theory and perceived linkages.

immediately apparent that Vroom's theory reinforces the notion that motivation is an individual phenomenon. For one person, an outcome that may have a high valence is money. For another individual, a high valence outcome may be respect. According to Vroom, if the outcomes of the process are not important to the individual, then there is no motivation. The notion that different rewards are important to different people is the source of the cafeteria-style benefit programs in which employees are allowed to choose their benefits within certain cost parameters. Whereas for one employee health benefits may be an important benefit, to another employee, health benefits may be less important than tuition reimbursement. To a third employee a dental plan may be more important than either health benefits or tuition reimbursement.

Because effort and outcome are connected through performance, there are actually two linkages that must be intact for an employee to perceive a causal relationship between effort and outcome. The first link is between *effort* and *performance*. Vroom called this link **expectancy**. The second link connects *performance* and *outcome*. Vroom called this link **instrumentality** (Figure 8.3). For a valued outcome to cause an employee to make an effort, the employee must perceive that the effort will lead to the desired level of performance (expectancy) and that performance will result in receipt of the valued outcome.

There are three ways that the expectancy link can be broken. First, the employee may not have the skills to achieve a level of performance that would result in the desired outcomes. (In school, the "E" for effort is something quite apart from the "A" for outstanding performance.) It does not take long for an inadequately skilled employee to recognize that no matter how hard he tries, he will not succeed. When that realization occurs, he quits trying.

Second, the performance appraisal system may not accurately recognize behavior as performance. Performance appraisals are mechanisms for interpreting employee behavior as it relates to performance criteria. They officially translate employee behavior into performance. Performance appraisal systems that provide faulty translations break the expectancy linkage. Take, for example, an emergency medical technician who possesses and applies a high level of technical skill, who is dependable, and who exercises good judgment. If this employee's performance is evaluated with a performance appraisal form that focuses only on subjective issues like friendliness and cooperation, important and positive aspects of his behavior will be overlooked. In addition, the employee will have only partial control over his performance because the evaluator's perception of the employee's attitudes and expressiveness would be more related to performance than technical work-related behavior (i.e., the evaluator's performance appraisal behavior contributes more to determining the employee's performance than his own work-related behavior). Performance appraisals that fail to focus specifically on job content are likely to be perceived as threats to the link between effort and performance. Finally, the employee may have the skills to do the job and may make an extraordinary effort to perform but still fail to succeed because he applies his skills and efforts in the wrong way. Take the cardiac surgeon who does a masterful job of replacing a mitral valve—on the wrong patient. Actual behavior must be aligned with behavioral objectives imposed by the organization to be interpreted as acceptable performance.

Instrumentality is the perceived relationship between performance and outcome. This link can be broken when the employee cannot see that performance is the proximal cause of receiving rewards. One reward that is commonly used as a motivator is a pay raise. However, raises frequently fail to motivate in spite of the fact that they have high valence for many employees. Forget, for the moment, that pay is a hygiene factor that may not be a very good motivator under the best of circumstances. Pay raises are rarely tied directly to performance. It is customary to award a raise in conjunction with a performance appraisal. However, if a raise is only a cost of living increase, then it is definitely not linked to performance in the mind of the employee. It is more linked to a simple fact of life—inflation. Even when the pay raise has a merit component, the causal relationship between the raise and performance is diluted by any cost-of-living increase that is concurrently awarded. If pay were a motivator for an employee, why would he be motivated to make an effort when the pay increase would be the same, or nearly the same, with or without his effort?

Another break in this link can occur due to inconsistent reward patterns. Assume that Jane has an anniversary date in January. She gets a raise on that date, and in her organization, there is only one performance evaluation and pay increase per year on the anniversary date. Assuming that a pay increase serves as a motivator for Jane, what happens if each year the amount of a pay increase varies with the budget for labor expense? Or, what if the actual amount of the pay increase is more dependent on profit margins earned in December than it is on Jane's performance? Obviously, Jane will see very little link between her performance and her pay raise. Her perception reflects reality because, in this example, there is very little correlation between performance and pay raises. The consequence is that, for her, pay increases lose their motivational potential.

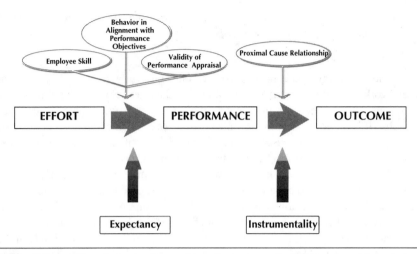

Figure 8.4   Key elements of expectancy theory, perceived linkages, and intervening variables.

The example of Jane brings up another way in which instrumentality may be weakened. Jane's raise is in January. According to the policy of her organization, she has no hope of another increase until the next January. What happens to Jane's motivation in February? It would not be surprising to see it go down, in spite of the fact that she just got a raise. Why? Because the work that she does in February probably has little to do with the raise that she will get the next January. In work, just as in entertainment, people tend to remember the last thing they see. (Hence, the importance of a strong closing number at the end of a show.) Managers doing a performance appraisal in January are likely to remember December and January performance more vividly than last February's performance. Therefore, because performance appraisals and subsequent pay increases are infrequent, pay increases fail to motivate throughout the entire evaluation period. To strengthen the relationship between performance appraisal and outcomes, performance evaluation should be an ongoing process. With continuous evaluation, employees and managers alike are reminded that performance is always important, not just at or near a predetermined performance appraisal time. Ongoing performance appraisal also gives the manager the opportunity to link performance to a common motive— the need for recognition.[16] While some items, like pay increases, may not be possible to bestow frequently, recognition for performance can be given continuously.

The expectancy and instrumentality linkages in expectancy theory illustrate how difficult it is in practice to motivate employees through a reward system. Figure 8.4 illustrates how these linkages can become blurred by intervening factors. The linkages between effort and the desired outcome are tenuous in many organizations. Unless managers clarify these relationships for employees and take actions that communicate the strength of the relationships, rewards will be of limited value in motivating employees.

Equity and Motivation

One of the ways that employees determine whether the rewards they get from their work are appropriate is to compare what they get to what others in similar positions get (i.e., they tend to compare their outcomes to the outcomes of other people). It is obvious that some people bring more skill, knowledge, and effort to a position. Therefore, there is a tendency to compare outcomes relative to inputs. For example, two physical therapists with approximately the same positions, similar skill sets, and similar time and effort commitments would probably suspect that they would have similar outcomes. If the outcomes vary significantly, then the therapist with lower outcomes (like paid time off and/or salary) would probably feel that she is being treated unfairly. If the physical therapist were to compare herself to a therapist in a supervisory position who had an advanced degree and worked longer hours, she would probably expect that her outcomes would be lower and would be unlikely to feel that she was being treated unfairly in such a situation.

According to **equity theory**, each individual mentally calculates a ratio of outcomes to inputs for himself (O_i/I_i) and a ratio of outcomes to inputs for some other individual, known as a referent (O_r/I_r), and then acts in a way that reduces the discrepancy between the two.[17] For example, if two pharmacy technicians do essentially the same job and have similar levels of performance, but technician A makes approximately $1.00 per hour more than technician B and technician B finds out about it, then technician B may try to do less work (i.e., decrease his inputs) to bring his outcome-to-input ratio in line with that of technician A. Alternatively, in the name of fairness, he could demand a $1.00 per hour raise. The apparent inequity in pay differential acts as a demotivator. It is the realization that employees may perceive inequities in pay structures that causes some managers to caution their employees not to share wage and salary information with their colleagues. (Perhaps it would be wiser to eradicate the inequities than to try to enforce a gag rule?) The lesson to be learned from equity theory is that not only is the valence of a reward important to employees, but so too is the amount of the outcome relative to the outcomes of co-workers.

Lessons to be Learned from Motivational Theories

Unfortunately, the motivational theories reviewed in this chapter do not converge into a neat list of activities that managers can pursue to motivate their employees. However, they do provide considerable insights into motivation that managers can apply on a daily basis as they work with employees as individuals and in groups.

1. *Each employee has different motives.* There is no reason to believe that each employee is going to react like any other employee to the

same set of motivational factors. Legal constraints, ethical guidelines that promote justice and fairness, and the need for organizational efficiency all promote the development of inflexible, uniform reward systems and working conditions. While these systems meet some organizational goals, they do not foster an environment where many different individuals with different motives can find fulfillment.

2. *Motivation is dynamic.* People do not sustain emotions consistently. How long can any one individual stay fighting mad without having to take a break to go on to something else, even temporarily? How long can anyone be passionately in love without other emotions intruding on the feeling? Motivation is no different. Different motives take precedence at different times. This characteristic makes it extremely difficult for managers to predict what motives can be appealed to and when.

3. *Motivation has more to do with the job itself than with the organization in which it is performed.* This characteristic also complicates managers' jobs. Managers have more control over the environment in which the job is performed than they do over the job content itself.

4. *Employee perceptions are an integral part of motivation.* It is pure folly to attempt to dissociate motivation from employee perceptions. It borders on arrogance for managers to assume that their view of workplace reality is the only reality and that what motivates them also motivates their employees.

5. *Seemingly routine policies and their implementation may influence motivation.* Pay ladders, seniority systems for promotion, seniority-based benefits, flex-time, telecommuting, flexible benefit plans, and other policies may significantly affect the way employees feel about the organization, especially when they compare the benefits they receive under these terms of employment with the benefits received by their colleagues. Employees who sense inequity in their treatment may behave so as to alleviate the inequity. The result could be avoidance behavior such as loafing or absenteeism.

Motivation in Healthcare

Much of the managerial function in healthcare institutions involves the management of professional employees (i.e., employees who, by virtue of expertise in their field, perform much of their work with relatively little supervisory oversight). It has been widely suggested that in managing professional employees, managers structure jobs so as to appeal to employees' pre-existing internal motivation to work independently. This means that, as far as possible, the manager needs to delegate to the employee the authority to make decisions relevant to his own work.

In addition, the manager should recognize that professional employees derive satisfaction from the successful application and augmentation of their skills. In fact, one study of a wide variety of clinical and administrative personnel found that "the most significant determinant of overall job satisfaction appears to be the extent to which the job provides for the individual's growth and self- actualization."[18] This finding was confirmed by a study of occupational therapists, which indicated that learning new skills and receiving recognition when a good job was done contributed to job satisfaction.[19]

The same study indicated that therapists' perceptions that their skills are inadequate for successful job performance contribute to job dissatisfaction. Another study indicated that perceived autonomy and self-esteem were associated with job satisfaction among occupational therapists.[20] In addition, as occupational therapists remain in a position, aspects of the job that they find most rewarding change. Occupational therapists with up to three years' experience found direct patient care to be the most rewarding aspect of their jobs. As therapists gain experience, program development and managerial/supervisory aspects of the job become more rewarding.[21] The above findings and the results of similar research suggest that managers can appeal to the motives of professionals by making ongoing learning opportunities available, providing opportunities to achieve, recognizing achievement, and making sure that duties that are assigned to professionals actually require professional-level skills.[22]

In healthcare institutions, where quality and cost-cutting reign, there is a tendency for control of employee activity to be tight. Thus, healthcare managers are caught in the middle of a dialectic tug-of-war between control and self-direction. In the current environment, it is difficult to find areas in which managers feel comfortable delegating to employees expanded control over their own work. However, creative managers can do so. One interesting example of successful delegation of authority and control comes from Children's Hospital Medical Center in Cincinnati, where a self-staffing system in a nursing unit resulted in increased autonomy, nurse satisfaction, and quality of care.[23]

One of the difficulties within healthcare organizations has been a mismatch between professionals motivated by achievement and/or advancement and organizations that minimize the number of positions in the managerial hierarchy. Even large clinical support departments of large hospitals frequently have only two or three levels (supervisor, assistant director, and director) of management. For example, lack of advancement potential has been shown to be one of the characteristics that leads to dissatisfaction among hospital pharmacists.[24] Lack of advancement opportunities has led to the development of clinical (or career) ladders that offer advancement opportunities outside the managerial hierarchy.[25] Formalizing growth opportunities into levels is also a way of providing recognition for achievement.

Although the concept of career ladders is appealing, in practice, they have met with mixed success. Among hospital nurses, low rates of participation in clinical ladder programs have been reported. Among the possible reasons for low participation is that opportunities for clinical advancement appeal to some but not to all nurses. Also, taken as a whole, nurses seem to be ambivalent about the ability of existing clinical ladder programs to meaningfully enrich their jobs.[26] Many clinical ladders fail to appeal to intrinsic motives such as skill enhancement and self-actualization because advancement up the ladder leaves nurses with the same functions and no increases in responsibility or accountability.[27] Institution of the clinical ladder concept requires that care be taken to keep the emphasis of the program on excellence in patient care.[28] Otherwise, clinical ladder grades can become nothing more than shallow substitutes for scarce managerial promotions.

Although professional employees are fundamental to the process of providing healthcare, there are many other employees as well. Even though they may not have the same level of clinical or managerial expertise as professional employees, technical support employees may be motivated by the same factors as their professional colleagues.

The motivation of nursing assistants in long-term care facilities has been the subject of considerable research because there is a very high rate of turnover (40%–75% annually)[29] among this group of employees. This level of turnover is a managerial problem because it means that considerable resources have to be spent to continually recruit, orient, and train new nursing assistants. However, administrators of nursing facilities are left wringing their hands about how to intervene because there is not much that can be done about the content of the nursing assistant's job. The nature of the job requires that assistants provide personal care for all facility residents. Because some residents suffer from dementia, they can be very difficult to care for. Some may even be combative. Lack of bowel and/or bladder control is another common problem among residents. Thus, nursing assistants are constantly faced with the unappealing task of keeping residents clean. Administrators tend to accept a high turnover rate as the unavoidable consequence of the interaction of undesirable job content with low wages commanded by this group of low skill workers. Given the seemingly immutable nature of job content, administrators see no opportunity for intervention. They could not be more mistaken.

The typical response of nursing facility administrators to the turnover problem is an example of making inaccurate assumptions about motives. Contrary to conventional wisdom, the thing that nursing assistants find most attractive about their jobs is the same thing that their professional kin find attractive—the opportunity to do something for others.[30,31] It is the personal feelings they have for patients that is the most frequently reported job satisfaction factor. Although they hold low paying positions, financial considerations are not their primary reason for leaving a job.[32] Instead, management style, management policies, and policy implementation are more likely to cause nursing assistants to be dissatisfied.[33,34]

Because managers and professional staff members would not be motivated by the work that nursing assistants do, they tend to assume that nursing assistants cannot be motivated by that work either. Clearly the road to appealing to nursing assistants' motives is to more actively involve them in planning the care of residents and to recognize the importance of their contributions, rather than to treat their work as less important because it requires less technical skill.

Conclusion

In the opening case, Anita is suffering from a lack of motivation. Her avoidance behavior is highly unusual for her and should certainly be taken as a warning sign to her (and to her immediate superior) that something is seriously wrong. Her lack of motivation is caused by both job content and context factors. She still apparently cares about the job in spite of the fact that it is more difficult than she had anticipated. She knows that her work is important, and it is that sense of importance that has motivated her in the past. There are any number of potential interventions that could be applied here. Her job could be restructured to relieve some of the pressure. The physical plant could be made more secure for her and for other employees. She might try to restructure her time so that she spends some time with the clients of the clinic. Managers sometimes become removed from the action on the front lines and lose touch with the significance of the tasks that they administratively support.

Anita also needs to reevaluate her assumptions about employee turnover. For example, she has made the assumption that the APN is leaving for a higher salary. This may not be true. Because the employee clearly and specifically stated how his expectations have not been met, there is every reason to believe that money is not at the heart of the motivational problem. If Anita had a better feel for the motives of her employees and intervened in the work situation to try to assure that employee needs were addressed, she might have fewer problems with turnover. That alone would relieve some of the stress she is feeling.

Motivation is a feeling that can change with the slightest change in a job, the work environment, or even the mood of the employee. In the best of all worlds, Anita will enjoy a much needed day off and come back to work with a renewed sense of purpose.

Endnotes

1. Abraham Maslow, "A Theory of Human Motivation," *Psychological Review 50* (1943): 370–396.
2. Donald D. White and David A. Bednar, *Organizational Behavior: Understanding and Managing People at Work*, 2nd ed. (Boston: Allyn and Bacon, 1991).
3. David C. McClelland, *The Achieving Society* (New York: Van Nostrand, 1961).
4. David C. McClelland and David H. Burnham, "Power Is the Great Motivator," *Harvard Business Review 73* (January-February, 1995): 126–139.
5. Frederick Herzberg, Bernard Mausner, and Barbara Bloch Snyderman, *The Motivation to Work* (New York: John Wiley, 1959).

6. Thomas D'Aunno and Myron D. Fottler, "Motivating People," in Stephen M. Shortell and Arnold D. Kaluzny, *Healthcare Management: Organization Design and Behavior*, 3rd ed. (Albany, NY: Delmar Publishers, Inc., 1994).

7. Robert J. House and Lawrence A. Wigdor, "Herzberg's Dual-factor Theory of Job Satisfaction and Motivation: A Review of the Evidence and a Criticism," *Personnel Psychology 20* (1967): 369–389.

8. Benedict Grigaliunas and Yoash Wiener, "Has the Research Challenge to Motivation-Hygiene Theory Been Conclusive?" *Human Relations 27* (1974): 839–871.

9. Jean M. Woodward and I-Chun Chen, "Effect of 'Mood That Day' on Pharmacists' Job and Career Satisfaction," *Psychological Reports 74* (1994): 393–394.

10. Frederick Herzberg, "One More Time: How Do You Motivate Employees?" *Harvard Business Review 65* (September/October 1987): 109–120.

11. Ibid.

12. Ibid.

13. Hal Leonard, "Quality Concepts for International Service Providers," presentation at the World Trade Center, St. Louis, (October 11, 1994).

14. Leonard Sayles, *Leadership: What Effective Managers Really Do...and How They Do It* (New York: McGraw-Hill, 1979).

15. Victor H. Vroom, *Work and Motivation* (New York: John Wiley, 1964).

16. Ruth Davidhizar, Joyce Newman Giger, and Victoria Poole, "Taking the Dread Out of Annual Performance Evaluations," *Healthcare Supervisor 13* (1995): 33–37.

17. White and Bednar, op. cit.

18. George Shouksmith, Karl Pajo, and Aksel Jepsen, "Construction of a Multidimensional Scale of Job Satisfaction," *Psychological Reports 67* (1990): 335–364.

19. Betty Risteen Hasselkus and Virginia Allen Dickie, "Doing Occupational Therapy: Dimensions of Satisfaction and Dissatisfaction," *American Journal of Occupational Therapy 48* (February 1994): 145–154.

20. Karen Jacobs, "Flow and the Occupational Therapy Practitioner," *American Journal of Occupational Therapy 48* (November/December 1994): 989–995.

21. Maureen Freda, "Retaining Occupational Therapists in Rehabilitation Settings: Influential Factors," *The American Journal of Occupational Therapy 46* (March 1992): 240–245.

22. Charles R. McConnell, "Supervising the Healthcare Professional," *Healthcare Supervisor 13* (1994): 1–11.

23. Jackie Hausfeld, Kathy Gibbons, Alisa Holtmeier, Maria Knight, Carla Schulte, Theresa Stadtmiller, and Kathie Yeary, "Self-staffing: Improving Care and Staff Satisfaction," *Nursing Management 25* (October 1994): 74+.

24. Larry D. Grieshaber, "An Evaluation of the Management of Pharmaceutical Services in Institutional Environments," doctoral dissertation, Purdue University, August 1977.

25. Janice L. Davis, "Clinical Ladders: A Plan that Works," *AORN Journal 49* (March 1989): 802–806.

26. S. Kay A. Thornhill, "Hospital Clinical Career Advancement Programs: Comparing Perceptions of Nurse Participants and Nonparticipants," *Healthcare Supervisor 13* (1994): 16–25.

27. Ann B. Hamric, Teresa R. Whitworth, and Anne Stier Greenfield, "Implementing a Clinically Focused Advancement System," *JONA 23* (September 1993): 20–28.

28. Maria J. Glenn and Janice Smith. "From Clinical Ladders to a Professional Recognition Program," *Nursing Management 26* (March 1995): 41–42.

29   Troy Gaddy and Gregory Bechtel, "Nonlicensed Employee Turnover in a Long-term Care Facility," *Healthcare Supervisor 13* (June 1995): 54–60.

30. Larry D. Grieshaber, Patricia Parker, and Judy Deering, "Job Satisfaction of Nursing Assistants in Long-term Care," *Healthcare Supervisor 13* (June 1995): 18–28.

31. Howard M. Waxman, Erwin A. Carner, and Gale Berkenstock, "Job Turnover and Job Satisfaction Among Nursing Home Aides," *The Gerontologist 24* (1984): 503–509.

32. Gaddy and Bechtel, op. cit.

33. Grieshaber et al., op. cit.

34. Waxman et al., op. cit.

9

Leadership:
Neuromuscular Disorders

In this chapter the reader will learn how:
◆ leadership deficiencies can be diagnosed
◆ leadership deficiencies are like neuromuscular disorders
◆ leadership traits can be recognized
◆ leadership styles vary
◆ leadership behavior patterns can be identified
◆ situational factors shape leadership behavior
◆ leaders accrue and use power
◆ transformational and transactional leadership differ.

The Firing of Bob Kline

Pattie H. (Director of Home Health Services): *"I don't know how I feel about it. I'm sorry for Mr. Kline, of course, but I think that it might be the best thing for Bracken Health System. He was a very nice man, and I liked the fact that he had an open door policy. But, he never came through the open door. I always had to go through it. And every time I did, I felt like I was going over my boss' head...but my boss wasn't doing his job, so I had to go to the top to get what my department needed. I just don't think Mr. Kline knew what was going on around here."*

Susan L. (Chief of Medical Staff): *"I really didn't know him very well. He was pretty easy going. All we ever talked about was the financial condition of the hospital. I guess he was good at watching* *the numbers, but, given his background, that was to be expected. I do know that every time I went up to the administrative office suite, everybody seemed to be running around like a chicken with its head cut off. I'm not sure what all those VPs were doing, but everybody seemed busy."*

Mack M. (Chief Operating Officer): *"Bob was a good finance man. I can't say he was my favorite person, though. I couldn't depend on him to make a decision. I felt that I spent most of my time covering my backside so that one of the VPs couldn't stab me in the back. A couple of them never miss the chance to make you look bad in front of the boss. Bob never gave me a hard time, but he didn't do much about them either."*

Michael V. (Chairman of the Board of Trustees): *"It was the hardest thing I have ever had to do. Bob had been here for 28 years. When the CEO job came up a few years ago, he was the natural choice. A loyal hospital employee and a nice guy that nobody ever had an unkind word for. He was a top notch CFO who knew where every penny went. Financially, this place was tight as a drum. Given the budget tightening going on everywhere, that was just the kind of man we needed at the helm.*

But after four years, it was obvious that Bob just couldn't take us where we needed to go. His people were always complaining about his lack of attention to detail and lack of insight into their functions. It became pretty obvious that the top management team was spending more time arguing with each other than getting anything done.

While all the other providers in this market were actively pursuing mergers, acquisition, and managed care opportunities, Bob just seemed to let us get left behind in the dust. He kept telling us how good our cost figures looked, but that doesn't matter much if you don't have revenue coming in. Stan Holmes, the vice president for Strategic Planning, found a couple of small healthcare companies for us to buy. Mack, the COO, set up some kind of practice management unit that he thinks will help us attract docs. Marty Sorens has been marketing the hell out of the hospital. But that isn't nearly enough to keep us up with the other systems. I just hope that we didn't wait too long to make a change."

Defining Leadership

What is leadership? What makes a leader? People recognize leaders and leadership when they see them. They also recognize situations in which leadership and leaders are absent. However, leadership is amorphous. Like water changes shape to fit its container, leadership changes to fit situational imperatives. Behavior that constitutes effective leadership in one situation may be monumentally unsuccessful in another. Imagine a drill sergeant's leadership applied in a preschool or in a think tank. Conversely, imagine a preschool teacher's leadership behavior applied in a juvenile detention facility. Likewise, the effective leader of the book club of Centerville, Kansas, may not be an effective leader of a band of guerrilla warriors in Peru, and vice versa.

Leadership is influencing others to take action. "Leaders inspire others to action; they create a sense of purpose and direction; and they personify the values of the organization. Leaders set the standards of performance for the organization as a whole as well as for the individual employees."[1] There are three defining characteristics of leadership. First, leadership is a process that hinges on the interaction between leaders and followers. Second, leadership is action-oriented. Third, leadership actions are goal-directed. Because leadership involves influencing others to take action, it is closely related to motivation. In fact, it is successfully appealing to individuals' motives that makes someone a successful leader.

When there is a leadership vacuum in an organization, the behavior of the organization resembles a neuromuscular disorder. Some organizations become paralyzed. They stay in one place without reacting to external stimuli. Like a neuromuscular disorder, the specific cause of organizational paralysis may not be easy to diagnose. A neuromuscular disorder results from a breakdown at some point in the long chain of events that occur between a stimulus and a muscular reaction. Identifying the origin of the neural conduction deficit is difficult. Similarly, the etiology of organizational paralysis may lie at any point between external stimuli and organizational reaction. In the opening case, Bracken Health System failed to respond to its changing environment.

A sensory deficit is one possible explanation for the lack of response. It is possible that neither Mr. Kline nor anyone he depended on in top management perceived the change. Given that changes in healthcare have been widely publicized, a cognitive deficit is a more likely explanation. Perhaps the change was perceived, but neither Mr. Kline nor his advisors knew how to react to it, or they decided not to act. Even when sensory and cognitive processes function appropriately, muscular responses may be impaired due to a neural or neuromuscular blockage. At Bracken, a plan of action may have been formulated but either not communicated at all or communicated in a way that failed to elicit an organizational response.

The Bracken case may be more accurately compared to a partial paralysis with episodes of spasticity. Some actions were taken in response to the changing environment, but they do not seem to be coordinated. Given the tension among the vice presidents, that is not surprising. If Mr. Kline provided direction, the direction either was unclear or was too weak to trigger a response. It is as though this organization did not have integrated brain function. To the external observer, there is no purposeful movement. The teams that worked on practice management, marketing, and acquisitions may have performed their work well, but there was no central stimulus to cause them to work together toward a common goal. Fortunately, in the world of management it is possible to perform a brain transplant. Bracken's board of trustees started the procedure by excising Mr. Kline. However, merely replacing him with a fully functional substitute will not quickly solve Bracken's leadership crisis. The new brain will be attached to an existing dysfunctional nervous system. Assuming that the new brain survives the organization's rejection of a foreign body, a new neural pathway will have to be established between the brain and the nervous system. Then, the brain will have to take control of that system. Rebuilding the neural network may be a very long process similar to stroke rehabilitation. It will certainly be months and maybe years before the organization, under the direction of a new CEO, will become an effective, coordinated corporate body.

It is obvious that the Bracken Health System needs an effective leader. Although most people recognize effective leaders and leadership in action, how will the board of trustees recognize leadership skills during the selection process? Even with internal candidates, it is unlikely that board members will have had the opportunity to observe closely enough to assess leadership skills or potential. Even after considerable exposure to Mr. Kline, they failed to detect his poor leadership skills. The board's first and vitally important step will be to identify the leadership skills that are required of the CEO. It can then devise a search strategy through which an assessment of each candidate's leadership skills can be made.

Leadership is important throughout the entire organization, not only at the top. Irrespective of organizational level, each manager has a role in influencing those at lower levels to action. Effective organizations are thoroughly infused with leadership, not merely endowed with it at the top. Because leadership is a fundamental component of management, it is crucial that managers at all levels understand what it is and develop self-awareness of their own leadership skills. Careers in management seem to develop and grow along with an individual's ability to influence others.

There are a number of ways to analyze and explain effective leadership. Each of these perspectives contributes to understanding this complex process. However, as the following discussion makes clear, no single explanation of leadership definitively points the way to becoming a successful leader.

Great Man Approach

Like so many members of the animal kingdom, humans have a great capacity for learning through imitation. Because people recognize leaders when they see them, it is not difficult to figure out who to imitate. Martin Luther King, Joan of Arc, Abraham Lincoln, Genghis Khan, and Mahatma Gandhi are a few of the names that are almost synonymous with leadership. Each one of these leaders created a special bond with a group of individuals who took up the cause of the leader. By following each of these leaders, individuals put their livelihoods, safety, and lives at risk. How did these leaders forge such a bond? What did they do that can be imitated?

All of these leaders shared three qualities essential to effective leadership: strong belief in people, pursuit of excellence, and bias for action.[2] A common theme that recurs in the communications of these leaders to their followers is the leaders' belief in their ability to overcome, to rise above their oppressors, to defeat their enemies, and to achieve their objectives. Excellence is also a common theme, although its definition varies from military triumph, to spiritual self-actualization, to creating just societies. All great leaders call their followers to action. While Genghis Khan and Joan of Arc literally led their troops into battle, Mahatma Gandhi led his followers into peaceful resistance. Both extremes are action, and both kinds of action resulted in success.

None of these leaders was born to a leadership position. Everyone knows about Lincoln's log cabin origins. Joan of Arc was the daughter of peasants. Khan was the son of a petty chieftain. Gandhi was born to a family with a history of participation in local politics, but began his own career as a lawyer in South Africa before returning at 45 years of age to India, where he had no political base. Without a ready-made entree into leadership roles, how did these people achieve extraordinary leadership status? They probably started by forming bonds with individuals.

Before groups respond simultaneously to leaders, many one-on-one relationships must be established.[3] Leaders encourage individuals to bring problems to them by being responsive to requests for assistance. By making their skills available to others, they create situations in which individuals become indebted to them. They also appear to be in constant contact with potential followers. In the Bracken case, Mr. Kline's failure to leave his office was perceived as a sign of lack of leadership. By maintaining a high level of contact, leaders become a source of information and assistance to others. Over time, consensus develops about who has the highest status in the group. The leader becomes a locus of information and goodwill.

If and when a time comes for action, the leader works the group before attempting to direct the group as a whole. In working the group, the leader discusses possible courses of action with other influential group members and garners their support. In essence, working the group is a process of taking advantage of the goodwill and respect that has been generated over time. With the support of key players in the organization, the leader takes little risk that the group as a whole will ignore her direction. Many individuals in contemporary organizations become leaders as a result of building goodwill and judiciously calling on others for support.

Perhaps one of the most important lessons of the Great Man Approach is that unanimity among followers is not required for success. In fact, given the diversity of human response to different situations, unanimity of support for any leadership decision is probably a pipedream. Given that it is difficult to get 12 jurors to agree to a verdict, how can one expect a department of 30–40 employees, or a health system of several thousand employees to achieve unanimity? Consensus is the best that can be expected. **Consensus** is general agreement. Leadership direction and specific decisions are bound to displease some people in the organization. Therefore, leaders must "absorb the displeasure, and sometimes, severe hostility, of those who would have taken a different course."[4]

Another important lesson to be learned from the Great Man Approach is that becoming a leader takes time. The trust that is the foundation of the relationship between leaders and followers takes time to build. The chairman of the board of trustees of Bracken Health System is rightfully concerned that it may be too late to save the system. Not only has Bracken already missed vital opportunities, but it may take months to find the right new CEO and then months or even years for that person to generate the kind of trust that will make him an effective leader of the organization.

Finally, the Great Man Approach clearly distinguishes leadership from position. Mahatma Gandhi, Joan of Arc, and Martin Luther King held no political office. Abraham Lincoln and Genghis Khan did. However, Lincoln and Khan gained their offices by virtue of being leaders first. **Formal leaders** have their leadership positions legitimized by holding organizational positions that give them the authority to direct the actions of others. **Informal leaders** hold no such position but still influence others. Organizations can and do have both formal and informal leaders in work groups. It is not at all uncommon, for example, to have a situation in which a department head is the formal leader of a group, but a nonmanagerial employee actually has as much or even more influence over the behavior of the staff. Such situations often lead to conflicts. Formal and informal leaders either learn to coexist, or one of them has to leave the situation.

The Great Man Approach to learning leadership does not provide all the insight into leadership that managers need. Each of the leaders used here as examples led their constituencies to a single, overarching goal. Lincoln's objective was to preserve the Union, Gandhi's to liberate India from British rule, King's to assure African-Americans an equal position in American society, and Joan of Arc's to maintain French sovereignty. Goals in the workplace are usually multidimensional. They include both quantity and quality of production goals. Workplace goals also lack the visceral impact of the goals pursued by these leaders. This limits the applicability of appeals to motives made by these great leaders. Managers can almost never use patriotism and freedom to rally employee support.

It is also not always possible to imitate the leadership techniques of great leaders. Few people, if any, can duplicate the oratory skills of Martin Luther King, the iron fist in a kid glove demeanor of Abraham Lincoln, the mystic and pious purposefulness of Joan of Arc, or the hunger strikes of Mahatma Gandhi. Nor would these techniques be successful in most situations. Would King's thunderous oratory inspire a laboratory staff to perform better, or would it inspire laughter? Would the vice president of Patient Care Services' threat of a hunger strike inspire employees to decrease absenteeism, or would it stimulate more absenteeism just to see what would happen? Would a CEO's call for employees to donate back 5% of their pay to the hospital because God told him to ask for the money result in employee donations, or would it result in commitment to a psychiatric unit? Behavior that serves leaders well in history-altering situations may not be appropriate in contemporary organizations.

Trait Approach

Considerable research has been done to identify traits that characterize effective leaders within more common organizational contexts. Research on leaders in a variety of situations indicates that several traits tend to differentiate leaders from nonleaders. These traits seem to fall into five categories:

- *Ability*. Leaders are able to solve problems, make judgments, and work hard. They have technical and verbal skills. They are intelligent, original, alert, and energetic.

- *Achievement*. Leaders tend to accomplish more relative to nonleaders. They are aggressive, authoritative, enthusiastic, persistent, and tolerant of stress.

- *Responsibility*. Leaders are dependable and seize the initiative. They are also self-confident and dominant.

- *Participation*. Leaders are active, social, adaptable, cooperative, sensitive, talkative, and tactful.

- *Status*. Leaders are popular and have relatively higher socioeconomic status than nonleaders.[5,6]

Naturally, not every leader will have all these traits. Nor will an individual with many of these traits necessarily be an effective leader. One of the problems with trying to determine what traits characterize effective leaders is that each individual can be described by any number of words or phrases, many of which have different meanings to different people. A boss that Dick may describe as aggressive, Jane may describe as assertive, and Joe may describe as off-the-wall. Needless to say, researchers have had difficulty uniformly ascribing traits to specific leaders. Also, research has been inconclusive about which traits are most important and most closely related to successful leadership. Is it more important, for example, for a manager to focus on being participatory or on developing technical skills? Nor, as the sidebar "Caring and Courage in Leadership" indicates, have all important leadership traits been explored. Therefore, the traits of effective leaders that have been identified are descriptive but do not prescribe a specific course of action for managers who want to be effective leaders. As interesting as the delineation of leadership traits is, observation of specific behaviors of leaders in organizational settings has resulted in few applicable insights.

CARING AND COURAGE IN LEADERSHIP

There are a number of questions about leadership in healthcare which suggest that there is a rich research agenda to be pursued. Among the more interesting that come to mind are:

1. What kind of academic preparation results in the most effective leaders? (Or potentially more threatening to academicians, Does academic preparation make any difference in leadership effectiveness?)

2. How do (or should) leadership roles and behavior change with the level in the organizational hierarchy?

3. How does the age of followers and leaders influence leadership?

4. How should leadership potential be assessed?

5. What can an organization do to develop its pool of internal leadership talent?

6. How does the gender of leaders and followers influence leadership?

For the healthcare industry, in which the majority of the workforce is composed of women, the latter item is of particular interest and importance. There is considerable evidence which indicates that women have had more limited opportunities to assume managerial leadership positions and have been perceived to have less leadership potential than men. Women in leadership positions tend to incorporate characteristics and behavior patterns that are more masculine than feminine.[1] Discomfort is generated by the dissonance between what women in healthcare believe is organizationally demanded of them to be effective leaders and what they believe is just.[2] Women possess an ethic of care that would seem to make them suited for contemporary managerial roles which support the work and effort of subordinates.[3] Yet caring is a leadership trait that has not been extensively researched. The Great Man Theory of Leadership and trait theories which emphasize characteristics that are considered masculine add to the sense of dissonance. Therefore, it becomes attractive to leave these aging explanations of leadership effectiveness behind.

Before these theories fade entirely from the managerial lexicon, there is yet another trait that deserves consideration by researchers and practitioners alike. It is a trait that is not easily measured nor is it always visible. Therefore, it is seldom taken into account in research studies. That trait is *courage*. As these words are being penned, the United States is engaged in a serious internal debate over maintaining peacekeeping troops in Bosnia. At stake is the American leadership role in NATO. The United States must either demonstrate the courage to risk the lives of its soldiers to keep the peace, or it must relinquish its leadership position. The disconcerting part of courage, of course, is that it involves risk. The question of whether a leadership position is worth the risk of losing lives is a thorny one. (Note how little courage has to do with wisdom. There are plenty of cemetery residents who were simultaneously courageous and unwise.)

Leaders always put themselves, and, frequently, others, at risk. With the mantle of leadership, they assume the ultimate responsibility for the decisions they make and the direction in which they choose to lead their followers. Their personal risk includes the loss of their job, their career, their reputation, and, maybe, even their life. They also risk losing the affection of their followers. They face the risk of legal liability for their actions. And, perhaps most important of all, they face the risk of living with their conscience at the end of the day. Our society rests on the courage of our organizational leaders.

"Courage which is displayed in everyday business life is not as spectacular as that displayed upon historic battlefields, but it is just as essential to the prosperity of mankind.

"In the business world the common need is for courage to be honest, courage to be truthful, courage to respect the rights of others, courage to be fair and not to take selfish advantage of the confidence and trust placed in you."[4]

One of the difficulties of the Great Man Theory and trait theories of leadership is that so much of what can be learned from them boils down to *charisma*. Charisma is difficult to understand and even more difficult to learn. But the key to charismatic leadership may well be the demonstration of courage. Leaders who are willing to risk their own comfort, safety, and well-being for some *core value(s)* communicate unequivocally the importance of pursuing those values. All of the great leaders used as examples in this chapter displayed courage in the face of adversity and attracted a committed, courageous group of followers as a result.

In the modern organization, we seldom have to face baton-wielding, machine gun-toting, para-military types. But if we are going to lead effectively, we do have to put our careers on the line. In the face of economic peril and threats posed by office politics and fickle markets, effective managers demonstrate old-fashioned gumption.

Endnotes

1. Bernard M. Bass, *Stogdill's Handbook of Leadership: A Survey of Theory and Research* (NY: Free Press, 1981).
2. Carolyn Rozier, "Power & PTs," Pt. 2, *PT Magazine 2* (November 1994): 42–46.
3. Richard L. Daft, *Management,* 4th ed. (Fort Worth: The Dryden Press, 1997).
4. Personal comment, R.B. Stewart, Professor of Financial Management and Vice President and Treasurer, Purdue University (1925–1961).

Behavioral Approach

Leadership Styles. Leadership styles are patterns of behavior that have been identified relative to the way organizational leaders handle decision making. Three leadership styles have been extensively studied:

- **Authoritarian** leaders make decisions for their groups and communicate these decisions to the group members.

- **Democratic** leaders allow members to reach decisions about their own activities. However, they do take the initiative in providing groups with assistance in reaching their decisions. They may provide the group with information required for decision making and/ or facilitate group processing by arranging group meetings.

- **Laissez-faire** leaders are almost nonleaders in that they provide direction and support to the group only when requested by the group to do so.

The empirical evidence on job satisfaction and motivation indicates that most people prefer to work in situations in which they have more rather than fewer opportunities to participate in making decisions about their own work. As noted in Chapter 8, for healthcare professionals there is a significant correlation between job satisfaction and independent decision making. Therefore, it is logical to expect that healthcare professionals would be less likely to follow a leader who employed an authoritative leadership style. The weight of the evidence seems to indicate that of the three leadership styles, the authoritative style is the least effective.[7] There is little doubt, however, that at times the authoritative style is clearly the preferred style. In an emergency room, patient outcomes would certainly be compromised if clinical teams employed democratic decision-making processes or if physicians took a laissez-faire approach to leading clinical teams. This example suggests that these styles may not be mutually exclusive, even within a single manager. The head nurse of an emergency room may use an authoritative style in an emergency situation, a democratic style in establishing staffing schedules, and a laissez-faire style in arranging departmental social events. The fact that all three styles may be used by the same leader at different times suggests that situational factors are considered in choosing appropriate leadership behavior.

Maintenance and Task Behavior. These are behavioral patterns that are defined relative to the goals that leaders attempt to achieve. Maintenance and task behavior patterns have been identified by two independent research efforts undertaken to classify leadership behavior based on how that behavior was perceived by employees.

In studies conducted at the University of Michigan, leadership behavior was identified as being either employee-centered or production-centered. **Employee-centered** leaders are perceived by their followers as being concerned with meeting the emotional and/or social needs of the group members. **Production-centered** leaders are perceived as being concerned with getting the work done.[8] It is not too difficult to identify these two types of leaders in almost any organization. Some managers seem to spend almost all of their time talking with employees about almost anything the employees want to talk about. They seem to be just as comfortable talking about an employee's family or vacation as they are about what is going on at work. When they are not talking about personal issues, they are doing things that build strong interpersonal relationships like sending sympathy cards and planning office birthday parties. These managers are employee-centered. Production-centered managers spend time talking to employees, but their conversation is limited to work-related issues. The production-centered manager is always focused on getting tasks done.

Employee-centered and production-centered behaviors are not mutually exclusive. Rather than confining their behavior to either extreme, most managers favor one pattern over the other. Also, managers may shift from one orientation to the other. This kind of shift is often seen prior to a Joint Commission on Accreditation of Healthcare Organizations visit. An employee-centered leader may become more production-centered as the impending accrediting team visit nears. After the visit, the manager may revert to employee-centered behavior.

In studies conducted at Ohio State University, similar patterns of behavior were identified.[9] These studies indicated that most organizational leadership behaviors could be divided into two categories: initiating structure and consideration. **Initiating structure** refers to those leadership behaviors that result in defining and structuring jobs and channels of communications. These behaviors would include scheduling, evaluating performance, originating and implementing new ideas and methods of processing work, and assigning tasks. **Consideration** behaviors are related to maintaining and strengthening the group itself and responsiveness to interpersonal needs of group members. Although investigators at the University of Michigan and Ohio State University were working independently to identify leadership behaviors, their work resulted in similar conclusions. The employee-centered behaviors identified by the University of Michigan researchers are very similar to the consideration behaviors identified by Ohio State University researchers. Likewise, production-centered behaviors are similar to initiating structure behaviors. The primary difference between the studies is that Michigan researchers considered employee-centered and production-centered behaviors to be mutually exclusive (i.e., managers either exhibited one set of behaviors or the other). Consideration and initiating structures were viewed as coexisting in the same manager (i.e., a single manager could exhibit either low or high levels of behavior in each of these areas). In fact, there seems to be a weak, positive correlation between these two sets of behaviors. Managers who display a high level of consideration also have a tendency to initiate structure.[10]

The fact that consideration and structure initiation behaviors can be exhibited in varying proportions by different leaders is the underpinning of Blake and Mouton's Leadership Grid®. Rather than using leadership *behavior* as the basis for their model, however, they use leadership *attitudes*. The attitudes that they use, *concern for people* and *concern for production*, would likely manifest themselves in the behavioral patterns described above. The theoretically feasible combinations of these attitudes in a single leader resulted in Blake and Mouton's identification of a set of leadership styles quite different from the democratic, autocratic, and laissez-faire styles noted above.

1. *Impoverished Management* is characterized by low concern for people and low concern for production. The manager does little either to sustain the group or to set the stage for the accomplishment of work.

2. *Country Club Management* is characterized by high concern for people and low concern for production. The manager works to create a pleasant work environment but does little to get the work of the group accomplished.

3. *Authority-Compliance* is characterized by low concern for people and high concern for production. The manager focuses on increasing efficiency of operations and is concerned for people only to the extent that they are necessary factors of production.

4. *Team Management* is characterized by high concern for people and high concern for production. The manager supports and facilitates the work of individuals and groups toward organizational goals through developing trustful and respectful relationships.

5. *Middle-of-the-Road Management* is characterized by moderate concern for people and moderate concern for production. The manager seeks to balance organizational and human needs by making trade-offs between the two so that, in the end, organizational goals are adequately met, and employees are reasonably satisfied.[11]

The practical value of the behavioral approaches to leadership is that they strongly suggest that effective leaders must divide their attention and energies between the personal needs and concerns of their subordinates and the accomplishment of organizational goals. If they do neither, then for all intents and purposes, they cannot be effective leaders in spite of their organizational titles. If they focus exclusively on the task, they risk losing the goodwill and support of the people they need to get the task done. If they focus on employees to the exclusion of the task, they run the risk of having a happy workplace where no work actually gets done. Since accomplishing work is the raison d'être of most organizations, the happy workplace could disintegrate.

As important as it is for managers to realize that they must not be single-minded in their leadership behaviors, the behavioral approach to understanding leadership still disconnects leadership from the infinite variety of situations that call for leadership behavior. A set of behaviors that works in one situation may be hopelessly ineffective in another. Even the experts who support the notion of leadership styles recognize that leaders switch from one style to another, especially when one style fails to garner the results they want to achieve.[12] Effective leaders must adapt their style to the situation in which they find themselves. Managers who do not adapt their styles are at high risk of failure when they move from one type of social institution to another.[13]

Situational Factors that Shape Leadership

When people think of leadership, they think of individuals who have become strong leaders. However, that conceptualization excludes the other equally important half of the leadership process—followers. In order for leaders to be able to influence followers, followers have to be willing to be influenced. Not only that, but the environment in which the leader/follower relationship occurs must facilitate the relationship.[14] Managers need to be able to identify the factors in their environment and in their work groups that will help them to determine what leadership style or behavior is most appropriate at any one time.

The **Situational Leadership Theory**[15] provides a way of linking leadership behavior to different situations. It begins with the idea that leadership behaviors include both consideration and initiating structure elements. Like the Leadership Grid®, it assumes that leadership styles arise from the relative emphasis that leaders place on people and production. However, rather than assuming that the Team Management leadership style is, for example, always the preferred style, it suggests that the preferred style is the style that best fits the follower's readiness. Readiness refers both to the follower's ability and willingness to do the job. The following linkages are made:

1. When the employee is unwilling and unable to do the job, a high production, low consideration style is appropriate. This requires that managers give specific direction in performing work and closely monitor performance to make sure that the work is actually performed as intended. The key leadership behavior in this style is **telling**.

2. When the employee is unable but willing to perform the job, a high production, high consideration style is appropriate. Because the employee is unable to do the job, the manager makes decisions but explains those decisions to the employee to maintain the employee's goodwill and cooperation. The manager also provides considerable direction to the employee in work performance. The key leadership behavior in this style is **selling** management decisions to employees.

3. When the employee is able but unwilling to perform the job, a low production, high consideration style is appropriate. The leader shares ideas with the employee and facilitates decision making on the part of the employee in order to give the employee an ownership

stake in the work of the organization. The key leadership behavior in this style is **participating** with employees in making decisions and structuring tasks.

4. When the employee is able and willing to perform the job, a low production, low consideration style is appropriate. If the employee can function without the manager's intervention, the most effective leadership behavior is to get out of the employee's way and allow the employee to function as independently as possible. The key leadership behavior in this style is **delegating**.[16]

Situational leadership theory is very instructive. A manager could classify each subordinate into one of these categories and use the corresponding leadership style as a rule of thumb for influencing that employee. However, two caveats about the strict application of this theory are in order. First, using different leadership styles with different employees can be perceived as unequal and inequitable treatment. This can lead to motivational problems if employees equate differential treatment with unfair treatment. Therefore, managers who choose different leadership styles must make it clear that their behavior is appropriate to each individual employee. For example, if the delegation style is used with only one employee, the manager needs to make it clear to other employees that delegation is not a result of favoritism. Rather, the manager delegates when employees demonstrate appropriate levels of ability and willingness. Second, managers need to recognize that individual employees change. For whatever reasons they may become more or less willing to complete tasks. As they encounter new tasks, their ability to perform may also vary. Therefore, managers may have to change their leadership styles over time with the same employees.

Linking Motivation and Leadership

Another way incorporating follower characteristics into a leadership framework can be accomplished is by approaching leadership from the viewpoint of the follower. Being influenced to action by another requires that the follower be motivated. Therefore, effective leaders establish relationships with followers that foster their feelings of motivation.

Recall that according to the expectancy theory of motivation, employees are motivated to perform when the outcomes of their performance are of value to them and when they believe that their expenditure of effort will lead to the achievement of those outcomes. It seems logical to assume, therefore, that for an individual to effectively play a leadership role, he would have to foster the followers' perceptions that there are valuable rewards available in the work environment and that if employees make an appropriate effort toward achieving those rewards, they will receive them. This is the premise of the **path-goal model** of leadership.[17] According to this model, the leader helps followers to focus on goals that are important to them and makes it clear to followers how their efforts will lead to the achievement of these goals. The path-goal model is an attractive explanation of leadership in organizational settings for three reasons.

First, it accommodates other explanations of leadership effectiveness. Nothing in this model excludes any other approach to understanding and explaining leadership. Great leaders focus the attention of their followers on important goals and lay out a path of behavior that leads to the achievement of these goals. The path-goal model is also consistent with explanations that focus on leadership traits and behavior. However, in this model, traits and behavior are secondary to effectively communicating goals and pathways to achievement. Leadership style becomes a means to an end. The style that best communicates goals and pathways is the most appropriate style. That style will depend on the leader's comfort, the followers' receptivity, and situational demands.

Second, the path-goal model recognizes that all situations, leaders, and followers are different. The constant variable in their relationships is the need to achieve goals. In this respect, the path-goal model recognizes that leadership is a multidimensional process that requires the right mix of leader, followers, and situation.

Finally, the path-goal model suggests specific tactics that managerial leaders can pursue to increase their effectiveness. These tactics include interventions at each point in the expectancy model.

1. *Employee level.* Maintain high contact with employees to determine what outcomes are important to them. Recognize that ongoing contact is important because employee goals change over time.

2. *Expectancy.* Determine the factors that employees perceive to be barriers to performance. Remove the barriers from the work environment or assist employees to successfully overcome them.

3. *Instrumentality.* Make sure that performance is directly tied to outcomes.

4. *Outcomes level.* Assure that outcomes of performance are of value to employees.

According to the path-goal model, clear and consistent communication is the key to effective leadership. The leader's role is to make sure that employees recognize what outcomes can be achieved and how these outcomes are consistent with their personal goals. The leader also has to make clear to employees the path between effort and desired outcomes.

It cannot be overemphasized that the path-goal model of managerial leadership is much more complex than merely holding out desirable rewards and guiding employees to them. Take the case in which a laboratory manager is getting pressure from physicians' offices for a faster turnaround time for lab results. A simplistic interpretation of the path-goal model might lead the manager to attempt to influence laboratory personnel to work faster by offering a reward of value to them such as a performance bonus. The manager would show the employees how the bonus is achievable by explaining how turnaround time is to be determined, how individual performance is directly related to turnaround time, and how decreased turnaround time is related to the amount of the bonus. Unfortunately, this simplistic application of the path-goal model is fraught with potential difficulties. Because emotional responses to external stimuli are short-lived, the motivation generated by these rewards is limited. Consequently, the reward level may have to be continually increased to stimulate the same degree of motivation. There are always limitations to the level of economic rewards that managers can offer. Eventually, the employee's need for a particular reward may become saturated so that a new reward will have to be devised. And, of course, since not all employees value rewards equally and since skill differentials may intervene in their achievement of rewards, equity issues will probably arise.[18]

There is also an inherent possibility of a lose/lose situation in the above scenario. If the employees do not take the bait and choose not to work harder to achieve the reward, then the manager loses because turnaround time does not improve in spite of the attempted intervention. He will feel frustrated and may even resent his employees for not having behaved in a way that was consistent with his expectations of them. The employees also stand to lose psychologically because they failed to achieve an outcome that was within reach. Even though not obtaining the reward may be a result of their own decision not to attempt to achieve, they are still emotionally cast in the role of losers for having not achieved a goal. Even if the employees do accept the challenge, work for the reward, and eventually achieve it, there may be a win/lose outcome. The manager wins because turnaround time is decreased. But, in spite of having achieved the reward, employees still stand to lose psychologically because they have succumbed to the *implied threat* of withholding rewards if they fail to perform. They will have, in effect, compliantly entered into a relationship in which they perceive that they have become dependent on the largesse of paternalistic managers.

The more successful application of the path-goal model requires that managers establish relationships with subordinates in which they are able to help employees to achieve their own goals rather than the manager's goals. This requires that managers work with their subordinates to define problems, attempt to learn what employees value, explore employee concerns and anxieties, and redefine problems with employees in such a way that solutions result in win/win outcomes. In the laboratory example, what the manager perceives to be a problem of slow turnaround time, employees may see as inadequate work processing systems that not only delay results but jeopardize quality. By putting these conflicting perceptions on the table, managers and employees can work toward a mutual understanding of the problem. This dialogue also gives each party the opportunity to voice concerns. In this example, employees are concerned about quality, and the manager is anxious about the potential loss of clients. Among the potential solutions here are hiring more personnel, automating procedures, and changing work processes. All of these address employee and managerial concerns and result in the achievement of everyone's goals. These permanent solutions may cost no more than a bonus system that might result in only temporary improvement. As this application of the path-goal model indicates, it is impossible to separate leadership behavior from concepts of motivation, teamwork, and problem solving.

Power

Power is closely related to leadership. Like leadership, power is the ability to influence the actions of others. However, there are important differences between the two. First, power is a process; power is an attribute. Leadership is exercised through relationships with others. Power is held by an individual and exists irrespective of its utilization. For example, a nursing supervisor may have the power to fire her assistant. The fact that she chooses not to exercise that power does not mean that it does not exist. In fact, by firing an assistant, the supervisor actually loses power over that person. If there are too many firings, the supervisor may not be allowed to hire another assistant or may be fired herself. By using her power, she loses her power. Leaders, on the other hand, do not exist except when engaged in leadership. Individuals may continue to hold a title (and power commensurate with the title), but if they are not providing leadership, they are not leaders.

Second, leadership requires that the leader appeal to the motives of followers. Power requires that powerless individuals acquiesce to the desires of the power holder/wielder. The focal point of leader/follower relationships is follower motivation. The focal point of power-based relationships is power holder/wielder motivation.

Third, power is usually based on an individual's ability to control the resources on which others depend.[19] These resources may include financial resources, information, interpersonal support, and manpower. Of course, the more control someone has over resources, the more powerful he is perceived to be. In organizations, power is highly correlated with position because people in higher positions can exert more control over key resources. Although managerial leadership includes discussions of resource utilization, it is much more dependent on the quality of interpersonal relationships than it is on the control of resources. James MacGregor Burns, a widely-read author on leadership, eloquently sums up the difference between power and leadership: "To control *things*—tools, mineral resources, money, energy—is an act of power, not leadership, for things have no motives. Power wielders may treat people as things. Leaders may not. All leaders are actual or potential power holders, but not all power holders are leaders."[20]

Because effective leaders have power, it is important to understand the types of power based on their source. These types of power include reward, coercive, legitimate, referent, and expert.[21] Reward, coercive, and legitimate power arise from the organizational position that an individual occupies. **Reward power** is the ability of an individual to control positive reinforcements. In the managerial context, this power comes from control over incentives like promotions, pay increases, schedules, and task assignments. **Coercive power** arises from the ability to control negative reinforcements. Negative reinforcements include demotions, pay cuts, and scheduling. **Legitimate power** arises directly from a position held by the power holder. This power includes power over procedures (e.g., scheduling), and activities (e.g., chairing meetings and evaluating performance). Reward, coercive, and legitimate power increase with higher organizational positions.

Expert power arises from an extensive and/or specialized knowledge of a field critical to the operation of an organization. In a clinic, if only one person understands the computer system, that person has expert power because she controls a critical resource. Specialized knowledge confers unique control to the person who holds it. **Referent power** arises from the attractiveness of an individual to others. People are influenced by individuals with referent power because they want to be like them. Charisma is a key ingredient of referent power.

To this list of kinds of power might be added information power.[22] **Information power** arises from an individual's knowledge of an organization. This knowledge relates to what is happening within the organization and/or how the organization interfaces with its environment. That knowledge can then be used to influence others.

Power and Lateral Relations

In the managerial context, power is important not only because the manager uses it to influence the behavior of subordinates, but also because it is used in relationships with other managers and departments. As a group's formal leader, the manager is responsible for representing the work group to other organizational constituencies. The group depends on the manager's power to protect the group's interests and to manage intergroup relationships in such a way that the goals of the whole organization are achieved. The broader the manager's power base (i.e., the more sources from which he draws his power), the more control he will have over relationships with other managers.

There are three ways managers obtain power in lateral relations.[23] **Networking** is establishing helpful relationships with other individuals in the organization. These individuals may be supervisors, subordinates, or peers. The key to successful networking is choosing highly influential persons with whom to network so that the manager gains access to the benefits of their power. For example, a manager in a hospital's radiology department may do well to establish a relationship with a member of the management information systems (MIS) staff so that the manager can take advantage of the staffer's expert power for the radiology department's benefit. Having this relationship may mean that the radiology department's MIS needs are met before those of other departments or that the radiology department will gain access to important information about new developments in the MIS area.

Coalescing is the formation of coalitions. Like networking, the objective of coalescing is to gain access to the power of others. However, the formation of a coalition may be more formalized because each partner enters into the relationship in the expectation of gaining specific benefits. The coalition may center around a single issue, in which case it may be short-lived. For example, coalitions may form around budget time to maximize economic resources available to different departments. The heads of the radiology and MIS departments, for example, may form a coalition to secure financing for a new MIS that will support the operations of the radiology department. The combined power of these department heads may be sufficient to secure a resource that neither one alone could have gotten.

Co-opting is bringing people of influence into a group in order to take advantage of their power. Consider the following case.

> *Mr. Perkins, the head of the health information department of a city-wide network of public health clinics, sees a need to restructure the process of generating and archiving medical records. He decides to form a task force composed of the administrators, directors of nursing, and medical directors of each clinic to review the current system and suggest improvements. He knows that the support of each of these individuals is crucial to designing and implementing an effective system. Although he knows that some of the people will probably not want to change the current system, he includes them anyway so that they will feel some ownership in the new system and, thereby, take advantage of their power to make the new system work.*

The higher the degree of organizational disagreement regarding common goals, the higher the individual manager's need for power.[24] Power is needed to protect and advance the interests of the group the manager represents. The more scarce and critical resources are to the manager's work group, the more the manager will wield power to secure them. It is interesting to note that power can generate power in organizations. Power can be used to establish rules, hoard information, and put partisan individuals into positions of power. Thus, the power of individuals and/or groups can become institutionalized.[25]

Transactional and Transformational Leadership

The kind of leadership that has been the focus of this chapter is commonly called **transactional leadership**. It is a term commonly used to describe the interactions between organizational leaders and followers that result in the accomplishment of the routine, ordinary work of the organization. **Transformational leadership**, on the other hand, is the process of inspiring followers to achievement that exceeds the ordinary (i.e., performance that exceeds routine expectations). Transformational leadership differs from transactional leadership not so much in the kinds of interactions between leaders and followers as it does in its outcomes. People who exceed their routine level of performance effectively expand the boundaries of organizational performance. Through their performance, they transform the organization.

How does a leader inspire extraordinary performance that transforms organizations? There are three essential steps in the transformational leadership process.

1. The leader must recognize the need to revitalize the organization. Without the impetus of this recognition, the status quo will remain dominant.

2. The leader must create a vision. Pushing performance boundaries requires that employees be able to visualize performance that does not yet exist. They need to conceptualize performance that they have not yet achieved or experienced.

3. The leader institutionalizes the transformation so that it becomes part of the organization's structure. As part of the structure, the transformation survives independent of the leader that initiated it.[26]

Inspiring people to stretch to their fullest performance potential requires that leaders stretch their leadership skills. Charisma, individualized consideration, and intellectual stimulation are cornerstones of transformational leadership.[27] Charismatic leaders are people in whom followers can place their trust. Transforming the organization results in everyone's being faced with the uncertainties inherent in a new, unknown work environment. It is crucial that the transformation process be spearheaded by leaders who inspire confidence. Because the unknown causes anxiety, transformational leaders must immerse themselves in individualized consideration. Each organizational member's concerns must be addressed with understanding and humanity. The leader must work with each member of the group to assuage his fears and to keep him focused on the positive outcomes to be gained by pursuing extraordinary goals. Transformational leaders provide intellectual stimulation to subordinates. They urge them to consider problems in new ways and to try new solutions that are in keeping with the constantly evolving environment.

The central theme of the transformational leader is the identification of a set of values that are imperative for the organization to achieve. These values are frequently referred to as an organization's **core values**. Charisma is used to secure the commitment of followers to the achievement of core values. The transformational leader uses every opportunity to communicate core values to the organization so that the commitment of followers is reaffirmed. An original commitment to core values generates the momentum toward transformation; reiteration helps sustain the momentum. By stimulating followers to analyze problems in new ways and develop solution strategies, transformational leaders take advantage of the commitment to move the organization toward the achievement of core values. Employee energy is directed to moving the organization forward. In addition, employees gain a personal stake in the transformation. As the realization of the transformation becomes a fact, the transformational leader helps individuals deal with the changes (operational and psychological) that the transformation generates. This involvement not only sustains the commitment to the current transformation, but sets the stage for the next transformation, which in today's world is inevitable.

The more unstable an organization's environment, the more critical is the need for transformational leadership. In a rapidly changing environment, organizations that survive are organizations that are flexible and readily adaptable to the new challenges they continually face. For the past fifteen years, the need for transformational leaders in healthcare has been enormous. Complacency and business-as-usual approaches are insufficient to meet the needs of today's healthcare organizations.

One final note about transformational leadership. Transformational leadership is not a process that excludes transactional leadership. Even great historical leaders spent their share of time in transactional leadership activities. After all, armies not only must be inspired to victory, but they must be fed, clothed, transported, and paid. Pacifists must not only be moved to action, but they must be organized, and demonstrations and protests must be orchestrated. Even for the greatest transformational leaders, there are many routine goals to be met that require transactional leadership skills.

Conclusion

Mr. Kline's tenure as CEO of Bracken Health System was marked by a lack of leadership. It is obvious that he failed to be a transformational leader at a time when the organization desperately needed a transformational leader. His reaction to a changing environment was to urge people to cut costs more than they had already done. Not only was this a poor strategy, but it indicates an extremely narrow range of leadership skills.

Mr. Kline seems to have been a likable person. While that is one of the traits associated with leaders, it alone is not sufficient to sustain a leader. There is no indication that Mr. Kline held any kind of power other than legitimate power. His open door policy was ineffective in establishing the relationships necessary for the exercise of transactional leadership.

Ironically, his rise to the top spot in the organization may have been precisely because he was likable. As a likable person who had performed well in the past, he probably had made few if any enemies at Bracken. As the CFO, he may have known several of the members of the Board of Trustees personally. These board members may have made the mistake of assuming that the interpersonal skills which made for a good social relationship would also serve Mr. Kline well in establishing leadership/follower relationships. Persons who are inherently transformational leaders have a difficult time rising to the top because they are perceived as disturbers who are always trying to change things. They are bound to step on organizational toes on the way up the ladder.

Why Mr. Kline did not adopt more appropriate leadership behaviors is unknown. Perhaps he did not recognize his leadership shortcomings. Performance evaluation for CEOs has not been standardized in the past in many hospitals.[28] Even when there is a formal appraisal, none of the trustees is involved intimately enough with the day-to-day operation of the organization to give much feedback on transactional leadership skills. When a lack of transformational leadership skills eventually becomes evident, the boat of opportunity has usually already left the dock. This is what happened in the Bracken case. Even if Mr. Kline intuitively felt that he was not as effective as he could be as a leader, he may not have known how to change. Or perhaps he could not find a new leadership style with which he felt comfortable. In any case, there was a leader/organization mismatch that had to be corrected. The only way to improve performance is "either by changing the leader to fit the situation or by changing the situation to fit the leader."[29] Because Bracken was in no position to change the situation, the leader had to change. Since he did not change himself, the Board of Trustees had no choice but to remove him. His successor faces the formidable task of rebuilding Bracken's damaged neuro-muscular networks.

Endnotes

1. Charles W. Joiner, *Leadership for Change* (Cambridge, MA: Ballinger Publishing Company, 1987).
2. Ibid.
3. Leonard R. Sayles, *Leadership: What Effective Managers Really Do and How They Do It* (New York: McGraw-Hill, 1979).
4. Douglas McGregor, *Leadership and Motivation* (Cambridge, MA: The M.I.T. Press, 1966).
5. Bernard M. Bass, *Stogdill's Handbook of Leadership: A Survey of theory and Research* (New York: Free Press, 1981).
6. Arthur, G. Jago, "Leadership: Perspectives in Theory and Research," *Management Science 28* (March 1982): 315–336.
7. Henry L. Tosi, John R. Rizzo, and Stephen J. Carroll, *Managing Organizational Behavior* (Marshfield, MA: Pitman Publishing, 1986).
8. Rensis Likert, *New Patterns of Management* (New York: McGraw-Hill, 1961).
9. Ralph M. Stogdill and Alvin E. Coons, *Leader Behavior: Its Description and Measurement* (Columbus, OH: Ohio State University, Bureau of Business Research, 1957).
10. P. Weissenberg and Michael J. Kavanaugh, "The Independence of Initiating Structure and Consideration: A Review of the Evidence," *Personnel Psychology 25* (1972): 119–130.
11. Robert R. Blake and Anne Adams McCanse, *Leadership Dilemmas—Grid® Solutions* (Houston: Gulf Publishing, 1991).
12. Robert R. Blake and Jane Srygley Mouton, "An Overview of the Grid®," *Training and Development Journal 12* (May 1975): 29–36.

13. McGregor, op. cit.
14. Fred E. Fiedler, *A Theory of Leadership Effectiveness* (New York: McGraw-Hill, 1967).
15. P. Hersey and K. Blanchard, *Management of Organizational Behavior,* 5th ed. (Englewood Cliffs, NJ: Prentice-Hall, 1982).
16. Ibid.
17. Robert J. House and Terence R. Mitchell, "Path-goal Theory of Leadership," *Journal of Contemporary Business* (August 1974): 81–97.
18. Sayles, op. cit.
19. Donald D. White and David A. Bednar, *Organizational Behavior: Understanding and Managing People at Work,* 2nd ed. (Needham Heights, MA: Allyn and Bacon, 1991).
20. James MacGregor Burns, *Leadership* (New York: Harper & Row, 1978).
21. John R.P. French, Jr. and Bertram Raven, "The Bases of Social Power," in Dorwin Cartwright, ed., *Studies in Social Power* (Ann Arbor, MI: Institute for Social Research, University of Michigan, 1959), pp. 150–165.
22. White and Bednar, op. cit.
23. Ibid.
24. Jeffrey Pfeffer, "Power and Resource Allocation in Organizations," in Barry M. Staw and Gerald R. Salancik, *New Directions in Organizational Behavior* (Malabar, FL: Robert E. Krieger Publishing Company, 1982).
25. Ibid.
26. Noel M. Tichy and Mary Anne Devanna, *The Transformational Leader* (New York: John Wiley & Sons, 1986).
27. White and Bednar, op. cit.
28. Richard L. Johnson, "Appraising Performance at the Top," *Hospital and Health Services Administration 23* (Fall 1978): 36–47.
29. Fiedler, op. cit.

10   Communication: Aphasia

In this chapter the reader will learn how:

◆ communication problems are diagnosed
◆ clear, precise, and constant communication is important
◆ common communication barriers can be identified
◆ oral communication skills can be improved
◆ effective meetings can be conducted
◆ effective letters, memos, policies, and procedures are written
◆ the process of improving communication skills is like working with aphasic patients.

Y'all Come!

What: *an employee meeting to discuss the new St. Clare's Community Center.*

Where: *the Sandberg Auditorium.*

When: *November 1 at 7:30 A.M. and again at 3:30 P.M.*

J. Crane (St. Clare's CEO, to the Public Relations staff): *This is great! It isn't too formal, and the word "discuss" shows that we are care about how employees feel about this project. The topic, time, and place are clear. We'll hit employees on all three shifts with these times. I think this announcement is right on target. The employees are going to be excited about this new building because it is going to serve primarily the St. Clare family of employees. I know they probably*

209

won't care about the new Board Room and Executive Cafeteria, but when they hear about its new day-care center, employee fitness facility, and professional library, they're going to be 100% supportive. That support is just what we need to kick off our fund-raising effort.

I know that it's awfully far in advance to make an announcement, but if anyone asks about a timetable, we'll be able to talk around it. It may be five years to ground-breaking, but there is plenty of other work to do before then. Let's put the announcement in everyone's paycheck.

K. Gray (Director of Admissions, upon reading the notice): *This is great! We've always needed a program that addresses the needs of the community. This will complement our Cancer Prevention and Wellness centers nicely. But since I'm management, I wonder if I'm supposed to attend.*

S. Rodriguez (RN, Nursery): *A community center? I thought this was a hospital! Isn't there already a community center over on Grant Avenue? Just another way to waste money, if you ask me.*

R. Smith (Housekeeping): *Nobody has ever discussed anything with anybody around here before. We're just going to be told how it's going to be and that's the end of that. I've got better things to do with my time.*

B. Lao (Payroll): *I heard that they're not even planning to break ground for this thing for 10 years. Anything could happen before then. Why bother going to a meeting about this now?*

K. Beauvais (Pharmacy): *7:30 and 3:30? Why do I have to go to two meetings about the same thing in the same day?*

R. Setiawan (Radiology, two weeks later): *Well, I never got the notice that the time had to be changed to 7:00 A.M. These people can't even schedule a meeting. How are they ever going to build a $10 million building?*

M. Monroe (Dietary, two weeks later): *What meeting? I didn't see a notice in my pay envelope. The only thing I care about in my envelope is the paycheck.*

Nothing is as important to the maintenance of an organization as communication. Each interpersonal relationship in the organization is based on the quality and quantity of communication between two individuals. A relationship cannot exist without communication. In fact, any two individuals in the same place cannot not communicate. Envision two people in an elevator who exchange neither words nor eye contact and who stand at opposite sides of the elevator. Through their lack of interaction, these fellow passengers communicate volumes.

They communicate that they are hesitant to communicate with each other. If they fidget, they may also communicate discomfort or nervousness. If they stand immobile and rigid, they may communicate fear. No matter how hard these people try not to communicate, they communicate.

Even when people attempt to communicate, they sometimes send messages that are perceived as something other than what they intended. The St. Clare's case is a typical example. The CEO believes that the message is clear and unambiguous. However, different members of the organization interpret it differently.

K. Gray thinks that a community center is a program. B. Lao thinks it is a building. K. Gray and S. Rodriguez think the center is for the external community, although the CEO conceives of it as being for the internal community. While the CEO believes the meeting time and place are unambiguous, K. Gray and K. Beauvais interpret the message differently than she would have anticipated. After the meetings occurred, R. Setiawan comes away with proof that what was communicated in the written announcement is inaccurate. J. Crane believes that the word "discuss" is synonymous with "collaborate," whereas R. Smith perceives that at St. Clare's, "discuss" is synonymous with "inform." In contrast to J. Crane's knowledge of planned ground-breaking, B. Lao believes that ground-breaking will be at a different date. This is an issue that the announcement did not even address. Nor have the two attempted to communicate about it. Yet, miscommunication already exists.

Although to J. Crane this announcement appears to be a simple, straightforward message, it has been interpreted in a number of different ways. In the case of M. Monroe, the message has not been received at all.

Diagnosis of Communication Problems

Externally, the signs of managerial communications disorders mimic lack of leadership. Individuals and groups appear to act independently without visible coordination. Activity appears to be disjointed and, possibly, even at cross purposes. A differential diagnosis between lack of leadership and communications disorders cannot be made from external observation alone. One must view the organization internally to distinguish between the two.

Problematic managerial communications are like aphasia. An individual has a concept of a message or information that someone else needs to know. Through communication, the individual attempts to transfer her concept to second party. A communications problem occurs when the concept that the second party possesses after the communication process is not the same concept that the originator had. This is the same kind of problem experienced by aphasic stroke victims. While these individuals formulate messages that they want to communicate verbally to others, their ability to complete the transfer of their messages is impaired. Rather than a coherent message, listeners may perceive only garbled vocalizations. An examination of the communications process shows how even the simplest attempts at communicating can go awry.

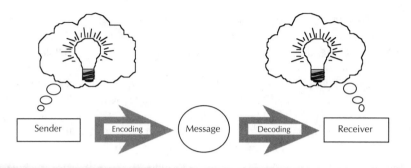

Figure 10.1   Basic communications process.

Communications Basics

The communications process has three basic components: sender, message, and receiver (Figure 10.1). In the first step of the process, the sender has a mental image. He then translates it into something that can be conveyed to and evaluated by the receiver. That something is frequently words. The process of translating the message to words (or into another medium that can be understood) is **encoding**. The message is an expression of an idea that is capable of being understood by someone else. Once the message is formulated, it is sent via a channel of communication. **Channels** are methods of communication. In organizations, common channels include telephones, memos, special announcements, E-mail, face-to-face conversations, voice mail, and reports. Once the message is transmitted, it must be decoded by the receiver. **Decoding** is the process of interpreting symbols (usually words) that have been received.

The St. Clare's case is a classic case of encoding and decoding errors. The phrase "community center" had a very specific meaning to J. Crane. The mental image that she had of this project had probably been shaped by the weeks, if not months, of thinking about the project and discussing it with project managers, top managers, and architects. What the phrase "community center" meant to her at the beginning of this project and what it meant on the day she approved the announcement may well have been two different things. But her intense involvement with the project caused her to forget alternative meanings of the words. In encoding this message, she would have done well to have reviewed the image that she wanted to convey and to have chosen words that specifically described the concept she had in mind. Both K. Gray and S. Rodriguez misinterpreted "community" to mean the community outside the hospital. Given that they spend a considerable amount of time working with members of that community, it is logical that they would make this assumption. However, this is still a decoding error on their part. They are part of an organizational community. In interpreting messages, it is a common error to accept the first interpretation that comes to mind rather than to search for the most accurate interpretation.

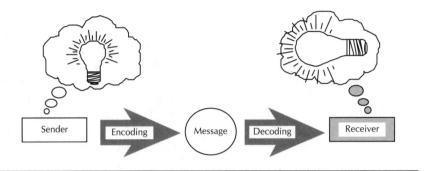

Figure 10.2   Basic communications process with contextual distortion.

One of the reasons for the encoding and decoding errors in this case is that the sender and receivers are coming from very different organizational contexts. While the CEO has been focused on strengthening the internal community, K. Gray and S. Rodriguez have been dealing primarily with members of the external community. Working in different contexts colors one's perceptions by infusing words with different meetings. Figure 10.2 shows how the idea of a light bulb can be changed by an individual's context. The sender's idea of a light bulb is a moderately sized object oriented vertically with the threads at the bottom. Perhaps this image came from light bulbs that go into the sender's table lamps. The sender chooses the words "light bulb" to convey this image. The receiver forms a slightly different idea from the words "light bulb." This image is larger and is oriented horizontally. Perhaps the receiver's image was formed as a result of the flood-lights that go into his wall-mounted outdoor sockets. In ordinary conversation, this slight difference may be insignificant. However, if the sender is a maintenance person who asks her assistant for a light bulb, she may well find herself holding the wrong object.

The difficult part of encoding and decoding is viewing the message from the other person's perspective (i.e., finding the common ground that allows for effective communication). For example, had J. Crane stopped to think that many employees typically work with members of the external community, perhaps she would have realized that "community" would probably be interpreted in a way other than what she had intended. Likewise, if K. Gray and S. Rodriguez had remembered that the CEO recently had been talking publicly about the need to build a strong internal community, they may have discovered the intended meaning of the message. It is interesting to observe that meanings are in people rather than in the words they use to convey their thoughts.

In addition to the difficulties of encoding and decoding, messages also have to travel through noise. **Noise** is anything that interferes with the transmission and/or reception of messages. Everyone who has listened to a radio is familiar with the concept of noise. Airway noise disrupts the flow of radio waves, with the result that the listener hears static and distorted sounds. Noise can be both physical and psychological. Physical noise is easy to understand. It includes environmental noise that can impair hearing, illegible print, and inaudible speech. Psychological noise includes unwillingness to listen, attention deficits, and distractions. Figure 10.3 shows how noise can distort a message. In this case, the word "light" is used to convey the sender's idea. The receiver interprets what he hears as the word "flight." Environmental noise, poor enunciation, or inattentiveness may have caused this distortion. This example shows how even simple messages must make their way through the porous physical and psychological walls that separate people.

Nonverbal Communication

Messages may be encoded into words or actions. Action messages are **nonverbal communication**. Successful clinicians are skilled in decoding nonverbal communication. For example, they watch for patients' reactions to palpation pressure during physical examinations. They look for puzzled expressions that may indicate a patient's lack of understanding. They note hand-wringing and furrowed brows that may indicate worry.

In the patient-practitioner dyad (i.e., two-way communication), nonverbal communication is particularly important because patients and practitioners do not always share the same working vocabulary. This difficulty is increasing with the increase of multiculturalism in America. Not only is it more difficult to find words that both sender and receiver can use, but the more diverse contexts of encoding and decoding make it less likely that the message will be understood. At the patient-practitioner level, this means more reliance on nonverbal communication. At the organizational level, it means that greater efforts need to be made to match patients to practitioners with whom they can communicate, that multilingual staff be employed, and that written materials be carefully prepared and reviewed for locally understood vocabulary.[1]

Nonverbal communication is an important communication channel, in spite of the fact that it is usually nonspecific. Only occasionally is nonverbal communication so specific that it is unlikely to be misinterpreted. For example, a scream from a person in a burning building is difficult to interpret as anything other than distress. However, what about the patient's wringing of hands? Such an action is seldom deliberate. It may indeed mean worry. Or it may indicate discomfort from arthritis or muscle spasm. Or it may be an unconscious, meaningless habit.

Because different people use nonverbal cues so differently, trying to learn the meaning of nonverbal messages is like looking up words in a dictionary. There is usually a primary meaning, as well as several secondary meanings (which supports the conclusion that meanings are in people rather than in words). The context in which the message is sent helps to clarify its meaning. Hand wringing that starts upon learning bad news, for example, is more likely to be the result of distress than arthritis.

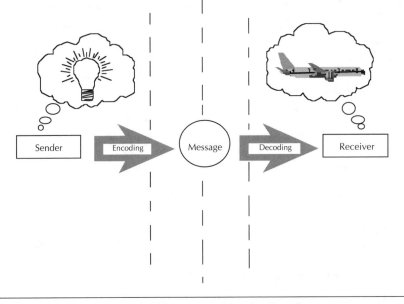

Figure 10.3   Basic communication process with noise distortion.

Some common nonverbal behaviors and their primary interpretations are given in Table 10.1. It is important to note, however, that not only are there alternate interpretations, but that some nonverbal behaviors mean entirely different things in different cultures. For example, nodding usually indicates agreement and shaking the head indicates disagreement. However, Bulgarians use the gestures in the opposite way. In parts of India, shaking the head is not negation.[2]

In addition, nonverbal behaviors are rarely exhibited in isolation.[3] They are combined with other nonverbal behaviors, and verbal messages that may alter, clarify, and/or deepen their meaning. Touching is an excellent example. The words and other gestures that accompany touching help to clarify its meaning. When the touch accompanies words of condolence, it reinforces the message of care and concern expressed by the words. When it occurs on the golf course between friends, it reinforces the idea of camaraderie and shared interest. When it happens on the golf course between business associates, it may reinforce the power that one player has over another. Or it may indicate a desire to make the relationship more friendly.

In addition to being culturally defined, the meaning of touching is influenced by family units. In some families, tactile communication is a primary channel of communication and is encouraged.[4] In others it is not. Cultural and familial variances in nonverbal behavior lead to encoding or decoding errors similar to the verbal message distortion depicted in Figure 10.3. A touch on the shoulder that is

Table 10.1   Some Representative Nonverbal Behaviors and Their Usual Meanings

Nonverbal Behavior	Primary Meaning(s)
Gestures	
Touching	Power; Caring
Avoiding eye contact	Desire not to interact
Establishing eye contact	Invitation to interact; Desire for inclusion/involvement
Leaning forward	Attentiveness
Leaning backward; Slouching	Indifference
Closed fist	Power; Force
Animated gestures	Excitement; Interest
Preening	Nervousness
Crossed arms	Mind closed to the message
Facial expressions	
Smiling	Happiness; Approval
Crying	Unhappiness; Happiness; Weakness
Tilting head up	Superiority
Tilting head down	Submission
Appearance	
Uniforms	Defined role/function
Casual	Indifference
Make-up	Concern about how others perceive the sender
More formal clothing than minimally required	Concern about how others perceive the sender
Flamboyant clothing	Craving attention; Poor taste

intended to convey care and concern could be interpreted as a superficial and insincere gesture to someone who grew up receiving hugs as a show of concern.

The importance of nonverbal communication cannot be overemphasized. When it is used together with verbal communication channels, nonverbal communication can be a powerful reinforcer. However, there are times when receivers perceive nonverbal communication to be in conflict with verbal messages. When this happens, they are far more likely to believe the nonverbal communication. Research has yielded a mathematical approximation of the importance of nonverbal communication relative to verbal communication.

Total impact = 0.07 verbal + 0.38 vocal + 0.55 facial[5,6]

In the formula above, "vocal" refers to sounds other than words (e.g., screams, laughter, and sighs). Words constitute the least important part of verbal communication.

In Western culture, facial expressions send potent nonverbal messages.[7] Receivers scrutinize senders' faces for nonverbal cues that support or refute the verbal message. For example, eye contact is strongly linked to veracity. "Look me in the eye and say that" is a challenge to a suspected liar issued with the belief that it is impossible to lie with a "straight face." The concept of a straight face includes not only eye contact but any facial expression that indicates nervousness or discomfort (e.g., stiffly robotic expressions, twitching, out-of-the-ordinary movements, and increased and/or irregular respiration). Of course, it is not impossible to learn to lie convincingly (i.e., to lie with a straight face). Conversely, people may communicate nervousness and discomfort when they are telling the truth. Despite the knowledge that interpretation of facial cues may be faulty, receivers still depend on their ability to detect truthfulness through the face. People believe not only that truthfulness in specific situations can be perceived facially, but that character in general can be read in the face. The old saying about wrinkles adding character to the face is based on this premise.

Another important dimension of nonverbal communication is physical space between the sender and receiver. Hall has identified several different distances at which Americans generally feel comfortable communicating for different purposes.[8] **Intimate distance** (physical contact to 18 in.) is the distance in which close, personal interactions take place. **Personal distance** (1.5–4 ft.) is the distance in which much interaction with friends and family takes place. In the closer range of this distance (up to 2.5 ft.), touching is possible. In the further range, the communicators are at arm's length. **Social distance** (4–7 ft.) is the distance for personal interaction. Most business and casual social interactions take place at this distance.

People become uncomfortable when there is a mismatch between distance and the intent of communication. For example, in crowded public places like busses and sporting events, people who do not want to interact at all are forced into intimate distances. Because this distance is uncomfortable, they develop defense mechanisms (such as deliberate avoidance of eye contact and stiff postures) to make it clear to each other that in spite of the intimate distance, they do not want to engage in intimate communication. Health practitioners experience this mismatch all the time. They perform personal care services that require communication at intimate distances. During the process of becoming health professionals, they acclimate to this dissonant situation. However, patients tend to be uncomfortable with this distance because it is unusual for them. This discomfort may contribute to the stress of being a patient.

People also become anxious when the person with whom they are communicating initiates a change in distance. For example, when a co-worker moves from a social distance to a personal or intimate distance to communicate something, the action may indicate to the receiver that the relationship is becoming more personal. This perception may or may not be accurate. If the message is about a project that both parties have been working on without the knowledge of anyone else, the personal distance may be required to discuss the project confidentially. If, however, the message is some juicy office gossip, moving closer to share it may indeed indicate that the relationship is becoming less collegial and more personal, since gossip tends to be shared more readily with co-workers who are also considered friends.

Managers have to be very aware of how distance can be perceived by others. A personal distance that a manager may perceive as communicating concern may be perceived by an employee as inappropriately personal—perhaps even sexually threatening. Likewise, a social distance that an employee feels is appropriate may be interpreted by a manager as aloofness and lack of involvement or concern.

Research in nonverbal communication indicates that the old saw "Actions speak louder than words" is axiomatic. In the managerial context, this leads to the conclusion that one of the best ways of communicating to employees what to do and how to do it is for the manager to become a role model for employees to follow.[9] At the supervisory level, managers communicate how to perform specific tasks through demonstration. For example, the simple task of appropriately answering a telephone and routing telephone messages can be communicated to employees through role modeling. When role modeling is combined with other communication channels, it can be a very powerful tool. For example, during orientation, employees can be taught how to answer the telephone. The supervisor can then role model the behavior. Finally, the supervisor can provide the new employee with feedback on how well he performs this task and offer specific suggestions for improvement. At the executive level, role modeling sets the tone for the whole corporate culture because employees put faith in the behavior they see. They hear words but listen to behavior.[10] In the St. Clare's case, R. Smith did not believe the word "discuss" because the image he decoded from that word was not the same as the image that he decoded from the behavior of St. Clare's management. He believed the actions he saw rather than the word he read.

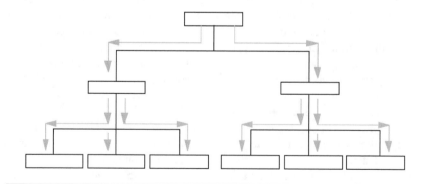

Figure 10.4   Chain network of organizational communication.

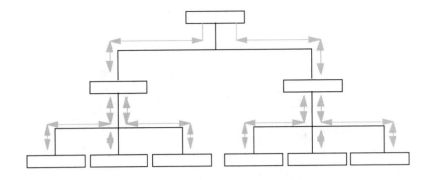

Figure 10.5   Chain network of organizational communication with afferent/efferent pathways.

Communications in Organizations

Communication in organizations follows pathways that are like neural networks. In the simplest pathway, the **chain network**, communication flows in a straight line through the formal organizational structure (Figure 10.4). The St. Clare's case is an example of chain communication in which the communication flowed from the top to the bottom of the organization. The only thing unique about this example is that the CEO communicated directly with employees rather than going through all the ranks in the hierarchy. An example of a message that would typically go through all the ranks would be the contents of the budget. The CEO would share the budget with top managers, who in turn would communicate appropriate parts of it to middle managers, who would communicate smaller parts of it to department heads, who would share even smaller parts of it with supervisors, who would communicate relevant budgeting constraints to individual employees. The chain network is similar to the central nervous system (CNS) in that communication is, to a large extent, under the control of top management. Top management controls the pathway by putting a hierarchical structure in place, enacting policies and procedures that establish parameters for communicating within the chain, and by initiating messages. This network is used by managers to give employees instructions and information they need to perform efficiently and effectively, and to share feedback on their performance. An interesting characteristic of the chain network is that unlike the CNS, which has separate nerves for afferent and efferent impulses, the chain pathway carries messages in both directions (Figure 10.5). In healthy organizations, top managers establish communication parameters that permit and encourage employees to provide managers with feedback and information. Just as a person cannot function without efferent impulses from peripheral nerves, an organization cannot function without communication up the chain network.

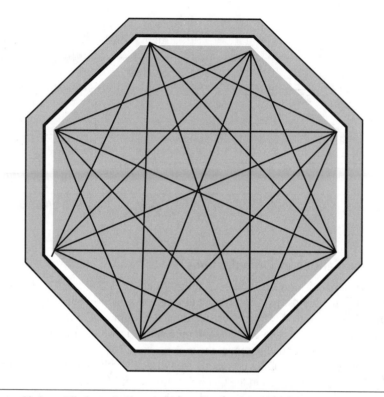

Figure 10.6   All-channel network of organizational communications.

Another common pathway, the **all-channel network**, occurs when all communicators interact with each other freely (Figure 10.6). Some all-channel networks are established deliberately when teams are formed. If the team is isolated from the rest of the organization, then management has considerable control over the kind of information that circulates through the channels. However, self-contained teams are hypothetical. All teams interact with other teams in some way so that the content of intrateam communications permeates team boundaries. Managers have little control over these leaks.

More commonly, all-channel networks form spontaneously among employees. Because they are an inherent component of any organization, all-channel networks are more central to the vitality of the organization than chain networks. In this way they are similar to the autonomic nervous system (ANS). Network communication facilitates the activities essential to the existence of the organization outside the conscious activity of top managers. It is through this network that the messages essential to the maintenance of interpersonal relationships in the organization are communicated. The **grapevine** is an all-channel network through which informal information is communicated.

For managers, the grapevine can be either a nemesis or a powerful communications tool. The messages in it may be destructive and/or inaccurate. Imagine the consequences if the following message were to get into a health system's grapevine: "Dr. Smith, you know, Chief of Surgery, is an alcoholic." If the story were true, the grapevine message could make an already difficult situation worse. Depending on the personalities and positions involved and how far the story has spread inside and outside the organization, the situation could become even more resistant to effective intervention than it inherently is. If the message is not true, the reputation of Dr. Smith, the health system, its medical staff, and management could be unjustly damaged.

Even job-related information becomes distorted in the grapevine. In the St. Clare's case, B. Lao heard through the grapevine that ground-breaking would occur in 10 years instead of the five years anticipated by the CEO. Given that the grapevine can spread inaccurate and damaging messages, it is no wonder that many managers see it as a weed that needs to be exterminated.

Nevertheless, when two employees gather together, there will be a grapevine. Rather than attempting the impossible mission of getting rid of this network, the effective manager uses it. The manager can effectively combat inaccurate information by putting correct information into the grapevine via informal conversations with employees. Also, through these conversations the manager can send out new information that he wants employees to know. Since each person in the grapevine has more than one contact, information can be disseminated much more quickly than it can through a chain network. A word of caution is in order though. Because messages become distorted in the grapevine and because not every employee is part of the grapevine, the grapevine cannot be used as the only channel of communication. The grapevine is an adjunct to formal communication, not a substitute for it. Communication through a chain network increases the likelihood that all employees will receive the same message. Well-cultivated and maintained grapevines can support the development of healthy network communications rather than crowd them out.

Communication networks and channels of communication are overlaid and overlapped in organizations. Individuals typically employ more than one channel of communication and are members of more than one network. Thus, the anatomy of an organization's communications is not easily dissected. However, managers must understand the anatomy and physiology of organizational communications to successfully use available channels and networks. Because up to 89% of a manager's time may be spent in verbal communication,[11] managers should emphasize this skill in professional development efforts.

Improving Verbal Communications—Managing the Environment

For effective communication to occur, an environment must be established in which noise is minimized. There are too many factors that are situation specific to generate a comprehensive list of suggestions for minimizing noise. However, there are three principles and some derivative guidelines that are universally applicable. From these, astute managers can identify more specific guidelines to apply in their unique situations.

PRINCIPLE 1:   Each individual message competes with other messages, concerns, and environmental factors for the attention of the receiver.[12]

The human mind is an awe-inspiring structure in that it simultaneously processes an enormous number of impulses quickly and efficiently. Decoding messages received by others is one of those many simultaneous processes. Marvelous as the brain is, there is a limit to its ability to accurately perceive and decode concurrent input. The more an individual's attention is divided among a variety of inputs, the less likely messages are to be accurately decoded. A number of steps can be taken to decrease competition for attention.

First, physical noise should be eliminated, if possible. If not, it should be minimized. Public address system music and radios are mere annoyances for some people and intrusive irritants for others. Even for those individuals who regard them as **white noise** (i.e., sound that fades into the background and minimally affects thought processes), these sounds interfere with hearing. If white noise cannot be eliminated, then verbal communication should occur in places where it is not present. Routine sounds of an office or work environment have the same effect. Although they often become white noise for people who become accustomed to them, they still impede hearing. Cubicle office and work space arrangements may decrease but do not eliminate this kind of noise.

Second, interruptions should be minimized. Managers should establish a communications environment in which it is assumed by everyone that the message currently being communicated is the most important message at any one moment. No other employee or colleague should assume that his message is more important. When the manager is in conversation with anyone, it should be understood that the only permissible interruption is for an emergency or impending disaster. The existence of this policy communicates the importance of effective communication in the organization. Such a policy can sensitize everyone to the importance of minimizing distractions in the communications process and thereby strengthen communications throughout the entire organization.

Finally, the environment should be comfortable. Excessive heat and cold can distract the receiver from the message being conveyed. Uncomfortable chairs and unusual decor can also be distracting. The receiver cannot concentrate on these external stimuli and simultaneously pay attention to the message.

PRINCIPLE 2: **Each individual message competes with other messages, concerns, and environmental factors for the time of the receiver.**[13]

Given that everyone receives thousands of messages a day, very little time is devoted to any one of them. Therefore, managers have to make appropriate time available to communicate. Several actions can minimize the competition of messages for time.

First, communication should be removed from regular work areas where other activities compete for time. It is unrealistic for managers to expect employees to focus simultaneously on what they are doing and pay attention to what managers are saying. So much of the work of healthcare workers is carried out in response to the needs of others (both patients and colleagues) that it is almost impossible to communicate effectively in the employee's work area without interruption. If the message is a very short simple one like, "I got that report you left on my desk yesterday," then the message may be effectively delivered at the employee's work station. However, discussing the format and/or contents of the report would probably require taking the employee away from her work station, even if the conversation would only be expected to last for five minutes. In the space of five minutes the phone could ring any number of times, and others might compete for the employee's time during the conversation. What could have been a 5-minute discussion with clear exchange of messages could easily become a 15- or 20-minute discussion ending in messages distorted by noise.

Second, time should be scheduled for communication. Both managers and employees have competing demands for their time. By allocating time specifically for communication and rigidly adhering to that allocation, managers can minimize the competition. Scheduling meetings is a common way to set aside time specifically for communication. Managers can also establish open door times during which communicating with employees becomes the manager's number one priority.

Finally, spontaneous communication should be postponed if the manager and/or employee really does not have the time for it. For example, if an employee comes in to talk about a vacation schedule and the manager is trying to prepare for a budget meeting the next day, the manager's attention is probably going to be divided between the employee's message and the materials waiting on his desk to be reviewed or prepared for tomorrow. Rather than giving the employee's concern a half-attentive hearing, the manager should probably schedule a time to talk when the employee will have the manager's undivided attention. The manager can communicate greater concern for the employee's problem by delaying the discussion and listening attentively than by listening inattentively right now.

PRINCIPLE 3: Even under the best of environmental circumstances and with the best planning, messages become distorted.

Managers cannot make effective communication happen by merely following a cookbook of good communications practices because there are other people involved in the process. Although managers can establish environments in which effective communication can occur and frame messages in generally understood language, they cannot control the perceptions of receivers. Effective communication frequently requires additional inputs.

1. *Repetition* confirms the receiver's perceptions. If the original message and its reiteration are incongruent, the receiver is alerted to a perceptual problem and clarification can be sought. Repetition with the same words will confirm listening comprehension (i.e., whether the words were heard correctly). Repetition of a message with the use of different words (**paraphrasing**) can be used to confirm understanding. For example, take the simple statement, "The sky looks ominous." This sentence could be repeated by the sender and successfully parroted back by the receiver. But if the receiver does not understand the word "ominous," effective communication has not taken place. However, if the second iteration of the statement is, "The sky looks foreboding," then the receiver may take the meaning from the second sentence. Also, from the second sentence, the receiver may determine that what he thought "ominous" meant may or may not be the case.

2. Verbal messages should be supported by appropriate *nonverbal behavior*. Because nonverbal behavior generates belief on the part of receivers, senders should infuse communications with it appropriately. In the St. Clare case, it seems to be important to J. Crane that employees be enthusiastic about the new community center. If she wants employees to share her enthusiasm she will have to communicate that enthusiasm. Saying, "I'm enthused about the new community center" with a deadpan face and in a flat tone of voice will not communicate the message she wants to communicate. She will have to use vocal inflections, energy level, and gestures to communicate enthusiasm.

3. Messages should be verified through *feedback*. One confirmation technique is to ask the receiver to repeat the message. Asking the receiver to repeat the message is a very simple technique that allows some misunderstandings to be clarified immediately. However, the manager who uses this technique needs to keep in mind that repetition confirms listening comprehension but not understanding.

Also, in most work situations, asking for verbatim repetition would be considered paternalistic because parents frequently use this technique to reinforce messages with young children. However, it is frequently possible to avoid paternalistic appearances by asking employees to paraphrase and/or summarize what was said. In group meetings, recording minutes provides an unobtrusive vehicle for employing the repetition technique. Because minutes should always be an accurate record of the communication that took place during the meeting, the group leader can ask for frequent repetition and paraphrasing in a very nonthreatening way for record-keeping purposes.

Unfortunately, healthcare practitioners have to work in distraction-filled environments. They may have little control over an occasionally chaotic environment. Because little can be done to prevent patient-, family-, or co-worker-generated distractions, simultaneous conversations in nurses' stations or office corridors, ringing telephones, and public address announcements, practitioners adapt as best they can to disruptive environments. It is imperative for each practitioner to realize, however, that this kind of environment leads to communications failures. In the clinical setting, how many medication errors can be attributed to the fact that physicians are interrupted while writing orders, or nurses are interrupted while preparing doses, or pharmacists do not hear drug names or doses correctly over the din of the pharmacy? Just because practitioners are forced to communicate in less-than-ideal circumstances in clinical settings does not mean that they should continue doing so in managerial situations. Practitioners who become managers should be more aware than anyone else of the difficulty of attempting to communicate in high noise environments.

Improving Verbal Communications—Listening

Because managers often initiate the communication process, they tend to focus their attention more on sending messages than on receiving them. To become better communicators, they make efforts to improve writing and speaking skills. While these efforts certainly lead to better communication, managers also have to continually improve in their roles as message receivers (i.e., they need to improve their listening skills).

Effective listening is not a passive activity. Hearing is passive. Listening requires an expenditure of energy (sometimes a considerable expenditure) to decode the message that is being sent. The amount of effort that is required to listen is inversely proportional to the clarity of the message. The more clear the message, the less the effort that is required to listen. Note how much energy is required to listen to someone who has little fluency in English. To decode the message requires that the listener first extract the words from the unfamiliar sound patterns generated by an accent, altered speech rhythms, and unusual grammatical constructions. Then, the listener has to evaluate the words and perhaps make mental substitutions that seem to be more consistent with the context in which the message is delivered.

Managers can hone listening skills just as they can improve speaking and writing skills. The realization that messages compete for the receiver's time and attention sets the stage not only for improving the sending of messages, but for receiving them as well. The following practices improve listening.[14]

- The listener must stay focused on the message. Just as managers need to minimize environmental distractions and noise when sending messages, they must do the same when receiving them. Even when there are no obvious external distractions, they do usually have more than one problem or issue to deal with at a time. Therefore, their minds can drift to other pressing issues while someone else is speaking. Paying attention means paying undivided attention.

- The listener should listen for key points. The conscious mind is a poor tape recorder. It does not record each of the millions of words it hears accurately. However, it is a very good assimilator of concepts. The listener should work at remembering the few key points or concepts the sender conveys and verify these by paraphrasing them back to the sender.

- The listener should avoid evaluating the content of a message too quickly. It is natural for people to evaluate content. In fact, it is encouraged. The whole idea behind educational efforts to increase critical thinking skills is to encourage people to evaluate and judge the content of messages. However, a busy manager may have a tendency to judge content too quickly. If he judges before he has heard the entire message, he may make errors because he has heard only a partial message. Or he may make judgments based on faulty understanding of the message because he acts before verifying that he has understood correctly. Managers should develop the patience to let the sender complete the message before interrupting or making judgments. The bottom line of the message may not be at all what the manager expects it to be.

- The manager needs to prepare to listen. The best way to prepare is to be as knowledgeable as possible about the subject to be discussed. For example, if an employee wants to talk about the schedule, the manager should review the schedule before discussing it. He might also ask the employee to define the scheduling issue in advance of a meeting so that they share the same frame of reference for understanding and discussing the issue.

Improving Verbal Communications—Meetings

Meetings seem to be the sustenance of organizational life. It has been estimated that healthcare managers spend 75%–80% of their time in meetings and make nearly all their decisions in a group setting.[15] When a meeting is limited to two people, the basic communications model can be an extremely useful tool in helping managers to understand and improve the process. As they seek to continually improve communications skills, this model should be constantly revisited. However, the team approach to task accomplishment requires that meetings frequently involve more than two people. The dyadic model still serves to explain the interactions between any two people in the group, but it holds fewer lessons for structuring and controlling the multilayered, complex communications processes that are inherent in meetings.

The foundation of a meeting is its purpose. Unfortunately, the purpose of a meeting is not always clear to either the chairperson or to the attendants. The need to have a meeting is frequently an intuitive response to a perceived problem. It is a knee-jerk, problem-solving process. However, the intuitively perceived need for a meeting is frequently not translated into a purpose that is clearly understood by everyone in attendance.

The purpose of **informational meetings** is the transfer of information, usually from managers, who call the meetings, to employees.[16] Because the purpose is relatively simple, informational meetings are limited in scope, form, and length. Informational meetings are efficient and effective ways of communicating to a large group of people. Although individuals may leave with different perceptions of the message, at least they all hear the same words in the same context. This can be extremely helpful because group members can identify discrepancies in understanding, as well as reaffirm and reinforce the message among themselves.

The purpose of **discussion meetings** is to share information, ideas, and opinions.[17] Discussion is pursued for a variety of reasons, including securing group agreement with a decision that has already been made, solving a problem, and gathering information that will serve as a basis for further discussion and problem solving.

The purpose of **staff meetings** is to foster communication among a group of co-workers.[18] Staff meetings are common in healthcare settings. They are usually scheduled at regular intervals with few changes in meeting times. Perhaps this is a legacy of the 24-hour-per-day nature of healthcare delivery. By having a standing time for meetings, staff members with variable schedules can plan ahead for meetings. Staff meetings are frequently used for both informational and discussion purposes. Content usually includes official announcements, personnel-related news, clarification of grapevine messages, discussion of current problems, professional development, and notification of changes in regulatory and accrediting requirements.[19]

Meetings are expensive, especially in healthcare. A one-hour meeting of eight staff members consumes eight man-hours of time. Assuming an average wage of $12 per participant, the meeting costs a minimum of $96. Assuming that an additional 25% of wages is added for benefit coverage, the cost is increased to $120. If the meeting is held during productive hours, additional staff may have to be paid to handle work that cannot be delayed. In settings that provide round-the-clock services, this is unavoidable. An alternative is to have an additional meeting to include employees who could not be pulled from their regular assignments. In either case, the cost of the meeting goes even higher. Obviously, the more highly paid the meeting participants, the more expensive the meeting. Therefore, unproductive meetings are costly.

Effective meetings are characterized by several attributes: (1) the issues addressed in the meeting are significant, (2) there is no wasted time, (3) attendants contribute in a meaningful way, (4) the outcomes are either high quality decisions or ultimately contribute to high quality decisions, and (5) power is used and shared appropriately in the group.[20] Two ingredients go into meetings that share these characteristics: planning and nurturing.

The cornerstone of effective meetings is the agenda. It is easy for busy managers to neglect the agenda. Some managers confidently attempt to conduct meetings without agendas, or they keep the agenda in their heads or in the form of notes written to themselves. This practice does not maximize the effectiveness of meetings. Written agendas should be prepared and distributed in advance. The written agenda helps attendants prepare to listen and to participate. When people know the topics to be discussed, they have the opportunity to reflect on them before the meeting and come prepared with their questions and comments. If the issues include the generation of alternative solutions to problems, advance notice allows the necessary time required for participants to come prepared with creative contributions.

The agenda is also used during the meeting to keep the discussion focused on important issues. During the meeting, the agenda becomes a tool for facilitating the meeting process. For groups that have a tendency to stray from the purpose of meetings, the written agenda can be a powerful control tool. Some groups have a tendency to stay focused on meeting objectives but have so much to contribute that agendas rarely are completed in the allotted time. Enhancing the agenda by adding time limits for the discussion of each agenda item can help the group to complete the entire agenda. If agendas are habitually not completed, each agenda should be reviewed for its compatibility with the meeting format and time allotment. Perhaps some informational items can be effectively communicated through some other channel, or different groups such as task forces can be formed to deal with some of the items.

The written agenda also serves to confirm meeting messages. For example, one agenda item may be, "Discussion of the February 1 institution of a new paid time off policy that adds eight personal hours per year to the current plan." This item straightforwardly states the new policy. Placing it on the agenda in this form alerts employees that they will probably have the opportunity to ask questions about the new policy and to comment on it. During the meeting, the manager can verbally reinforce the written agenda item and expand on it as needed.

During the course of a meeting, discussion of each agenda item should end with a clear plan of action, and that plan should have target dates attached so that everyone is aware of expectations. For example, if one agenda item is a discussion of patient waiting times in an ambulatory care setting, the discussion should end with a statement of what the next step in the problem-solving process will be and when that step will be completed. This is particularly important for participants who are responsible for the next step. It also alerts all other discussion participants about the deadline for input if they have some additional thoughts on the topic after the meeting.

After the meeting is over, minutes should be prepared and distributed. By reconciling the minutes with each participant's recollection of the proceedings, messages are clarified. Also, minutes help inform interested parties who were not included in the meeting or who were unable to attend.

Improving Written Communications

Providing clinical care is hazardous to writing skills. Operational and legal concerns cause practitioners to write in stylized ways that do not serve them well in communicating with nonclinicians. These clinical styles cannot be effectively applied to communications about nonclinical issues. Much of the writing done by practitioners is in the form of notes. Clinical notes contain abbreviations, incomplete sentences, limited vocabulary, and copious medical jargon. They also fail to provide sufficient descriptive detail for anyone not trained in a clinical discipline because it is assumed that anyone who has need to review the notes will have a sufficient knowledge base to accurately fill in the gaps in a clinically logical way.

Skill in making clinical notes does not translate into managerial writing skill. Learning to make useful, intelligible clinical notes takes considerable practice. So does effective writing for managerial purposes. The clinical setting does little to foster the development of managerial writing skills because it affords scant opportunity to practice those skills. Even the writing skills that were adequate for preparing academic papers and reports atrophy quickly when they are not used. The following recommendations will help practitioners to improve writing skills immediately.

1. *Use reference materials extensively.* Language continually evolves. Accepted formats for memos and letters change. So do acceptable grammatical constructions and spellings. In the clinical setting, practitioners who fail to modify their clinical practice so that it is consistent with currently accepted standards are considered incompetent. Similarly, managers who fail to keep up with changing writing rules may be perceived as incompetent or ineffectual.

2. *Proofread.* Writing reflects the writer's thought process. However, thoughts seldom occur with sufficient clarity and logic to make them intelligible to others. Therefore, they must be modified as they are put on the page. The problem is that the mind works faster than fingers write or keyboard. It even works faster than the mouth dictates. The result is that words which actually appear on paper are not always as clear or grammatically correct as the writer thinks they are. Therefore, proofreading for clarity and correctness is imperative.

For the writer who is out of practice, it is helpful to have someone else proofread. It is difficult for writers to read their own words in the same way that others read them. Other readers can point out ambiguities, poor or improper word choices, and grammatical errors. A word of warning—good proofreaders are hard to find. Search out someone who is good at spotting errors. People who read extensively and read a wide variety of material can usually spot writing problems quite well.

3. *Use all the technology available.* Word processing programs can be enormously helpful to writers. Features that check documents for misspellings should always be used. However, proofreading for spelling errors is still essential because these features will not catch homonym problems (e.g., "two" used in place of "too" or "to").

4. *Write in short, simple sentences.* The purpose of managerial writing is to communicate clearly, not to entertain. Unless the document is very long, which is rare for most managerial communications, the reader does not have the opportunity to become bored. Long sentences and long descriptive passages are more subject to error than short, simple statements. It is better to err on the side of being boring than to make mistakes.

5. *Use common vocabulary.* People who write infrequently sometimes try to make themselves and their writing appear erudite by choosing the proverbial $10 word when $2 words work just fine. Unfortunately, the vocabulary that one can use effectively to convey messages is more limited than the vocabulary that one can understand in context. Therefore, although writers give themselves a pat on the back for coming up with such great sounding words, they end up using words incorrectly, and the message is distorted. Also, using vocabulary in writing that is not part of a writer's working oral vocabulary can make the person appear arrogant and pretentious to people who regularly work with her.

Writing is a mirror of the writer's thoughts. The words that appear on paper represent the writer in the writer's absence. When those words are read and decoded by the receiver, the writer is not there to explain the meaning or to provide all the nonverbal nuances that support and clarify verbal communication. The written message stands on its own. Therefore, the extraordinary time and effort that go into producing written communications should be considered by writers as time well spent.

Cultural Communications Barriers

The bad news about the increasingly multicultural work force in healthcare is that it complicates the already difficult task of managerial communication. The good news is that the multicultural workforce mirrors the multicultural community and is, therefore, better able to serve it. The more diverse workforce also brings a broadened perspective to bear on solving the organization's problems and achieving its objectives. The manager's task as it relates to increasing cultural diversity is twofold. First, the manager must establish communications networks that allow the organization to take full advantage of these various perspectives. Second, the manager has to develop expanded communication skills that make it possible to overcome cultural communication barriers. He must also mentor his staff in these skills.

Culture is a way of looking at the world that is shared by a group of people. It includes the group's beliefs about what is important and about what behaviors are appropriate in different situations. The perspective and belief systems of the group are manifested by normative behaviors in etiquette, traditions, rituals, dress, cuisine, and artistic endeavors. Although culture is frequently associated with nationality, they are not synonymous. Culture can span national boundaries. For example, the word "Hispanic" refers to a system of beliefs that span several national boundaries in Latin and Central America. On the other hand, a single country may contain several distinct cultural groups. For example, the Quebeçois constitute a distinct culture within Canada. Although culture establishes norms within a group, it is important for managers to realize that not all individual behavior arises from the norm. In America, for example, making eye contact and smiling are generally considered to be signs of friendliness. However, there are individual Americans who interpret these expressions as signs of insincerity or frivolity.

Although individual behavior may deviate from cultural norms, it is important for managers to understand cultural norms to help them deal with people that they do not know as individuals. Realizing that cultural norms influence individual behavior gives managers insight into what they might otherwise consider unusual or inappropriate behavior. In America, interpreting culture is particularly difficult because different individuals, families, and cultural groups assimilate at astonishingly different rates and in different ways. These differences must be taken into account to avoid inappropriate generalizations.

Culture defines rules of etiquette that structure communication. Within a culture, abiding by these rules is a symbol of respect for others. The problem for managers is recognizing culturally defined gestures of respect and responding to them appropriately. One gesture of respect and courtesy in many other cultures is not interrupting other speakers. This is true among Thais[21] and several other Far Eastern cultures. Silence in the presence of authority figures is common in Asian cultures.[22] How might silence be interpreted by an American manager in a dyadic interchange? In the American context, silence might be interpreted as disinterest, disengagement, disagreement, lack of understanding, or even defiance. Respect would normally not be an interpretation because Americans express respect in more active ways. At the other extreme, in some cultures (notably French, Italian, and Arabic)[23] interruptions and simultaneous conversation is a sign of enthusiasm and interest in the conversation. This behavior might be interpreted as disrespectful and rude by many Asians and even Americans.

Culture also influences nonverbal communication. In China, for example, eye contact tends to be sustained. Arab cultures also employ eye contact in communication more than Western cultures. It is the reliance on eye contact that contributes to the closer distances used in Arabic communications. By way of contrast, eye contact is considered to be an invasion of privacy in Japan. In space conscious Japan, large arm movements also indicate an invasion of privacy. However, in Arab cultures, large arm gestures reinforce the spoken word and endow it with emotional content.[24] Although managers do not need to adopt the same nonverbal communication patterns as their employees, it is helpful to understand that the nonverbal cues they observe do not necessarily mean the same thing as the nonverbal cues to which they are accustomed. Also, managers can improve communications by becoming sensitive to the fact that people who are adapting to a culture other than the one in which they grew up may not be comfortable with organizational communications, or they may inadvertently send mixed verbal and nonverbal messages. Managers should use as much repetition and feedback as possible to verify the content of messages.

Language is a potential obstacle to communications. The United States is a large country that is relatively linguistically homogenous. Many U.S.-born Americans have little, if any, experience with foreign languages. Lack of exposure magnifies the problem of language because Americans have fewer linguistic alternatives and are less prepared to find alternate ways of communicating than people from countries with more linguistic diversity. Managers are vulnerable to errors both in over- and underestimating language skills of people for whom English is a second, third, or fourth language. Managers should realize that foreign accents do not necessarily indicate that speakers lack facility in English. People who have studied languages know that understanding comes before the ability to speak. Even when the learner gets to the point that the correct words come to mind, the accent tends to linger because getting the sounds exactly right is the last step in developing fluency. Therefore, managers have to evaluate feedback carefully to make sure that the message is understood without treating the employee as a linguistic incompetent. At the other extreme, managers may overestimate language skills. Effective communication in any language requires far more than solid grammar and vocabulary. Every language is infused with subtleties of meaning which are mastered only after extensive experience with using the language on a daily basis. Once again, this phenomenon means that managers must verify comprehension of messages, even with employees whose mastery of English seems to be adequate.

It is easy for managers who deal with culturally diverse work forces to feel that the burden of overcoming communication barriers falls disproportionately on managers as opposed to employees. Many managers believe that it is the employees' responsibility to adapt to the dominant culture of the workplace rather than the workplace (and its management) adapting to them. It is certainly true that the employees do have a duty to adapt. However, managers seldom see the cultural adaptations that employees have already made before they get to the workplace and the multitude of small but significant adaptations they make every workday. The fact that they have found a place in the American work force means that they have already made tremendous progress in cultural adaptation. Also, managers must remember that leading employees is a managerial responsibility, irrespective of the characteristics of those employees. Dealing with cultural diversity is part of that leadership responsibility.

Conclusion

The results of the meeting announcement by St. Clare's CEO were not the results that she anticipated when she sent the message. This is an all too common occurrence. What is troubling about this case is the fact that the message came from the CEO. Because CEOs set the standard for so much of the behavior that occurs in organizations it is not too farfetched to assume that weakly drawn messages like this one are pervasive at St. Clare's. If they are not yet the order of the day, they may well become prevalent if the CEO stays at St. Clare long enough. Once poor communication practices become part of the corporate culture, eradicating them is extremely difficult. It is easy for people to communicate in a lackadaisical way. It is more difficult and time-consuming to carefully encode and decode messages. The only way to improve organizational communications is for each individual to develop and utilize effective communication skills. Intervention to improve communication skills includes the same approaches used in the rehabilitation of aphasics.

First, a holistic approach is essential.[25,26] Encoding and decoding messages is a complex process that has psychological, sociological, and cultural dimensions in addition to technical verbal and nonverbal components. Efforts at improving the process must, therefore, be comprehensive. Learning grammar, vocabulary, and nonverbal cues alone is insufficient. Increasing communication effectiveness also requires augmenting understanding of human behavior.

Also, it is important to remember that the communications process is a means to an end. Therefore, the content of messages must be considered in conjunction with the process of communicating them. The content and its importance in relationship to organizational objectives and other messages needs to be considered when choosing an appropriate channel and way of encoding the message. Thus, in this case, the short note in a pay envelope was not an appropriate way to communicate such an important message.

Second, rehabilitation of aphasic patients is built on the constant evaluation of speaking skills and feedback to patients to reinforce progress toward effective speech.[27] Managers need the same kind of feedback about the effectiveness of their communications. If no one tells J. Crane about how her announcement was understood, she will never know that what she did was ineffective. Nor will she have any clues about how to improve the way she makes these announcements. Because most people have difficulty offering constructive criticism to their superiors, it is unlikely that this CEO will be made aware of her deficiency. Aphasic persons cannot assess and modify their communication deficits without the intervention of therapists. Likewise, managers need assistance with assessing and improving communication skills. Because communications are essential to the life of organizations, assessment and improvement of communication skills should be part of each manager's professional development agenda. And because communication is a two-way process, improving communication skills should be an objective of all employees.

Endnotes

1. Nancy Ann Jeffrey, "HMOs Say 'Hola' to Potential Customers," *Wall Street Journal 77* (November 30, 1995): B1, B6.
2. Iris Varner and Linda Beamer, *Intercultural Communication in the Global Workplace* (Chicago: Irwin, 1995).
3. Mark L. Knapp, *Nonverbal Communication in Human Interaction* (New York: Holt, Rinehart & Winston, 1972).
4. Ibid.
5. Albert Mehrabian and Morton Wiener, "Decoding of Inconsistent Communications," *Journal of Personality and Social Psychology 6* (1967): 109–114.
6. Albert Mehrabian and S. R. Ferris, "Influence of Attitudes from Nonverbal Communication in Two Channels," *Journal of Consulting Psychology 31* (1967): 248–252.
7. Paul Ekman and Wallace V. Friesen, "Nonverbal Linkage and Clues to Deception," *Psychiatry 32* (1969): 88–106.
8. Edward T. Hall, *The Hidden Dimension* (Garden City, NY: Anchor Books, 1969).
9. Ruth A. Shearer and Ruth Davidhizar, "It's Not What You Do But How You Do It: Tips for the Manager," *Healthcare Supervisor 13* (1994): 12–16.
10. Thomas A. Atchison, *Turning Healthcare Leadership Around: Cultivating Inspired, Empowered, and Loyal Followers* (San Francisco: Jossey-Bass Publisher, 1991).

11. Henry Mintzberg, *The Nature of Managerial Work* (Englewood Cliffs, NJ: Prentice-Hall, Inc., 1980).
12. Jonathon S. Rakich, Beaufort B. Longest, and Kurt Darr, *Managing Health Services Organizations*, 3rd ed. (Baltimore: Health Professions Press, 1992).
13. Ibid.
14. Donald D. White and David A. Bednar, *Organizational Behavior: Understanding and Managing People At Work*, 2nd ed. (Boston: Allyn and Bacon, 1991).
15. Susan E. Ogborn, "Running Effective Meetings, Running Effective Groups," *Healthcare Supervisor 13* (1994): 69–77.
16. Charles R. McConnell, *The Effective Healthcare Supervisor*, 2nd ed. (Gaithersburg, MD: Aspen Publishers, Inc., 1988).
17. Ibid.
18. Ibid.
19. William Umiker, *Management Skills for the New Healthcare Supervisor* (Gaithersburg, MD: Aspen Publishers, Inc., 1988).
20. Dave France and Don Young, *Improving Work Groups: A Practical Manual for Team Building* (San Diego, CA: Pfeiffer and Company, 1992).
21. Varner and Beamer, op. cit.
22. Sondra Thiederman, *Bridging Cultural Barriers for Corporate Success: How to Manage the Multicultural Workforce* (New York: Lexington Books, 1991).
23. Ibid.
24. Varner and Beamer, op. cit.
25. Libby Kumin, *Aphasia* (Lincoln, NE: Cliff Notes, Inc., 1978).
26. Martha Taylor Sarno, "Aphasia Rehabilitation," in Martha Taylor Sarno and Ollie Hook, eds., *Aphasia: Assessment and Treatment* (Stockholm, Sweden: Almqvist and Wiksell International, 1980).
27. Ibid.

11 Managing Change: Hypertension

In this chapter the reader will learn:
- ◆ how to determine the different levels and types of change
- ◆ why individuals and groups resist change
- ◆ how to overcome resistance to change
- ◆ how to plan a change process
- ◆ how to assess and resolve conflicts that commonly accompany change.

Bitter Medicine

February—Mary Ortiz is the vice president of Operations of Compton Pharmaceutical Services (CPS). CPS is a successful and growing business with three divisions that operate at different sites. Its Packaging Division repackages pharmaceuticals for physicians and retail pharmacy dispensing. Its Retail Division operates twelve retail pharmacy outlets concentrated in the local metropolitan market. Its Direct Dispensing Division provides mail-order pharmaceuticals nationwide. About 45% of the dispensing business is local. An additional 15% comes from within the state. CPS' executives know that to continue CPS' growth in the rapidly changing healthcare environment, it must gain access to the managed care market through contracting with managed care companies to provide pharmaceutical services to managed care clients. The executives decide to do three things to position CPS to compete for these contracts:

237

1. Expand hours at all local retail outlets to make them more attractive to local managed care plans;

2. Increase productivity in the mail order division by implementing prescription production targets for technicians and pharmacists; and

3. Initiate more vigorous quality control standards in the Packaging Division and tie merit raises to order processing accuracy.

Mary announces these plans to the division managers on February 28 and asks them to draw up plans for implementing these changes so that they are in place by the end of March.

March 15—Three pharmacists and five technicians in the retail division have resigned in the past two weeks because they cannot rotate through the additional shifts required by extended hours. Two other pharmacists have resigned to accept other positions. They say that their new jobs offer them more opportunity for professional development.

April 10—A committee of pharmacists and technicians from the Packaging Division asks for a meeting with Mary to voice their complaints about the new productivity standards. They feel that the standards are unreasonable. Mary refuses to meet with group. She tells the group that the development and implementation of standards are the responsibility of the Division Manager.

April 15—Turnover and absenteeism in all the divisions are up. Mail order deliveries are slower. At two different times and locations, retail outlets have been unable to fill prescriptions because no pharmacist was available to work.

April 18—Data from the first two weeks of April show no improvement in order processing performance in the Repackaging Division.

April 20—A pharmacist in the Direct Dispensing Division has sought treatment for a stress disorder that he claims was brought on by the new production targets. Although mental health services are not covered by CPS' health plan, he threatens to sue for damages if CPS does not pay for the treatment and time lost when he has to be away from his job because of stress.

May 15—CPS loses a bid to provide services for the largest managed care plan in the state. Through the industry grapevine, Mary learns that the bid was lost because CPS provided inadequate access to service and had too little data to support its quality control claims.

Compared to many managers, CPS' executives were ahead in planning to meet external challenges. They recognized that they could not stay in the comfort zone of the business niches that they had identified and successfully exploited. They knew that CPS would have to change in order to continue to operate successfully. The changes that the executives sought to make were appropriate to the changing market. The fact that CPS lost a contract based on access and quality deficiencies verified that the executives' concern about these issues was warranted. The origin of the productivity initiative is not as clear. However, services were being expanded and quality increased in anticipation of contracts that had not yet materialized. Expansion has to be paid for, and it is possible that the executives were trying to finance expansion through productivity gains. Irrespective of its origin, productivity is a legitimate concern of any organization, and establishing productivity goals is a widespread and justifiable management practice. The changes that CPS managers chose to make were appropriate. Had they been successfully implemented, CPS may have become a successful provider of managed pharmacy services. Instead, CPS seems to be in a worse position in May than it was in February. The medicine ordered by the executives was the tonic that the organization needed, but it seems to have been too bitter for the members of the organization to swallow.

Change is one of the most difficult challenges that managers face. Because change is intrinsic to organizational life (indeed, to life itself), it would seem that managers and employees would have so much experience with it that changing would be as natural as breathing. It is not.

Managing change is similar to managing hypertension. Like change, hypertension is a condition that evolves differently in different individuals. Hypertensive patients and organizations undergoing change respond to interventions in somewhat unpredictable ways.

Hypertension is one of the most common health problems. However, the fact that healthcare providers have considerable experience in managing the disease does not mean that treatment always results in positive outcomes. Each hypertensive patient is different. Patients respond differently to various treatment modalities. They exhibit different levels of compliance with prescribed treatment regimens. Stability of blood pressure varies from one patient to another. The approach to the treatment of hypertension varies with disease severity, underlying etiology, and patient acceptance. Likewise, the appropriate approach to managing organizational change depends on the characteristics of the contemplated change, and the different responses of individuals and groups to change.

Attributes of Change

One of the reasons that managers have difficulty managing change is that there is very little empirical evidence to support one managerial approach over another. Most of the conventional wisdom in this area comes from personal experience and anecdotal evidence provided by consultants who help different kinds of organizations work through different kinds of changes. The dearth of research results that support the relative merits of different change strategies stems from three barriers to field-based research. First, successful change depends on so many different variables that isolating and controlling them to determine the relative significance of any one variable is extremely difficult. Second, the course of change is unpredictable. Once a change is initiated, any number of circumstances can arise that may cause managers to terminate the change process, significantly alter the course of the change, or replace the initial change with an entirely new change. Therefore, it is difficult for researchers to study change processes that have been carried through without significant alteration. Third, because implementation of change takes time, the variables on which successful implementation depends also change. For example, one of the factors that plays a role in the implementation of change is leadership. If there is a change in leaders during the change process, the relative influence of individual leaders and different leadership styles is almost impossible to identify. These research barriers are the result of the dynamic nature of the change process.

The factors that are barriers to researchers also present major challenges to managers deeply involved in initiating or implementing change. The purpose of this chapter is to help managers understand the change process so that they can manage it more effectively. Recognizing that all change is not the same is the first step to understanding change and formulating an effective strategy for managing each change.

Although change never looks exactly the same in any two organizations, it has four clearly discernible attributes:

1. Change is a process, not a discreet, isolated event.
2. Change is a personal experience.
3. Change is experienced.[1]
4. Change results in uncertainty.[2]

Managers who have a tendency to lose sight of the big picture tend to conceive of change as an event rather than a process. During World War II, the Battle of the Bulge was an event; liberating Europe was a process. The Battle was not isolated from the overall objective. The event and the process were connected and interdependent. In the CPS case, the specific operational changes were disconnected from the overall process of changing CPS into a competitive managed care provider. As each of the division managers went about implementing these changes, there was no evidence that a unified sense of purpose was generated throughout the organization. Without a sense of purpose, there was nothing to garner the commitment and support of employees. Compare this to the commitment of the soldiers who fought in the Battle of the Bulge. They were aware of the importance of the Battle to the success of the entire European mission.

There were no interdivisional support systems at CPS. If such systems had been in place, isolated change events could have been integrated into an organization-wide process. For example, all three operational changes could have been undertaken under a quality improvement initiative that would have linked the efforts with a management information system (MIS). The MIS could have supported quality improvement objectives in all three divisions. All three divisions could have developed quality, accessibility, and productivity improvement objectives that could have been interrelated. Gains in one division could have supported gains in another. For example, new customers in the retail division who needed maintenance medication could have become customers of the mail order division. The MIS could have identified these customers so that CPS could have provided service to them in the most efficient, cost-effective manner. Because different kinds of changes were delegated to each division, CPS' divisional activities were disconnected from the objectives of the organization as a whole.

Change is a personal experience because each individual and group reacts to it differently. Feelings are an intrinsic part of change because employees respond to change emotionally. They either embrace change or reject it with their hearts, not their minds. This makes managing change difficult for managers who are more task-oriented than process-oriented. Managers who attempt to deny or ignore emotional responses to change run the risk of losing the ideas, alternative solutions, and perspectives that employees can contribute to the process. By denying the emotional aspect of the process, managers may also divorce themselves from their own emotions,[3] which jeopardizes their ability to work effectively. Repressing and ignoring feelings is no more healthy in one's work life than it is in one's personal life. Refusing to deal with emotions at work has as much potential for producing unhealthy and unhappy results as it does at home.

The impact of change cannot be fully comprehended until it is experienced. It is much different to talk about adding a 12-hour shift on Sundays than it is to work it. Planning to lay off 10 people is a far cry from seeing them leave at the end of their last day. Deciding to implement a quality control program feels much different than experiencing the triumph of exceeding quality control expectations. Change on paper and change in discussion do not comprise change itself. Change is a process that is experienced.

Change always results in uncertainty. Only a few of the outcomes of some changes can be anticipated with some degree of certainty. For example, automating a juice pouring function in a dietary department may predictably result in the layoff of a worker whose primary responsibility is pouring juice. However, other outcomes are not so easily predicted. Will the displaced worker quit? Will he seek a transfer to another department? Will he become violent if he is fired? Will supportive co-workers sabotage the juice dispenser? Will enthusiastic employees identify other functions that could be automated? Even a relatively small change such as this one has several possible consequences, not all of which can be anticipated. The physician who makes a change in the drug regimen of a hypertensive patient tries to anticipate the occurrence and gravity of unintended side effects. The manager must be equally concerned about the side effects of organizational changes. The only certainty is that every change opens the organization to new vulnerabilities and new opportunities. The uncertainty of managers and employees is not knowing what those vulnerabilities and opportunities are. Uncertainty results in the wall of resistance that managers often meet when implementing change.

The four attributes of change are universal. They become more pronounced and significant at higher levels of change. Identifying the level of change can help managers anticipate how difficult and long the change process will be. At the lower levels, change is easier and quicker. At the higher levels, it is more difficult and takes longer.[4]

Levels and Types of Change

The first level of change is **change in knowledge**. Change at this level is easiest to bring about because it is achieved through the effective communication of knowledge. Note that easiest does not mean easy. As Chapter 10 emphasized, effective communication is anything but easy. The second level is **change in attitude**. This level is much more difficult to achieve because it involves changing emotional responses. Managers are accustomed to communicating rational concepts. However, communication of rational concepts is frequently insufficient to change emotions. The third level is **change in individual behavior**. Bringing about this level of change is usually preceded by the two previous levels (i.e., first changing individual knowledge, then changing the emotional response, which ultimately results in a change in behavior). An individual's knowledge and attitude must be aligned with managerial objectives for individual behavior to change. The fourth level of change is **change in group behavior**. This level of change is the most difficult to achieve because groups do not always exhibit monolithic behavior. Some individuals are more amenable to change than others so that during the change process, the shift in group behavior more nearly resembles the movement of an amoeba rather than that of a paramecium (see Figure 11.2). The group becomes less cohesive and orderly as some individuals adopt the change more readily than others.

Successful implementation of the changes at CPS required changes in group behavior. Therefore, CPS executives should have anticipated that the changes would be difficult and that their acceptance among employees would be uneven. It is not surprising that these changes had not been fully or successfully implemented before CPS made its managed care bid.

It is also important for managers to recognize that changes vary based on their temporal relationship to causative events.[5] **Developmental change** is an evolutionary change. It is the kind of change that is an intrinsic part of existence. In healthcare, new technologies and regulatory mandates are evolutionary changes in the HSO environment. These new developments cause HSOs to respond (i.e., evolve and change) to maintain their existence. **Traumatic change** takes place in response to sudden internal or external events. A managed care plan's loss or gain of a large group of enrollees would cause a traumatic change as new personnel are cut (or added) and systems are modified to handle the significant change in workload. Although the line between development and trauma is more difficult to draw in management than it is in medicine, the fundamental distinction is the same. **Managed change** is undertaken in anticipation of future events. This was the kind of change that CPS attempted. Executives undertook change to be prepared to meet future managed care challenges. Because it is anticipatory, managers have the opportunity of undertaking managed change pursuant to analysis and planning. Managed change is similar to preventive care. Just as prevention, trauma, and development require different medical strategies to optimize health, different kinds of changes require different managerial strategies to optimize organizational performance.

The changes at CPS were traumatic. In clinical work, managing trauma cases requires close attention to patient progress and development of complications. It also requires an extraordinarily high commitment of resources. The same degree of attention and commitment is required to successfully manage traumatic organizational change. One reason for CPS' poor outcome may have been the failure to recognize the amount of trauma these changes would inflict, which resulted in too little time and attention being committed to their implementation. The difference between the amount of resources required to manage traumatic change and developmental change is roughly equivalent to the difference between the resources required to manage hypertensive crisis and mild hypertension.

Another way of differentiating changes is based on their comprehensiveness. In this scheme, there are two kinds of change: incremental and total. **Incremental change** is the type of change that CPS attempted. Three distinct problem areas were identified, and three specific changes were initiated to address these problems. The rest of the organization and its operations remained the same. **Total change** involves completely overhauling the organization. This kind of change is referred to as **reengineering**. Reengineering may be thought of as reconstructing the organization and its processes from the ground up.[6]

Given the extraordinary changes in CPS' environment, reengineering may have been appropriate. CPS executives seem to believe that CPS' business is providing pharmaceutical products to niche markets. This business mission is too narrow. CPS' real business is making pharmaceutical products available and usable to consumers, wherever they are. This reconceptualization of CPS' core business should cause CPS managers to reevaluate the current divisional structure and the work that each person does in the organization. Reengineering might result in an organization in which repackaging and mailing are done at each retail site to decrease delivery and order processing time. Or it might result in more centralization of billing, order entry, and order processing with a more decentralized delivery system. Whatever it would look like, the reengineered organization would have a new set of job descriptions, operating policies and procedures, and communications patterns that would better serve all CPS clients. Reengineering is more time-consuming and wrenching that incremental change, so it is not to be undertaken lightly. However, reengineering is necessary when the market for an organization's products and services changes dramatically.

Resistance to Change

In the beginning, Change begat Uncertainty. Uncertainty begat Fear.
And Fear begat Defense Against Change, who is also called Resistance.

Resistance to change is common at all levels of the organizational hierarchy. It is a natural phenomenon that all managers encounter. Managers would do well to accept resistance as a given and not to take its occurrence personally.[7] What is it about change that causes fear? There are several possible sources of change-induced fear.[8] First, because no one works alone in an organization, changes may threaten hierarchical, collegial, and/or social interpersonal relationships. Some changes threaten power bases and the resources over which individuals have control. Change opens the door to turf wars that could result in shifts in the prerogatives of employees and loss of budget for managers. Second, fear may also arise from an individual's having to face an inadequacy. Even a knowledge level change can trigger this fear. Imagine a middle-aged manager who has viewed computers as a clerical tool. In a reengineering effort, it is decided that all managers will receive training in the use of a relational database program that will allow them to update and exchange vital data quickly without having to go through a data processing department. Because the manager may be afraid that his computer illiteracy will come to light, he may resist the change. Third, some individuals may fear that change reflects badly on their past performance. After all, if things are going well, they reason, why change? The division managers at CPS, for example, might have been afraid that the changes reflected some inadequacy in their performance and that as a result their jobs or advancement opportunities might be in jeopardy. CPS executives did not seem to realize that resistance might come from division managers.

Fear is not the only etiological basis of resistance.[9] Some individuals may resist because they do not understand a change. It is difficult to leave the comfort of understanding (even in a bad situation) for the disorientation of not understanding. The people who are affected by a change may not share the same assessment of the need for change as the change initiator(s). This perceptual difference is critical because it is difficult for people to go along with changes that they believe are bad, especially if they perceive them to be bad not only for themselves but also for the organization. Some individuals may resist because they do not like the change initiator's attitude. Many people find it hard to support the objectives of people they do not like, even when those objectives are mutually beneficial. There are plenty of people who "bite off their noses to spite their faces." Others simply have a low emotional tolerance for change of any kind. Some people are more emotionally attached to routine and rooted in the present than others.

It has also been suggested that people resist change when they feel that the change is made for change's sake (i.e., that the change is an end rather than the means to an end). If people do not perceive that a change has a purpose, they will resist the change.[10,11] The bottom line is that if people do not believe that there is a good reason to change, they will have to be dragged along kicking and screaming.

Managers typically view resistance to change like clinicians view hypertension. It is a pathological process that needs to be controlled because if it is left unchecked, extensive damage (and, in severe cases, even death) may ensue. However, hypertension can be a useful and necessary reaction that preserves vital physiological functions in times of stress. Resistance to change also results in some outcomes that help maintain organizational stability. On the positive side, an analysis of resistance can lead to the identification of low job satisfaction and its causes. Resistance can also help managers to identify communication weaknesses. It may compel change initiators to more clearly define the nature of change and the reasons for it. It may also cause a useful reconsideration of the possible negative outcomes. Finally, resistance may result in increased organizational assistance for those individuals who are most affected by the change.[12] The initiation of change and resistance to it can be viewed as a dialectic process through which a change that is more mature and better suited to meeting the organization's needs emerges.

Overcoming Resistance to Change—Things to Do

People who have been through a major organizational change can reflect on the experience and identify factors that facilitated the change. They can also identify actions that would have made the change go more smoothly if they had been utilized. The management literature is filled with suggestions for managing change that come from experienced managers. The reader and interpreter of this literature must be aware, however, that managing change is not a one-size-fits-all process. Managers should start the process by identifying the level and type of change proposed. Next, they should make an assessment to determine how it is likely to affect employees. Then they will be in a position to choose from the long list of suggestions those strategies that best address the needs of their work groups. Therefore, the recommendations offered here should be viewed not so much as commandments, but rather as guidelines that have proven effective in other organizations.

Two broad principles should guide the manager's approach to decreasing resistance to change. These are (1) recognition and validation of employee concerns regarding change, and (2) appropriate modification of managers' and employees' expectations. Recognition and validation of employee concerns is the psychological dimension of managing change. As millions of people are displaced in today's rapidly evolving workplace, the fear of losing one's job is well-founded. Today's employees are under more pressure than employees in the past several generations because high quality employment opportunities are extremely limited and the odds of replacing one's current job with another of equal income are steadily decreasing.[13] Other fears regarding change are equally valid. The manager needs to be as definitive as possible in identifying and discussing with employees their fears and concerns. The manager should early and quickly dispel the fear of those things that are unlikely to result from the change. He should deal openly and honestly with the outcomes that employees are justifiably afraid of, especially if those outcomes are likely to occur. A clinician who is about to perform a painful procedure does not lie to the patient and say that it will not hurt. Instead, he helps the patient to cope with the pain by explaining its intensity and duration. Sugarcoating reality would only serve to destroy the patient's trust in the clinician. Likewise, successful change depends on a mutually supportive relationship between managers and employees. If managers expect individuals to do the right thing for the organization, then the organization, through its management, must do the right thing for employees. "Leaders generate loyalty by being loyal."[14]

Building trust during the stress of change depends on two factors: predictability and capability.[15] People want to know what to expect. Whether they are likely to survive the change unscathed, or be better off, or lose their position, they want to know. Although managers can seldom guarantee outcomes, they can help build a sense of predictability by establishing ground rules that will guide the change process. These ground rules might include how decisions regarding change implementation will be made, how procedures may be automated, how team leaders will be chosen, and how layoffs will be determined. With these kinds of ground rules, employees can assess their own vulnerabilities and opportunities and start planning accordingly. The other major component of trust is capability. For managers and employees to trust each other in evolving roles, they must believe that they are capable of fulfilling those roles. For example, assume that a change calls for more employee decision making. The manager who has used an authoritative, control-oriented style may not believe that employees are capable of making decisions. Conversely, the employees who have worked for this manager may not believe that the manager is capable of allowing them to make decisions. The result is mutual lack of faith in each other's capabilities. Professional development and constant expansion of work roles are the keys to increasing and demonstrating capability.

The second broad principle that should guide management of change is appropriate modification of expectations. Modification of expectations does not mean that lofty hopes and dreams of employees and managers have to be quashed. But it does mean that their expectations have to be realistic. In times of change, managers are in a position to help employees modify their expectations because managers have a deeper understanding of conditions within and outside of the organization. This enlightened point of view can be particularly useful in helping employees recognize paradigm shifts. For example, in the first 40 years or so of the post-World War II era, career success was equated to advancement within an

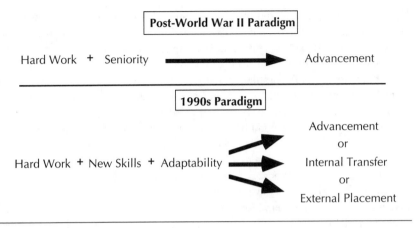

Figure 11.1   Paradigm shift in career development expectations.

organization. The road to advancement was paved by hard work and longevity in the organization (Figure 11.1). Today, career success is not defined by advancement alone. The recent wave of downsizing has severely limited advancement opportunities. In these times of declining employment opportunities, the definition of success in the workplace must also include ongoing employment. Ongoing employment may be within the same organization, in another organization, or in a new independent business. Not only is the definition of success evolving, but hard work and seniority are no longer the keys to success. Hard work remains, but seniority has largely been replaced by continual development of new skills and adaptability. Managers can assist employees by helping them to recognize these changes and by supporting their efforts to develop new skills. Employees who are well positioned to take advantage of change are less likely to resist it.

Within the broad framework established by these two overarching principles of change management, several specific tactics for decreasing resistance to change have been found to be successful.

Define goals and explain benefits. Defining goals infuses the change with its purpose. Managers should repeat goals frequently throughout the process to keep employees focused on the long-term purpose of the change, rather than being consumed by the short-term pain of change. Because the natural reaction to change is resistance, benefits must be clearly identified. Like goals, benefits must be reinforced through repetition. "If there is a single rule of communications for leaders, it is this: when you are so sick of talking about something that you can hardly stand it, your message is finally starting to get through."[16]

The more difficult the change, the more important it is to keep the benefits front and center. Explaining benefits is more difficult to do with planned change than with developmental and traumatic change. With the latter kinds of change, employees can recognize the need to change as the result of a causative factor in the internal or external environment. But planned changes occur before causative factors occur. Therefore, the need to change is less apparent. This could have contributed to part of the problem at CPS. Had a large increase in current business forced the lengthening of retail store hours or necessitated increased productivity, employees may have been more willing to adapt.

No change will go smoothly if managers and employees perceive goals and benefits differently. St. John's Mercy Hospital in St. Louis is one of many examples in which management's stated goals and benefits of reengineering are inconsistent with employees' perceptions of the goals and benefits. According to a local report, managers believe reengineering will "reduce costs and make patient care more streamlined, seamless and, they hope, better."[17] The hospital's change agent consultant says the "aim is to preserve and enrich nurses' jobs."[18] Meanwhile, a number of nurses publicly claim that the change will result in poorer patient care and a loss of nursing jobs. They point to several organizational changes that support their perceptions. Some nurses are talking about unionizing and meeting with a statewide nursing group to discuss their rights.[19] Without implying that anyone is specifically to blame for lack of consensus, it is obvious that managers and consultants have not convinced the nursing staff of the need for the changes. If the central focus is decreasing cost, then that should be the goal, and the benefit of cutting costs needs to be emphasized. If the central focus is improving patient care, then the benefits of improving care need to be emphasized. The worst possible strategy is to claim that the goal of reengineering is to increase quality of care when the real goal is cost cutting. The quality of care veil is readily transparent to discerning employees. Failure to come to consensus in this organization has exposed it to bad publicity, created morale problems among the staff, and made it vulnerable to intervention by third parties.

Identify what will not be changed. People need to have some sense of grounding and continuity during change. Emotionally, they may feel that their whole work world is being turned upside down. If the change involves new work hours and/or employment status, they may feel that their whole lives are being disrupted. To be reminded of the things that remain constant is reassuring. This kind of reminder is even more important with groups and individuals who have been through several changes and with employees who are cynical as a result of bad experiences with change.

Make the change exciting. This may be easier to do with developmental changes and knowledge-level changes than with other kinds of change. Among healthcare professionals, new technologies can create excitement because they make the work of care providers easier and safer. They may also result in better clinical outcomes, which results in clinician gratification. When employees are being hurt by a change, attempts at creating excitement may appear callous. However, for the health of the organization, managers need to find all the silver linings they can and communicate benefits at every opportunity. Even traumatic changes frequently have positive outcomes that need to be made clear to change survivors.

Boost confidence. Because capability is crucial to the trust relationship, examples of capability need to be identified and brought to the attention of everyone. For example, if the change involves increased employee decision making, then examples of strong, independently formulated decisions need to be brought to everyone's attention. The fact that the decisions were arrived at without the participation of managers emphasizes the capability of employees to function within the framework of new rules. Short-term performance standards can also be established so that the group will have several opportunities to recognize and celebrate success during the change. For example, at CPS the quality control goal may have been a 20% reduction in order filling errors. Short-term goals may have been to decrease product count errors by 2%, decrease order quantity errors by 3%, and decrease billing errors by 4%. Achieving each one of these goals could be an occasion to celebrate and to reinforce the employees' belief that they could achieve the overall quality control goal.

Allow adequate time for the change. The manager's change mantra should be **patience**. Because resistance to change is an emotional response, people need time to work through their emotions. If managers are going to create a mutually supportive environment, they must allow sufficient time for discussion of the change and the employees' response to it. They must allow employees time to find their own ways of coping with the change. As employees cope, managers may have to listen to employee concerns more than once. Managers must realize that people do not always make emotional adjustments rapidly. At CPS, the early turnover in the retail division may have been avoided if employees had had more time to work through their responses to the change. They may have had time to realize that most retailers would eventually have to increase accessibility with the result that other opportunities may not have appeared so attractive. In this case, expectations about work hours would have to be modified. This takes time. Given enough time, employees may have more fully and rationally considered the negative effects of the change, as well as the positive aspects of working at CPS, and decided to stay. Or they may have had time to work out the logistics of new work schedules.

The process of an individual's working through an organizational change has been compared to the mourning process.[20] The first stage of the working through process is **shock**. During this stage, the individual may feel somewhat numb. The individual is prone to outbursts of anger and panic. He tends to be closed to assimilation and rational processing of information. Obviously the more traumatic the change, the more profoundly felt will be the shock.

Shock is followed by **disbelief**. During this stage the individual begins to yearn for what is lost or is about to be lost. This stage is characterized by irrational emotions such as self-reproach for unavoidable or uncontrollable circumstances

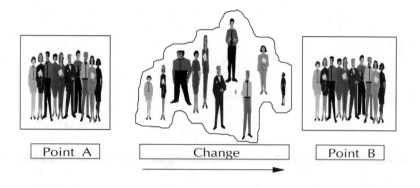

Figure 11.2   Group cohesiveness during change.

and denial of reality. Fight or flight behavior is symptomatic as people seek to maintain the status quo. They may fight by stubbornly continuing current behavior patterns and by directing their energy to proving that no change is necessary. At CPS, the flight response was evident as people in the Retail Division sought to maintain the status quo by finding new employment. The Direct Dispensing Division employees chose to fight by complaining about new standards.

The third stage is **discarding**. This is the phase during which the individual accepts the fact that change is inevitable. This is a crucial stage in the working-through process. During this phase the individual confronts the reality of change. The employee may feel defeated by circumstances over which he has no control.

Acceptance may be accompanied by feelings of sadness. If the new situation is too unpleasant, the individual may still exhibit flight behavior.

Realization is the final stage of working through change. In this stage, the individual begins to accommodate to the new order of his organizational life. Sadness begins to recede as the dominant emotion and he begins to focus more on his new role. Throughout this phase, less time and energy are spent in mourning the past, while more time and energy are spent planning for the future.

Because each individual moves through these stages at different rates, managers have to tailor support and intervention activities to individuals, not to groups as a whole. Figure 11.2 illustrates how groups react to change and how group cohesiveness may be affected. Before the change, the individuals at Point A are close together to represent cohesiveness. The figures are different to represent diverse roles, but they are similar in size to indicate that the roles played by individuals are roughly equal in importance. During the change process, the group is in disarray. The person at the far right of the center graphic seems to be moving through the process more quickly. At this stage of the change, the manager should probably concentrate on helping her to define and adjust to her new role. The figure at the far left may still be in the shock stage. The appropriate intervention with her may be to provide significant opportunities to vent her anger so that she can exhaust this emotion and begin to move beyond the shock stage. The different sizes and shapes of the figures represent the different scope and importance of individual roles during the change. The lack of alignment and fit reflects the disruption of group cohesiveness. Once all group members work through the change, roles can be normalized and cohesiveness reestablished as indicated by the final grouping at Point B. Because some changes require that group roles be added, deleted, or redefined, the post-change group will not always look exactly like the pre-change group.

A model that is very similar to the mourning/working-through model described above is the death and dying model of Kubler-Ross.[21] This model is well-known to clinicians who work with terminally ill patients. Kubler-Ross identified five stages that people go through when they learn of a terminal diagnosis:

1. Denial (shock)

2. Anger

3. Bargaining

4. Depression

5. Acceptance

These stages closely mirror the stages of mourning. In fact, this model may be thought of as a special type of mourning for the impending loss of one's own existence. People whose current sense of identity, life-style, or livelihood stands to be extinguished by an organizational change would go through these stages. Clinicians and managers alike must recognize these stages and adapt their behavior accordingly. What experienced clinicians come to realize about this process is that it is unalterable. Therefore, the clinician's role is not to disrupt the process, but rather to support patients as they go through it. Managers too often find themselves trying to change the process. For example, when anger surfaces, they attempt to suppress it. Or when bargaining behavior begins, they allow themselves to be drawn into dead-end negotiations. Managers must realize that employees faced with change will go through these stages whether or not managers want to accommodate them.[22]

Provide forums for communication. Having meetings to discuss change looks easy on paper. In reality, these meetings are among the most difficult managerial tasks. In open forums managers are exposed to employees' anger and despair. As messengers of bad news, managers are often the targets of employees' negative emotions. "Don't shoot the messenger" was never said by a threatened employee. The open forum can become the shooting range on which managers are verbally and emotionally wounded. Forums can be used to allow employees to vent their emotions so that they can move on in working through the change. They can also be used to share information and to clarify change-related issues. Thus, open forums are useful, but seldom pleasant.

One-on-one meetings can also be used to achieve the same objectives. In one-on-one meetings, there is no opportunity for an employee's negativism to be reinforced by other employees during the meeting, and the manager may feel a bit safer. However, these meetings take an extraordinary amount of time and subject the manager repeatedly to employee anger and frustration. Whether the manager chooses open forums, one-on-one meetings, or a mixture of the two, the point is that interaction must be personal. Satisfaction surveys, suggestion boxes, and similar low contact communication channels are too sterile to provide the kind of emotional venting and support the employees need.

Get people to buy into the change. When people are faced with a situation in which they must behave in a way that is inconsistent with their feelings, they experience **cognitive dissonance**. Cognitive dissonance is psychologically un-comfortable. When people experience cognitive dissonance they do not perform at their best.[23] The manager's responsibility is to align emotions and behavior so that employees feel comfortable with, and are eager to pursue, the desired behavior.

The best way to do this is to transfer ownership of the change from management to employees. With planned changes, this is most easily accomplished by having employees generate the ideas for the necessary change. At CPS, this could have been done by forming a broadly representative employee task force to develop a plan to make CPS competitive for managed care contracts. To help the task force come up with appropriate changes, managers could have provided it with information about what managed care plans look for in purchasing contracted services. A well-informed employee group that wanted CPS to succeed would probably have come up with changes that were similar to what the executives mandated. The task force could have facilitated the proposed changes by promoting its ideas to colleagues.

Employees can be involved in both developmental and traumatic changes, although time constraints may preclude their involvement to some extent. At the very least, employees should be involved in deciding how best to implement change. They may not gain ownership of the change, but they will become owners of the change process. Managers should keep employees focused on finding as many win/win solutions as possible. Managers know that they have succeeded in transferring ownership of the change when people begin to forget who had the original change and change implementation ideas.

Transferring ownership of the change to employees has been the keystone of change implementation strategies for decades. "Make your change their change" has been the stock advice of business consultants. To managers who face the challenges of the workplace of the 1990s, this advice may have a hollow sound. Think about today's typical hospital employees. In the past 10–15 years, how many reorganizations have they been through? How many CEOs have they seen come and go? How many cutbacks and layoffs? How many motivational programs? How many half-finished projects and programs? Is it realistic to expect a group of employees who have been pummeled and disillusioned by change after change to embrace even more changes under the guise of reengineering and quality improvement initiatives? It has been suggested that when working with groups that have become cynical secondary to experiencing multiple changes, the ownership transfer strategy will not work. Cynical employees will not get excited about and accept ownership of any change. The only option managers have with such a group is to impose the change by mandate and then to let the positive outcomes generate the enthusiasm and excitement. Today's cynical employees may not be willing to believe in the change before positive results are seen.[24] The catch-22 with this approach is that unenthusiastic employees may undermine the change in spite of management's dictates. At CPS, that may have happened in the Packaging Division, where there was no improvement in quality in spite of management directives.

Avoid blame. Managers should be careful to avoid blaming anyone or anything for a change and should downplay accusations made by employees. Accusations should be minimized for three reasons. First, blame is a negative emotion. During a time when so many feelings are negative, adding another is counterproductive. Organizations can become moribund when individuals and groups wallow in negativism and self-pity. Negativism feeds on itself. The only way to break out of the cycle is to allow people to vent negative feelings and then to move them on to the positive aspects of change. Second, accusations can stop the working-through process. As long as the target of anger is present, anger will be slow to dissipate and may be rekindled indefinitely. For example, at CPS, if Mary is blamed by the employees of the retail division for expanded hours, then every time she comes into contact with them, the feelings of anger are likely to return. The progress of working through the change at CPS could become arrested in the anger stage. Finally, accusations set the stage for poor working experiences and relationships. If Mary is blamed for the change, then the next time she tries to work with employees on any other operational issue, she will probably get a cold reception.

Reasons for Change Failures—Things Not to Do

Communicate too little. Managers are so busy that they often fail to communicate, or they abbreviate the communication process.[25] Perhaps this is due in part to America's action-oriented organizational culture. The productive manager is perceived to be a busy manager, rather than a talking manager. However, to successfully implement change, managers must add communication to their portfolio of activities. It also bears repeating that communicating a message once is never enough. Only constant communication is sufficient communication.

Incompletely integrate point-of-use factors. Change is too often formulated from the point of view of change makers, not from the point of view of change users.[26] In the CPS case, there was no consideration of how production standards would affect employees. There was no consideration of whether the roles of supervisors and employees would change. Apparently, there was no recognition that some employees would be affected more than others. When it became obvious that there were employee concerns, the change initiators did not listen. Their failure to take employee concerns into account doomed the change to failure and opened the door to a lawsuit.

Fail to allocate enough time. Because managers are under pressure to produce results quickly, they seldom allow time for employees to psychologically work through the change. However, some processes cannot be compressed. Managers frequently face a trade-off: move quickly and significantly increase the risk of change failure and of employee disenfranchisement, or move slowly and significantly increase the chance of success and support of employees. Demands for immediate gratification and short-term returns too often sway managers to opt for the former alternative. Not only does this strategy dim the prospects for long-term success, but it is unfair to employees. If there is one duty that employees and managers owe each other, it is respect. Failure to allow employees a reasonable opportunity to adjust is a demonstration of disrespect.

Fail to integrate all changes. One of the problems in the acute care of patients with multiple diagnoses is coordinating the work of all of the specialists who focus on separate problems. Treatments prescribed by an oncologist may change renal function, which will cause the nephrologist to change diuretic therapy, which causes the infectious disease specialist to change the dose of the antibiotic, and so on, and so on. In most organizations, several different changes are usually happening simultaneously. There is a tendency to apply specific fixes to specific parts of the organization independently. Unfortunately, many of the fixes are prescribed with the assumption that the rest of the organization is static. Individual changes may end up failing because no one takes a global view of the organization to make sure that all of the changes are consonant.[27]

Fail to clarify expectations. What is the purpose of the change? What are the projected outcomes? How will current positions be affected? How will career and professional development opportunities be affected? These questions should be answered as early, honestly, and accurately as possible in the process. Failure to do so guarantees that employees will resist the change.

Ignore the emotional aspects of change. Change leaders assume that employees, as rational individuals, react rationally to change. They assume that if they communicate the reasons for the change clearly and justify the change and implementation plan, employees will jump on the change bandwagon. Unfortunately, those leaders forget the emotional dimension of change. Managers also need to remember that what they perceive as rational may not be what employees perceive as rational. Research in social change indicates that merely informing people and expecting them to follow a rational course of action in light of new information is generally insufficient to bring about change.[28]

The Change Process

Organizational change requires planning, implementation, and stabilization. In the management literature, this sequential process is referred to as **organizational**

development.[29] Organizational development is like remodeling. The result of a remodeling project is reconfigured space through which activities of living and/ or working flow. Organizational development results in a reconfiguration of individuals regarding the work they do. Anyone who attempts a remodeling process starts with a blueprint so that the outcome of the project is clear to the designer, the builder(s), and the client. Cosmetic surgeons use the same kind of process by using computer-generated images to define the outcomes of surgical procedures. Organizational change requires a well-defined goal statement to guide the process. Unfortunately, goals are too seldom formulated in a document that is regularly consulted during the change like a blueprint is consulted during remodeling. Once the new configuration of employees and activities has been determined, a plan for transforming the organization has to be drawn up.

The plan for making a change is divided into three basic steps: unfreezing, substituting, and refreezing.[30] **Unfreezing** is the process of disrupting the habitual behavior of employees. Unless redirecting force is applied to organizational behavior, people will continue the status quo. Appropriate unfreezing interventions vary with the level and type of change. In some cases, merely providing information is sufficient to unfreeze. For example, providing clinicians with information about the transmission of HIV was sufficient to cause many of them to exercise more care in handling body fluids. Providing appropriate information is perhaps the most effective way of unfreezing behavior to initiate a developmental change. Unfreezing behavior is the most difficult part of the implementation plan because it requires dislodging employees from their current behavior patterns. Individuals tend not to abandon those patterns until they become uncomfortable with them.

Substituting is the replacement of old behaviors with new behaviors. To maximize the employees' ownership in the change, they should search for and adopt new behaviors on their own. Many hospitals, for example, used employee committees to reformulate body fluid precaution procedures in response to concern about HIV transmission. Committee members were likely not only to substitute these procedures for their old behavior but also to advocate their adoption throughout the organization. When time exigencies prohibit allowing employees to search for their own substitutes, more directive measures may have to be taken to bring about a substitution. For example, some kind of incentive can be attached to the substitute behavior to make it more attractive than the status quo behavior.

Refreezing is the institutionalization of the new behavior. Bringing positive outcomes to the attention of employees and reinforcing new behavior patterns are typical refreezing activities. The goal of refreezing is the reestablishment of comfort levels that employees felt prior to the change.

A person who is responsible for organizational development is a **change agent**.[31] Identifying the appropriate change agent is a critical step in the organizational development process. Managers are not always the best choices. Some of them do not have the range of skills required. Others may themselves be resistant to change. Still others have such strong interpersonal relationships with individuals who would be negatively affected by change that it is difficult for them to initiate the change process. Among the skills required of change agents are building and maintaining relationships and teams; resolving conflict; communicating values, skills, and knowledge; relating effectively with powerful and powerless groups; and facilitating the utilization of resources.[32] Change agents may be either internal or external. External change agents are management consultants whose only role in the organization is to manage organizational development. There are two clear advantages to using external change agents. First, they can assess the organization and its needs almost impartially. Their only allegiance is to the person who hired them. Thus, the consultant is as independent as possible. Second, change agents can absorb the anger of employees that might otherwise be projected onto managers. When the work of external change agents is done, they carry vented anger away with them, rather than leaving it to fester in the organization. The clear advantage of using an internal change agent is knowledge of the organization. The internal change agent is more likely to know where pockets of resistance are likely to be strongest, who holds what kind of power in the organization, and between whom the most important alliances are made. Once a change agent is identified, top managers must remain involved in the process. If they withdraw, employees may assume that the change is not really very important. Top managers must continue to communicate about the change and visibly support the change agent.

It has been suggested that organizational development efforts that reconfigure the entire organization, or large parts of it, require the leadership of a powerful coalition of people.[33] This may not hold true in small organizations. However, once the organization is large enough that no one person is in constant contact with everyone, then a coalition may be needed to spearhead a transformational change. When the organization is very large, a management team may need to be assembled whose sole responsibility becomes leading change.[34] Among the functions of the team are securing and distributing required resources, getting people to talk about the change, coordinating messages and activities, and creating opportunities for people to work together to make important change decisions. The leadership team also deals with emotional responses to the change and provides training and educational support.[35]

The key to the success of the change team lies in the choice of its members. At a minimum, the following roles need to be filled:

1. *Inventors* are individuals who bring trends and data together into change concepts that are clearly defined. Inventors pull disparate elements together in a way that allows others to understand what it is that needs to be done.

2. *Entrepreneurs* see and pursue opportunities. The key element that this member brings to the team is a strong tendency to act.

3. *Integrators* work with individuals to secure support for change.

4. *Experts* either have or acquire the skills and technical knowledge needed to effect change.

5. *Managers* facilitate the work of others by delegating and prioritizing.

6. *Sponsors* secure support and resources from top management.[36]

Changes that transform large segments of organizations frequently require more than one person in each of these roles. For example, clinical, data processing, and physical plant experts may be needed on a team that intends to completely overhaul an integrated HSO. Like the solitary change agent, the change team needs the visible support of top management to validate its work in the eyes of everyone in the organization.

Conclusion

When clinicians treat hypertension, they consider several factors in designing a therapeutic approach, including the patient's compliance patterns, the severity of the condition, and the side effects of medication. One of the biggest treatment barriers that clinicians face is the fact that most cases of hypertension are asymptomatic. Getting patients to change eating and exercise patterns with which they are comfortable is very difficult because the potential benefits are not easily sensed. In hypertensive cases, physicians tell the patients that the options for lowering blood pressure are not pleasant, and that they will not feel much, if any, better in the short run as a result. However, in the long run, therapy leads to decreased risk of other cardiovascular and renal disease. Therefore, the patient may live longer and/or be healthier.

Managers face the same challenges with many types of change. The change medicine is frequently unpleasant. Even when the change is perceived to be for the better, routines and relationships are still disrupted. The benefits of the change are not always immediately apparent. Nor do they always make people feel better, especially in the short term. But the change can eventually improve the viability and health of the organization.

Clinicians use several common tactics with hypertensive patients to secure compliance. First, they explain the disease and the consequences of doing nothing. Second, they provide emotional support to the patient. They assess the patient for signs of denial, anger, bargaining, depression, and acceptance so that they can counsel the patient appropriately. If the disease is mild, they allow patients time to work through these emotions. If the disease is life-threatening, they act more aggressively to secure a commitment to treatment. Third, they involve the patient as much as possible in designing the therapeutic regimen. First-line treatments for a mild case of hypertension include diet, exercise, and single-entity diuretics. If the clinician explains the advantages and disadvantages of each and the patient subsequently chooses one or the other, then the patient has assumed at least partial ownership of the therapeutic regimen. Clinicians could expect that compliance with a regimen of the patient's choice would be better than with a regimen of the physician's choice. These same tactics generally work with getting people to accept organizational change. Communicating, responding to individuals' emotional needs, and mutual participation are the keys to managing change. In today's cynical workplace, concern for individual well-being is the single most important component of organizational development.

Endnotes

1. Thomas A. Atchison, *Turning Healthcare Leadership Around: Cultivating Inspired, Empowered, and Loyal Followers* (San Francisco: Jossey-Bass Publishers, 1991).
2. Murray M. Dalziel and Stephen C. Schoonover, *Changing Ways: A Practical Tool for Implementing Change within Organizations* (New York: AMACOM, 1988).
3. Jeanie Daniel Duck, "Managing Change: The Art of Balancing," *Harvard Business Review 71* (November-December 1993): 109–118.
4. Paul Hersey and Kenneth H. Blanchard, *Management of Organizational Behavior: Utilizing Human Resources*, 3rd ed. (Englewood Cliffs, NJ: Prentice-Hall, 1977).
5. Atchison, op. cit.
6. Michael Hammer and James Champy, *Reengineering the Corporation: A Manifesto for Business Revolution* (New York: Harper Collins, 1993).
7. Emily Huebner and Pamela Ballou Nelson, "Managing Change—The Challenge of the '90s," *CARING Magazine 13* (October 1994): 94–101.
8. Manfred F. R. Kets de Vries and Danny Miller, *The Neurotic Organization* (San Francisco: Jossey-Bass Publishers, 1984).
9. Huebner and Nelson, op. cit.
10. John H. Zimmerman, "The Principles of Managing Change," *HR Focus 72* (February 1995): 15–16.
11. Dalziel and Schoonover, op. cit.
12. Huebner and Nelson, op. cit.
13. Jeremy Rifkin, *The End of Work* (New York: G. P. Putnam's Sons, 1995).
14. Atchison, op. cit.
15. Duck, op. cit.
16. Ibid.
17. Denise Smith Amos, "St. John's Shakes Up Nursing Staff," *St. Louis Post-Dispatch 118* (January 14, 1996): 1E, 8E.
18. Ibid.
19. Ibid.
20. Kets de Vries and Miller, op. cit.
21. Elisabeth Kubler-Ross, *Death: The Final Stage of Growth* (New York: Touchstone Books, 1986).
22. Richard A. Moreno, "How to Manage Change to Reduce Stress," *Management Review 66* (November 1977): 21–25.
23. Ibid.
24. Duck, op. cit.
25. Linda Burnes Bolton, Carolyn Aydin, Geraldine Popolow, and Jane Ramseyer, "Ten Steps for Managing Organizational Change," *Journal of Nursing Administration 22* (June 1992): 14–20.

26. Dalziel and Schoonover, op. cit.
27. Duck, op. cit.
28. Gerald Zaltman and Robert Duncan, *Strategies for Planned Change* (New York: John Wiley and Sons, 1977).
29. John A. Wagner III and John R. Hollenbeck, *Management of Organizational Behavior* (Englewood Cliffs, NJ: Prentice-Hall, 1992).
30. Edgar H. Schein, *Organizational Psychology*, 3rd ed. (Englewood Cliffs, NJ: Prentice-Hall, 1992).
31. Wagner and Hollenbeck, op. cit.
32. Ronald G. Havelock and Mary C. Havelock, *Training for Change Agents* (Ann Arbor, MI: Institute for Social Research, University of Michigan, 1971).
33. John P. Kotter, "Leading Change: Why Transformation Efforts Fail," *Harvard Business Review 73* (March-April 1995): 59–67.
34. Duck, op. cit.
35. Ibid.
36. Dalziel and Schoonover, op. cit.

Unit IV
Controlling

12

Quality:
Sports Medicine

In this chapter the reader will learn how:

◆ important quality is in healthcare

◆ problems arise related to quality of service

◆ quality is defined

◆ quality is assessed and measured in healthcare

◆ continuous quality improvement techniques can improve quality

◆ empowerment and training improve quality

◆ quality improvement relates to quality assurance and outcomes assessment

Mondays were usually hectic at the EastSide Care Center (ESCC) of Metro Health Plan (MHP), the largest HMO in a large Midwestern city. MHP is a staff model HMO which has a twenty-year history of relatively steady, but unspectacular, growth. Through a series of acquisitions and contractual arrangements, MHP established a formidable network of providers and services. Competing managed care plans neither offer the same breadth of services nor cover the geographical area as well. ESCC is one of twelve MHP ambulatory care centers. In addition, MHP's extensive home health services, four outpatient surgery centers, and agreements with six area hospitals support MHP's leading position in the market.

For George Soledad, MD, administrator of ESCC, Monday, May 5 was busier than most. The weekly executive committee meeting chaired by the CEO caught George off-guard. The CEO announced that she was forming a team to develop a Total Quality Management program for MHP. She appointed George, one of three physician administrators at MHP, to the team. The CEO justified the program by saying that improving quality is necessary to maintain MHP's leading competitive position. George was not sold on the whole idea. MHP had grown through sound strategic moves and, to his way of thinking, MHP had already secured its competitive position by forming alliances that virtually locked out any serious competition. He wants to provide high quality services, but the kind of comprehensive program the CEO described would use resources that George thought could be better used actually providing service.

The remainder of George's morning and afternoon had been spent in a flurry of typical administrative activities. He had a meeting with the law firm defending MHP in a liability action taken against an ESCC nurse. She had mistakenly phoned an order to the ESCC pharmacy for hydralazine 25 mg. po qid prn instead of hydroxyzine 25 mg. po qid prn. Substituting the antihypertensive for the antihistamine had caused an automobile accident when the patient had a hypotensive episode. George also had to deal with a new patient who was upset about having a second phlebotomy because the ESCC laboratory personnel mixed up some routine blood chemistry samples. He also had to stop a loud argument between Dr. Craig and nurse Smithe about the lack of certain supplies in an examination room. He also dealt with the usual complaints about late appointments and clinician deviations from approved treatment protocols. On the positive side, he got a couple of "thank you" notes from grateful patients. He also got a monthly report that showed that MHP enrollment was up by nearly 350 members over the previous month.

All in all, it had been a hectic, but not impossible, Monday. As he headed home for the day, he wondered how he and the other quality committee members could do just enough on this quality issue to keep the CEO satisfied until she came across the next management fad.

The Malcolm Baldrige National Quality Improvement Act of 1987 established an award program to recognize up to six American companies annually (two each in manufacturing, small business, and service) that best achieve quality. The award program is a unique, joint public-private venture run by the National Institute of Standards and Technology and financed by private business and industry. It took a monumental shift in the international balance of economic power to bring government and private industry together in this project. The aim of the Baldrige program is threefold: to promote quality awareness, to recognize quality achievements of American business, and to publicize successful quality strategies.[1] It is well-known that during the 1970s and 1980s, the inflation-adjusted earnings of the average American worker significantly decreased. At the same time, the national debt soared. Between 1981 and 1988 alone, it tripled.[2] During the same period, the economic success of Japan was in full-swing. While American manufacturers were finding it more and more difficult to sell products in the global marketplace, Japanese producers were finding willing buyers and expanding their markets. Economists, politicians, and business leaders looked for the etiology underlying the dramatic reversal of fortunes of these two economic powers. Certainly economic policy played a major role in the change, but there was another crucial causative factor—QUALITY. Buyers in markets all over the world, including the United States, recognized that the quality of Japanese products had surpassed the quality of American products. In a period of less than 40 years, on the ashes of World War II the Japanese built a manufacturing industry that generally provided the highest quality consumer products in the world. In the same period, the United States became a producer of many second rate goods and services. Complacency bred of success caused America's international market decline.

In the opening case, it seems that MHP's success in the market lulled George into a similar state of complacency. He does not seem to realize that the routine administrative problems he handles are symptomatic of poor quality work processes. Although MHP has no competitors to take advantage of those weaknesses today, the very existence of quality problems opens the door to competition.

In the American economy, healthcare is unique in being more domestically oriented than most other businesses because healthcare services generally have to be delivered where the patient is. There is, however, some international market for healthcare-related products and services. For example, well-known tertiary care centers provide services to foreign patients. Professional programs have international students. Manufacturers of health-related products are usually involved in international markets. However, until recently HSOs have been somewhat shielded from the economic forces which have made it imperative that American businesses focus on quality for survival.

That happy state of affairs has now changed for HSOs. It has not been the need to compete with foreign firms that has compelled HSOs to focus on quality. However, equally potent forces have made quality a high priority of HSOs. Among these forces are:

1. *Competitive pressures.* Providers have to offer higher quality services to capture larger market shares.[3] Under conditions of managed competition, service purchasers are looking for value. Value includes not only price, but the quality of services provided for the price. HSOs must provide high quality services to have a competitive advantage in the market.[4,5]

2. *Cost pressures*. Higher quality products cost less to produce on a per unit basis. This allows HSOs to price services competitively.[6]

3. *Process transfer*. For decades, healthcare providers have modified practices and organizations to cope with new technologies and escalating costs. Because tried and true strategies such as cost-containment have failed to adequately address these issues, healthcare managers have turned to quality improvement techniques that have been effective in improving performance in other industries.[7]

4. *Highly variable practice patterns*. Significant geographic variation in medical practice has been documented.[8–10] These findings give rise to questions about which medical care patterns are most appropriate. Where the utilization of high-cost alternatives is high, is that because the alternatives are appropriate or because they generate revenue? Where utilization of high-cost alternatives is low, is it because these alternatives are inappropriate or because no one will pay for them?[11]

These factors resulted in the rapid and widespread diffusion of quality improvement initiatives throughout the health services industry. The 1992 edition of the Joint Commission on the Accreditation of Healthcare Organizations (JCAHO) *Accreditation Manual for Hospitals* required that hospital CEOs have training in continuous quality improvement methods.[12] As a result, more than two-thirds of hospitals have pursued quality improvement programs.[13] Also, the Healthcare Financing Administration (HCFA) has developed a program, the Healthcare Quality Improvement Program (HCQIP), to strengthen quality improvement programs in healthcare delivery.[14] HCFA has undertaken several other projects to improve the quality of care delivered to Medicare and Medicaid recipients.[15–17] Recent research has focused on the development of quality indicators in nursing facilities,[18,19] dialysis centers,[20] and community settings.[21] The development of health systems that consist of a number of different kinds of providers suggests the need to develop additional quality indicators that reflect how well a continuum of care functions.[22]

Being on the sidelines while other manufacturing and service industries implemented quality improvement programs has allowed healthcare providers to take advantage of the wealth of knowledge gained in other settings. Much research and experience have been generated in areas like defining and measuring quality, and implementing quality improvement programs. An avalanche of literature has been generated that addresses different aspects of quality improvement.[23] Healthcare organizations have the opportunity to replicate successes and avoid failures.

There are no pathologies that are strong analogies of organizations in need of quality improvement. The best medical analogy is theoretical. Imagine an individual who is physiologically average with the ability to adapt to ordinary changes within her emotional and physical environment. Assume that this person develops the desire to become the best tennis player in the world. Health providers have much to offer her: ongoing dietary assessment and nutritional counselling to match diet to new activity levels, cardiovascular evaluation, exercises to improve eye-hand coordination, muscle strengthening regimens, and counselling to help her cope with the stress of training and competition. The process of transforming this physiologically average person into a top-flight athlete is a good analogy because it embodies two important aspects of quality improvement. First, creating this hypothetical athlete would require a holistic effort. Heart, lungs, skeletal muscles, aerobic processes, reflexes, coordination, and emotional coping would have to be significantly enhanced. Similarly, improving product and service quality is a holistic effort that requires the involvement of all parts of the organization. In today's world, improving quality means improving every aspect of performance. Comprehensive efforts to improve quality are called **Total Quality Management (TQM)**. Second, there are no absolute limits to how much athletic ability can improve. In fact, to be the best requires constant improvement. World records are destined to fall as athletes, trainers, coaches, and physicians find better ways of training and competing. Likewise, total quality is a goal that is never achieved because each time quality goals are met, the goalposts are moved a few inches further down the field. There is no end to doing things better. Therefore, **Continuous Quality Improvement (CQI)** is also used to describe quality improvement efforts. In the management literature, TQM and CQI are frequently used interchangeably, although they refer to different aspects of the same process.

Because TQM/CQI have been quickly disseminated throughout healthcare services, most clinicians have had some experience with quality improvement. Unfortunately, in the hectic atmosphere of most healthcare delivery sites, clinicians may be involved in quality improvement activities without learning the theoretical framework that gives rise to specific processes. Lack of understanding of quality improvement principles short circuits many TQM/CQI programs. The remainder of this chapter will provide a framework for understanding quality improvement programs and their application in healthcare.

Defining Quality

Before managers can undertake meaningful quality improvement programs, they must know where they are headed (i.e., they must have a clear concept of what quality is). Because quality, like beauty, is in the eye of the beholder, the range of perceptions of quality is almost limitless. Fortunately, through experience in a variety of industries, some consensus has developed among management theorists regarding the meaning of quality. People who are unfamiliar with the TQM/CQI literature, however, may not share this perception. It is imperative, therefore, that at the beginning of any quality improvement initiative, the working definition of quality be clearly and frequently communicated.

There are two dimensions of quality: conformance to specifications and meeting customer requirements.[24] These two dimensions have evolved from the seminal work of a handful of quality improvement experts—W. Edwards Deming, Joseph M. Juran, and Philip B. Crosby, to name a few. Their models of quality improvement form the basis of much of the research into healthcare quality. The methods of quality improvement that these men pioneered in other fields have been widely adopted by healthcare institutions. Therefore, it behooves healthcare managers to know about the focus of the work of these individuals and the theory behind it. These quality improvement pioneers have written extensively. Anyone who is responsible for designing and/or implementing quality improvement programs is well-advised to delve into their material.

Quality—Conformance to Specifications

This dimension of quality has been most closely associated with Deming. Deming's original interest was in the use of statistical methods to improve the quality of manufactured goods. During the economic boom following World War II, his exhortation to American manufacturers that quality was important fell on deaf ears. What sense did it make to spend money, time, and effort to improve quality when there was already more demand for many products than manufacturers could meet? In economically devastated Japan, however, Deming found an audience eager to do whatever it took to make products that the world would buy. The core of Deming's original work is **quality control (QC)** (i.e., ensuring that goods and services meet design specifications).[25]

As Deming's work in quality evolved, he focused more on improving production processes. Deming's premise is that processes must be in control before they can be improved. To determine whether processes are in control, performance must be tracked over time and variation from average performance noted and accounted for. Deming uses a **control chart** to track performance. Figure 12.1 is a control chart for billing errors. Each mark on the horizontal axis of this control chart represents a different day. Each mark on the vertical axis corresponds to the percentage of bills that contained an error. For most of the days shown on this chart, the percentage of bills issued with an error was above or below the average. It is not realistic to expect that performance will be the same every day. However, Deming suggests that to control a process, performance should center closely around the average. To achieve control, outstanding variation should be investigated. The **upper control limit (UCL)** and **lower control limit (LCL)** lines on the control chart mark the variation limits beyond which performance is evaluated. UCLs and LCLs are established by observing the process, plotting the results on a control chart, and then applying a statistical formula that takes into account how evenly the points are distributed around an average.[26] In this example, only one point is above the UCL. Deming would suggest investigating this occurrence to discover its causes. In this case, an inadequately trained new employee may have started work that day, or maybe an erroneous entry which caused errors in

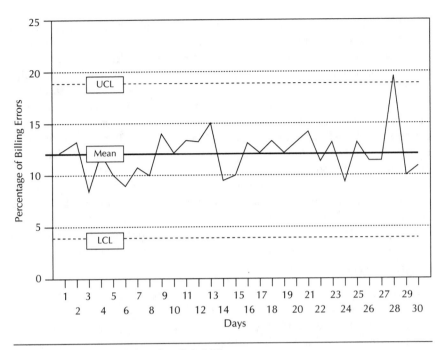

Figure 12.1   Control chart for clinic billing errors.

several bills was made into a billing data base. Deming would use the results of the investigation as the basis for modifying the process to prevent the extraordinary variances. Variations below the LCL should also be investigated. The control chart in Figure 12.1 indicates that on no day did billing error rates fall below the LCL. If this had occurred, the variation may have been caused by overscheduling, which gave each billing clerk more time to process bills. Or perhaps the supervisor may have had a chance to review more statements that day and correct errors before they left the department. Deming would suggest trying to duplicate conditions that led to extraordinarily good performance so that the line representing the average number of errors would be moved down. Deming's ultimate goal of moving performance toward more desirable levels is the link between his quality control work and CQI.

The quality control piece of Deming's work is closely related to quality assurance (QA) efforts in healthcare. **QA** includes identifying quality-related problems, implementing solutions to address those problems, and reviewing results to ascertain that the problems are solved and that no new tangential problems have been created. Once problems have been resolved, quality efforts are redirected to other problem areas.[27]

Deming's work in applied statistical methods to improve processes led to his developing a TQM philosophy. For Deming, quality cannot be achieved in a piecemeal manner. As QA has been generally applied in healthcare, it has addressed specific problematic outcomes without effective articulation of distinct QA projects to improve processes. Thus, the scope of activities and level of organizational commitment to QA is quite different than that required for TQM.

QA is essentially an inspection process that has been applied to clinical outcomes. The goal of QA has been to identify individuals who exceed a threshold of errors.[28] This "bad apple" approach to improving quality is costly and time-consuming. QA is a retrospective process that does not address defective processes. The inspection basis of QA establishes a counterproductive relationship between QA staff and providers. In contrast, the TQM philosophy articulated by Deming rests on the assumption that individual employees are not the cause of poor quality. What employees need to improve quality is not monitoring and correction, but rather knowledge, support, and processes that facilitate rather than impede performance.[29] The inspection approach of QA does not utilize the potential of well-intentioned, competent practitioners to improve healthcare quality.[30]

Quality—Meeting Customer Requirements

Juran's short definition of quality is "fitness for use."[31] Fitness for use is determined by whoever uses the output of a process. According to Juran, there are two aspects of fitness for use. The first aspect is product or service performance. Examples of performance include efficient product performance, how rapidly services are performed, product attractiveness, ease of product or service use, and accessibility. The second aspect of fitness is freedom from deficiencies. Examples of deficiencies include product failure, lateness of delivery, incorrect billing, and inaccessible or unavailable product service. Product performance and deficiencies are two sides of the same coin. Products that perform well result in customer satisfaction, whereas deficient products result in dissatisfaction.

Like Deming, Juran includes quality control in his approach to quality improvement. However, he sees quality control as the second of three processes used to manage quality. The first of those processes is **quality planning**. Quality planning is the process of determining who the organization's customers are, determining the needs of customers, translating customers' needs into processes that result in products which meet those needs, and operationalizing the requisite processes. Applying quality control methods to work processing results in data that is used to improve performance. The third of Juran's quality management processes is quality improvement. Quality improvement is changing production processes to either prevent poor quality outcomes or to significantly enhance overall product performance.

Crosby's approach to quality improvement relies less on quality control than either Deming or Juran. He emphasizes prevention. Because every defect represents a cost, errors are to be avoided, not controlled. Doing things right the first time so that there are zero product defects is the basis of Crosby's quality improvement philosophy.[32]

Quality in Healthcare

The complexities of providing healthcare services have made the direct application of definitions of quality from other fields problematic. Because healthcare delivery has both technical and interpersonal components, evaluating quality of care has to include both aspects of care delivery. Also, evaluating quality of care from the customer's point of view is complicated by the fact that practitioners and institutions frequently serve more than one constituency. Service is provided not only to patients, but to families of patients, referring physicians, and third parties.[33] Quality improvement programs must be comprehensive so as to include services provided to the full range of constituencies and to accommodate the conflicts that are generated in serving multiple masters.

There are also a number of factors that give rise to extraordinary variability in healthcare. Many of these factors cannot be controlled. For example, the emotional response of individuals to the stress of illness, physiological responses to medication, and the natural progress of pathologies is extremely variable. Controlling clinical processes may not be able to eliminate, or even significantly reduce, variation in clinical outcomes. Managers must "understand that random fluctuation exists in a stable production process."[34]

Achieving quality in healthcare is a bit like shooting at a moving target. On the technical side, new technologies become available quite rapidly. New drugs, laboratory procedures, and imaging techniques make some practices obsolete before the process of delivering care can be fully evaluated and variation minimized. On the customer requirements side, rapidly changing reimbursement and accessibility parameters create a playing field of shifting sand. As soon as the organization begins to improve quality under one set of conditions, the conditions change. Therefore, many quality improvement efforts in healthcare are fated to yield short-lived results. It is only natural that healthcare providers become frustrated when they perceive that all the hard work that goes into improving quality results in few long-term quality gains. One dimension of quality of healthcare delivery is how well providers respond to constantly changing conditions.

It was reported in a 1990 study by the Institute of Medicine (IOM) that more than 100 different definitions or parameters of quality of healthcare have been noted in the literature. From this review, the IOM proposed that the following definition captures the essence of quality of care. "Quality of care is the degree to which health services for individuals and populations increase the likelihood of desired health outcomes and are consistent with current professional knowledge."[35] This definition is broad enough to encompass wide variations in individual perceptions of quality ("desired health outcomes") and recognizes that outcomes of care are not certain ("increases the likelihood of desired health outcomes"). However, in its attempt to be inclusive of variation, the definition is too broad to suggest specific measures of quality that healthcare providers should use for quality assessment purposes.

Just as the work of Deming, Juran, and Crosby provides the theoretical framework of TQM/CQI, the work of Avedis Donabedian is the theoretical foundation for the evaluation of quality in healthcare. Donabedian suggests that assessing quality in healthcare should include an assessment of structure, process, and outcome. **Structure** is the setting in which healthcare is delivered. It includes not only physical facilities, but also the administrative organization that supports healthcare delivery. Clearly drawn job descriptions, committee composition consistent with institutional mission and goals, and human resources sufficient to achieve the mission and goals are part of the institutional provider's structure. **Process** is the application of knowledge, judgment, and skill to improve health status. Evaluation of process requires, first, that standards for decision making be established, and, second, that the degree of adherence to those standards be recorded. **Outcomes** include clinical outcomes (survival, functional level, recovery) and affiliated outcomes (attitude, satisfaction, disability, rehabilitation).[35] In Donabedian's model, the relationship among structure, process, and outcome is enabling rather than causative. Structure is important because it makes it possible for process to occur. Process is important because it makes improved health status (outcomes) more likely. If these three components are erroneously viewed as strictly causative (Figure 12.2a), then the model poses some difficult problems in application. For example, the existence of an Infection Control Committee does not guarantee effective infection control processes. Merely establishing a committee does not mean that the quality of the infection control process will improve, nor does the appropriate application of infection control measures (process) necessarily mean that nosocomial infection rates will go down. Factors other than infection control procedures contribute to nosocomial infections. However, without an appropriate underlying structure and effective and efficient processes, the achievement of high quality outcomes is unlikely. Structure, process, and outcome also tend to merge in healthcare. In practice, there are a number of intermediate outcomes that become fodder for further processing. For example, the status of the post-operative hip replacement patient is an outcome of a surgical process. The patient then becomes the input into a rehabilitation process, which, in turn, results in a functional status outcome (Figure 12.2b). This makes assessment of structure, process, and outcome anything but clear-cut.[37]

Measurement is fundamental to the development of an effective healthcare quality improvement program. Measurements themselves must be of high quality to be useful.[38] Quality measurements in healthcare are referred to as **quality indicators**. Effective quality indicators measure important aspects of care and accurately reflect the level of quality. No single quality indicator is sufficient to accurately reflect quality of healthcare delivery. Any useful quality assessment effort includes a range of indicators that are weighted to prevent skewed representations of quality. It is the selection of indicators and the relative importance assigned to them that has generated much of the controversy over quality assessment in healthcare.

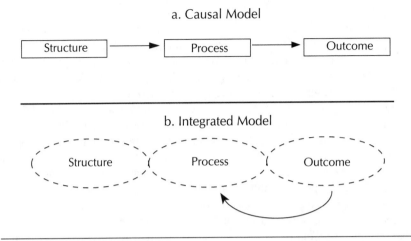

Figure 12.2   Structure, process, outcome model of quality assessment.

Outcomes Measurement

In recent years, the emphasis of quality assurance and quality improvement efforts has shifted from a structure and process orientation to an outcomes orientation. Note that the IOM definition of quality of care cited above focuses on outcomes. This shift is consistent with a trend in American business to focus almost exclusively on bottom-line performance. The rationale behind the emphasis on outcomes assessment is that when the outcomes of healthcare delivery are poor, the quality of structure and process is irrelevant. Food may be served hot and taste good. Medication may be appropriately prescribed and correctly and promptly administered. Clinicians and support staff may be attentive, helpful, and courteous. But when patients still have poor outcomes, none of that really matters. While this right-to-the-point approach is attractive for its simplicity, there are some risks inherent in relying on it too heavily.

Outcomes assessment is summative (i.e., the results are useful only for retrospective evaluation of quality). The data from outcomes studies only indicate where process weaknesses may exist. They do not help providers prevent poor outcomes during the care process itself. Sometimes it takes months, or even years, to generate valid outcomes data. Many quality improvement management decisions cannot wait that long.[39] In contrast, process measures can be used for formative purposes (i.e., they can be applied during the care process to improve the chances of high-quality outcomes). For example, one feasible hospital care process indicator may be the degree to which the choice of antibiotic therapy is consistent with culture and sensitivity results. Data collected for the purpose of quality assessment can be used immediately to improve outcomes. Each time it appears that an inappropriate antibiotic has been chosen, the prescribing physician can be notified and changes made if indicated. Thus, process assessment is consistent with Crosby's emphasis on prevention.

The fact that the relationship among structure, process, and outcome is not strictly causal means that outcomes reflect quality of structure and process in only a limited way. High quality outcomes do not necessarily mean that high quality care was given; poor outcomes do not necessarily mean that poor quality care was given. In isolation, outcomes can be misleading indicators of quality of care.[40] There are several factors that can disrupt a causal link leading from structure through process to outcome. Perhaps the most troublesome is the patient population served. Assume that hospital A serves an indigent inner city population and hospital B serves a predominantly wealthy suburban population. Ask 100 healthcare providers which hospital is likely to have the better outcomes and the large majority would probably say hospital B. At first glance, that may be due to the fact that hospital B would be expected to have resources to provide higher quality structure and process. However, if the respondents were told to assume that the quality of structure and process was equal at the two facilities, many of them would still predict better outcomes at hospital B because there is a qualitative difference in the patients typically served by these kinds of facilities. Patients of hospital A tend to present with more advanced pathologies and poorer nutritional and physical status than patients of hospital B. Therefore, they are at greater risk. The prognosis for these patients under comparable quality of care circumstances is worse. Variable case mixes and health status of populations served make comparisons of outcomes difficult. However, there are now software systems that help compensate for these differences by correlating patient admission severity with clinical outcome data.[41]

Outcomes are attractive quality indicators because laymen and third-party payers understand them as bottom-line performance measures. Most people perceive that a mortality rate of 1 per 100 admissions is better than a mortality rate of 2 per 100 admissions. Without the context of data that describes case mix and severity, and without process quality indicators, the natural conclusion is that the quality of care must be worse at the hospital with a 2 per 100 admissions mortality rate. Technically oriented process measures may not be much help to the layman trying to evaluate quality.[42]

From a quality improvement point of view, outcomes measures do little to help providers pinpoint which aspects of care delivery are most in need of improvement. They reflect the totality of healthcare. The integrity of supplies, the efficiency and effectiveness of diagnostic technology, the appeal of prescribed diets, and the work of all care and service providers are among the almost innumerable factors that influence outcomes. Retrospective review of outcome measures does not indicate which of these factors significantly influenced outcomes.

On the other hand, outcome measures are valuable when the totality of healthcare, including the patient's contribution in terms of self-care, is important.[43]

Whereas process measures are usually limited to the choices that are made in providing care, outcomes measures capture the skill with which choices of action are carried out.[44] Also, a few outcome measures can be used to identify problem areas that are most in need of quality improvement. For example, poor surgical outcomes indicate that more attention should be directed to operative and perioperative care.

The large outcomes databanks that are generated by government agencies, third-party payers, and research institutions make it increasingly possible to quantify the relationship between process and outcome. For example, the outcomes of coronary artery disease (CAD) patients who have percutaneous transluminal coronary angioplasty can be compared to the outcomes of CAD patients who undergo coronary artery bypass grafts. By determining which kinds of patients tend to have better outcomes with which procedure, it is theoretically possible to develop clinical practice guidelines that optimize outcomes. The Agency for Healthcare Policy and Research (AHCPR) is currently engaged in producing such guidelines. By February 1996, it had published seventeen guidelines.[45] It is, of course, difficult to write guidelines that take patient preference into account.[46] However, AHCPR has considered and incorporated this crucial component of care into its work. It must be remembered that each patient has a unique response to any given therapeutic plan. Therefore, using guidelines based on aggregate outcome data may not be appropriate for any given patient. Yet providers in today's managed care environment are more likely than ever to feel pressured to apply standardized care regimens to improve outcomes for the mythical average patient.[47]

Outcome measures that are commonly evaluated fall into three categories. **Technical outcomes** include clinical outcomes that have been evaluated for many years. They include morbidity, mortality, changes in health or functional status, and adverse events. **Interpersonal outcomes** include patient and family satisfaction, emotional and spiritual peace, referrals, compliance, future return for care, malpractice actions, and donations. A third set of outcomes arise from the amenities of the facility. Amenities are facility cleanliness, attractiveness, comfort of surroundings, and accessibility to conveniences. **Amenities outcomes** include patient and family satisfaction, referrals, and donations.[48] Obviously, amenities and interpersonal outcomes overlap.

Satisfaction

Fitness for use is ultimately determined by the end-user of products and services. Therefore, it is not surprising that measuring patient satisfaction has become an important part of quality assessment programs. Although patient satisfaction is an important quality indicator, its measurement is difficult. Interpretation of patient satisfaction data is not an exact science and using satisfaction data to improve quality may conflict with technical imperatives.

Just as patient variability influences outcomes, it also influences patient satisfaction. Patient satisfaction may not accurately reflect quality of care.[49] Patients' perceptions of care can be influenced by their preservice expectations of the service provider. An interesting interaction has been demonstrated between how patients select a provider and their reported satisfaction and evaluation of quality. When patients rely on their own opinion to choose a hospital, they tend to say they are more satisfied and that they received higher quality of care. When they rely on the opinion of others, they are less satisfied and rate quality lower.[50] Thus, the actual quality of care is not accurately reflected in the survey results. Patients may use experiences with other providers as comparative markers by which they establish expectations and judge subsequent providers. Their expectations of quality of care and service are derived from their prior experience. When their expectations are met or exceeded, they state that they are satisfied, and when their expectations are not met, they state that they are dissatisfied.[51]

The health status of respondents also influences their reported satisfaction. A recent report indicated that the health status of patients correlates positively with reported satisfaction (i.e., the less sick the patient, the more satisfied he is with his healthcare provider).[52] This suggests that to compare patient satisfaction with different providers, the health status of the population served should be taken into account, just as case mix and severity must be accounted for in comparing clinical outcomes.

Patient satisfaction measures are currently of limited use in measuring technical aspects of quality of care. Patient perceptions of technical quality are limited to the care they actually received. They have no way of knowing whether that care is appropriate compared to the range of feasible alternatives. They also do not have the knowledge to judge how well the care they received was rendered. They may perceive that a procedure was painful, for example, and, consequently, tend to be dissatisfied with the care. But whether that pain could have been avoided had the procedure been performed differently is not always possible for them to determine.

Maximizing the potential of patient satisfaction data to inform TQM/CQI efforts requires that survey instruments be carefully constructed and administered. Researchers like to use short, simple surveys that are easy for patients to complete and easy for surveyors to score. Such surveys have items such as, "On a scale of 1–5 with 5 being the highest, how did you like our food?" These surveys are easy to do, but they do not yield data that indicate how food service can be improved. An even more profound problem is that they do not address patients' unmet needs at all. Satisfaction surveys tend to focus on services that were provided, not those that were omitted. For surveys to meet the needs of TQM/CQI programs, they must identify patient needs.[53]

Measuring patient satisfaction should also be an ongoing effort that incorporates assessments at varying intervals after contact with the provider. A patient's perception of satisfaction may be quite different six months after a surgery than it is six days post-op. Satisfaction with healthcare service is inextricable from outcomes. As the patient's post service course evolves, perception of quality changes. Because decisions to utilize health services are made at varying intervals after service, patients' satisfaction six months or even six years after the service is as important as satisfaction six days after.

Patient satisfaction will continue to be a focus of quality improvement efforts because meeting the needs of patients is part of the definition of quality and because patients who are dissatisfied with one provider find others. Dissatisfaction is correlated with disenrollment from health plans.[54] Satisfaction of hospital patients seems to drop right to the bottom line. Net revenues, earnings, and return on assets have been related to patient satisfaction.[55] Deming suggests that merely satisfying customers, however, may not be enough to retain their patronage. Customers who are merely satisfied may still switch service providers under the assumption that they might not lose much but might gain substantially.[56] Patients have to be excited about service to be loyal. The way to move beyond patient satisfaction to patient excitement is to provide quality above and beyond what patients expect.[57]

Improving communication with patients seems to be the key to improving patient satisfaction. In the ambulatory care environment, performance in communication has been related to patient satisfaction. Both the amount and clarity of information patients receive are important.[58] In the acute care environment, patients need to be more informed of what to expect during and after procedures.[59] Communication is one of five characteristics that patients use to define healthcare quality. The others (empathy, reliability, responsiveness, and caring) are closely related to communication.[60]

Benchmarking

TQM/CQI are internally focused activities. In contrast, benchmarking is externally focused. **Benchmarking** "is the search for industry-best practices that lead to superior performance."[61] The best practices are then copied to achieve improved quality. Benchmarking is frequently incorporated into TQM/CQI programs because it can speed up the process of quality improvement. Instead of implementing incremental changes that move the organization closer to ideal performance, the processes that the best performers currently use can be adopted to move the organization immediately to the highest known level of quality. Although benchmarking is not inconsistent with TQM/CQI, it is not the same thing because it establishes a standard of performance that TQM/CQI philosophies reject. The zero defects and continuous improvement concepts reject the notion that the best performance in an industry is good enough. In the context of TQM/CQI, benchmarking can be thought of as one of several ways that can be used to improve quality.

Two kinds of benchmarking have been identified.[62] **Competitive benchmarking** is the comparison of an organization to competitors that produce the same product or service. For example, comparing the performance of one hospital's surgical services to another hospital's surgical services is competitive benchmarking. Note that competitive benchmarking does not mean that the objects of comparison are in the same market. By definition, one of the hospitals must provide the best surgical services. The best surgical services may not be provided by a local competitor. **World-class benchmarking** is the comparison of an organization to another organization outside the industry. For example, a hospital may choose to compare its billing process to the billing process of a utility company if the utility's billing function is recognized as the best billing process. Although the clients of the two organizations are very different, there still may be procedural lessons to be learned from the utility that are transferable to the hospital.

The steps in the benchmarking process include planning, analysis, integration, and action.[63] The planning stage is critical because it includes deciding what to benchmark and against which organization's performance to compare. Because there are many indicators of quality and performance, choosing what to benchmark can be difficult. The ultimate goal of any organization is to serve its customers. Therefore, outcome measures are obvious choices for benchmarking. In addition, some structure and process indicators can also be benchmarked, especially when they appear to be highly correlated with outcomes. Also, organizations may choose to concentrate benchmarking in those areas in which they have experienced the most difficulty in achieving significant quality improvement.

The Pareto Principle should also be applied to selecting indicators to benchmark. **The Pareto Principle** states that when several factors contribute to an outcome, relatively few of those factors account for the majority of the outcome. Those few factors are called the **vital few**. The remainder are called the **useful many**. If an organization controls or changes the vital few, it will exert a much greater influence over outcomes than if it controls or changes the useful many. The way to determine the vital few is to (1) list all the factors that stand between the organization and its goal, (2) arrange the list in order of importance, (3) identify the vital few factors and deal with those individually, and (4) identify the useful many and deal with those as a class.[64] Ranking factors is difficult when they cannot be quantified and statistically tied to outcomes. However, subjective ranking still keeps the organization focused on identifying and addressing the factors that are most important to improve. Additional criteria for selecting healthcare processes to improve have been suggested. They include choosing processes that both managers and employees believe need to be improved, processes that are clearly defined, and processes for which data are readily available and the effects of interactions easy to study. Processes for which change is currently planned or already underway should not be ranked.[65]

It has been suggested that applying the Pareto Principle to identify processes to improve may not be politically palatable in hospitals.[66] For example, there may be a tendency to avoid those projects that require change that might be unpopular with physicians. It is more comfortable for managers to choose processes that use resources that are under their direct control.

Identifying the industry's best performers is also difficult. Outcome data are not always available. Even when they are, one organization seldom has the best outcomes in all areas. For example, one rehabilitation provider may have the best clinical outcomes with stroke patients, while another has better outcomes with occupational injuries, while another has the best performance in utilization of facilities, and yet another has the best billing processes. To build a comprehensive benchmarking program, a single organization may have to find several benchmarking partners. Because data are not always available to indicate who the single best performer is in any one dimension of quality, the benchmarking partner usually ends up being an organization that is reputed to perform well. In a collaborative effort, benchmarking partners may actually end up learning each other's best practices in different areas. Collaborative benchmarking has been successfully used within a single healthcare system to identify best practices among system members.[67]

Analysis includes reviewing and comparing data to identify competitive gaps (differences) in performance. Analysis also includes identifying why the industry leader's performance is better. Understanding the reasons for outstanding performance is essential for the next step in the process—integration. Integration requires that benchmarking findings be converted into operational goals and objectives. In the action step of the process, these objectives are operationalized.

Implementation of TQM/CQI

Guiding Principles

Implementation of TQM/CQI is difficult because it requires a change that affects every aspect of the organization's operation. It is a managed change that requires changing group behavior. The Deming's Fourteen Points for Management (Table 12.1) provide a framework for implementing TQM/CQI These principles make quality the core of the organization's activities. Experience in applying these principles in healthcare and other industries suggest the following corollaries.

1. *Involve top management and the board in TQM/CQI.* Points 1 and 2 indicate that the goal of maximizing quality must be infused throughout the organization. The role of the organization's leaders is to create a corporate climate that incorporates and reinforces a total commitment to quality.[68] Top managers facilitate improvement by creating a climate in which professionals can redesign their own work.[69] That degree of organizational dedication can be stimulated and sustained only by the active involvement of the board, top managers, and senior medical staff, particularly in the initial stages.[70] Although the leadership team may not actually

Table 12.1   Summary of Deming's Fourteen Points and Commentary

Deming's Points	Commentary
1. Create constancy of purpose toward improvement of product and service, with the aim to become competitive and to stay in business, and to provide jobs.	*The focus of the organization should be not only on solving problems of today, but on preventing future problems.*
2. Adopt the new philosophy.	
3. Cease dependence on inspection to achieve quality.	*Inspection occurs too late to prevent errors, and dependence on it creates significant rework costs to achieve high quality.*
4. End the practice of awarding business on the basis of price tag.	*High quality products cannot be made from inferior materials. Savings on inferior materials are no savings at all in the long run.*
5. Improve constantly and forever the system of production and service, to improve quality and productivity, and thus constantly decrease costs.	*Reaching a performance standard is never an endpoint in the quality improvement process.*
6. Institute training on the job.	
7. Institute leadership.	*Leaders remove performance barriers and know the work they supervise so that they can help employees improve performance.*
8. Drive out fear, so that everyone may work effectively for the company.	
9. Break down barriers between departments.	*Quality is the responsibility of the entire organization, not a department.*
10. Eliminate slogans, exhortations, and targets for the work force asking for zero defects and new levels of productivity.	*Slogans frustrate employees whose performance is hampered by the process, not their lack of effort.*
11a. Eliminate work standards (quotas) on the factory floor. Substitute leadership. 11b. Eliminate management by objective. Eliminate management by numbers, numerical goals. Substitute leadership.	*Numerical goals suggest the possibility of punishment. The possibility of punishment creates fear. Drive out fear.*
12a. Remove barriers that rob the hourly worker of his right to pride of workmanship. 12b. Remove barriers that rob people in management and in engineering of their right to pride of workmanship.	*Never advise employees to produce work that is inferior to what they are capable of producing.*
13. Institute a vigorous program of education and self-improvement.	
14. Put everybody in the company to work to accomplish the transformation.	*Quality is everyone's responsibility.*

Note: adapted from W. Edwards Deming, *Out of Crisis* (Cambridge, MA: MIT, 1982).

implement quality improvement changes, it empowers members of the organization to do so, facilitates efforts by decreasing barriers to implementation, and constantly reinforces the organization's commitment to quality. The board can institutionalize the commitment to quality by articulating it in the mission statement.[71] The board also has a role in maintaining continuity in quality improvement efforts. Top executives come and go and quality improvement programs can be sidelined in their wake. The board is the stable factor in organizational management.

2. *Involve physicians in TQM/CQI.* In healthcare, it requires the participation of the board (for mission and continuity), administration (for facilitating improvement efforts), and physicians (for technical expertise and insight into medical care processes). Involving physicians is much easier said than done. Successful physician involvement depends on (1) overcoming the negative connotation of quality as essentially a surveillance process that results in punishment, (2) conceptually linking the best interests of the organization to the best interests of physicians so that they do not feel that participation is a matter of donating uncompensated time, and (3) including physicians in improving processes that are most important to them.[72]

3. *Institute continuous employee education and training.* Employees cannot exceed current levels of performance if they do not know how to do so. Employees need knowledge in quality improvement skills, technical skills, and organizational skills. In the area of quality improvement skills, employees must understand the TQM/ CQI philosophy, control charts (Figure 12.1), flow charts, and cause-and-effect charts. **Flow charts** are diagrammatic representations of the sequence of steps in a process. Figure 12.3a is a generic flow chart. Figure 12.3b is a flow chart for treating a bunion. The process begins with an appointment, which results in an office consultation. The patient makes a decision whether to have a bunionectomy. If the decision is yes, the bunionectomy is performed, and appropriate post-op care is rendered until maximum function is achieved. If the decision is no, then orthotic treatment is pursued until maximum function is achieved. Within this process, many other decisions are made. For example, how the treatment will be paid for, when to schedule treatment, and how long to continue treatment. The value of flow charts is in helping everyone understand process. Flow charts can be used to help employees identify how complex processes can be simplified and

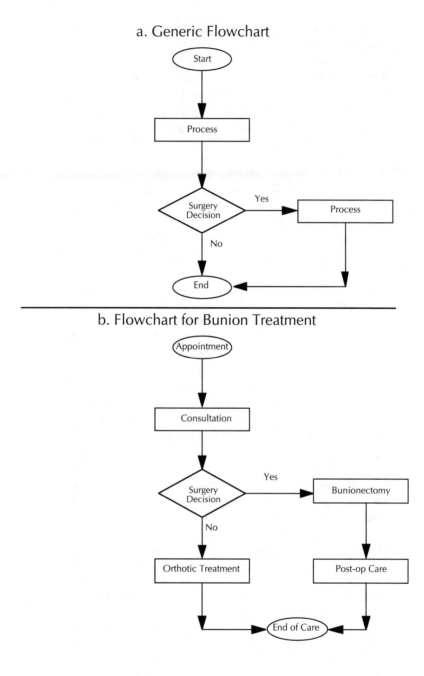

Figure 12.3   Flow charts.

improved.[73] Critical pathways and clinical practice guidelines can incorporate flow charts to illustrate decision-making alternatives at different treatment stages.

Cause-and-effect diagrams are tools to help organizations analyze problematic situations. Problematic situations are set equal to effects. Then, by working backward from the effect and asking "Why?", a diagram of interrelated causes is constructed (Figure 12.4).[74] Take the situation in which the problematic situation is a back-up of pre-op patients outside the operating room (OR). In response to the first "Why?", scheduling may be mentioned. In response to the question "Why is scheduling a problem?", several answers may emerge, such as surgeons' failing to request enough OR time, scheduling the most variable procedures first, and scheduling errors themselves. Asking "Why do scheduling errors occur?" might elicit responses like procedures being scheduled under the wrong date, the hearing deficit of an OR scheduler, and the computer program's allowing double posting. By the time all the "whys" have been asked and answered, a complete picture of the causative factors and their interrelationships emerges. The final diagram resembles a fish skeleton and is, therefore, also referred to as a **fish bone diagram**.

Using the cause-and-effect diagram helps organizations treat real problems rather than the symptoms that the problems cause. In organizational terms, pre-op logjams are not problems. They are the result (i.e., symptoms) of underlying etiologies. Eliminating the troublesome results requires treating the underlying etiologies.

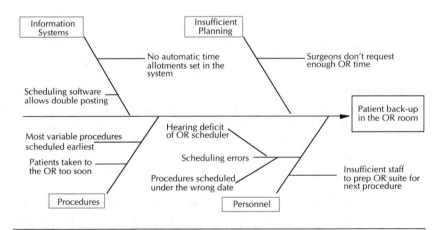

Figure 12.4 Cause-and-effect diagram.

Focusing on decreasing pre-op waiting times without identifying the causes is like treating a fever without identifying and treating the fever's cause.

The technical skills that employees need to improve are as varied as their jobs. Optimizing quality requires that employees have skills beyond those required to do the jobs they currently do. For example, few housekeepers have data processing skills. But without those skills, how will they discover if data processing can be incorporated into housekeeping processes to make them better? Likewise, how does an information systems analyst understand how data processing can be applied to housekeeping if he does not fully understand how housekeeping is done?

Deming's points 9, 10, and 14 speak to building organizational skills. Quality is not a departmental issue. The whole organization must be involved. This requires that employees improve communications skills and learn how to work effectively in interdisciplinary teams. Employees must learn how to overcome the interdepartmental rivalry and empire-building practices to which they have become accustomed. Employees must be supported in their efforts to overcome the communication barriers that have resulted from departmentalization and hierarchical organizational structures.

4.   Make the improvement of processes, not numbers, the focus of quality improvement. Deming is an adherent of Theory Y management. He believes that the cause of poor quality is in work processing, not in people. Therefore, the road to improving quality does not include threatening employees (point 8), cheerleading (point 9), or holding them to numerical performance standards (point 11). According to Deming, employees are already motivated to perform well. They perform well if organizational barriers do not impede their achievement. When processes work well, there is no need to rely heavily on inspection because employees will produce high quality results. Quantitative measurement does have a place in evaluation of processes. Some sampling of product is required to assure that processes are in control. Deming's approach, however, suggests that evaluation of work performance should focus more on employees' contribution to quality improvement than their reaching numerical goals.

Strategies and Models

There are several models that describe a sequence of events required to implement TQM/CQI.[75] Probably no one model is more correct or appropriate than another. They all can serve an organization well as a means of assuring that there is a shared understanding about how quality will be improved. The two models presented here embody the key steps usually incorporated in quality improvement models.

Juran conceives of quality improvement as a sequence of breakthroughs mediated by organizing activities (Figure 12.5).[76] For Juran, a breakthrough is a change that moves an organization to a higher level of performance. The breakthrough in attitude is a recognition that it is desirable to improve. The Pareto analysis is used to identify which changes would result in the biggest increase in quality. The next breakthrough, a breakthrough in knowledge, must be preceded by an organizational redesign that creates two groups. One group, the steering arm, directs the acquisition and utilization of new knowledge. The other group, the diagnostic arm, collects and analyzes data. The two groups work together toward a diagnosis, which is the application of research and analysis to generate knowledge needed for action. The knowledge breakthrough occurs when enough knowledge to support action exists. Breakthrough in culture occurs when resistance to change has been overcome and the members of the organization are willing to institute the changes suggested by the breakthrough in knowledge. Breakthrough in performance occurs if the changes result in performance improvement. At the end of the sequence, control is used to make sure that the performance gains are maintained.

The FOCUS-PDCA® model has probably been the most commonly used model in healthcare. The model was developed at the Health Corporation of America.[77] FOCUS is an acronym that describes the following sequence of steps in the quality improvement process:

1. Finding a process to improve
2. Organizing a team that knows the process
3. Clarifying current knowledge of the process
4. Understanding the cause of variation
5. Selecting the process improvement[78]

The parallels to Juran's sequence of breakthroughs is obvious. Both sequences include identifying projects, organizing groups, learning about the process, and choosing a course of action. PDCA stands for **Plan, Do, Check, Act**.[79] PDCA is a cyclical sequence of activities. A factor that leads to process variation is selected for change. A course of action is planned, the plan is done, it is checked to assess how well it worked, and results are acted on to maintain gains and/or further improve the process.

Quality Circles

No discussion of quality would be complete without mentioning quality circles. **Quality circles** are groups of employees who meet voluntarily to solve their own work-related problems in an organized way.[80] Quality circles were

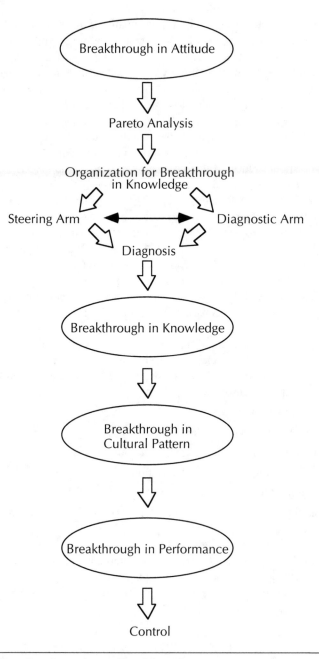

Figure 12.5   Juran's sequence of breakthroughs.

effectively used in Japan as a way of increasing employee participation in quality improvement. Their success has not been widely duplicated in the United States. Successful utilization of quality circles requires a long-term commitment. Members need to work together over an extended period to hone process improvement. This is inconsistent with the hit-and-run approach to problem solving that has characterized American business. Another problem has been that quality circles in America have seldom been empowered to act on their decisions. Their role has been advisory only. When management fails to act on recommendations, employee enthusiasm evaporates. Quality circles are, therefore, doomed to failure in organizations dominated by Theory X managers, who do not believe that employees can make decisions. Finally, like any group that attempts to improve processes, quality circles need to know how to improve. Members of quality circles become frustrated without adequate knowledge of how to evaluate and improve process and product quality.

Conclusion

In the MHP case, George Soledad is convinced that TQM/CQI is a passing management fad. Given the rapidity with which management fads come and go, it is not surprising that he feels that way. However, under all the jargon, theory, and rhetoric spawned by a renewed interest in quality, there lies the reality that quality improvement has long been an important part of American culture in general, and of healthcare in particular. Increasing athletic performance, expanding the boundaries of knowledge in all fields, and producing more profound and meaningful art have been objectives that have been embraced and publicly supported by Americans. In healthcare, clinicians and managers alike have long been committed to improving personal performance. MHP's CEO failed to make it clear that TQM/CQI is nothing more than a road map to help the organization achieve the level of performance to which most of its members already aspire.

In today's cost conscious healthcare environment, she might have done well to have shown how not implementing a TQM/CQI program is costing MHP money. Crosby estimates that achieving quality increases profit by 5%–10% of sales.[81] He identified three different kinds of costs of quality. **Prevention costs** are the costs of activities to prevent product or service defects. In healthcare, these costs include supplier reviews, consumer education, marketing research, continuing education, training in quality improvement, labor cost of quality teams, and preventive maintenance. **Appraisal costs** are related to product and service inspection. In healthcare, these costs would include billing audits, QA, accreditation reviews, utilization review, safety inspections, equipment inspections, and health status determinations. **Failure costs** arise from performance that falls below requirements. In general, these failures result in doing the work again, scrap, liability actions, after-service follow-up, and redesign of work process. Failure costs may result from both failures that involve clients (**external failures**) and failures that involve only members of the organization (**internal failures**). At

MHP both kinds of failures are evident. External failures include the medication error, the repeat phlebotomy, and the late appointments. Internal failures include the dispute between Dr. Craig and nurse Smithe, and deviations from treatment protocols. Although they may not reach customers, internal failures are very expensive because they result in overtime, delays in work processing, and wasted labor costs. Note how much labor cost was wasted at MHP by having three highly paid people engaged in a dispute over a routine inventory issue. One study of costs of quality conducted in a healthcare system similar to MHP found that failure costs accounted for more than 80% of total costs of quality.[82] The conclusion is obvious. Investing in prevention and appraisal is well worth the potential savings in failure costs.

For a significant quality improvement effort to take place at MHP, Dr. Soledad and his colleagues will have to be convinced that the effort is worthwhile. The CEO has to do a much better job of communicating the importance of TQM /CQI. Dr. Soledad's time could be better spent improving processes and supporting the efforts of employees than putting out fires. In fact, inevitably he will have no choice. Opportunists exist in every industry. Staying in the competitive lead requires staying in front of them. Somewhere in his future, there is a finely tuned, highly trained competitor poised to push him and MHP out of the lead.

Endnotes

1. Lloyd Dobyns and Clare Crawrod-Mason, *Quality or Else* (Boston: Houghton Mifflin, 1991).
2. Ibid.
3. George W. Whetsell, "Total Quality Management," *Topics in Healthcare Financing 18* (1991): 12–20.
4. Lawton R. Burns and Lee Roy Beach, "The Quality Improvement Strategy," *Healthcare Management Review 19* (Spring 1994): 21–31.
5. Marsha Gold and Judith Wooldridge, "Surveying Consumer Satisfaction to Assess Managed-Care Quality: Current Practices," *Healthcare Financing Review 16* (Summer 1995): 155–173.
6. Whetsell, op. cit.
7. Maria A. Friedman, "Issues in Measuring and Improving Healthcare Quality," *Healthcare Financing Review 16* (Summer 1995): 1–12.
8. John E. Wennberg and Alan Gittelsohn, "Small Area Variations in Healthcare Delivery," *Science 182* (December 14, 1973): 1102–8.
9. John E. Wennberg, Jean L. Freeman, and William J. Culp, "Are Hospital Services Rationed in New Haven or Over-utilised in Boston?" *The Lancet 1* (May 23, 1987): 1185–9.
10. John E. Wennberg, Jean L. Freeman, Roxanne M. Shelton, and Thomas A. Bubolz, "Hospital Use and Mortality among Medicare Beneficiaries in Boston and New Haven," *New England Journal of Medicine 321* (October 26, 1989): 1168–73.
11. Arnold M. Epstein, "The Outcomes Movement—Will It Get Us Where We Want To Go?" *New England Journal of Medicine 323* (July 26, 1990): 266–270.

12. Mary T. Koska, "New JCAHO Standards Emphasize Continuous Quality Improvement," *Hospitals 65* (August 8, 1991): 41–45.
13. Kirk A. Mahlen, "Achieving Superior Performance Through Process Improvement," *Healthcare Financial Management 47* (September 1993): 45–46+.
14. Barbara J. Gagel, "Healthcare Quality Improvement Program: A New Approach," *Healthcare Financing Review 16* (Summer 1995): 15–23.
15. Rodney C. Armstead, Paul Elstein, and John Gorman, "Toward a 21st Century Quality-Measurement System for Managed-Care Organizations," *Healthcare Financing Review 16* (Summer 1995): 25–37.
16. Stephen F. Jencks, "Measuring Quality of Care Under Medicare and Medicaid," *Healthcare Financing Review 16* (Summer 1995): 39–54.
17. Marsha Gold and Suzanne Felt, "Reconciling Practice and Theory: Challenges in Monitoring Medicaid Managed-Care Quality," *Healthcare Financing Review 16* (Summer 1995): 85–105.
18. David R. Zimmerman, Sarita L. Karon, Greg Arling, Brenda Ryther Clark, Ted Collins, Richard Ross, and François Sainfort, "Development and Testing of Nursing Home Quality Indicators," *Healthcare Financing Review 16* (Summer 1995): 107–128.
19. Peter W. Shaughnessy, Andrew M. Kramer, David F. Hittle, and John F. Steiner, "Quality of Care in Teaching Nursing Homes: Findings and Implications," *Healthcare Financing Review 16* (Summer 1995): 55–83.
20. William M. McClellan, Pamela R. Frederick, Steven D. Helgerson, Risa P. Hayes, David J. Ballard, and Michael McMullan, "A Data-Driven Approach to Improving the Care of In-Center Hemodialysis Patients," *Healthcare Financing Review 16* (Summer 1995): 129–140.
21. Marie E. Cowart and Jean M. Mitchell, "Florida's Medicaid AIDS Waiver: An Assessment of Dimensions of Quality," *Healthcare Financing Review 16* (Summer 1995): 141–153.
22. Stephen M. Shortell, Robin H. Gillies, and Kelly J. Devers, "Reinventing the American Hospital," *Milbank Quarterly 73* (1995): 131–160.
23. The number of references cited for this chapter relative to other chapters of this book is greater because these references constitute a reading list that is recommended for clinicians/managers who are responsible for quality improvement programs.
24. Ronald Fortuna, "The Quality Imperative," in Ernest C. Huge, ed., *Total Quality: An Executive's Guide for the 1990s* (Homewood, IL: Richard D. Irwin, Inc., 1990).
25. William M. Pride, Robert J. Hughes, and Jack R. Kapoor, *Business*, 5th ed. (Boston: Houghton Mifflin, 1996).
26. Mary Walton, *The Deming Management Method* (New York: Dodd, Mead &Company, 1986).
27. Kathleen N. Lohr, ed., *Medicare: A Strategy for Quality Assurance*, Vol. 1 (Washington: National Academy Press, Institute of Medicine, 1990).
28. Ellen J. Gaucher and Richard J. Coffey, *Total Quality in Healthcare: From Theory to Practice* (San Francisco: Jossey-Bass, 1993).
29. W. Edwards Deming, *Out of the Crisis* (Cambridge, MA: Massachusetts Institute of Technology, Center for Advanced Engineering Study, 1982).

30. Donald M. Berwick, "Continuous Quality As an Ideal in Healthcare," *New England Journal of Medicine 320* (January 5, 1989): 53–56.

31. Joseph M. Juran, *Juran on Planning for Quality* (New York: The Free Press, 1988).

32. Philip B. Crosby, *Quality is Free* (New York: McGraw-Hill, 1979).

33. Glenn Laffel and David Blumenthal, "The Case for Using Industrial Quality Management Science in Healthcare Organizations," *Journal of the American Medical Association 262* (November 24, 1989): 2869–2873.

34. J. Edward McEachern and Duncan Neuhauser, "The Continuous Improvement of Quality at the Hospital Corporation of America," *Health Matrix 7* (1989): 7.

35. Lohr, op. cit.

36. Avedis Donabedian, "Evaluating the Quality of Medical Care," *Milbank Memorial Fund Quarterly 44* (July 1966): 166–206.

37. ———. "The Role of Outcomes in Quality Assessment and Assurance," *Quality Review Bulletin 18* (1992): 356–360.

38. Armand V. Feigenbaum, "TQM: Healthcare Can Learn from Other Fields," *Hospitals 66* (November 20, 1992): 56.

39. Friedman, op. cit.

40. Donabedian (1992), op. cit.

41. Jane C. Linder, "Outcomes Measurement: Compliance Tool or Strategic Initiative?" *Healthcare Management Review 16* (Fall 1991): 21–33.

42. Donabedian (1992), op. cit.

43. Ibid.

44. Ibid.

45. Personal communication, AHCPR staff, February 21, 1996.

46. Epstein, op. cit.

47. Jodi Halpern, "Can the Development of Practice Guidelines Safeguard Patient Values?" *Journal of Law, Medicine & Ethics 23* (Spring 1995): 75–81.

48. Renee A. Stiles and Stephen S. Mick, "Classifying Quality Initiatives: A Conceptual Paradigm for Literature Review and Policy Analysis," *Hospital and Health Service Administration 39* (Fall 1994): 309–326.

49. Friedman, op. cit.

50. Joby John, "Referent Opinion and Healthcare Satisfaction," *Journal of Healthcare Marketing 14* (Summer 1994): 24–30.

51. Faye W. Gilbert, James R. Lumpkin, and Rajiv P. Dant, "Adaptation and Customer Expectations of Healthcare Options," *Journal of Healthcare Marketing 12* (September 1992): 46–55.

52. Jane G. Zapka, F. Heather Palmer, J. Lee Hargraves, David Nuenz, Howard S. Frazier, and Cheryl K. Warner, "Relationships of Patient Satisfaction with Experience of System Performance and Health Status," *Journal Ambulatory Care Management 18* (January 1995): 73–83.

53. Mary T. Koska, "Surveying Customer Needs, Not Satisfaction, Is Crucial to CQI," *Hospitals 66* (November 6, 1992): 50+.

54. Zapka, et al., op. cit.

55. David H. Furse, Michael R. Burcham, Robin L. Rose, and Richard W. Oliver, "Leveraging the Value of Customer Satisfaction Information," *Journal of Healthcare Marketing 14* (Fall 1994): 16–20.

56. Deming, op. cit.

57. Gaucher and Coffey, op. cit.
58. Zapka, et al., op. cit.
59. Koska (1992), op. cit.
60. Michael R. Bowers, John E. Swan, and William F. Koehler, "What Attributes Determine Quality and Satisfaction with Healthcare Delivery?" *Healthcare Management Review 19* (Fall 1994): 49–55.
61. Robert C. Camp, *Benchmarking* (Milwaukee, WI: ASQC Quality Press, 1989).
62. Craig Anderson and Peggy A. Rivenburgh, "Benchmarking," in Mara M. Melum and Marie K. Sinoris, *Total Quality Management: The Healthcare Pioneers* (American Hospital Publishing, 1992).
63. Eleanor Anderson-Miles, "Benchmarking in Healthcare Organizations: An Introduction," *Healthcare Financial Management* (September 1994): 58–61.
64. Joseph M. Juran, *Managerial Breakthrough*, 2nd ed. (New York: McGraw-Hill, 1995).
65. Donald M. Berwick, A. Blanton Godfren, and Jane Roessner, *Curing Healthcare: New Strategies for Quality Improvement* (San Francisco: Jossey-Bass, 1991).
66. Margarete Arndt and Barbara Bigelow, "The Implementation of Total Quality Management in Hospitals: How Good is the Fit?" *Healthcare Management Review 20* (Fall 1995): 7–14.
67. Robert G. Gift, Tom D. Stoddard, and Kirk B. Wilson, "Collaborative Benchmarking in a Healthcare System," *Healthcare Financial Management* (September 1994): 80–96.
68. Austin Ross, *Cornerstones of Leadership for Health Services Executives* (Ann Arbor: Health Administration Press, 1992).
69. Paul B. Bataldan and Patricia K. Stoltz, "A Framework for the Continual Improvement of Healthcare: Building and Applying Professional and Improvement Knowledge to Test Changes in Daily Work," *Journal on Quality Improvement 19* (October 1993): 424–447.
70. C. J. Bolster, Elizabeth Falter, and Laura Hooper, "Bringing Theory into Practice—Applying Improvement Thinking, Part II," *Clinical Performance and Quality Healthcare 1* (1993): 163–171.
71. Robert F. Casalou, "Total Quality Management in Healthcare," *Hospital & Health Services Administration 36* (Spring 1991): 134–145.
72. Berwick et al., op. cit.
73. M. Daniel Sloan, *How to Lower Healthcare Costs by Improving Healthcare Quality* (Milwaukee, WI: ASQC Quality Press, 1994).
74. Whetsell, op. cit.
75. Gaucher and Coffey, op. cit.
76. J. M. Juran, *Managerial Breakthrough*, revised ed. (New York: McGraw-Hill, 1995).
77. McEachern, op. cit.
78. Ibid.
79. Ibid.
80. Mike Robson, *Quality Circles in Action* (Aldershot, U.K., 1984).
81. Crosby, op. cit.
82. Brett J. Waress, Derick P. Pasternick, and Howard L. Smith, "Determining Costs Associated with Quality in Healthcare Delivery," *Healthcare Management Review 19* (Summer 1994): 52–63.

Stress:
Anxiety and
Depression

In this chapter the reader will learn:

◆ how to diagnose problems that arise from stress in the workplace

◆ what causes stress in the workplace in general and in healthcare in particular

◆ how to help employees cope with stress

◆ how to recognize potentially violent employees

◆ how to minimize the threat of workplace violence

◆ what legal ramifications of intervention strategies used to deal with potentially violent employees can occur

On the Edge

Okay. He knew he had to do something about it, but what that something was going to be, he did not know. Rob wished that his degree in optometry had included more than just Psych 101.

He had hired Jack eight months ago. Jack was in his early thirties and had worked as an optician for several different companies, including a couple of well-known retail optical chains. He was pleasant and came with good references. He was a confident and physically imposing interviewee. He later told Rob that a promising professional football career had been cut short by a knee injury.

Everything was fine for the first two months. Then Jack had become quite depressed. He went so far as to tell Rob that he had even had thoughts of committing suicide, but that he thought that he could probably never follow through with it. Although Jack had initially established good relationships with the customers, he began to withdraw to the optical lab, doing the repair work that other opticians did not like to do. Rob noticed that Jack seemed to be spending more time with Marlena, a young married sales clerk. That did not bother Rob until one day he found them together in the lab touching each other in a way that he considered inappropriate in a workplace. He let both of them know that this behavior was inappropriate and that they should save their displays of affection for their own time. Rob had witnessed no further behavior of this kind.

Jack's moodiness became more pronounced over time. One day he seemed to be ecstatically happy. The next, he was desperately depressed and despondent. Sometimes, he seemed to be unnaturally calm, and at other times, he was extremely irritable. Occasionally, he would go into the storeroom and kick and throw empty boxes to vent his anger.

Today, Sally, another optician, had sat in Rob's office in tears. She had overheard one of Jack's outbursts in the storeroom, and she told Rob that she was afraid. She said that if Rob ever left the premises, that she would not stay there alone with Jack. As far as Rob knew, Jack had not threatened anyone, nor even raised his voice to them. But his mood swings and storeroom outbursts were creating tension that was unfair to other employees. Rob had to admit to himself that even he was a bit afraid of Jack. But how to confront him? As the founding optometrist of Visionary Options, Inc., Rob wanted to protect his employees, but he also wanted to protect his business. He considered his alternatives. Did he have grounds to fire Jack? Should he simply issue a verbal reprimand? Should he make Jack's continuing employment contingent on getting counselling? On the other hand, maybe Jack just did not know that his outbursts were overheard and that they frightened others. Maybe just letting him know that would be enough to put an end to the whole thing. After all, this approach had put an end to Jack and Marlena's public displays of intimacy. As he reached for the phone to call his lawyer, he could not help but wonder if Jack was about to go over the edge.

Stress has become as much a staple of work life as time cards, bosses, and paid time off. At best, stress makes work life unpleasant. At worst, it manifests itself in debilitating illness and/or violence. Clinicians are accustomed to seeing stress in their patients because illness and stress frequently coexist. The stress that is seen in clinical settings is frequently manifested as anxiety and/or depression. Because they so often deal with these problems, healthcare providers are uniquely prepared to recognize and deal with work-related stress.

The Visionary Options case illustrates how similar clinical stress and workplace stress are. Rob and Sally are clearly anxious. Jack is anxious and depressed. His suicidal ideation, coupled with his inappropriate behavior, are signs that mental health intervention may be indicated. Rob, of course, is not professionally qualified to intervene clinically. However, he does have the responsibility to use managerial interventions to alleviate the anxiety and depression that Jack's behavior is generating in the organization.

The manager's role in stress management is complicated by several factors that are apparent in the Visionary Options case. First, managers cannot become clinically detached like clinicians can. Clinicians can establish emotional boundaries that protect them from feeling patients' pain. Managers are physically and emotionally inseparable from the work environment. The constancy of their presence keeps them from emotionally distancing themselves. Second, stress in the workplace is not easily contained. At Visionary Options, Jack's stress was at the center of a maelstrom that pulled other employees into its vortex. Finally, dealing with workplace stress is complicated by laws that shape the formal relationships among employers and employees. In formulating a strategy for dealing with this problem, Rob has to consider his legal relationship with Jack and the other employees. He also has to consider the firm's liability for Jack's actions.

Stress is epidemic in the workplace. Therefore, managing stress must be a central concern of managers. Hit-and-run strategies that focus on individual cases are insufficient to deal with a problem of this magnitude. Fortunately, managing stress is not unrelated to other managerial strategies that have been suggested in previous chapters. Motivated, satisfied work forces that function well in teams to produce high quality products are likely to experience relatively little work-related stress.

The Nature and Importance of Stress in the Workplace

Stress is one of those concepts that is difficult to define, but that people readily recognize when they experience it. Recognizing stress in others, however, is not always easy. "Stress is the manifestly uncomfortable feeling that an individual experiences when he or she is forced to deviate from normal or desired patterns of functioning."[1] This definition has two important components. First, stress is a feeling. As such, it is not something that is always readily apparent to others. Managers may detect signs of stress like short temper, lassitude, or fidgeting, but these may also be signs of other problems. Stress may be effectively masked so that managers are not aware of it. Second, stress is associated with a lack of fit between what an individual does and what he wants to do. This dissonance creates an inner feeling of tension.

Because stress is a feeling and feelings are not observable, it is tempting for managers to ignore stress altogether. Indifference to stress can be rationalized by conceiving of stress as part of every job in every organization. Therefore, dealing with stress should default to the holder of the job—the employee. If the consequences of stress were insignificant, this would be a rational (albeit ethically questionable) approach. Unfortunately, stress results in significant organizational damage. Therefore, it is incumbent on managers to intervene to minimize stress and its negative outcomes.

Connecting stress to specific negative consequences has been difficult due to inconsistencies in defining and measuring stress and its effects. The loss to American business in terms of productivity alone is estimated to be between $50 and $150 billion.[2] As pressures to increase quality and productivity escalate, it can be expected that these costs will continue to increase. There is evidence that the economic success of Japan has been subsidized to some extent by stress.[3] The continual search for more efficient and effective production methods has created extraordinary employee stress. Job stress has become so pervasive that the Japanese National Institute of Public Health has defined a syndrome (karoushi) that includes cumulative fatigue, exacerbation of pre-existing hypertension, and fatality.[4] Similarly, among nurses, it has been observed that as workload-related stressors (patient load and percentage of patient contact time) increase, blood pressure levels at work and after work increase.[5]

Several studies have linked stress to decreased productivity, increased absenteeism, increased turnover, and decreased employee health.[6] One study suggests that stress results in decreased organizational commitment. However, decreased commitment was not linked to decreased performance, especially when employees considered the task to be significant.[7] Because the nature of the work in healthcare is perceived by most people to be important, employees have a tendency to perform well even when they feel stress and are marginally committed to their organizations. However, healthcare managers cannot afford to depend on employees' commitment to their professional mission to guarantee efficiency and effectiveness. Just because healthcare providers feel that providing high quality care is important and continue to do so under stress, does not mean that their response to stress may not include disruptive behavior. Besides job task performance, stressors have also been linked to sabotage, interpersonal aggression, hostility and complaints, and theft.[8]

The emotional component of karoushi is similar to burnout. **Burnout** is emotional exhaustion that results from the accumulation of job-related stress. As clinicians are well aware, when stress reaches this level, physical and mental exhaustion usually coexist with emotional exhaustion. Healthcare practitioners are at increased risk of burnout because their work requires them to work extensively with others.[9] Not surprisingly, burnout results in organizational dysfunction. It has been associated with decreased morale, decreased performance, drug and alcohol abuse, absenteeism, turnover, and tardiness.[10] Fortunately, burnout is not the inevitable consequence of stress. The ability of individuals to adapt to stress also plays a role in the development of burnout.[11] Therefore, if managers intervene at the onset of stress with strategies that help employees adapt, some of the devastating effects of burnout can be avoided.

Effective managerial intervention requires that managers recognize the signs and symptoms of stress, that they understand the sources of stress, and that they be able to help employees cope with stress.[12] There are several signs and symptoms of stress (Table 13.1). These signs and symptoms may be manifested by individuals or groups. These are nonspecific indicators that may result from any number of physical conditions or that may be inherent personality traits. Therefore, a diagnosis of stress is only made after talking with employees. Through communication not only is the diagnosis confirmed, but the sources of stress are identified. Determination of sources of stress is important so that treatment can focus on underlying problems rather than on symptoms. Once the source(s) of stress is identified, managers can help employees identify appropriate coping mechanisms or refer them to someone who can.

Table 13.1   Signs and Symptoms of Stress

Poor performance by capable individuals
Lethargy
Absenteeism
Personality changes
Alcoholism
Attitude that annoys colleagues
Poor/inappropriate interaction with patients
Hypercritical behavior
Hyperactivity
Distrust of supervisors and peers
Complaints or sick days due to ulcers, prolonged colds, muscular pain, headaches, and gastrointestinal disorders
Risk-taking
Avoiding others
Increased smoking, alcohol, caffeine, or prescription drug consumption
Job errors
Mood swings
Clock watching
Fault finding
Seeking a transfer

Source: Cathy M. Anderson, "A Departmental Stress Management Plan," *Health Care Supervisor 8* (June 1990): 1–8.

Sources of Stress

Stressors are the forces that cause unwelcome deviations from normal or desired patterns of behavior. Stressors come from the individual's environment. Note that some stressors may cause stress in spite of the fact that the outcomes of impending events may be very good. Weddings are a good example. Although they are generally joyful occasions filled with positive expectations of future happiness, most people in the wedding party find weddings to be stressful. Weddings are stressors that cause behavior to deviate, albeit in a positive way, from the norm. Employees being considered for promotions, who have attractive new job offers or who are about to move into beautiful new work spaces, are likely to feel stress. Although these stressors result in discomfort and impinge on performance, they do not merit much managerial attention. Because of their potential to result in positive outcomes, employees find ways to adapt to these pressures. Employees may adapt to this kind of stress relatively well because they see it as part of the price to be paid for moving forward. It is the stressors that employees associate with negative outcomes that should be a cause of managerial concern. Those stressors are all too plentiful in most HSOs.

Patient-Generated Stressors

Job stress is directly related to an individual's perception of risk. The more risk associated with an action, the more apprehensive (i.e., stressed) an individual will be. Risk is inherent in dealing with patients. Healthcare providers are at risk of contracting communicable diseases. They are at risk of traumatic injury from combative patients. They are at financial and professional risk arising from potential allegations of providing inadequate care. They are at risk of being the targets of verbal abuse. A recent study of allied health professionals indicated that stressors arising from patient care activities significantly contributed to job-related stress.[13] Of the 15 most significant stressors reported by radiologic technologists, only one patient-generated stressor (abusive patients) was mentioned. However, nuclear medicine technologists included uncooperative patients, very ill patients, AIDS patients, and exposure to diseases among their most significant stressors. Medical technologists included exposure to HIV. It would be expected that because medical technologists are removed from the bedside that stress directly caused by patients would be less. Not surprisingly, as providers of bedside care, hospital nurses have voiced their fear of HIV.[14] The more nurses are exposed to AIDS patients, the more distressed they are likely to become.[15] AIDS is a powerful manifestation of the risk that has always been inherent in caring for patients.

Work Content Stressors

Many stressors arise from the process of accomplishing tasks. It is sometimes difficult to separate these stressors from stressors that come from the work environment. For example, in healthcare, interruptions are stressors. Are interruptions an inherent part of providing care, or do they arise from the environment? Probably both. Therefore, the classification of stressors as work content stressors or work context stressors is not exact.

Task complexity has been related to stress. Jobs which are so routine that they result in boredom may cause stress.[16,17] The simplicity of jobs that require little or no creativity or problem-solving creates stress due to the mismatch between the skill and/or knowledge of employees and job requirements. On the other hand, jobs that are too complex also create stress because employees cannot meet performance requirements.

Physical strain required by a job also results in stress.[18,19] Although automation is increasing in virtually every industry, many areas of healthcare practice still require physically strenuous activities. Clinical work is still very much hands-on work. Many physicians, especially surgeons, do very strenuous work. Many nurses, physical therapists, and occupational therapists have physically demanding jobs. So, too, do support personnel who transfer supplies and maintain facilities.

Work which leaves little or no room for error is stressful. Air traffic control is the quintessential example of work in which there is no tolerance for error. The parallel to healthcare is obvious.

Several job content stressors were noted in Frazer and Sechrist's study of allied health professionals. Radiologic technologists included disrespectful physicians, lack of respect, and malfunctioning equipment among their most significant stressors. Nuclear medicine technologists reported equipment malfunctions, add-on examinations, difficult procedures, and interruptions. Medical technologists noted equipment breakdowns, interruptions, lack of respect from physicians, and lack of respect from other healthcare workers. Respect issues are included here because they are so universally reported by allied health workers that lack of respect seems to be inherent in the job. However, perceived lack of respect may certainly vary in intensity from one work environment to another.

Work Context Stressors

Much of the stress research in organizational behavior has focused on context stressors. Stress has been linked to the fit between individuals and their organizational roles. Stress can result from role ambiguity and role conflict. **Role ambiguity** occurs when individuals do not understand what is expected of them. Role conflict occurs when there are clear, but conflicting demands. For example, in managed care organizations, physicians experience role conflict when their role as a patient advocate conflicts with their role as fiscal agents of their employers. **Role conflict** and role ambiguity have been linked to tension, fatigue, absenteeism, turnover, anxiety, and physical and psychological strain.[20] **Role scope** is the number of expectations placed on an employee. As noted above, when the scope is too large, the task gets too complex and stress results. When role scope is too narrow, it may lead to boredom, which also results in stress.

Much of the job-related stress experienced by American workers can be traced to work context stressors. The physical environment can contribute to stress. Among the physical stressors that have been identified are density and crowding, lack of privacy, vibrations, sound, temperature extremes, air movement, background color, and computer terminals.[21] The increased use of electronic work processing has introduced another potential stressor to many workplaces. Electronic monitoring of employee activities has resulted in "higher levels of job boredom, psychological tension, anxiety, depression, anger, health complaints and fatigue."[22] While it is tempting to make use of any technology that helps track employee productivity, the long-term negative effects on employees can easily outweigh any short-term productivity gains.

A recent study of university faculty and staff, and corporate managerial, professional, and clerical personnel found that the five most severe stressors were inadequate salary, lack of opportunity for advancement, insufficient personnel to handle assignments, inadequate support by supervisors, and lack of recognition for good work.[23] Frazer and Sechrist's findings were similar. Radiologic technologists' rankings of stressors included inadequate pay, unnecessary examinations, lack of staff, uncooperative radiologists, nonsupportive radiologists, demanding radiologists, management rules, poor patient care, overwork, department organization, and demanding physicians. Stressors reported by nuclear medicine technologists included uncooperative physicians, lack of staff, workload, salary, poor communication with physicians, and lack of staff cooperation. Stressors of medical technologists included poor management practices, difficult co-workers, lack of time, workload, lack of staff, excessive paperwork, insufficient time to complete work, stat abuse, responsibility without authority, and improper specimen handling.[24] The enumeration of these stressors indicates that considerable organizational stress is caused by things that happen in the work environment. Managers are severely limited in their ability to lessen stress that originates with patients. They can do a bit more to help employees deal with stressors that are inherent in the job. They have even more control over environmental factors.

Dealing with Stress

There are two basic strategies for dealing with stress in the workplace. Stressors can be eliminated from the environment, and employees can adapt in ways that lessen the stress they feel. Neither strategy will eliminate stress completely. Some stressors cannot be eradicated, new stressors continually appear, and adaptation has its limits. In wartime, for example, a soldier's ability to adapt to combat conditions over a long period of time is finite. Because stress is a personal phenomenon, some individuals will be able to adapt more easily and readily than others.

Eliminating stressors from the work environment is closely related to job satisfaction and motivation issues. The difference between job content and job context motivators (Chapter 8) is completely analogous. To reduce stress, the manager must address the job context issues that lead to stress (and simultaneously cause job dissatisfaction). As the research cited in this chapter and in Chapter 8 indicates, the most important of these issues are mutual respect, appreciation, workload, staffing, salary, and managerial policies and their implementation. The appropriate prescription for reducing stressors varies with the quality of the organization's leadership, its mission, and the resources with which it has to work. In working with anxious and/or depressed patients, practitioners try to establish an atmosphere that is warm and supportive—an atmosphere that is inviting. The hope is that the patient will feel safe, comfortable, and sufficiently at ease so that he will be open to discussing and resolving underlying problems. To minimize stress, the job environment should be structured in a way that leads to the creation of a warm, welcoming, and supportive workplace.

Helping employees to cope is the second important managerial stress intervention. **Coping** is the adaptive effort that individuals make to manage the demands that cause their stress.[25] There are two different ways in which people cope with stress. **Problem-focused coping** consists of taking action to change one's behavior or to change the environment so that there is less dissonance between the two. When behavior and environment are aligned, stress dissipates. **Emotion-focused coping** consists of attempts to decrease the emotional distress caused by stressors. Such efforts might include not thinking about stress-inducing situations or denying that they exist.[26] When individuals can control the environment and/or their job-related behavior, problem-focused coping is preferred to emotion-focused coping. However, when an individual perceives that he has no control and that no one is likely to intervene to lessen the dissonance, then he must depend on emotion-focused coping to ease his discomfort.

There are positive, emotion-focused coping activities. Meditation, for example, provides not only a respite from job-related stress, but from other stress as well. The meditative mini-vacation physically and emotionally revitalizes the individual and helps him focus attention, increase control over thought, and increase his ability to handle emotions.[27] Meditation is an attractive coping mechanism because it has no adverse side effects on the organization.

Some forms of emotion-focused coping lead to negative outcomes. Wishful thinking, denial, substance abuse, and overeating may provide temporary escape, but they emotionally and/or physically harm the individual and may make stressful situations even worse. One study found that nurses who report using these negative forms of coping also report more burnout, emotional exhaustion, depersonalization, and a weaker sense of accomplishment.[28] Unfortunately, the longer employees are in a job, the more likely they may be to resort to emotional escape coping activities that result in burnout.[29]

Stress counselling in the workplace has been shown to be beneficial. It has decreased anxiety, somatic anxiety, depression, and psychosomatic symptoms of stress, and increased self-esteem.[30] Employee assistance programs frequently provide stress counseling. Today's managers are fortunate that EAPs are widely available for employee referral because EAPs can deal with a broad range of stress-related issues. An individual's response to job-related stressors is influenced by many factors and stressors outside the workplace. In the Visionary Options case, it is reasonable to conclude that Jack's outbursts at work are related to stress in his personal life.

Coping with stressors is like juggling. Each stressor is an object that the individual has to handle very carefully to maintain a manageable rhythm and balance in his life. People who cope with several external stressors naturally have more difficulty coping with a job-related stressor than people who deal with fewer external stressors because they have more stressors to juggle. Because effective coping requires finding ways to juggle all the stressors in an employee's life (including personal stressors), few managers are skilled or confident enough to offer substantial help. EAPs are there for just that purpose.

Training in positive, emotion-focused coping techniques is valuable, especially for those employees with longer tenure who appear more likely to pursue negative coping strategies. There is evidence that progressive muscle relaxation, biofeedback, meditation, and breathing exercises are effective.[31] Training in reappraisal may also be helpful. Reappraisal is an evaluation process during which individuals reassess their positions within the context of their environments. Sometimes when people take the time to reconsider the causes of their stress, they reach the conclusion that in the overall scheme of things, their situation is not as bad as they originally perceived. Thus, their stress is decreased.[32] Training in any of these techniques should not be triggered by observed signs and symptoms of stress. Instead, training is appropriate organizational prophylaxis. Employee response to these kinds of programs varies widely. Some employees find that these activities are extremely useful, and they appreciate ongoing programming so that they continue to re-establish a kind of emotional anchor in positive thinking. Other employees have little use for them. They feel that the techniques do not address the cause of their stress. They may actually experience additional stress as a result of participating in programs that they feel do no good. Of course, neither response is wrong. Positive, emotion-focused coping techniques are helpful, but they are no panacea.

Exercise merits special mention because so many organizations promote employee exercise programs as a way of decreasing the utilization of health benefits. Like meditation, it provides an escape from job-related stress. While people concentrate on achieving a physical goal, they are not concentrating on stressors. Exercise is an effective diversion. As healthcare providers know, regular exercise also results in better health overall, including improvement of stress-related physiological outcomes like heart rate and blood pressure. Unfortunately, organizational research does not consistently support a correlation between exercise and stress level.[33] For healthcare providers, however, the stress reduction benefits of exercise are intuitively attractive. At the very least, people who are physically healthy have fewer stressors than physically unhealthy people because they do not have to deal with as much stress that stems from illness. Therefore, they have more energy and emotional reserves to cope with other stressors.

Behavioral changes that reduce stress frequently require joint employee-manager efforts. The first step in formulating a behavioral change strategy is to clearly determine the cause(s) of stress. The second step is for the employee and manager to identify alternative solutions to the stress-related problem. For each alternative, they must assess their capability to implement the solution and anticipate how behavioral changes could result in new stress. Consider the following case:

> *Dan, the head nurse of the cardiopulmonary stepdown unit, walked into the utility room and found Melissa, an LPN, sobbing. When she regained her composure, she told Dan that she felt like she was at the end of her rope. She had no choice about working, but she felt like she hardly saw her husband or her children, and she never had any time for herself. Things had only gotten worse since the recent change to four 10-hour shifts. She could not see the children off to school before the morning shift, and she was not home when they returned from school. After dinner, she was so tired that she could not do anything. The extra day off was spent just catching up from the other four days. Dan and Melissa agreed that shorter shifts would decrease her stress.*

It has been suggested that short shifts are one way to decrease stress among nurses.[34] This would be a reasonable alternative in the case of Melissa. However, Dan and Melissa have to consider several other factors. Does Dan have the authority to change one individual's shift? Would patient care suffer (which may result in more stress)? If an exception is made, what conflicts might arise that would generate more stress? If all nurses went back to shorter shifts, how many of them would suffer more stress? When the shorter shift alternative is viewed in this way, both Dan and Melissa might reject this alternative as being likely to generate more stress than it would relieve. They may need to continue to search for other ways to ameliorate Melissa's stress.

Because workload is a stressor in healthcare, employees and managers need to look for changes that decrease or redistribute workload to minimize stress. Process improvements that minimize the number of unplanned occurrences (such as stat orders) and interruptions are very helpful. In some areas, work can be organized so that all unplanned work is funneled through one person so that other employees can work at a planned pace with few if any interruptions. Employees can then rotate through the hot spot so that their high-stress time is limited.

Although socially and psychologically demanding work is a risk factor for coronary heart disease, the primary work-related risk factor is lack of control over how to use one's skills to get the work done.[35] There is evidence that perceived lack of control is related to a number of poor health outcomes.[36] It is the organizational structure and job design, rather than the work itself, that appears to result in stress-related illnesses. This is an important point for healthcare managers to remember because too often, stress experienced by healthcare providers is attributed to the pressure of the work rather than to the pressure of the workplace.

Lack of autonomy is one of the most significant factors in nursing stress and burnout. To decrease stress and burnout among nurses, it is important to find ways to increase the control that nurses have over making decisions about how they do their work.[36-39] On the face of it, this seems to be incongruent with the TQM mandate of minimizing variability. However, as long as everyone is aware of outcome objectives, then individuals can be given some latitude in deciding how best to achieve those objectives. Ultimately, the increased ability to decide how work will be done may lead to decreased variability in the final product. For example, take a hospital pharmacist who has a specific number of activities to complete in a shift. Among those activities are completing reports of adverse drug reactions (ADRs) and doing concurrent reviews of antibiotic therapy. Most pharmacists in the department do antibiotic reviews first thing in the morning so that they can make progress notes in the chart that physicians can see when they make working rounds. Since the deadlines for ADR reports are more forgiving, they leave these reports to the end of the shift and work on them as time allows. However, Pharmacist Smith prefers to do ADR reports first thing in the morning because he finds that he has greater access to the medical records that he needs at that time of the day. He leaves antibiotic reviews to later in the day when more culture and sensitivity reports are available, which allows him to make recommendations based on more complete data, although he does have to spend more time calling physicians during their office hours. Obviously, there are advantages and disadvantages to both practice patterns. However, as long as the outcomes are within acceptable limits of variability, stress will be minimized by allowing the pharmacists to schedule their own work.

When no problem-focused alternatives alleviate stress, the employee may have to be separated from the environment. In institutional nursing, sometimes this can be accomplished through internal transfer. In some other departments, it is possible to move employees from one job to another. In physical therapy, for example, moving from geriatric rehabilitation to intensive care may present a therapist with a new practice environment that has fewer stressors. In community settings, this kind of flexibility is more difficult to achieve. In home healthcare, for example, if stress arises from providing care in the home and no coping techniques have worked, the employee may have no choice but to find another job.

Because many coping techniques are helpful, managers should be familiar with them and be prepared to help employees explore coping options as soon as stress occurs. Doing so can prevent serious consequences of stress. One of the most serious consequences of stress with which managers have to be concerned is violence.

Importance of Workplace Violence

In the United States, fifteen people are murdered at work every week.[40] In spite of their prevalence, workplace murders are always shocking because people are being killed doing something that is culturally valued (i.e., attempting to earn a living by going to work). The emotional impact of workplace mortality generates extensive media coverage. Unfortunately, workplace violence that results in injury does not garner the same attention. About 1 million people are victims of violent crimes at work annually. From 1987 to 1992, an average of 13,068 rapes, 79,109 robberies, 264,174 aggravated assaults, and 615,160 simple assaults occurred each year.[41] Hundreds of thousands of victims and co-workers are shaken and scarred by violence. Violence destabilizes work groups and makes peak performance impossible. Months and even years of work that go into team building and quality improvement can be eradicated in a few violent moments.

Not only is this level of violence psychologically and physically devastating, it is also very expensive. Each violent incident results in 3.5 days of lost work. In addition to days covered by sick and annual leave, employees incur $55 million in lost wages.[42] The economic impact on employers is also substantial. Not only is productivity disrupted, but some employers have had to pay damages to families of murder victims. Violence also typically results in a significant increase in worker-compensation premiums.[43] The high economic and human costs of violence make preventive measures imperative.

Early Detection of Violence-Prone Individuals

Violence in the healthcare environment can arise from three sources: patients, patients' families and visitors, and employees. Dealing with potentially violent patients should be part of every healthcare provider's training program. Unfortunately, it is not. Even less attention is paid to violent significant others of patients. When it comes to helping patients and their significant others work through a normal range of responses to illness (e.g., crying, withdrawal, projecting, and verbal venting), clinicians receive at least rudimentary training. However, many of them are not trained to deal with the far less common, but potentially devastating, violent response. In healthcare delivery, a violent response becomes disconnected from its roots in the disease process, and responsibility for managing the responses passes from the care provider to security. Frequently, before the hapless clinician can hand the hot potato off to security, he becomes a victim. As police and criminal justice systems increase their use of hospitals as a resource for dealing with drug overdose, severe mental illness, and other aberrant behavior cases, the level of exposure to violent patients will increase.[44]

Illness itself can create extreme stress. Add to that the fact that many patients feel that they are helpless pawns of an overwhelming and frightening healthcare monster (the system), and it becomes obvious that violence should always be considered as a possible illness response. Dealing with violence that is rooted in pathological processes is beyond the scope of this chapter. Suffice it to say that management has a responsibility to protect employees from foreseeable patient violence. The best protection from patient violence is training, especially in de-escalation techniques. [45]

Violence associated with employees seldom arises without advance warning. Violence-prone employees usually exhibit behaviors that are warning signs of impending violent outbursts. Unfortunately, these warning signs are not unique to violence-prone individuals. For example, one warning sign is irritability. Irritability is a common personality trait. How fortunate for everyone that all people who are irritable do not become violent! Identifying a violence-prone employee is like recognizing a syndrome. Spotting one sign or symptom is usually not enough to make either a diagnosis or a prognosis. It is a pattern of signs and symptoms that should lead the manager to be concerned about violent behavior.

The typical violent employee:

- is a white male in his 30s or 40s
- is a marginal performer
- tends to be a loner
- identifies strongly with his job
- has few or no healthy outlets for anger
- has difficulty accepting authority
- has a history of frequent job changes
- has a history of substance of abuse
- has a history of depression, paranoia, violence, or encounters with violence
- has a history of conflicts with co-workers and/or supervisors
- is frequently angry
- has a fascination with weapons or the military
- has a fascination with media reports of violence
- has poor self-esteem
- has an unstable family life
- has unresolved physical or emotional injury claims.[46–49]

Of course, not every violent employee shares these characteristics. Conversely, many people with one or more of these characteristics do not become violent. However, the clinician who has dealt with violent patients will recognize familiar patterns in this list. For example, the employee who has a history of breaking policies and procedures is similar to a violent juvenile who habitually breaks the rules at school and at home, or the violent patient who has a history of disregarding the law.

In addition to these characteristics, a number of behaviors are warning signs of impending violence. They include:

- making verbal threats
- using physical intimidation (including flashing weapons, gaining access to restricted areas, and stalking)
- exhibiting obsessive behavior (including holding a grudge against co-workers and/or managers, and being preoccupied with being right)
- being intolerant of criticism
- abruptly changing behavior patterns
- blaming others for personal problems
- verbalizing frequently about violent events
- complaining frequently (including complaints about lack of fair treatment, workload, and physical and psychological stress)
- experiencing episodes of lack of temper control
- asking for help (including requests for time off or seeking help from an EAP)
- discussing sexual problems (including harassing behavior)
- talking about sleep disturbances, physical ailments, or problems at home[50–53]

The last point is very important. People whose home life is relatively stress free and who have healthy outlets for aggressive tendencies outside the workplace are less likely to act on their violent tendencies at work. However, when neither work nor home environments provide appropriate outlets and/or when both environments are stressful, violence may erupt in either one or both.

Sources of Violence

Most acts of employee violence are the result of anger that the employee has not been able to express to his satisfaction in other ways. The more immutable the object of his anger, the greater his sense of frustration becomes and, hence, the greater his anger. Violence becomes the only way that some employees perceive that they can make anyone hear how intensely angry they are.

One of the more interesting aspects of employee anger is the employee's own contribution to it. In many ways, today's workplace is an extremely complex and unforgiving place. Many organizations make minimal efforts to accommodate the individual needs of employees. Employees who are bright are treated essentially the same as employees who are dull. Except for the protections accorded to some of them by the ADA, physically impaired employees are treated the same as physically unimpaired employees. Employees with heavy responsibilities at home are treated the same as those with virtually no outside responsibilities. Employees whose personal characteristics (be they positive or negative) deviate too far from the norm feel out of step with the organization. Employees who have low-self-esteem or who have poor coping skills are especially vulnerable to frustration and anger that arise from the perception that because it is rigid, the organization is unaccommodating and uncaring. Behavior that most employees accept as part of ordinary organizational life these employees may find threatening or offensive.[54] Therefore, self-esteem and coping skills are characteristics to keep in mind when evaluating employment candidates or potential team members, because employees with these characteristics are more likely to find organizational life difficult and stressful.

One of the most important causes of workplace violence is the loss, or threatened loss, of a job.[55] Large-scale mergers, downsizings, and reorganizations have created a kind of mass paranoia about job loss. In our rapidly changing economy, most people have friends, relatives, and/or acquaintances who have lost jobs. This fact would probably just result in a level of stress with which most people could cope if jobs were plentiful. They are not. Even highly skilled individuals can be unemployed for long periods because of corporate obsession with credentialism and very narrowly conceived job specifications. At the same time, transferability of skills is undervalued. (It would be interesting to know, for example, how many home health agencies would hire nurses with mediocre performance records in home healthcare rather than institutional nurses with outstanding performance histories.) A loss of a job in today's economy could translate into the loss of everything that an employee has worked for years to achieve. If a loss of this magnitude threatens an employee's family and/or his self-worth, and he perceives that he is incurring this loss unjustly, he may become violent.

The rigidity of hierarchical organizations also contributes to anger and violence.[56] Most hierarchical organizations are not hospitable. People have difficulty being heard. Even if they are given an opportunity to voice their concerns, the slowly grinding wheels of bureaucracy make it appear as if the organization is unresponsive. Indeed, sometimes employee concerns get ground between those bureaucratic wheels as if they were insignificant grains of millet. Along with their concerns, the unique skills and creativity that individuals bring to the workplace become grist for the mill. The devaluing of skills and ideas is a source of frustration and anger.

Organizational leadership can contribute to violence. Complex, rigid organizations, in and of themselves, can make employees feel that their workplaces are impersonal and uncaring. But add to that environment managers who treat employees as though their feelings are unimportant, and the workplace becomes overtly hostile to some employees. Many employees who have become violent note that even more than specific actions taken against them by managers, it was the dehumanizing manner in which they were treated that triggered violent behavior.[57]

Preventing Employee Violence

Respect

Managers who are starved for simplistic answers to managerial problems have one here. Respect. Respect for employees as humans who have feelings, responsibilities at work, responsibilities outside of work, ideas, aspirations, and fears. Respect for employees does not mean that managers have to automatically give in to employee demands or agree with employees' opinions. It does mean that managers must recognize that employees have valid ideas and feelings and that their ideas and feelings should be taken seriously. To minimize the potential for employee violence, managers need to demonstrate respect for employees in several different ways.

Respectful Listening

There is one characteristic of violence about which almost everyone agrees. Violence gets attention. When an employee kills a supervisor or a co-worker (or several of each), there is no doubt that people far and wide get the message that the perpetrator was unhappy. In many cases, perpetrators resort to violence as the only way they know to make sure that someone gets their message.

Many acts of violence could be averted if the perpetrator perceived that his complaints or concerns were heard and taken seriously. There are undoubtedly experienced managers who read these words and think, "I do listen and I do care, but no matter what I do or say, people are going to believe what they want. You just can't satisfy everybody." Too often, the actions of these managers do not communicate how concerned they really are.

One thing that a manager can do to indicate that he truly cares is to take notes when listening to an employee's concern. (How many people bother to take notes when they do not care about what is said?) *After* the employee has completely stated his concerns, the manager can work from his notes to clarify and restate the employee's position. This action provides the employee with concrete evidence that he has been heard. Follow-up action will undoubtedly be required to reconfirm the manager's commitment to work with the employee to resolve the difficulty. However, respectful listening is the first step in that process.

An important part of respectful listening is allowing the employee to completely express his feelings. When the employee is angry, the manager has to allow the employee to vent his anger. This is more difficult than it sounds. Frequently, the manager will himself become angry during the process. He may feel that the employee's complaints are unjustified, or he may feel that the employee's anger is being projected onto him unfairly. Irrespective of how the manager feels, he must let the employee vent. Venting his own anger, becoming argumentative, or trying to reason with the employee is counterproductive and shows more concern for his own well-being than for that of the employee. The manager needs to find his own way of coping with stress and venting anger apart from interpersonal interactions with employees.

Respectful Follow-up

Listening must be followed by action. For his own well-being, the manager cannot shoulder all employees' problems. However, he must recognize that after anger is vented, it can rebuild if there is no effective follow-up. The second time around, respectful listening may not be an effective way of de-escalating the potentially violent employee. Therefore, a plan of action which requires that the employee share responsibility for finding solutions to situations that result in anger is indicated. Allowing an employee to vent his anger is never a pleasant experience. After the crisis is over, there may be some hesitancy on the part of both the employee and the manager to interact. The employee may be embarrassed by his angry outburst. The manager may carry around his own anger about the incident, or he may not know how to reestablish a healthy relationship. The initial contact after an employee vents his anger is awkward. Nonetheless, it is important that the manager not avoid the employee.[58] A healthy relationship has to be reestablished as soon as possible. Both the employee and the manager have to move forward and deal with the factors that resulted in the angry outburst.

Respectful Feedback

One element of follow-up behavior is providing feedback. Typically, feedback is given in the form of negative criticism, silence, advice, and positive reinforcement.[59] About the only time that silence is appropriate is when the only things that the manager can think of to say would make an already difficult situation worse. Silence is the most indefinite form of communication. Withholding verbal cues that would help an employee understand feedback communicates disregard for the employee. It is never easy to be the recipient of negative criticism. Negative criticism should therefore be delivered with respect for the employee's feelings. Negative criticism should be offered along with a plan of action that will help the employee improve. This coupling leaves the employee with a feeling of hopefulness rather than helplessness. Advice and positive reinforcement generally are well-received and pose less of a problem for managers to deliver. The main issue with advice and positive reinforcement is to remember to give it. Problem-focused managers too often forget to acknowledge the positive.

In an effort to soften the blow of negative criticism, some managers combine it with positive reinforcement. This is a well-meaning step that can have unintended poor outcomes. Combining the positive and negative is often perceived by employees as a mixed message. When managers use this technique habitually, employees begin to dread getting a pat on the back because they know that a kick in the pants will follow. This technique also tends to divert attention away from problematic behavior. Ultimately, it is probably more beneficial to deliver negative and positive feedback at appropriate times rather than to dilute or skew employee response to either one by routinely combining them.

Respectful Discipline

The whole concept of discipline conjures negative images like detention, humiliation, beatings, and verbal abuse. Managers would probably do well to relieve themselves of the idea that they should ever be disciplinarians in the workplace. Counselling, collaborating, coaching, negotiating, and challenging are more respectful and positive ways of conceptualizing relationships among adults. However, to be consistent with contemporary literature, the term discipline is reluctantly used here.

The first step in respectful discipline is to choose an appropriate time and place for the interaction.[60] The manager needs to approach employees when he feels up to dealing with a difficult situation. The end of the work week is usually not a good time because some employees need an opportunity to vent soon after the disciplinary session. A weekend may allow anger to escalate to violence. The place is also crucial. Respect requires that discipline never take place in front of other employees.

Any disciplinary action should focus on the employee's behavior, not the employee. Statements like "You have a motivation problem" and "Your attitude about your job is bad" should be avoided. First, these statements are inappropriate because motivation and attitude are attributes that cannot be seen. Some behaviors may be indicative of low motivational levels or of disliking one's job. But no correlation between any one behavior and any one feeling is so strong that managers are justified in making such definitive assessments. Second, these kinds of remarks are inflammatory. Because the focus of such statements is an employee's feelings and feelings are virtually inextricable from personality, the statements may be offensive. A natural response to offensive language is anger. By focusing on well-documented, specific behavior the manager is more likely to be able to achieve behavioral changes without personally offending and angering the employee.

No matter how behaviorally focused and rational the disciplinary session, employees are likely to become defensive. The manager has to remember that this is a natural response to negative criticism. At the time that the employee states his defense, he may also vent anger. An "I don't want any excuses" approach simply leads to employee frustration and repression. This is where respectful listening should be used in the disciplinary process. After the employee has vented his anger, the manager should calmly discuss the employee's explanations without allowing himself to be drawn into an argument or diverted from the problematic behavior. The manager also needs to realize that sometimes there are valid explanations for undesirable patterns of work performance. In fact, the manager's interpretation of observed behavior may be erroneous. Accepting valid excuses and working with employees to prevent recurrences is not a sign of managerial weakness. A weak manager is one who stubbornly holds to a plan of disciplinary action in the face of evidence that the employee is not at fault.

Even managers who demonstrate the utmost respect for employees may find themselves in potentially violent situations as a result of disciplinary actions. A disciplinary meeting may represent a threat that is the final straw to a stress-laden employee. If the manager senses that the employee is losing emotional control or is becoming enraged, the meeting should be terminated.[61] This is not the time to say something like, "Darren, this is just the kind of outburst I've been talking about. Now shut up and listen for a change." Darren's rage could easily escalate to violence on the spot. Intimidation is not the safest way to handle an enraged employee.

Respectful Termination

Whether it occurs as a result of a simple lack of sufficient workload or it results from a long history of poor performance, termination is traumatic. Respectful termination requires that employers handle termination with compassion, even when it results from the employee's own actions. It is the callousness with which many employers handle termination that frequently leads to violence. The following practices indicate to employees that employers recognize and are concerned about their loss.

1. Take sufficient time to terminate the employee. Because termination is difficult for managers, they try to get through the process as quickly as possible. Termination is a grave action that merits a significant expenditure of time. Employees who are simply handed a pink slip and given a few hours (or minutes) to remove their possessions are likely to feel that the former employer had no regard for their feelings, or even their lives. What kind of regard can such an embittered employee be expected to have for the employer?

2. Assist employees in preparing for other employment. Outplacement services can be used to assist employees in searching for new positions. Specific training can be offered to increase marketable skills. Severance pay buys employees time to find a new position. These actions are expensive, but they are not nearly as expensive as murder. Even when employees are potentially violent, providing some kind of support in terms of severance pay and/or training may be enough to avoid a violent outcome. These actions communicate more care and concern than words do.

3. Choose the appropriate person to terminate the employee. In the case of ordinary layoffs, the appropriate person is usually the employee's immediate supervisor. This is the manager who probably has the strongest interpersonal relationship with the employee.

When the termination results from poor performance (especially performance that is characterized by aggressive tendencies), it is usually kinder and safer for a higher authority, who has no direct history of dealing with the employee's behavior, to handle the termination.[62] When there is concern about potentially violent behavior, the organization's EAP or independent mental health professionals should be consulted for advice about how to best proceed with the termination.

4. Terminate in a timely manner. Respect for other employees requires that managers act as expeditiously as possible to terminate individuals for poor performance, especially when poor performance includes aggressive behavior. Allowing these employees to remain on the job is an emotional burden for everyone. No employee should be allowed to successfully use intimidation to keep his job.

Once the decision has been made to terminate, there is no purpose in rehashing performance issues with the employee. The termination meeting is not the place to review past behavior, nor the place to argue with or berate the employee. Nor is it the place for negotiation or discussing what the employee could have done to have kept his job.[63] The time for these activities is past. The termination meeting should focus on the circumstances that necessitate the layoff, on policy, and on the facts that show that policy was broken. Out of respect, the employee should be allowed to vent (as long as violence is not imminent), and the manager should express concern for the employee's welfare. Arguing and negotiating are not part of that process. Above all, a vindictive "I told you so" approach is contraindicated.

The Legal Dimension

In the Visionary Options case, Rob's immediate concern appears to be the legal constraints on the actions he can take to deal with Jack's behavior. His first concern, of course, should be the safety of his clients, other employees, and himself. However, the legal aspects of this situation constitute a valid secondary concern. Actually, by making safety the primary concern, Rob's and Visionary Option's liability exposure will be minimized. Rob has to walk a legal tightwire here while he balances his duty to individuals who come into contact with Jack within the context of his employment at Visionary Options, and Jack's rights as an employee and an individual.

In general, the courts have held that employers may be liable to victims of violence. This liability arises from negligent hiring, negligent supervision, and negligent retention.[64] In respect to hiring, the employer's duty is to protect employees and clients from injuries caused by employees that the employer knows or should know pose a risk of harm to others.[65] Notice the phrase "should know." Employers cannot escape this duty by turning a blind eye in the hiring process. The courts have generally held that employers have a duty to investigate applicants as a way of preventing violence. A thorough review of references should include questions about tendencies toward violent behavior.

In the Visionary Options case, Rob faces a situation in which he could be held liable for negligent supervision if Jack causes an injury at work. Rob knows that Jack's behavior is a cause of concern among his employees. He himself is fearful. Rob has options that he can pursue to prevent injury. For example, he could enlist the aid of a mental health professional, refer Jack to counselling, assign him to work in which he has minimal contact with others, or terminate him. The best way to avoid liability under the theory of negligent supervision is to intervene as expeditiously as possible.[66] In this case, Rob could become liable under the theory of negligent retention as well. When it becomes foreseeable during the course of employment that the employee is unfit due to violent tendencies, the employer may become liable as a result of continuing employment that puts others at risk.[67]

The circumstances surrounding violence and jurisdictional requirements are so variable that it is virtually impossible to assess risk of liability on an *a priori* basis. Although Visionary Option's exposure appears to be significant, it is generally limited to violent acts that Jack might commit within the scope and course of his employment.[68] If Jack were to harm his wife, for example, this act would be outside the scope of his employment, and under ordinary circumstances no liability would attach to Visionary Options.

Protecting employees is a legal concern, not only as a result of civil liability exposure, but also as a result of the Federal Occupational Safety and Health Act (OSHA). In general terms, OSHA requires that employers establish a safe and healthy workplace for employees. It also requires that, in certain situations, employers respond to interemployee threats of violence by taking preventive measures.[69]

If liability from risk of injury were the only issue, Rob's intervention plan would be fairly easy. He would separate Jack from co-workers and clients immediately. On the face of it, termination would appear to be the optimal alternative. However, it must be remembered that safety is always the primary consideration, and immediate termination may not be the safest alternative. It may therefore actually increase liability exposure. The other concern that Rob has to consider is the legal duty of Visionary Options to Jack.

Several of the alternatives to dealing with potentially violent employees could result in violations of employee rights.[70] If the employer warns other employees that a potential perpetrator has violent tendencies, he could be guilty of defamation. **Defamation** results from communicating something that is both false and results in injury. Defamation is a complicated issue because, in some instances, statements may be false and result in injury (such as a damaged reputation), but are considered by the courts to be privileged (i.e., allowable). In order to be privileged, the communicator usually has to believe that the statement is true and limits communication to people who have a need to know within a business context. Spreading unsubstantiated rumors for the fun of it would obviously not qualify as privileged communication. Acting on hearsay evidence without appropriate investigation may not give the manager sufficient reason to believe the statement is true and would jeopardize the privileged status of a warning to other employees.

Investigation is an essential element of dealing with potentially violent behavior. However, the employer has no more right than a law enforcement agency to invade an employee's privacy. To avoid litigation arising from invasion of privacy, employers should limit intrusion to a level of activity that a reasonable person would not find offensive. They should also avoid disclosing findings to the public.

A fairly new legal consideration in dealing with potentially violent employees is the ADA, which affords protection from discrimination against qualified individuals with physical or mental disabilities. If violent tendencies stem from a mental illness, hypothetically, an employer would have to make reasonable accommodations. But are there any reasonable accommodations for violent tendencies in the workplace? Although total isolation and leaves of absence are theoretically possible in some cases, are they reasonable? Eventually, case law will probably provide the answers to these questions.

Another concern that arises from ADA is hiring practices. The prospective employer should refrain from asking questions about a candidate's physical and mental health history to avoid the appearance of discriminatory hiring practices. However, it has been suggested that pre-employment reference checking should include questions that focus specifically on workplace behavior.[71] As long as the line of questioning focuses on actions rather than the causes of actions, the exposure to ADA violation appears to be less than liability exposure for negligent hiring in the event that these questions about behavior are not asked and violence results.

In the Visionary Options case, Rob needs the advice of legal counsel. Defamation, privacy rights, and the ADA are extremely complex areas of the law. Rob needs to discuss the case with counsel so that the material facts of the case can be clarified and an informed expert opinion rendered. Rob could have strengthened his legal position before he got to this point by mounting a strong legal offense. This would have been done through explicit, unequivocable policies that communicated zero tolerance for workplace violence. Such policies should be very specific in defining unacceptable behavior. The stronger an employer's documentation that the employee got the zero tolerance message, the better. Employees may be asked to sign that they received copies of policies. They can be required to go to an orientation where the policy is stated orally. They can be asked to take periodic quizzes that demonstrate their knowledge of zero tolerance policies. These measures generate documentation that employees knew the employer's stance on violent behavior.

Conclusion

There is a general feeling in America that life is getting harder. More and more families depend on multiple wage earners. The national debt is soaring. Real wages are down. It seems to many people that the harder they work, the further behind they get. Boards of directors and CEOs feel the same way about their organizations. The more they do to move organizations ahead in an environment of economic and technological turbulence, the further behind they seem to be. Consequently, they push everyone to be more productive, and yet more productive, and even more productive. Against this background of personal and workplace pressure, stress and violence are epidemic.

It is easy for managers to throw up their hands in surrender and declare that there is nothing they can do because stress and violence are societal problems, and, as such, they are far too large for a single manager to deal with. As this chapter has shown, this is not true. There are several techniques that can help employees cope with stress, and treating employees with respect can lower the incidence of workplace violence. These strategies work, but they take time, and time is one thing that managers have too little of.

Managers sometimes do not realize how much of their time is devoured by employee stress. Managers spend a tremendous amount of time compensating for the absenteeism, turnover, and poor performance that stress produces. If managers spent that time helping employees deal with stress, two things would happen. First, managers would probably find themselves with more time than they ever imagined because the stream of stress-generated work would begin to dry up. They might also find employees taking on many tasks that had previously gone undone. Second, the workplace would be a more pleasant place. Being around anxious, depressed people all day is nobody's idea of a good time. What better payoff could there be for spending the time it takes to provide employees with the stress management support they need?

Endnotes

1. Timothy P. Summers, Thomas A. DeCotis, and Angelo S. DeNisi, "A Field Study of Some Antecedents and Consequences of Felt Job Stress," in Rick Crandall and Pamela L. Perrewé, eds., *Occupational Stress: A Handbook* (Washington, DC: Taylor & Francis, 1995).
2. Mark O. Hatfield, "Stress and the American Worker," *American Psychologist 45* (1990): 1,162–4.
3. Walter Tubbs, "Karoushi: Stress-death and the Meaning of Work," *Journal of Business Ethics 12* (November 1993): 869–878.
4. Jeremy Rifkin, *The End of Work* (New York: G.P. Putnam's Sons, 1995).
5. Marilyn L. Fox, Deborah J. Dwyer, and Daniel C. Ganster, "Effects of Stressful Job Demands and Control of Physiological and Attitudinal Outcomes in a Hospital Setting," *Academy of Management Journal 36* (1993): 289–318.
6. Charles D. Spielberger and Eric C. Reheiser, "Measuring Occupational Stress: The

Job Stress Survey," in Rick Crandall and Pamela L. Perrewé, eds., *Occupational Stress: A Handbook* (Washington, DC: Taylor & Francis, 1995).

7. Willian H. Hendrix, Timothy P. Summers, Terry L. Leap, and Robert P. Steel, "Antecedents and Organizational Effectiveness as Outcomes of Employee Stress and Health," in Rick Crandall and Pamela L. Perrewé, eds., *Occupational Stress: A Handbook* (Washington, DC: Taylor & Francis, 1995).

8. Peter Y. Chen and Paul E. Spector, "Relationships of Work Stressors with Aggression, Withdrawal, Theft and Substance Use: An Exploratory Study," *Journal of Occupational and Organizational Psychology 65* (1992): 177–184.

9. Stephen P. Robbins. *Organizational Behavior: Concepts, Controversies, and Applications* (Englewood Cliffs, NJ: Prentice-Hall, 1989).

10. E. Dara Orgus, "Burnout and Coping Strategies: A Comparative Study of Ward Nurses," in Rick Crandall and Pamela L. Perrewé, eds., *Occupational Stress: A Handbook* (Washington, DC: Taylor & Francis, 1995).

11. Bonnie L. Roach, "Burnout and the Nursing Profession," *Health Care Supervisor 12* (June 1994): 41–47.

12. Cathy M. Anderson, "A Departmental Stress Management Plan," *Healthcare Supervisor 8* (June 1990):1–8.

13. Gregory H. Frazer and Scott R. Sechrist, "A Comparison of Occupational Stressors in Selected Allied Health Disciplines," *Healthcare Supervisor 13* (September 1994): 53–65.

14. Kathleen Montgomery and Charles E. Lewis, "Fear of HIV Contagion as Workplace Stress: Behavioral Consequences and Buffers," *Hospital & Health Services Administration 40* (Winter 1995): 439–456.

15. Jennifer M. George, Thomas F. Reed, Karen A. Ballard, Jessie Colin, and Jane Fielding, "Contact with AIDS Patients as a Source of Work-related Distress: Effects of Organizational and Social Support," *Academy of Management Journal 36 (*1993): 157–171.

16. Hendrix et al., op. cit.

17. John A. Wagner III and John R. Hollenbeck, *Management of Organizational Behavior* (Englewood Cliffs, NJ: Prentice-Hall, 1992).

18. Ibid.

19. Connie Lindborg and Ruth Davidhizar, "Is There a Difference in Nurse Burnout on the Day or Night Shift?" *Healthcare Supervisor 11* (1993): 47–52.

20. Ronald J. Burke, "Sources of Managerial and Professional Stress in Large Organizations," in Cary L. Cooper and Roy Payne, eds., *Causes, Coping and Consequences of Stress at Work* (Chichester, U.K.: John Wiley & Sons, 1988).

21. Ibid.

22. M. J. Smith, P. Carayon, K. J. Sanders, S-Y. Lim, and D. LeGrande, "Employee Stress and Health Complaints in Jobs With and Without Electronic Performance Monitoring," *Applied Ergonomics 23* (1992): 17–28.

23. Spielberger and Reheiser, op. cit.

24. Frazier and Sechrist, op. cit.

25. Richard S. Lazarus, "Psychological Stress in the Workplace," in Rick Crandall and Pamela L. Perrewé, eds., *Occupational Stress: A Handbook* (Washington, DC: Taylor & Francis, 1995).

26. Ibid.
27. David Fontana, *Managing Stress* (Leicester, U.K.: The British Psychological Society, 1989).
28. Orgus, op. cit.
29. Stephen J. Halovic and John P. Keenan, "Coping with Work Stress: The Influence of Individual Differences," in Rick Crandall and Pamela L. Perrewé, eds., *Occupational Stress: A Handbook* (Washington, DC: Taylor & Francis, 1995).
30. Cary L. Cooper and Golnaz Sadri, "The Impact of Stress Counseling at Work," in Rick Crandall and Pamela L. Perrewé, eds., *Occupational Stress: A Handbook* (Washington, DC: Taylor & Francis, 1995).
31. Lawrence R. Murphy, "Workplace Interventions for Stress Reduction and Prevention," in Cary L. Cooper and Roy Payne, eds., *Causes, Coping and Consequences of Stress at Work* (Chichester, U.K.: John Wiley & Sons, 1988).
32. Richard S. Lazarus and Susan Folkman, *Stress, Appraisal, and Coping* (New York: Springer Publishing Company, 1984).
33. Steve M. Jex, Paul E. Spector, David M. Gudanowski, and Ronald A. Newman, "Relations between Exercise and Employee Responses to Work Stressors," in Rick Crandall and Pamela L. Perrewé, eds., *Occupational Stress: A Handbook* (Washington, DC: Taylor & Francis, 1995).
34. Roach, op. cit.
35. Robert Karasek and Töes Theorell, *Health Work: Stress, Productivity and the Reconstruction of Working Life* (New York: Basic Books, 1990).
36. Daniel C. Ganster, "Worker Control and Well-Being: A Review of Research in the Workplace," in Steven L. Sauter, Joseph J. Hurrell, Jr., and Cary L. Cooper, eds., *Job Control and Worker Health* (Chichester, U.K.: John Wiley & Sons, 1989).
36. Roach, op. cit.
37. Orgus, op. cit.
38. Fox et al., op. cit.
39. David C. Glass, J. Daniel McKnight and Heiddis Valdimarsdottir, "Depression, Burnout, and Perceptions of Control in Hospital Nurses," *Journal of Consulting and Clinical Psychology 61* (February 1993): 147–156.
40. *Homicide in the Workplace*, Centers for Disease Control and Prevention (March 9, 1995).
41. Ronet Bachman, *Violence and Theft in the Workplace*, U.S. Department of Justice (July 1994).
42. Ibid.
43. Helen Frank Bensimon, "Violence in the Workplace," *Training and Development 48* (January 1994): 26–31.
44. *Guidelines for Preventing Workplace Violence for Healthcare and Social Service Workers*, U.S. Department of Labor, Occupational Safety and Health Administration (1996).
45. A concise overview of de-escalation strategies can be found in Carol A. Distasio, "Violence in Health Care: Institutional Strategies to Cope with the Phenomenon," *Healthcare Supervisor 12* (June 1994): 1–34.
46. Bensimon, op. cit.
47. Michael Mantell and Steve Albrecht, *Ticking Bombs: Defusing Violence in the Workplace* (Burr Ridge, IL: Richard D. Irwin, 1994).

48. Carol A. Distasio, "Employee Violence in Healthcare: Guidelines for Healthcare Organizations," *Healthcare Supervisor 13* (March 1995): 1–15.
49. Marianne Minor, *Preventing Workplace Violence: Positive Management Strategies* (Menlo Park, CA: Crisp Publications, 1995).
50. Ibid.
51. William E. Lissy, "Workplace Violence," *Supervision 51* (April 1994): 20–21.
52. Mantell and Albrecht, op. cit.
53. Distasio, op. cit.
54. Seth Allcorn, *Anger in the Workplace: Understanding the Causes of Anger and Violence* (Westport, CT: Quorum Books, 1994).
55. Bensimon, op. cit.
56. Allcorn, op. cit.
57. Bensimon, op. cit.
58. Allcorn, op. cit.
59. Minor, op. cit.
60. Allcorn, op. cit.
61. Distasio, op. cit.
62. Mantell and Albrecht, op. cit.
63. Minor, op. cit.
64. William C. Martucci and Denise Drake Clemow, "Workplace Violence: Incidents—and Liability—on the Rise," *Employment Relations Today* (Winter 1994/1995): 463–470.
65. *Terror and Violence in the Workplace*, 2nd ed. (San Francisco: Littler, Mendelson, Falstiff, Tichy & Mathiason, PC, 1995).
66. Martucci and Clemow, op. cit.
67. *Terror and Violence*, op. cit.
68. Martucci and Clemow, op. cit.
69. Minor, op. cit.
70. *Terror and Violence*, op. cit.
71. Michael Barrier, "The Enemy Within," *Nation's Business 83* (February 1995): 18–24.

Index